What others are saying about June Keith:

"There are a million stories in Key West and June Keith seems to know them all."
— **Dave Barry,** Pulitzer Prize-winning columnist. Author.

"June Keith certainly is an engaging writer. She is a pleasure to read."
— **Alan Shearer,** *The Washington Post*

"A June Keith column is like a Key West sunset—once it begins you're hooked until it ends."
— **Kenley Jones,** Correspondent, NBC News

"You'll fall in love with her, and the Keys."
— **Captain Tony,** Key West Mayor Emeritus. Saloonkeeper.

"Her love for the people of Key West makes one wish her type thrived all over small-town America."
— **Gene Gabriel Moore,** *Southern Voice*, Atlanta

"Keith knows first-hand, that Key West has the kind of sweaty, raunchy appeal you either surrender to—gloriously—or you walk away from, shaking your head in disgust. Either way, the town stays under your skin."
— **Jeanne Malmgren,** *St. Petersburg Times*

"The best Keys guide. Current. Opinionated. Poetic. Honest."
— **Joel Carmel,** The Book Nook, Key Largo

June Keith's
Key West &

SECOND EDITION

Palm Island Press
THE FLORIDA PUBLISHERS

Food

Hotels

Beaches

Diving

The Florida Keys

Fishing

History

Writers

Festivals

Attractions

Museums

Wildlife

For Fannie Elizabeth Rogers

Copyright © 1997, 1999 by June Keith
Illustrations © 1997 by David Harrison Wright
Interior design by Troy Scott Parker, Cimarron Design

Second Edition
Third printing, revised

Published by
Palm Island Press
411 Truman Avenue, Key West, Florida 33040 U.S.A.
SAN 298-4024

Library of Congress Cataloging-in-Publication Data

Keith, June
    June Keith's Key West and the Florida Keys.
        p. cm.
    Includes index
    ISBN 0-9643434-5-2
    1. Florida Keys (Fla.)—Guidebooks. 2. Florida Keys
(Fla.)—History. /. Title. //. Title: Key West and the
Florida Keys.
F317.M7K45 1997   98-67545
917.59'4104'63

Table of Contents

The Lower Keys:
A Land That's Mostly Water; A Sea That's Mostly Sky 279

Middle Keys and Marathon: Nothing Succeeds Like True Grit 333

Sooner or Later Everyone Comes to Key Largo 467

Without a hint of irony,
everybody calls it Paradise.

– CHARLES KURALT

❀

Paradise Found

THE FLORIDA KEYS ARE LIKE NOWHERE ELSE ON THE PLANET. In a photograph shot from a space shuttle, the Keys appear to be a handful of white pebbles thrown by some giant hand into the shallow, green-blue waters of the Florida Bay. The amazing Overseas Highway and its 42 bridges whipstitch a 130-mile trail from mainland Florida all the way to Key West. The coral islands of the Florida Keys are small, rarely as wide as two miles, usually much narrower. Each has its own attractions, auras, and powerful personalities. There are five regions in the Keys, and you will find wonders worth seeing in each of them.

This book is a guide and a companion designed to answer most often-asked questions about what there is to see and do, as well as where there is to eat and sleep, in the Florida Keys. You'll find descriptions of famous attractions like the free daily sunset celebration, dolphin swims, festivals and annual events, historic bars and renowned restaurants, and America's only living coral reef. You'll also learn the locations of not-so-well-known places, like secret gardens, funky diners, beachfront bistros, and off-the-beaten-path retreats.

In this book you'll meet Jimmy Buffett, and the ghosts of Ernest Hemingway and Tennessee Williams. You'll learn of our spectacular swashbuckling history, and the precious legacy of our early citizens: the world's largest outdoor museum of 19th-century architecture.

With this book you'll reap the benefits from my long-term love affair with Key West and the Florida Keys. I came for a weekend twenty-two years ago and never left, a common story in Paradise.

Outside of Key West addresses are identified by mile markers, small green signposts with white numbers. Mile markers tell you where you are on the Overseas Highway, the "Main Street" of the Keys. You really can't get lost in the Florida Keys, unless, of course, you want to....

This book is a result of independent research and years of Keys living. Descriptions are based on personal visits and interviews. Prices are always subject to change, of course, as is the management and ownership of businesses.

No one paid to get into this book, and no one paid to get out of it. Welcome to Paradise!

– June Keith

The
Last Resort
Key West

Old Town Area

Key West Bight

Mallory Square

Garrison Bight

CAROLINE STREET

EATON STREET

FLEMING STREET

SOUTHARD STREET

PALM AVENUE

SIMONTON STREET

WHITEHEAD STREET

DUVAL STREET

TRUMAN AVENUE

WHITE STREET

1

Fort Zachary Taylor

UNITED STREET

ATLANTIC AVENUE

Key West

Stock
Island

NORTH ROOSEVELT BOULEVARD

1

*To
Lower
Keys*

FLAGLER AVENUE

Salt ponds

Key West International Airport

A1A

SOUTH ROOSEVELT BOULEVARD

Key West

Frangipani

A Brief History of Key West

SPANISH EXPLORER Ponce de Leon is credited with discovering Florida
and claiming it for Spain in 1513. When de Leon's expedition sailed
past the southernmost islands of Spain's newest land acquisition, his
sailors viewed the dense and twisted mangroves along the islands' shores
and called them *Los Martires*, which translates as "the martyrs."

On a later visit to Florida in 1521, Ponce de Leon was killed in a
battle with Florida Indians protesting Spain's intentions to turn the savages into Christians. Along with several missionaries, de Leon died after
being shot by a poison arrow.

A century later the island of Key West began to appear in charts and
maps of the Caribbean with the name *Cayo Hueso* or Bone Key. This,
according to legend, was because the bones of dead Indians lay scattered
on the beach when the first explorers came ashore.

As European settlers began chasing northern Indians off land along
the U.S. east coast, tribes were forced to push farther south. The Calusa
Indians of South Florida were forced by stronger, more warlike Indians
from northern Florida southward and into the Keys. The Calusas fled
from island to island until they reached Key West and could go no farther. Here they fought a final bloody battle that left their sun-bleached
bones strewn on the beaches. The hardiest of the Calusas escaped in
boats to Cuba, where they eventually spawned a strain of long-legged
Cubans.

In 1815, Spain awarded the remote and generally useless island of Key
West to Juan Pablo Salas, a St. Augustine native who'd proven himself,
in word and in deed, invaluable to his country.

Salas later sold the island, which he'd made no move toward civiliz-
ing, to American businessman John Simonton for $2,000. Simonton
recognized the potential of the island's deep-water harbor. Convincing
others of this, he divided the island into quarters and sold three of them
to fellow businessmen Whitehead, Fleming and Greene.

It is unclear exactly why the name Key West replaced *Cayo Hueso*. Perhaps it is the name *Cayo Hueso* twisted on an English-speaking tongue. (Say *Cayo Hueso* five times fast and see what happens.) Perhaps because the name refers so appropriately to Key West's westernmost position in the island chain. In any event, by the time Simonton and his friends took over and started naming island streets after themselves, Key West had become the working name of the place, and eventually it stuck.

After arranging his finances and naming a street after himself, Simonton contacted the U.S. Navy and suggested to them that since Key West is strategically located in the northern Caribbean, it might be a perfect place for them to set up a base of operation.

The USS *Shark*, captained by Lieutenant Matthew C. Perry, sailed into the harbor in 1822 with orders from the Secretary of the Navy to investigate the potential of the island and its harbor, "with a view to further measures for its occupation and for the establishment of a port of rendezvous and for commerce."

Just what Simonton and his pals were hoping for!

Lieutenant Perry's report to his superiors in Washington was very favorable. But the news wasn't all good. Perry reported that there was "among the decent folks on the island tending to their legitimate seafaring interests, a small band of desperados who have paid but little regard to either law or honesty." But the island's God-fearing settlers would keep this wild bunch in line, he suggested.

Lieutenant Perry claimed Key West in the name of the United States in March 1822 and hoisted the U.S. flag. Sailors aboard the *Shark* fired a thirteen-gun salute. Then, their job done, Perry and the USS *Shark* sailed away.

The desperado problem, however, proved to be more unmanageable than Perry had estimated. Pirates of the area continued to plunder, maim and kill in spite of the U.S. presence. In 1823 Captain David Porter was appointed commodore of the West Indies Anti-Pirate Squadron. Porter's mission was to protect American citizens and U.S. commerce from pirates. He was also charged with the duties of suppressing the slave trade and establishing a naval base on Key West.

The island, Porter reported back to his superiors in Washington, was certainly no place for a naval base. There was no fresh water, and the place swarmed with mosquitoes and sandflies. Nonetheless, Porter went

ahead and assembled a fleet of shallow draft vessels known as the
Mosquito Fleet and, in spite of several outbreaks of yellow fever among
his ranks, made fast work of flushing pirates from the area.

Wrecks Ashore

These were pre-lighthouse days, so passage around the Florida Keys, even
after the pirates had been chased out of the region, remained a dangerous
endeavor. The reef area that lies seven miles to the south of Key West
was an extremely hazardous passage when the weather kicked up or when
captains unfamiliar with the Keys' tricky, shallow waters sailed up onto
the razor-sharp edges of the reef.

Just off Florida Keys shores, the busy trade routes were being used regularly by vessels loaded down with every kind of cargo imaginable. In a
few short years, wrecking and salvaging became Key West's primary business. Sharp-eyed citizens stood watch in high towers and searched the
horizon for ships foundering on the reef. The first to arrive on the scene
and offer assistance, became the captain in charge of salvaging as much
of the cargo as possible.

By prior agreement, ship owners and their insurers shared recovered
cargo with the salvagers of Key West. Half a recovered cargo, after all,
was better than no cargo at all. The wrecking captain, in turn, then
divided his share of the proceeds among his assistants. Much of the salvage was finally auctioned off, conveniently, in Key West, since federal
legislation forbade any salvaged goods taken from U.S. waters to leave
American ports.

Consequently, Key West was quickly becoming quite a prosperous port
city. From its incorporation in 1828 until the 1850s, it was considered the
richest city, per capita, in the United States. Wharves, shipyards and
chandleries soon lined the harbor shore. Buyers from New York, Charleston, and Havana bid on salvaged goods such as fine wines, silks, laces,
silverware and furniture from all over the world. Key West grew rich, if
not in cash, then at least in fine possessions as wrecking proceeds trickled
down into settlers' hands. Mothers and daughters might show up in
church wearing new dresses made from a salvaged bolt of silk. The entire
citizenry might find itself handsomely shod in fine leather shoes salvaged
from a wrecked ship en route to New York. Wealth was everywhere!

But in addition to the profitable wrecking and salvaging industries, fishing, turtling and salt manufacturing had become crucial to the island's economic survival. Between the years of 1830 and 1861 Key West supplied much of the nation's salt, which, before refrigeration, was the chief method of food preservation. It was gleaned not from salt mines but from the sea. Shallow tidal pools on the south side of the island were covered with large, flat evaporating pans which filled with salt water during the wet spring and summer months. When the tidal pools receded during dry winter months, the water evaporated, leaving 340 acres of crystallized salt drying in the pans. Later, during the Civil War, Union soldiers closed down the salt industry when it was discovered that local Confederate sympathizers were smuggling Key West salt into the Confederacy. The salt industry resumed at the war's end, but was wiped out by a hurricane in 1876. By then, salt mines had been discovered on the mainland anyway.

To try to slow down the increasing wrecking that continued into the 1850s, the government began stationing "light boats" and, later, lighthouses, on the dangerous reefs. Sturdier, safer steamships began carrying the valuable cargo that once had been shipped aboard wooden schooners, which were dependent upon the wind and weather.

By 1855 Key West's population had grown to 2,700, and progress had dealt the business of wrecking some serious blows that would ultimately lead to its end.

Southernmost Yankees

Florida seceded from the Union in 1861. Meanwhile, in Key West, Fort Taylor, strategic to the defense of the city's harbor, was quietly commandeered by a troop of Union soldiers in the predawn hours one April morning that same year. It was expected that the townspeople would attack the fort, but that did not happen, and soon more troops arrived, assuring that Key West would be the only southern city to remain in Union hands for the duration of the war. There were, to be sure, plenty of Southern sympathizers in Key West, but with Union soldiers everywhere, they couldn't do much to support the Confederate cause. Key West was the only place in the country where you had to go north to join the South.

At that same time, the East Coast Blockade Squadron was headquartered in Key West as well. The squadron's mission was to stop blockade runners from sailing contraband to the Confederate troops via the Gulf of Mexico. Nearly three hundred blockade runners were arrested; their ships were impounded and anchored in Key West Harbor. America's most famous blockade runner is the fictional character, Rhett Butler of Margaret Mitchell's *Gone With The Wind*.

The New El Dorado

Because Key West's climate was so much like its nearby neighbor Cuba, only ninety miles away, it did not take long for someone to recognize the area's potential for cigar manufacturing. The first cigar factory was established on Wall Street in 1831. As Key West grew, so did the business of cigar manufacturing.

During the Cuban Revolution that began in 1868, thousands of Cubans emigrated to Key West to find better lives working in the cigar industry which the influx of manpower greatly expanded. Soon the cigar business was bringing over a million dollars into the city annually. By 1871, Cubans employed in the cigar industry were a powerful political force. The original San Carlos Institute, a center of nationalistic politics, was constructed on Duval Street. In the city-wide election of 1876, several Cuban-born men were elected to political offices, including that of mayor.

The devastating fire of 1886, which is believed to have been started in the San Carlos Institute, burned down nearly two thirds of the city, including several important cigar factories and many cigarmakers' houses. But the cigar industry recovered quickly and went on to reach its peak of production in 1890. By then 129 cigar factories operated on the island. Workers produced an amazing 100,000,000 cigars annually.

Cigar factory employees enjoyed excellent salaries and working conditions. Workers often donated up to 10% of their earnings to support Cuba's fight for independence from Spain. Attempting to interrupt the flow of cash to Cuban revolutionaries, however, Spanish agitators sparked conflicts among workers and instigated labor strikes, often based on the flimsiest of excuses. A major strike in 1890 occurred when workers claimed that pay was unfair for making various qualities of cigars. Factory owners paid the same wage for making all cigars, whether cheap ones or very expensive smokes.

To entice cigar manufacturers out of Key West and over to Tampa, incentives such as tax-free land and cheaper labor were offered to Key West factory owners. In Tampa, there were no unions. One by one the cigar manufacturers began to abandon Key West and its strife. So the great shift occurred. By the turn of the century, Key West had lost its position as America's leading producer of hand-rolled Cuban cigars.

Cleaning up with Sponges

Another important industry that started in Key West and moved to a more supportive venue was sponging. An enterprising businessman sailed a shipload of Keys natural sponges to New York City in 1850 and very quickly found a clamoring market for them. By 1890 Key West was the commercial sponging capital of the world.

Natural sponges are soft skeletons of animals that once had lived in the shallow waters surrounding the Keys. Prying them from the ocean floor, drying, cleaning and bleaching them in preparation for the marketplace was, and still is, a smelly and back-breaking job. Nonetheless, sponging was an important business. At the turn of the century, Key West's sponging fleet was 350 boats strong and employed 1400 men, who harvested up to 165 tons of natural sponges a year.

In time Key West spongers began indiscriminately harvesting sponge beds, ignoring laws designed to preserve the supply. In 1904 several sponge companies were established to take advantage of the rich sponge beds in Tarpon Springs, on Florida's west coast just north of Tampa. Once again Key West's remote location worked against it. Tarpon Springs spongers and merchants had a much easier time getting their wares to the world's shipping routes, and Tarpon Springs soon replaced Key West as the world's prime producer of sponges.

Eventually a weird and deadly sponge fungus destroyed all of the beds in the Florida Keys, and cheap synthetic sponges were invented to take the place of the expensive, natural ones. In the last twenty-five years sponge beds have become healthy and productive again. Several small businesses are harvesting Keys sponges today.

Remember the *Maine*

The battleship USS *Maine* sailed into Key West Harbor in June,1896. Officers and crewmen from the ship were soon incorporated into the community, making many friends and romantic liaisons here.

In late 1897, in a show of America's military strength as well as her support for American business interests in Cuba, President McKinley ordered the USS *Maine* to sail on to Havana. On February 15, 1898, the *Maine* was ripped apart by an explosion in Havana Harbor. Of 354 American crew members aboard, 266 were killed. Those who didn't die were badly burned. Many of the injured were taken by ship to Key West, where they were cared for by nuns at the Mary Immaculate Convent, which had been turned into a temporary hospital. The dead were also returned to Key West, the place where they'd known their last happiness. A special plot in the Key West Cemetery, where many of the victims of the explosion are buried, is a marvelous and moving monument to this bleak chapter in American history.

The cause of the explosion was never determined. Nonetheless, nine weeks later, on April 22, 1898, Spain and the U.S. officially went to war. A short war. It didn't take long for Spain to realize that the Spanish armed forces were no match for America's military might. After a three-month fight on two fronts half a world apart, the U.S. found itself in possession of an empire stretching from the Caribbean to the far Pacific. Not only did Spain grant Cuba its independence; by the time the peace treaty had been signed on August 12, 1898, Spain had also ceded Puerto Rico to the U.S. and cut a deal to sell the Philippine Islands to them for $20 million.

The Missing Link

By the turn of the century, Key West was one of the country's most sophisticated cities, with electricity, streetcars, telegraph cable and regular performances by touring European opera and ballet companies. These performances were frequently mounted in the San Carlos Institute, which was also called, during those palmy days, the San Carlos Opera House.

Moreover, the Overseas Railroad arrived on the island in January of 1912. It connected the entire Florida Keys with the rest of America via a

128-mile railroad to Miami. The railroad also became a link to Cuba. Passengers were able to train to Key West and then board a steamship that would carry them across the Florida Straits to Havana.

The Overseas Railroad, with its remarkable bridges and causeways, was labeled the "Eighth Wonder of the World." When the first train pulled into Trumbo Point in 1912, the event sparked the biggest celebration the island had ever seen.

The railroad that had cost visionary Henry Flagler $25,000,000, and nearly 700 men their lives, was an unfortunately short-lived enterprise. In 1935 the railroad was destroyed by a vicious hurricane that killed nearly 600 people in the Upper Keys. At the time of its demise, the company was deeply in debt, with no hope of recovery in sight. And so the railroad right-of-way and the bridges were sold to the State of Florida, which used them for an overseas highway that eventually opened in 1938.

Smuggling

The jagged coastline of the Florida Keys, with its many inlets, nooks and coves, has long been a perfect entry way for a variety of contraband coming into the country by boat. Nowhere is entry into the U.S. so easy as it is here. To cross the border into the United States, one merely comes ashore. In the 1920s, when the sale and consumption of alcoholic beverages in the U.S. became illegal, the Florida Keys became infamous as a gateway for rumrunning. Havana is only ninety miles from Key West. Beer and rum purchased in Cuba doubled in value when they reached America's shores and doubled again and again as they changed hands, until at last the expensive booze finally trickled down to the consumer. Whiskey, rye and scotch, smuggled from the British Isles via Nassau, followed the same course. Certainly great fortunes were made bootlegging.

When it all ended with the repeal of Prohibition in 1933, hoodlums and syndicates, as well as a surprising number of ostensibly law-abiding citizens, found themselves at the end of a magnificent era of easy money and fortune building. Among the most daring smugglers to accumulate impressive fortunes was Grace Lithgoe of San Francisco. Lithgoe stayed in the Keys for five years, defying capture and finally retiring a rich woman. It is hinted that several of Key West's most famous old families came by their original riches through smuggling.

Aside from the bootleggers, Key West citizens didn't pay much attention to Prohibition. The bar that became Sloppy Joe's, where Hemingway drank both during and after Prohibition, was boldly called "The Blind Pig," a slang term used for anonymous-looking storefronts that hid bars during Prohibition. It seems somewhat like calling a brothel "The Whorehouse," but it's also very typical of the island, where nobody spends much time on subtlety.

Later, marijuana smuggling, which flourished in somewhat the same way as rum smuggling had half a century earlier, reached its glamorous zenith in the early '80s. A new generation of citizens became wealthy, and the restaurants, bars, and trendy shops of Key West prospered. But as the stakes escalated, the game turned dangerous. Finally the once-thriving cottage industry collapsed: some of the players went to jail; others were tricked out of or robbed of their cash; still others blew amazing fortunes on the high life. Only a lucky handful invested in property, businesses and homes.

Southernmost Hooverville

By the time the Great Depression had hit in the 1930s, the bootleggers were the only people in Key West making any money. The wrecking, sponging and cigar industries were long gone. By 1934, 80% of the popu-

Gingerbread trim from Prohibition days with rum and wine bottles, hearts and spades, for those in the know.

lation of 11,000 was on relief. Property owners were unable to pay taxes. The situation seemed hopeless, so city fathers did something that had never been done before in American history: They tore up the city charter and told the federal government that they could no longer survive as a city. At first, the federal government considered evacuating the entire town and moving the citizens to Tampa. But then they came up with a better plan: Turn the city of Key West into a tourist destination!

Julius Stone was sent to do just that. It was his idea to bring Works Projects Administration (WPA) artists to Key West to paint island scenes designed to attract curious travelers. WPA artists also created guidebooks with lists of local tourist attractions for forthcoming visitors. (Ernest Hemingway's house on Whitehead Street was attraction number 18.)

In addition, Stone rallied the townspeople to landscape the streets and beautify the town. He talked Pan American World Airways into resuming service to the city. His efforts led, furthermore, to the resurrection of the Casa Marina and numerous other Key West hotels, motels and guesthouses. It was during Stone's commission, as well, that the Federal Building on Simonton Street and the open-air City Aquarium were both built.

To further promote his vision of Key West as a tourist town, Stone wore pink, yellow or green bermuda shorts and sports shirts. Cubans called him *El Paraquito* (the parakeet) because of his preference for pastel outfits. Stone's success at turning around the helpless town did not go unnoticed. Newspapers around the country carried stories about the lucky workers in Key West who worked in Bermuda shorts. The headline "Workers Go to Work in Shorts," in the mid-1930s, was titillating indeed.

After the hurricane of 1935, Stone was also instrumental in transforming the hurricane-ravaged Overseas Railroad bed into the Overseas Highway, a mammoth project that put hundreds of people to work and brought thousands of people to the Keys. Even President Roosevelt came for the three-day-long celebration of the formal opening of the Overseas Highway in 1938.

Military Town

Meanwhile, the government began work on the Key West submarine base, preparing for the possibility of war, in the late 1930s. The construction and maintenance of the base provided jobs for many citizens who found gainful employment throughout World War II. Just as it did across the rest of America, WW II put the citizens of Key West back on their feet, too.

Key West became a military town during the war and remained so for many decades. The Navy stationed 25,000 personnel on the island and hired many civilians. The backbone of Key West's economy at that time was the Naval presence. Then the island suffered another setback in 1974 when the Navy closed the submarine base and withdrew enormous numbers of its people. Overnight, it seemed, half of the population of Key West was suddenly gone. Businesses collapsed, and the downtown area became a ghost town once more. Stores, bars and restaurants were boarded up. Duval Street buildings were abandoned and left to crumble in the sun.

The Last Resort

This state of desolation did not last long. Once again, it was decided that tourism was the city's only hope for economic recovery. The restoration and preservation of downtown Key West, fully supported by local and state governments, steadily picked up steam. Tourism became everybody's objective for the future. In the early 1980s a county-wide Tourist Development Commission was formed to promote the Keys throughout the world. The TDC collects a "bed tax" which amounts to millions of dollars annually, all funneled into advertising and promotion for the island.

The Key West of today is unmistakably a tourist town indeed, hosting millions of visitors each year. The town's need to attract and satisfy its paying guests colors just about everything that happens here.

Architecture

A
s YOU EXPLORE the streets of Old Town Key West, you might feel as if you've time-traveled back to an early New England town. The most fantastic of Key West's wooden houses were built in the 1800s, when the island's wealthiest citizens were making huge fortunes from wrecking, sponging, and cigar manufacturing. In those early days, when the city of Key West was among the wealthiest in the country, homes were lavished with elegant details and elaborate gingerbread trim. But those prosperous times passed, and Key West, by the 1930s, was among the poorest U.S. cities.

Through the years old houses were often allowed to run down by descendants of the once-large families who originally occupied them. Many were divided into ramshackle apartments.

In 1886, while the city's lone fire engine was in New York undergoing repairs, nearly two-thirds of the town burned to the ground. After that fire, federal and municipal buildings were constructed predominantly of brick. Tin roofs on homes replaced wooden shingles because they stopped the spread of fire from one roof to the next; they deflected sunlight and heat, and they also assisted in water collection. Rain ran easily off the roofs into cisterns.

From just after the Civil War until the early 1900s the cigar industry was one of Key West's primary sources of income. To house the workers and their families, factory owners constructed neighborhoods of small cottages. Today, these century-old houses, built predominantly in the "shotgun style," are scattered throughout Old Town Key West.

In much of the rest of America the prosperity of the post WW II-era brought about the construction of suburban homes, created for smaller families. Large wooden houses, difficult to maintain and largely run down by time, were destroyed to make way for modern brick and mortar construction. But fortunately in Key West, few property owners had the money to dismantle their white-elephant houses or to replace them with more modern materials, so here they remain.

Key West is recognized today as a model city of historic preservation. The city's one-hundred block historic district of wooden houses is the largest in the country. These remarkable houses of Old Town Key West, which have survived America's headlong march into progress, will continue to survive. Since the beginning of Key West's preservation movement in the 1960s, city and state preservation laws have been implemented and strictly enforced, insuring that our old houses will continue to provide the world with a glimpse into a magical chapter of America's history.

The pioneering citizens who built these houses of the 19th century speak to us across many generations, from a time when architectural style was dictated by need, and then by culture, and finally, for the lucky few who could afford it, by subjective expression.

The Houses of Old Town

If you find your fundamental knowledge of architecture challenged in Key West, you're not alone. The architecture on this island is difficult for anyone to identify and label specifically. Keeping track of which type of pillar, post or column signifies the stylistic roots of Greek, Roman, or Queen Anne can become a mind-boggling exercise. When someone is bold enough to come out and name the architectural style of a place, you can be sure that someone else will soon come along to disagree. There is no right or wrong to this. The debate can never end.

Most of the wooden homes borrow features from a variety of styles, which were brought to the island from many places, and adapted to withstand weather conditions quite foreign to the rest of America. The people who built them were sometimes legitimate building contractors, sometimes ship carpenters, and sometimes pioneering Americans with enormous enthusiasm and good, old-fashioned common sense.

In describing the wooden architecture of Key West, the word *vernacular* has become interchangeable with *conch* as in "vernacular architecture" or "conch house." Here are the five major classifications of architectural styles represented in Key West's conch houses.

Classic Revival

A popular architectural style in the early 1800s was the classic revival, a style made popular in England. American builders and carpenters adapted the style according to their tastes and needs. The style is identified by well-proportioned rectangular forms, gabled roofs and columned porches. Balance is a determining factor. The majority of the houses in

A Classic Revival style Key West house—"The Gingerbread House"

the historic district are classic revivals. The house many consider to be the fanciest house on the island is the classic revival at 615 Elizabeth Street, "The Gingerbread House."

Eyebrow

The eyebrow house, an offshoot of classic revival, is unique to Key West. There are about 100 of these on the island. Adapted to keep sun and heat out of upstairs rooms, the windows of an eyebrow house are set beneath a heavy roof overhang, supported by corner beams.

Examples of this distinctly conch adaptation are at 816 and 823 Eaton Street. Once you get the hang of recognizing the eyebrow house, you'll spot them frequently.

An Eyebrow house

A Bahamian style house

Bahamian

Bahamian style houses are designed to withstand tropical heat and storms. Features are wide, wrap-around porches, and floor to ceiling wooden-shuttered windows, designed to take the best advantage of prevailing breezes. Spacious and rectangular, the no-nonsense styling of the Bahamian house is stunning in its simplicity.

The houses at 730 Eaton and 408 William streets are true Bahamian houses, actually constructed on Green Turtle Cay in the Bahamas and barged to Key West in 1846.

Queen Anne

Queen Anne styled architecture, a category of the broader division of Victorian, was popular in the 1880s, when the residents of Key West were still enjoying a thriving economy. A predominant element of Queen Anne style is a pointed turret on one side of the house. Beyond that single identifying point, just about anything goes. Queen Anne is the most lavish style you'll see here.

Queen Anne-style—"The Southernmost House"

Key West's quintessential Queen Anne house is the very last one on Duval Street, on the ocean at the southern corner of the island. It's called *the* Southernmost House, although there is controversy over whether or not it truly is the southernmost house. There is no question of its authenticity as a perfect example of Queen Anne architecture.

Shotgun

Shotgun houses, also known as cigarmakers' cottages, are the island's smallest homes. Shotguns sit on raised foundations and are recognizable by their very simple design: a hall that runs from the front door to the back, with a parlor and one or two bedrooms leading off it. On the out-

Shotgun houses

side, the little houses feature a door on one side and one or two windows, depending upon the width of the house.

A much-photographed block of shotguns is the 400 block of Truman Avenue, where a row of cigarmakers' cottages have been restored to look much as they did when they were constructed around the turn of the century.

Gingerbread Trim, Conch Architecture's Unifying Trademark

The fancy swirls, designs and forms cut out of wood and used as decorative trims on Key West's wooden houses are known as gingerbread. With a memorable dash of whimsy, gingerbread trim is the unifying trait of conch architecture. It is the memory of gingerbread trim that visitors to America's largest outdoor museum of wooden houses remember most clearly when they recall Old Town Key West.

Some Notes on Getting Around

EY WEST is a small island, roughly two miles by four miles. The downtown area, where visitors spend most of their time, is smaller still. A hike from one end of Duval Street to the other is less than a mile and will take you from the Atlantic Ocean to the Gulf of Mexico. Those accustomed to walking will find downtown destinations no more than an easy stroll away.

Cars are generally a bother here. If you're bringing a car to Key West, make sure there's parking available at your hotel or guest house. (Many do not have off-street parking.) Metered spaces downtown are $1 per hour; $.25 per hour at Smathers Beach. You'll find private lots, with varying prices, throughout downtown.

At 300 Grinnell St., there is a Park & Ride garage. Park and ride a shuttle around the island. Parking there is inexpensive, and the shuttles are pretty regular. Park & Ride info: 292-8160.

Currently the city is experimenting with a residential parking program. Spaces on side streets marked "RP" indicate these spots. If you don't have Monroe County plates, or a residential sticker issued by City Hall, do not use these spots. You will be ticketed. Key West has a large and active fleet of meter readers. Cops write parking tickets, too. Illegally parked cars are often towed.

Taxis
Call Five 6's Cabs at 296-6666 or Friendly Cab Company at 292-0000.

Charter Van, Limo or Bus
Call Eggs Transport (see page 136) at 294-0190 or 304-4035.

Bikes
Once you understand how the island is laid out you'll want to see it like a native: on a bike. The island is small and flat, and features near perfect weather year round. Roughly 15% of local residents rely exclusively on bikes for local transportation.

A bicycle path hugs the north and south sides of the island. It's got its fair share of bumps and potholes, so you need to keep your eyes open. Restoration is ongoing. Only bikes and pedestrians are authorized to use the bike path, so it's safe, easy and fun. To bike all the way around the island via the bike path, which will disappear entirely in some places, you'll probably need about an hour and a half, so start out early in the morning or later in the afternoon, when the sun is not so high in the sky. Don't try this trip on a very windy day; if you hit hard wind you'll feel as if you're pedaling your bike under water.

Remember that pedestrians have the right-of-way on sidewalks. If the sidewalk is clear, you're welcome to ride your bike on it. Weaving your bicycle around pedestrians on busy downtown sidewalks is actually illegal! Bicycles move with motor traffic, and follow the same laws as cars. In Key West, you will get a ticket for going through a stop signal, or for riding your bike at night without a light.

Bicycle Rentals

Standard rates for bicycle rentals are $5 a day; $25 a week; $75 a month. Some guesthouses and hotels provide bicycle rentals to their guests. Wherever you are in Key West, chances are you're within walking distance of a dozen or so bicycle shops that will rent you a bike.

Mopeds and Scooters

Key West's narrow streets, good weather, and scarce parking make mopeds and scooters a very popular and affordable mode of transportation. However, the island's lax helmet laws make them potentially deadly.

Ambulances in Key West respond to an average of 300 moped accidents each year, accounting for nearly half of all traffic accidents. Tourists are involved in three-quarters of them. Fortunately, most accidents involving mopeds result in little more than road rash, the agonizing yet non-life-threatening scrapes on knees and elbows that have skimmed along the pavement. Serious moped accidents involve head injuries—concussions, skull fractures, brain contusions or hemorrhages. Statistics also show that 20% of moped drivers involved in accidents are intoxicated.

Moped rental stands are everywhere, often sharing space with bicycle rental shops. Moped rentals are usually around $15 a day, or $100 a week. You must be at least eighteen years old and a licensed driver with a credit card to rent one. If you want a helmet, just ask for one.

*The wind blows so hard the ocean gets up on its
hind legs and walks right across the land.*

– E. G. Robinson's sidekick describing a hurricane
in the film *Key Largo*.

Frost Free in Paradise—
Keys Weather

THE WEATHER IS DIFFERENT in the Keys. It is temperate year round.
We never, ever have frost. That's why they call it Paradise. Were it
not for the possibility of hurricanes, the Florida Keys would have the
world's most perfect weather. The sun shines here just about every day
of the year. It rains only half as much as it does in the rest of Florida.
The reason has to do with land mass and convection currents. What it
all means is that when skies are dark and wet over Miami and
Ft. Lauderdale, skies in the Keys remain blue and clear.

Afternoon showers in the rest of Florida are common. They happen
when the land heats up and the moist air from the ocean hits it. In the
Keys, the land mass is missing from the equation. Hence, the Keys get
only about thirty-eight inches of rain each year. Key West is the driest
city in Florida.

Highs and Lows

Highest temperature ever recorded in Key West was 97 degrees. Coldest
was 41. On summer's hottest days the Florida Keys have the advantage
of being situated between two very powerful bodies of water, the Gulf of
Mexico and the Atlantic Ocean. The trade winds keep even the hottest
days tolerable.

Usually we have a week or two of cold weather just around Christmas time, which also happens to be the very busiest time of the year down here. When temperatures drop into the 50s outdoors, the temperature is also in the 50s indoors since older Keys homes rarely have insulation or heating systems. So we locals wear many layers of clothes, and even socks beneath our sandals. We probably look mighty peculiar to tourists.

Water temperatures in the Atlantic Ocean are in the lower 70s during the Keys' cooler months. By July and August, the water warms up to the mid-to-upper 80s, and humidity makes it difficult to dry off after a shower.

Florida Weather Report
305-207-9672
Toll-free from the Keys. Call the National Weather Service in Miami for a taped weather report for the Keys, any hour of the day or night. Also, sunrise, sunset and tide schedules.

Conch, An Endangered Species

THE WORD IS pronounced *konk*. If you pronounce the *ch* in conch, like the *ch* in crunch, everyone will know that you're very new to the island. The regal queen conch is Monroe County's much beloved mascot. A Conch is a native of the Florida Keys; conch refers also to any person, place or thing relating to the Florida Keys, which is known as the Conch Republic. People not born here, but who are dedicated citizens of seven years or more are called Freshwater Conchs.

Conchs suffer conch madness. They live in conch houses. Their sons play for the Fighting Conchs, the name of the high school football team. Their daughters kick up their heels in a girls' drill team known as the Conchettes. Conch Capers is the name of the annual local variety show. Conch cruisers are the cars that work fine here, but you wouldn't dare drive one out of Monroe County. Conched out is what you are feeling when you positively, absolutely must get out of the Keys for a couple of days or go nuts.

Eating Conch

Conch chowder comes cream-style or tomato-style like Manhattan clam chowder. Sometimes people order conch chowder, taste it, and tell the waitron there's been a mistake. "I ordered conch chowder," they say, "not clam chowder." The two are close cousins. Order conch chowder in a Cuban restaurant some time; that's where it's best.

Cracked conch steak is a slab of conch pounded until it's tender or passed through a tenderizer, then batter dipped, and pan or deep fried. Eating this delicacy can be a challenge if it is not properly tenderized. A good place for a conch steak is the Rusty Anchor, out on Stock Island. Somebody in a fish store once told me that the conch tenderizer machine is a real hassle. Not to operate; that's easy. But cleaning the machine after the conch has been tenderized takes so much time the entire process is not cost efficient.

Conch fritters can be another one of the world's great taste treats— chewy, spicy, crisp on the outside and tender on the inside. They are not difficult to make. Sadly, chefs often skimp on the conch. There should be lots of conch meat in a conch fritter. Otherwise, you're getting what one of my Bahamian neighbors scornfully describes as dough fritters.

Another treat, conch seviche, is seen on menus less frequently. Too bad. Conch meat cooked and tenderized by lime juice is sublime. Don't be afraid to try it.

Nowadays the conch in stores and restaurants is imported from the Bahamas. The Keys conch population has been nearly annihilated by hungry divers.

The World's Biggest Conch

See the colossal conch, homage to conch spirit, in front of the Key West High School at 2100 Flagler Avenue. Here's a photo opportunity not to be missed. The monument is constructed of metal scraps and built by the metal shop students at Key West High under the direction of former shop teacher and artist George Carey. Carey, a Conch, is descended from a long line of sea-faring Careys including Captain George Carey, who back in 1859 built the Heritage House at 410 Caroline Street.

Blowing Conch

The distinctive sound of a blowing conch travels for distances of over two miles. The shell was used as a musical instrument in Mesopotamia over 4,000 years ago. In some African and island cultures it still serves as a ceremonial trumpet. During Key West's annual Old Island Days, a conch-blowing contest attracts many contestants. It's one of those only-in-Key West activities that draws lots of media attention. Of course, these conch blowers are only required to blow one mighty blast, not recognizable melodies like *The Flight of the Bumblebee* or the *Sabre Dance*.

Rimsky-Korsakov on the conch shell? Impossible you say? Not for Reverend and Mrs. Thurlow Weed. In the mid-70s the accomplished conch shell musicians appeared as guests on television's game show *To Tell The Truth*. Mr. and Mrs. Weed also appear in the 1978 film *The Key West Picture Show*. Reverend Weed was, and remains long after his death, the undisputed king of queen conch playing in Key West.

A Walking Tour
of
Historic Old Town Key West

T HIS WALKING TOUR covers one-and-three-quarter miles of Old Town
and one and three-quarter centuries of history. Plan on taking around
two leisurely hours to complete it.

The tour begins in Mallory Square, in front of the Key West Chamber
of Commerce. There is municipal parking on nearby Mallory Dock. A
frequently heard question here is "where is the sunset pier?" It's right
here. At Mallory Dock. A good time to start the walk is about two hours
or so before sunset. That way, you'll be heading into the cool of the evening and arriving back at Mallory Dock in time for the world's coolest
sunset.

Here in Mallory Square in 1822, American sailors raised the U.S. flag,
symbolizing the purchase of Florida from Spain. The streets of Old Town
Key West radiate from this initial settlement, and many of the stately
structures you see here were built well over a century ago. These buildings, once warehouses, icehouses and chandleries (stores selling all
manner of ships' supplies), are today home to a glittering variety of shops,
saloons and bistros.

The Chamber of Commerce is located in a building that was owned
in the 1800s by one of the town's wealthiest citizens, wrecking master
Asa Tift. The valuable salvaged cargoes from wrecked ships were stored
here. The Shell Warehouse next door is in what used to be Tift's Ice
House. Before electricity, Key Westers imported ice from New England.
Great chunks of pond ice were shipped to Key West, then packed in saw-
dust and stored in the former ice house you see here.

Mr. Tift was so successful at his various enterprises that he built himself a fine mansion on Whitehead Street, which you can visit today. It's called the Hemingway House and Museum.

In Mallory Square you'll see several crusty characters created out of papier mache. They are more than happy to pose for photographs. In front of the Shell Warehouse, there is a conch fisherman just in from the sea. Out in the square, another fisherman on a bicycle sells fish. And on a bench just outside of the Key West Aquarium sits an old sea captain smoking a pipe. Many people particularly enjoy posing with the shark outside the aquarium, which was built by the Works Projects Administration in 1934 and was the island's first tourist attraction.

If you're fascinated by wrecking, the industry that turned this little seaport town into the richest small city in America in the mid-1800s, you'll love the Shipwreck Historeum, where you'll meet Asa Tift, your guide, through exhibits which recreate the shore-side bustle and drama of the wrecking business.

Lined up in front of the Sponge Market are Old Town Trolleys. Trolley tours depart Mallory Square every half hour. Just past the aquarium is the Clinton Market, a large, cream-colored brick building. In its earliest days this was once a coal storehouse. Until the early 1930s it was a naval administration building. Today the building is a complex of shops, air conditioned to near freezing temperatures and full of exactly the kind of merchandise you'd expect to find in a busy tourist center.

Continue on to Front Street.

That great, red brick building, next on the right, with the uncharacteristic chimneys is the Custom House. Built in 1891, it was abandoned in the 1950s and saved from the bulldozers in 1973, when it was added to the National Register of Historic Places. The architectural style is Romanesque revival. The Key West Art and Historical Society is in charge of its current restoration; a museum and art and cultural center is planned.

This tiny, nicely tended triangular park just in front of the Custom House is Clinton Square. It contains a monument to the Union soldiers and sailors who lost their lives here during the Civil War. The men didn't die in battle—the only shots fired here were for practice. They died from yellow fever. For the duration of the war, Key West, the southernmost city, was peacefully held in Northern hands.

Whitehead Street, 200 Block

Just ahead on the corner is Mel Fisher's Maritime Heritage Museum. On July 20, 1985, Mel Fisher and his faithful treasure salvors discovered the mother lode of the Spanish galleon *Atocha*, which sank in 1622 with a cargo of gold and silver bars, jewelry, and coins, altogether valued at over $200 million. Don't be surprised if Mel Fisher himself is there to greet you. On exhibit: treasure that lay unclaimed on the ocean floor for more than 360 years.

Cross Whitehead Street.

The Audubon House and Gardens is at 205 Whitehead. The three-story house was home to Captain John Geiger, his wife, and their nine children. When John James Audubon came to the Keys in search of flamingos in 1832, he stayed at the Geiger house. Several original Audubon engravings commemorate the visit.

Just past the Audubon House driveway is a replica of gingerbread trim that was used during Prohibition to indicate the personality or theme of the house on the property. The rum and wine bottles and the hearts and spades advertised to those in the know that gambling, liquor and loose women were available behind a fence like this.

On your right, across the street, still stands an old Navy cistern, one of the biggest cisterns on the island. Before water was brought to the Keys via a pipeline from the mainland during World War II, residents relied upon rainwater, which they collected and stored in cisterns like this. Nearly every home had a cistern of some sort. Key West was the first city of its size to get electricity, in 1887, and the last to get running water, in 1942!

Also on your right you'll find the Presidential Gates. Installed in 1906, these gates were designed to be opened for U.S. Presidents only. The last president to pass through them was John F. Kennedy in 1962, who came here along with the Joint Chiefs of Staff during the Cuban Missile Crisis. Other presidents to pass through the gates were Presidents Dwight Eisenhower and Harry Truman. (To visit Truman's Key West retreat, known today as "The Little White House Museum," go through the Presidential Gates, on into the Truman Annex, and straight ahead about a block.)

In 1987 a private citizen bought the 103 acres of the non-active Navy base and an offshore island for $17 million. The buyer was Pritham Singh, who once lived a hand-to-mouth existence here in Key West. In the late '60s he sold sea shells by the seashore at sunset. In the '70s, he sold seashore property in Maine and was so good at it that he made a fortune. One day he read in the *New York Times* that the Navy base was to be auctioned off on the following day. Singh hopped a jet, came to town, and sealed the deal twenty-four hours later.

You are welcome to walk through the Presidential Gates and stroll through the remarkably transformed property. Some houses and condominiums are available for sale or rent here. You can't miss the sales office. If you're interested, take lots and lots of money.

Turn left onto Caroline Street.

Caroline Street, 400 Block

Lots of women go crazy in this town, and everyone in Key West has at one time or another wondered which one of them Jimmy Buffett is singing about in "There's a Woman Going Crazy on Caroline Street."

On your right is the garden of Kelly's Caribbean Restaurant and Grill and first home of Pam Am Airlines. The first roundtrip ticket to Havana, Cuba, was sold here in 1927. Kelly is Hollywood actress Kelly McGillis, who starred in movies *Top Gun* and *Witness*.

Next door to Kelly's at the end of the driveway, you can see the green exterior of the Robert Frost Cottage, named for the American poet who spent sixteen winters here. The cottage sits on the property of the Heritage House Museum at 410 Caroline. The house was built by Captain George Carey in 1834—one of the oldest houses in town. Notice the fresh-water well to the left of the front door. Legend has it that Indians, as well as sailors and pirates, came ashore to use this well. The hand-rolled glass windows of the house are original.

At 429 Caroline, at the corner of Duval, you can see the house of Dr. Joseph Yates Porter, Florida's first health officer under whose leadership yellow fever was eradicated. Dr. Porter's bigger claim to fame is, however, the fact that he was born in this house in 1847 and died here, too, in same bedroom in 1927, eighty years later. The entrance, with its double doors, wide staircase, twin Grecian urns, gingerbread trim, and stained glass conch shells, is worth a good look.

The Bull and Whistle Bar, at the corner of Caroline and Duval, is popular for its very laid-back attitude, open air bar, and all-day, live entertainment. The cement-cast bull, charging through the Caroline Street wall of the Bull & Whistle, was created by sculptor June Tvardzik in 1978. We can't quite imagine why.

Cross Duval and continue on Caroline.

Caroline Street, 500 Block

On the left, the historic Fogarty House, now housing Key West's own Hooters Restaurant. In this once proud mansion Dr. and Mrs. John Fogarty entertained Presidents Cleveland and Taft, and railroad baron Henry Flagler. Dr. Fogarty was mayor of Key West and hosted a joyful week-long celebration when the Overseas Railroad arrived in January, 1912.

Next door you'll find the Curry Mansion, built in 1905 by Milton Curry, son of William Curry, Florida's first self-made millionaire. The tour through this many-leveled Victorian mansion is very different from most. In the Curry Mansion you are free to sit at the grand dining room table while a companion shoots your photo. You are invited to spend all the time you like in the library, which is full of goodies, and to poke and peek at will. The Curry Mansion is also a very gracious guesthouse.

You'll next come to Ann Street on the left. At the corner of Ann and Caroline is the building that once housed Pauline Hemingway's interior design shop. After her divorce from Ernest Hemingway in 1940, Pauline became an interior decorator. The building is now actually two houses joined—223 Ann Street and 525 Caroline Street. The Caroline Street address was Pauline's shop.

In the yard at 531 Caroline is a large, East African tulip tree. The tree's tulip-like, orange blossoms appear in the wintertime. There is a jasmine bush and a frangipani tree. Both produce incredibly sweet-smelling flowers. The jasmine has tiny white flowers. Frangipani flowers are waxy with four petals. This house belonged to John Spottswood, a Monroe County Sheriff and state senator. Spottswood was a good friend of

President Harry Truman. For many years after leaving office, the Trumans maintained their friendship with the Spottswoods. Mrs. Spottswood recalled that although she'd heard that Truman cursed often, she had never heard him swear. She called the first lady "Mrs. T" and never "Bess."

Straight ahead, on the lefthand corner of Caroline and Simonton, is the Cypress House, a fine exhibit of classic Bahamian architecture. The house that originally stood on this corner really was made of cypress, but it burned, along with two-thirds of the island, in the great fire of 1886. The house you see today was built in 1888 out of Dade County pine. The exterior is painted with a sealant to maintain its natural appearance. The Bahamian features you'll see here are tall, floor-to-ceiling windows, high ceilings, and porches on both levels. Beneath the Cypress House are two cisterns where collected rainwater is used to water the garden and fill the pool. A 40-by-40 foot roof can catch up to 4200 gallons of rainwater in a year!

Turn right here and head up Simonton Street.

Simonton Street, 300 Block

On the left is the old Post Office and Federal Building built in 1934 of petrified coral rock quarried from Windley Key, 80 miles to the north in the Upper Keys. The quarry from which this stone was taken is now home to Theater of the Sea, a theme park.

Now on the right at 314 Simonton we come to the Casa Antigua Apartments, Ernest Hemingway's first stop when he arrived in Key West in 1928. From his second-floor apartment, he must have had a panoramic view—across the tin roofs and treetops, all the way to the Atlantic in one direction and the Gulf of Mexico in the other. It is easy to imagine how Hemingway became instantly enamored of the island.

At the back door of the gift shop, you enter a courtyard and garden full of tropical foliage. Look for a peacock and a very blue tiled pool. Take a camera. If you buy something worth $10 or more, you can visit the garden for free; otherwise, it will cost you $2. But remember, this Eden-like oasis is newly created. In Hemingway's day, this courtyard held an automobile dealership and a repair shop.

As you walk up Simonton, notice the mahogany trees along the side-walks on both sides of the street. These were planted by the Civilian Conservation Corps (CCC) in the 1930s when young men were taken off relief and given jobs such as beautifying their towns.

Sign of Sanford, at 328 Simonton, is the workshop, studio and show-room of artist Sanford Birdsey. Her storefront windows are a throwback to the days when window shopping was a favorite pastime.

Cross Eaton Street.

Simonton Street, 400 Block

On the corner of Simonton and Eaton sits the First Methodist Old Stone Church. The Indian laurel tree in the front yard is a member of the ficus family, which is well represented on this island. The church is constructed of two-foot-thick coral rock walls quarried from this same property. After the rock had been removed from the earth, the quarried site was used as a cistern. The cistern was so large it supplied water to the church as well as many neighbors and often ships that came into the harbor. The caps of the cisterns are still visible in the side yard.

This stone church replaced an old wooden one. As the new church was slowly constructed of coral rock, the much smaller wooden one remained inside. It took the congregation fifteen years to complete the stone church, and, when it was done, the old wooden church was dis-mantled and removed, piece by piece, through the newer front doors. In 1892 the first service was held in the Old Stone Church you see today.

At 410 Simonton we now see the William Kerr House. There is no other house quite like this one, built around 1880 by architect William Kerr for his bride. The architectural style is carpenter's gothic. Kerr was an Irishman hired by the government to oversee the construction of the beautiful Custom House in 1891. He also designed the Old City Hall and the Old Stone Church. In front of the Kerr house notice the lush philo-dendron growing up the massive trunk of a mahogany tree.

At the intersection of Fleming and Simonton, you're standing at the heart of Key West's antique district. The tall brick building on the right is one of the few survivors of the Great Fire of 1886 that destroyed much of the town. After the fire, residents took a hard look at the destruction and realized that buildings of brick and houses with tin roofs were the ones that had survived. These elements were incorporated into the reconstruction of the city. Tin roofs have been popular in Key West ever since.

Cross Fleming Street.

Simonton Street, 500 Block

The elegant Marquesa Hotel and Cafe was once a flophouse, as dark and foreboding twenty years ago as it is bright and inviting today. In the mid 1980s a young woman was murdered here. Her body was discovered the following morning by a passerby who saw her feet, one wearing a sandal, one not, poking out from under the house (shades of *The Wizard of Oz*).

Those pretty silver buttonwood trees that line the block were planted by the Marquesa Hotel. The seeds from these trees resemble the buttons of an earlier day; hence, the name buttonwood.

The name of Dr. Maloney, the original resident of 508 Simonton, is still visible in the stained glass above the door. Today Maloney's former home is a collection of ramshackle apartments.

Free School Alley, home of Nancy's Secret Garden, begins here in the middle of the block on your left. Nancy invites visitors to bring a picnic and to dine at a table beneath the canopy of her spectacular tropical jungle. There is an entry fee of $6 to help pay for the upkeep of this fantastic collection of palms and exotics.

The building at 525 Simonton (Old Island Realty), built in 1890, is an excellent specimen of classic revival architecture, one of the five main styles represented in Key West's historic district. Current owners have received many awards for this restoration. Twin palms in front are particularly healthy Washingtonias, easily identified by their height and tiered grass skirts. There are several other Washingtonia palms on the island, but none so noble as these.

In 1905 the aforementioned Dr. Maloney sold the building at 530 Simonton, now a wellness center, to the organizers of B'nai Zion. Begun in 1887, it is the oldest organized Jewish congregation in Florida. The island's first Jewish settlers were escaping religious persecution in Russia, heading for new lives in Cuba and South America, when their ships wrecked on the reefs and they found themselves, as many other travelers did, stranded in Key West. Today the congregation has a modern synagogue on United Street.

Before 530 Simonton was a synagogue, it was home to a saloonkeeper who dabbled in wrecking. The captain's walk, from where enterprising seamen searched the horizon for signs of a shipwreck, is still on the roof.

Cross Southard Street.

Simonton Street, 600 Block

Just past the intersection of Southard and Simonton, on the left side, you'll see a good example of a gumbo limbo tree and how the owners of the property have detoured their white picket fence to allow for the tree's thickening trunk. The gumbo limbo is also called the "tourist tree" because of its peeling, red skin.

Coming up on the corner of Simonton and Angela streets, you'll see Key West City Hall. The infamous police station is housed here, and so is Fire Station #1. Our police and fire departments were once rife with felonious recruits. In 1976 the fire chief, with the strange but true name of Bum Farto, was charged with two counts of sale and delivery of cocaine. Before his sentencing, he rented a car in Key West and headed out of town. A month later the car was found parked on a side street, but Bum has never been seen or heard from again. Ten years later his wife, who supported herself by baking birthday and wedding cakes, successfully petitioned to have her missing husband declared legally dead so that she could collect his pension. If he is alive, Bum Farto is now 77 years old.

Then in 1984, the assistant police chief was charged with delivering cocaine in fried chicken boxes. He is about to be released from prison.

Turn left onto Angela Street.

Angela Street, 600 Block

This block of Angela has the distinction of having the highest elevation on the island: 18 feet above sea level. When you reach the end of the block, you are at the top of Solares Hill.

The Philip Burton House is at 608 Angela. If Key West historians and tour guides follow true to form, this house will probably become known as the Liz Taylor House because Elizabeth Taylor visited here often. Her host was her father-in-law, Shakespearean scholar Philip Burton. Burton was once headmaster at the Port Talbot School in South Wales, where he met, and adopted, a brilliant student named Richard. The great actor eventually became the fifth and sixth husband of Elizabeth Taylor.

Professor Burton, a great scholar and a kind neighbor, was known for his tireless dedication to local theater and his enjoyment of long, solitary walks. He bought this little house on Solares Hill in 1974 and lived here until his death in 1995.

If you were to continue straight ahead, you would come to the city cemetery, a wonderful place to visit in the cool of the early morning or the late afternoon.

Turn left onto Elizabeth Street.

Elizabeth Street, 600 Block

You'll now see on the right a row of cigarmakers' cottages, or shotgun houses, so called because of their design: a hall begun at the front door and extending back the length of the house. Then a parlor, one or two bedrooms, and finally the kitchen were connected off to the side of the hall. If you were to look through the front door of the house, you would see clear through to the backyard—as if you were looking down the barrel of a shotgun. The open doors at the front and back of the house allowed for a cooling ventilation. Addresses 621, 623, 625, 627 and 629 Elizabeth are all shotgun cottages once lived in by Cuban cigarmakers and their families. Today cottages such as these rent for around $1,000 a month and sell for around $200,000. If you can find one for sale...

The house at 620 Elizabeth is a typically New England-style home, illustrative of the strong ties between New England and the Florida Keys. The gold-colored ceramic star indicates that this house has been restored to its original condition. The pink star, which you see less often, indicates that the residence was once part of an Old Island Restoration Foundation house tour.

Turn right onto Bakers Lane.

Bakers Lane

In the middle of the block, more or less, you'll see a marker for Bakers Lane. Turn here and stroll down this typical Old Town lane for a look at a cozy cluster of cottages whose occupants enjoy the peace and quiet of a nearly car-free neighborhood. However, they do have to put up with ardent fans of writer James Leo Herlihy who make the pilgrimage to his home nearly every day of the year to pay homage to the man who penned the heartbreaking novel *Midnight Cowboy*. Herlihy lived at 709 Bakers. Notice the 1960s-era gingerbread trim on Herlihy's house. Inside, on the door, there is a hinged flap over a peep hole. On the flap Herlihy had written: "God is at the door. Let us see what face he is wearing now."

The Gingerbread House at 615 Elizabeth was a wedding gift from Benjamin Baker to his daughter in 1885. In both corners of this white-picket-fenced yard stand small lignumvitae trees. You can recognize them by their tiny blue flowers and/or red berries, depending upon the time of year. The only tornado ever to hit the island tore this house off its foundation in 1972. Because of the damage, the distressed property sold at a rock-bottom price of $22,500 that same year. Since then, the house has been updated and has changed hands frequently. In May 1993 it sold for $715,000!

This is perhaps the island's most classic example of gingerbread trim. In the mid 1800s, after the invention of the jigsaw, builders and carpenters identified their work by the fanciful detail of the scroll ornamentation, or gingerbread. It was the the very last thing to be installed on a new house. When the popularity of gingerbread grew nationally, Sears and Roebuck then began selling it in their catalog. Unfortunately, as a result of its mass production, gingerbread trim has lost its individuality.

Moving along to the end of the block, beginning at 608 Elizabeth, we see three new houses built in 1996 and designed to fit in with the historic architecture already present for over 100 years. Here in the historic district, anything new has to be constructed in the style of neighboring houses, built a century earlier.

Cross Southard Street.

Elizabeth Street, 500 Block

The house on the right-hand corner, 701 Southard, has two steep gables for collecting rainwater. The more slanted roof area you have, the more water you collect.

On the left side of Elizabeth Street in the backyard of 631 Southard, is a healthy Key lime tree, which bears fruit year round. In front of Kinky's Construction, at 522 Elizabeth, are two colossal Spanish lime trees. The female of the two produces green fruit in spring and summer months, ripening in August. Next to her, on the right, is a male Spanish lime.

In the yard at 518 Elizabeth there is a pretty flowering tree called poor man's orchid, identifiable by its double-lobed leaves and orchid-shaped flower in the winter. Also, you'll find a fragrant jasmine bush.

Next door at 516 Elizabeth, we see a good example of an eyebrow house, an architectural style unique to Key West. There are roughly one hundred others on the island, each featuring the heavy roof overhang that protects upper-story windows and, thus, the second floor of the house as well, from the direct rays of the sun.

On the roof of 514 Elizabeth, see a roof opening called a scuttle, designed to let hot air flow up and out through the attic, while cooler air flows into the house via doors and windows on the first level. The popular island circulation system is borrowed from ships. When it rains, the scuttle quickly and easily shuts tight. By the way, it rains very infrequently in Key West. Our average rainfall is thirty-eight inches a year, the least amount of any city in Florida.

If you now look toward the right-hand corner of the library parking area, you'll see a huge West Indian almond tree. Around it grow the broad-leaved vines of a prolific philodendron plant. Toward the back of the lot, almost directly centered, is a magnificent jacaranda tree, with feathery, light-green leaves and lavender blossoms that appear in both spring and summer. The marbled wood of the jacaranda is used for the dashboard of Mercedes Benz cars.

Next to the wheelchair ramp on your left there is a woman's tongue tree, which you can recognize by its long seed pods that rattle incessantly when the wind blows. Hey, what does that have to do with women's tongues?

Turn right onto Fleming Street.

Fleming Street, 700 Block

Now walk to the end of the block and turn right. On your left are the Jerry Herman Houses, at 701 and 703 Fleming Street. Jerry majored in architecture at the University of Miami. While his minor was music, he was such a skilled pianist and composer that his mother encouraged him to pursue music as well as architecture. And so he did, and the rest of the story is Broadway history. Jerry went on to compose music and lyrics for hits such as *Hello Dolly*, *La Cage Aux Folles* and *Mame*. Thanks, Mrs. Herman!

Jerry's love of architecture and design have not, however, deserted him. Through the years he has restored several Key West properties, none so dramatic as these two fine specimens of Victoriana. The two were identical twins until 703 was fitted with solar generating panels, a modern corruption that knocked it out of the running for several historic preservation awards.

Next, our pink library at 700 Fleming is South Florida's first public library, organized in 1892. For forty-four years the library service was run by the Key West Women's Club. Then in 1959 it moved into this home of its own.

In the library's side yard a palm garden was recently installed. It features twenty-six varieties of palm trees that grow in the Caribbean Basin, from Florida to South America. The garden is open from 9:30 a.m until 5:30 p.m.

At the end of the block, on the left, is the Fleming Street United Methodist Church, erected in 1912. Today a congregation of the Southernmost Church of God in Christ worships here. This church, which replaced an earlier wooden structure destroyed by a 1910 hurricane, is built in a castle style of architecture, alluding to the Kingdom of God.

Turn left onto William Street.

William Street, 400 Block

At 421 William, on the left side of the building, there is a stairway to heaven. The man who was to become my husband lived in the third floor apartment of this house years ago. I climbed that stairway many times.

Another house farther down at 415 William, has been restored to look very much as it did when it was built in 1898. The Key West Bed and Breakfast is the first of a row of beautifully restored historic homes, several of them now used as guesthouses. The Island City House, at 411 William, is one of the largest wooden structures on the island. See how far back from the street it extends? The Gideon Lowe House, or Whispers, at 409 William, is another successful restoration. Notice the yellow elder tree on the left side of the house. This tree flowers three times a year, so it's nearly always in bloom.

Across the street on the left side we see two houses that were barged in 1847 to Key West from Green Turtle Cay in the Bahamas. The yellow house at 408 William was owned by Captain Richard Roberts. The house next door that fronts on Eaton Street was owned by his brother-in-law, Captain John Bartlum. In those days, it was easier and cheaper to barge than to build. The nearest source of hard lumber was 700 miles away in the Florida Panhandle. And these houses, built by shipbuilders using wooden pegs, were easily disassembled, transported and then reassembled.

Turn left onto Eaton Street.

Eaton Street, 700 Block

The Calvin Klein house at 712 Eaton was built in the 1890s by a prosperous grocer, Richard Peacon, who lived here with his family for many years. Locals were shocked in 1980 when fashion baron Calvin Klein paid $975,000 for the octagon-shaped house after it was spiffed and polished to pretty perfection by interior designer Angelo Donghia. Donghia had paid only $45,000 for the place six years earlier. Of course, to Calvin Klein, a guy who charges $100 for a pair of $20 jeans, the price tag must have seemed fair enough. Klein's frequent guest, Brooke Shields, seemed to enjoy visiting Key West more than her host. Klein didn't spend much time here, and a few years after making the famous deal, he sold the house at a huge loss. Why didn't Calvin Klein like Key West? One trolley tour driver says he left because the octagon house didn't have enough closet space. Nowadays it is not at all unusual to pay a million bucks for a pretty property in Paradise.

Turn right onto Peacon Lane.

Peacon Lane or Grunt Bone Alley

Across the street from Calvin's is Peacon Lane, also known by an earlier name, Grunt Bone Alley. Currently there's a sign on this corner, but it may be gone by the time you get to this short thoroughfare only the length of a city block. People seem to love snatching the Grunt Bone Alley sign.

In the first yard on the left side of the lane, you can recognize two travelers palms by the overlapping appearance of their wide, tight stalks near the earth. Each of these fronds, it is said, contains a quart of rainwater—good news for travelers in the tropics in the days before the pipeline delivered fresh water from the mainland.

The Henry Faulkner House is at 328 Peacon. Before he died in a car crash in 1981, Faulkner willed this house to poet Stefan Brecht, son of Bertolt Brecht, with the provision that he never sell it, or dispense with any of the furniture Henry had collected and stored therein. So Brecht, who does not live in Key West, rents the house to a local woman who has lived here for over a decade. She is forbidden to dispose of one stick of Henry Faulkner's termite-infested furniture. Furthermore, she is not permitted to clear out the attic or to alter the premises in any way. So she lives with the gargantuan mirrors in their magnificently carved wooden frames and the art-deco-era chandeliers and lamp treatments that Henry installed thirty years ago. "That's fine," she says. "Imagine all the great energy in here!"

Although Faulkner was a profoundly talented painter whose stylistic flowers, birds, butterflies and slanting houses epitomize the era of the '60s, he longed to be taken seriously also as a poet. He sang jazz in a falsetto voice and claimed to be a large black woman trapped inside a small white man's body. Faulkner's friend, writer James Herlihy, wrote *Midnight Cowboy*, the novel that became the hit movie. It is said that Herlihy modeled the character of Ratso Rizzo after his friend, Henry Faulkner.

Faulkner's Key West house was the setting for several scenes in the film *Criss Cross*, about a go-go dancer's adventures here in the late '60s. The film stars Goldie Hawn and is an excellent physical portrayal of '60s-era Key West. Aside from the fact that the making of the film employed hundreds of Key West people over the slow summer of 1990, and a lot of us got to see Goldie Hawn and Kurt Russell up close, there is little else that is positive to say about it. The film is now on video, but it's understandably difficult to find.

Goldie, by the way, is a true beauty with luminescent skin and a pleasing personality. Kurt's not too bad either.

Now, retrace your steps to the corner of Eaton and William Streets for more historic sights.

Turn left onto William Street.

William Street, 300 Block

On the right corner, look for a huge rubber tree, another member of the ficus family. The rubber tree, popular on the mainland as an indoor plant, grows outdoors year round in this frost-free city. Notice how trees of the ficus family drop thin, aerial branches that return to the earth and take root on their own. Eventually these spindly aerial branches merge to form bigger, sturdier new trunks. Someone has tied a bundle of new branches into a knot, and they have melded quite beautifully, exhibiting the ficus family's strange capabilities.

At 328 William you'll see the "birthday cake" house, so named because of its gingerbread trim in the shape of dripping icing along the roof line and the row of gingerbread flaming candles on the fence around the yard.

Farther down, the little eyebrow house, with the double scuttles, at 309 William, has been in the same Key West family for over 150 years. To the immediate right is Sawyer Lane. Look straight down the lane and you will see, on the left, a massive breadfruit tree. It is the tallest tree in the neighborhood—you can't miss it.

Breadfruit resembles a big, green volleyball and is delicious peeled, baked, and smeared with butter, or cut into chunks and fried in oil. Breadfruit was the cargo on the HMS *Bounty* when a group of mutinous sailors set Captain Bligh adrift at sea in 1789. The breadfruit trees had been loaded onto the ship in Tahiti for delivery to wealthy plantation owners in the West Indies who were to use breadfruit as cheap food for their slaves. Legend has it that Captain Bligh was lavishing the precious supply of fresh water on the breadfruit rather than on the thirsty crew. Another version of the mutiny on the *Bounty* says many members of the crew had fallen in love with Tahitian women, or at least with the Tahitian women's easy virtue, during a five-month layover and were damned cranky when the ship finally sailed, leaving their lovers behind. It didn't take much to get them mad.

At the end of the block on your right, you'll now see the white building with red trim that fronts on Caroline Street. You're now nearing the Key West Bight, a unique, curving waterfront and seaport area.

Caroline Street, 800 Block

The historic Red Doors Building here is a far cry from its previous incarnation. At the height of Key West's shrimping industry, the Red Doors was a notoriously rough shrimpers bar, nicknamed by locals the "Bucket of Blood." Fights broke out every fifteen minutes downstairs, while upstairs, rooms were rented out by the hour. The first known example of Key West timeshare.

Don't miss all the great food and drink stops here. The first is B.O.'s Fishwagon at 801 Caroline. A bit farther up the street is Pepe's, at 806 Caroline, one of the island's oldest and most beloved eateries. Still farther along, at 920 Caroline is PT's, where pool and pot roast rule. For a sandwich to go, stop in at the Waterfront Market on the Bight and visit the long, inviting deli and sandwich counter. Fresh fruit, veggies, bakery items, fish, and beer and wine are all available here.

Cross Caroline Street and head toward the waterfront.

William Street, 200 Block

On your right you can't miss The Wyland Wall, on the Waterfront Market. It took Wyland a week to paint this reef scene. He paints by airbrush, from the bottom of the wall to the top. In the summer of 1993, Wyland traveled from Maine to Key West, stopping at a new location each week to paint a different mural. He painted thirteen murals, in thirteen stops in thirteen weeks! This is the last one on his expedition.

This waterfront area of the Key West Bight includes the seaport and Land's End Marina farther on up Caroline. It is the largest single section of waterfront on the island still free of hotels or condominiums. The City purchased the bight from a shrimp and seafood exporting conglomerate in 1992 for $18.5 million. A red brick harborwalk and wooden pier is planned for the entire waterfront. Locals are hoping the restoration will not zap the area clean of its hard-earned, funky charm.

This calm, sheltered harbor was once home to Key West's shrimping fleet. After nocturnal shrimp were discovered in the Tortugas in 1949, shrimping flourished. Nearly 400 boats dragged their nets across the ocean's floor each night, pulling up tons of the world's favorite shrimp, Key West Pink Gold, from the nearby waters. During the season, lasting from November through July, shrimpers went to sea for two weeks at a time. They were paid very well, but out at sea there was no place to spend their money. Consequently, when the shrimpers returned to shore, they were rich, randy and ready to party. When things didn't go their way, they fought, often quite viciously. Hence, the notorious Bucket of Blood.

The ever-popular Schooner Wharf Bar is on the waterfront too, on your right. Farther down the brick harborwalk, you'll come to a two-story waterfront building that belongs to Jimmy Buffett. His recording studio is inside.

In the Lazy Way shops farther on, you'll find fortune and tarot card readers, and local artists and craftspeople creating jewelry, hats, painted T-shirts, and gauzy dresses.

Turn right and then make a quick left onto Greene Street.

Greene Street, 600 Block

On your left you'll next see there are two interesting shops: Joseph's Antiques, in the shed at 616 Greene, and the Sea Store at 614 Greene. Bill Ford of the Sea Store is the Audubon spokesman for the Keys. He'll tell you what birds are being spotted, what birds aren't, and where you should go to see the ones that are. (Call 294-3438 for a taped message of the same information.)

The long, white-painted brick building on the left was built by William Curry in 1878. (You remember William Curry—America's first self-made millionaire who came to town as a penniless youth in the early 1800s. We love this guy!) This was one of his many downtown holdings, an auction hall and tobacco warehouse. Key West Handprint Fabrics is housed here now, but, sadly, handprinting is no longer done here. Fabric is printed in Miami instead, but you still can buy fabric by the yard or purchase a dress or shirt made of handprint fabric.

Cross Simonton Street.

Greene Street, 500 Block

A crazy quilt of culture and commerce here. At the Key West Aloe Factory you can view a working laboratory and buy outlet merchandise of perfume and luscious aloe lotions as gifts or tiny, luxurious vacation toiletries.

Watch cigars being hand rolled and buy a souvenir sample of the fragrant Cuban symbol at the Conch Republic Cigar Factory next door to the Kozuchi Japanese Restaurant and Sushi Bar. The Eastern eatery operates inside a very tiny and neatly appointed space across the street from an equally good Thai place. At Kozuchi's, the Japanese beer is very cold, and the sushi bar is the real thing.

Old City Hall, at 510 Greene Street, has undergone a recent restoration, but, in spite of all the thousands of dollars spent, the four clocks on the tower up top still don't agree on the time. The original city hall was built of wood and, consequently, was burned in the fire of 1859. It was rebuilt, again in wood, but it again burned in the fire of 1886. The current brick building was designed by everybody's favorite architect William Kerr in 1891. On the ground-floor level of the building, notice the high archways of an open-air market. The upstairs was used for offices and meeting rooms of the mayor and city commissioners.

The old City Hall building was abandoned in 1962 for the current, much more modern City Hall at Simonton and Angela streets. In 1991, Old City Hall was renovated and brought back to turn-of-the-century splendor. Now that it is considered chic to be 100 years old, City Commission meetings go on here once again.

Thai Cuisine, a restaurant across the street at 513 Greene, is a great restaurant, and, like its name, very unpretentious.

Sloppy Joe's Bar on the corner has been many things to many people, but it's best known as Hemingway's favorite watering hole and home of the annual Hemingway Look-alike Contest that goes on each July 21 on the occasion of the writer's birthday.

Cross Duval Street.

Greene Street, 400 Block

Captain Tony's Saloon is now where the original Sloppy Joe's Bar was founded by Hemingway's good buddy Captain Joe Russell, nicknamed "Sloppy Joe" by the writer. In 1937, in response to a rent hike, Sloppy Joe's Bar moved lock, stock and barrel to its current location. So Captain Tony's is actually the place where Hemingway did his late afternoon drinking.

In December 1936 a writer named Martha Gellhorn came to this bar with the purpose of meeting Hemingway. They met and began a love affair which eventually led to the demise of Hemingway's second marriage. The couple married in October 1940, less than two weeks after his divorce from Pauline. Pauline, wife number two, was the mate with whom he shared his Key West years, considered by most critics to be the most significant time of his writing career.

Captain Tony himself is not around much anymore. He might be at home, visiting with some of his thirteen kids, or being interviewed by some adoring reporter, or on the road with Jimmy Buffett, who likes to pull him up to center stage at his concerts and introduce to his fans the man for whom the song "Last Mango in Paris" was written.

Carved above the stage at Captain Tony's are these words: "Everybody is a star at Captain Tony's." Without the Captain, the place has definitely lost some of its elan. But the beer's still cold.

Cross Greene Street, head into Kino Plaza.

Kino Plaza

Directly across the street from Captain Tony's, walk through a brilliantly colored canopy of bougainvillea into Kino Plaza. Straight ahead you'll see the Kino Sandal Factory, where you *have* to buy a pair of leather Kino's that will last you forever, especially if you don't wear them in the snow— and for only $6!

From Kino Plaza, turn right onto Fitzpatrick Street, which quickly becomes Tift's Alley. And now you're back at Mallory Square once again.

Writers

*The passion we have to create
is all we know of God*

– TENNESSEE WILLIAMS

♥ ♥ ♥

Pulitzer Prize Winners
who live or have lived in Key West
and the years in which they won

Robert Frost	1924, 1931, 1937, 1943
John Hersey	1945
Tennessee Williams	1948, 1955
Ernest Hemingway	1954
Wallace Stevens	1955
Elizabeth Bishop	1956
Richard Wilbur	1957, 1989
Phil Caputo	1972
Joseph Lash	1972
Annie Dillard	1974
James Kirkwood	1976
James Merrill	1977
Alison Lurie	1985

Some Key West Writers

Ellis Amburn
Currently living in Key West, this Texas-born writer has ghostwritten autobiographies with Priscilla Presley, Zsa Zsa Gabor and Shelley Winters. In addition, he has written biographies of Roy Orbison, Janis Joplin and Buddy Holly. His books are intensely researched and much respected. "I write the books I'd like to read myself," Ellis says. His most recent work is a biography of Jack Kerouac, beat-era author of *On the Road*. Ellis is currently at work on a biography of Liz Taylor.

Elizabeth Bishop
Poet Elizabeth Bishop bought a house at 624 White Street in the late 1930s. There she recorded her impressions of Key West and the people she met here in several wonderful essays. For a great view of the island as it was in the 1940s, read *Collected Prose*, which was published posthumously in 1984. While she lived in Key West Bishop took up painting. It wasn't very good, but she did it, and that's what mattered. One of her watercolor images graces the cover of her *Collected Prose*.

Bishop stayed on the island for many years, fishing, swimming and biking. Then, in the '50s, she left and never came back, as if she'd absorbed all she could of the place. She was no longer a Key West resident when she was awarded the Pulitzer Prize in 1956.

John Malcolm Brinnin
John Malcolm Brinnin, another Nova Scotia-born poet, died in 1998 at the age of 82. He began wintering in Key West in the '40s. Brinnin was a writer of remarkable refinement. His mellifluous speaking voice lives on at the Audubon House where his is the voice of Captain John Geiger, who leads an audio taped tour of the historic house. John Malcolm immortalized his relationship with Truman Capote in the book *Sextet*. Brinnin's most famous work is the fascinating and heartbreaking memoir, *Dylan Thomas in America*.

Philip Burton

Dr. Burton lived at 608 Angela Street from 1974 until his death in 1995. The Shakespearean scholar, actor, writer and director was the step-father of actor Richard Burton. Dr. Burton was sometimes visited here by dear friend and two-time daughter-in-law Elizabeth Taylor. Burton's autobiography is *Early Doors: My Life and the Theater*. His most famous scholarly work is *The Sole Voice: Character Portraits from Shakespeare*.

Phil Caputo

Phil Caputo doesn't live in Key West anymore. But he visits often because he has a passion for fishing, which he describes brilliantly in an 1988 essay called *The Ahab Complex*: "...an obsession to pursue and conquer a monster of the depths regardless of the consequences to one's bank account, career and family life." He shared the 1972 Pulitzer Prize for an investigative series on political corruption in Chicago. Caputo's nonfiction book *A Rumor of War* is said by many to be the quintessential Viet Nam book. It is also the book that put Caputo on the literary map for all time.

John Dos Passos

Manhattan Transfer, The 42nd Parallel, The Big Money and *Mid-Century*. In 1928 Dos Passos took a train to Key West and stayed. In a letter to his pal Ernest Hemingway, he described the island as a quiet and isolated place—a good place to write. In 1934, Dos Possos was introduced to his future wife Kathy at Hemingway's Whitehead Street home. The couple lived for a while in the house at 1401 Pine Street.

Nancy Friday

She's a writer of social commentary and sexy, uncatagorizable stuff like *My Secret Garden*, a collection of women's sexual fantasies (excellent late-night reading). Her many best-selling books including *My Mother/Myself* and *Women on Top* have made her wealthy and famous. Nancy is tall and commanding and always wears a fresh hibiscus tucked behind her ear. In Key West she strides importantly through the places she visits and has been known to set unwary people in her path spinning like tops. But on television talk shows, she's patient and very gracious.

Robert Frost

Frost's elegant poetry won him four Pulitzer Prizes. He wintered in a garden cottage at 410 Caroline Street as a guest of the famous hostess, Jessie Porter Newton. He also stayed at 707 Seminole Street. Frost didn't care much for Key West. In letters back home in New England he described it as shabby and dilapidated, which it surely was at the depths of its degradation in 1935. But he found the weather irresistible and spent sixteen winters here, beginning in 1934. Frost wrote no poems about the island. In Key West, he said, he simply enjoyed "barding around."

James Leo Herlihy

Herlihy lived for three years in what is sometimes referred to as "the hippie house" at 709 Bakers Lane. The house's gingerbread trim features jigcut peace signs. Herlihy's '60s novels *Blue Denim* and *Midnight Cowboy* were made into films. *A Story That Ends With a Scream, and Eight Others* includes several short stories set in Key West. Herlihy's friends in Key West were playwright Tennessee Williams, artist Henry Faulkner, and novelist-playwright Jimmy Kirkwood.

John Hersey

Hersey wintered for many years in a compound on Windsor Lane where his neighbors were Richard Wilbur and John Ciardi. His books include the 1945 Pulitzer Prize winner *Hiroshima*. A final contribution just before his death in 1994, *Key West Tales*, is a collection of odd, sad stories written quite beautifully in Hersey's seductive and seamless prose.

David Kaufelt

As a copywriter in a New York advertising agency, David Kaufelt penned "Choosy mothers choose Jif," the slogan that launched a peanut butter empire. Kaufelt's 1973 novel *Six Months With An Older Woman* was translated into a two-hour movie for TV. Lately, Kaufelt has begun publishing mysteries with names like *The Fat Boy Murders*.

Jimmy Kirkwood

He owned a house at 1023 Catherine Street but wasn't in town often. Kirkwood co-wrote the Pulitzer Prize-winning play *A Chorus Line*. The son of silent screen star Lila Lee, Kirkwood was also an actor as well as a writer. His wonderful books are *Good Times/Bad Times*, *American Grotesque*, *P.S. Your Cat Is Dead!*, *Some Kind of Hero*, *Hit Me With A Rainbow* and *Diary of a Mad Playwright*.

Kirkwood lived between New York, Los Angeles and Key West and sent memorable Christmas cards to a select group of friends. The Christmas postcards featured pictures of Kirkwood and celebrity friends. Scribbled in red ink across the front: "Merry Christmas from the Kirkwoods." One year the "Kirkwoods" were Jimmy and Elizabeth Taylor. Another time, Jimmy, Mary Martin and Carol Channing.

Alison Lurie

She won a 1985 Pulitzer Prize for *Foreign Affairs*. Her novel *The Truth About Lorin Jones* is partially set in Key West. Lurie's latest, *The Last Resort*, is entirely set in Key West, which is about the only good thing the reviewers have to say about it. Once a professor of English at Cornell University, Lurie now divides her time between Key West, Ithaca and London.

John Leslie

The adventures of Key West native and private eye Gideon Lowry are skillfully told by local writer John Leslie. Who-done-it devotees love these mysteries. Lowry loves lazy cats, swaying palms, and reminiscing about the good old days in Paradise. But oh! The troubles he sees! Dig Leslie's sultry titles: *Love For Sale*; *Killing me Softly*; and his latest: *Blue Moon*.

Tom McGuane

Jimmy Buffett's great friend lived at 1011 Von Phister and at 123-25 Ann Street before that. Two of his novels are set in Key West: *The Bushwhacked Piano* and *Ninety-two in the Shade*. The latter was made into a movie which was filmed in Key West in 1975. Locals still talk about the rowdy Hollywood crowd that came to perform in that film. Elizabeth Ashley, Margot Kidder, Peter Fonda, and Warren Oates reportedly adapted easily to the island's free-wheeling ways.

McGuane is currently married to Jimmy Buffett's sister, Laurie. They live in Montana.

James Merrill
Yes, the Merrill Lynch brokerage house Merrill. For the last sixteen years of his life, he spent half the year in a cozy cottage in Key West and the other half in Connecticut. Today Merrill's house is on the Literary Walking Tour, although sadly, many of the folks on the tour confess to never having heard of James Merrill. "Who?" they say. "What did he write?" In the course of his amazingly successful career in poetry, Merrill won the Pulitzer Prize, and he twice won the National Book Award in poetry. His epic poem *The Changing Light at Sandover* is a favorite of Ivy League and Seven Sisters professors.

Evan Rhodes
For many years the movie star handsome Rhodes lived in the elegant eyebrow house at 621 Catholic Lane. Later he moved up to Sugarloaf Key. Some of his books: *An Army of Children, On Wings of Fire, Bless This House, Forged in Fury, Valiant Hearts* and *A Distant Dream*. Rhodes also wrote the libretto for a musical based on his novel *The Prince of Central Park*. The musical went all the way to Broadway in 1985. However, it closed after only eighteen performances.

Leigh Rutledge
Cat Love Letters. Diary of a Cat. The Gay Book of Lists and *When My Grandmother was a Girl*. Leigh's dedication to hopeless causes, lost souls and sentimentality is becoming legendary. His Key West house is large, *very* large, you might think, for one guy and his partner. The extra space belongs to his cats. There are usually thirty of them wandering around. All of them suffer with heart-breaking injuries or diseases deemed terminal. Leigh performs the miracle of bringing his beloved cats back from death's dark door. Newspaper reporters and *People Magazine* writers ask Leigh questions such as "How many pounds of kitty litter do you use in a week?" "Would you ask someone how many rolls of toilet paper they use in a week?" Leigh huffs.

Laurence Shames

The books: *Florida Straits. Scavenger Reef. Tropical Depression. Sunburn.*
Shames's South Florida-based novels are described as comic thrillers and
are found on the mystery shelves at the bookstore. Shames came to Key
West from New York, where he wrote the "Jake" column for *Glamour
Magazine* for several years and an ethics column for *Esquire Magazine*
from 1982-1983.

Shel Silverstein

He's a Grammy Award-winning songwriter, a cartoonist and the author
of the world's best-selling poetry books for children: A *Light in the Attic,
Where the Sidewalk Ends, Falling Up.* Among his hit songs are "The Cover
of the Rolling Stone" and "A Boy Named Sue." Silverstein lives on an
Old Town street behind a jungle of tropical foliage designed to discourage
curiosity seekers. Soft-spoken and earthy, he can be seen walking the
sidewalks of Key West in baggy shorts and sandals, poking through the
stacks at the public library, dining at local restaurants, and regularly
stretching at yoga classes. Silverstein is shy. Very shy.

Wallace Stevens

One of America's most renowned poets was also an insurance exec from
Hartford. Stevens discovered Key West on a business trip to Miami.
Throughout the decade of the 1930s, he wintered at the grand Casa
Marina Hotel. Although Stevens was here during Hemingway's Key West
decade, the two were not friends. Wallace is said to have avoided both
Hemingway and Dos Passos. His one literary buddy was Robert Frost, and
even that relationship was a rocky one. When Stevens drank, he grew
resentful and confrontative. A fistfight once broke out between
Hemingway and Stevens followed by many versions of how the fracas
came about and who got the best of whom. By 1940, both Hemingway
and Stevens were gone from the island, never to live here again.

Stevens won the National Book Award in 1950 and the Pulitzer Prize
in 1955. Because Tennessee Williams enjoyed reading aloud Steven's
poem *The Idea of Order at Key West*, it was read at Williams' funeral in
1983.

Thelma Strabel

Following a career as a fashion reporter in Paris, Strabel wintered in Key West in the late 1930s. She loved the place so well that she stayed for several years. In an article about Key West she wrote for the *Saturday Evening Post*, she described the island as "quiet and careless and charming."

Her novel *Reap the Wild Wind* set in 1830s-era Key West, is the story of two wreckers who fall in love with the same local temptress, foxy Loxi Claiborne. The novel was first serialized in the *Saturday Evening Post* and later appeared in book form. A very young, very hunky John Wayne stars in the movie version. In one memorable scene, Miss Claiborne of Key West shocks the gentle folk of Charleston when she sings a naughty song at a genteel party.

Strabel herself became the talk of Key West when she built a house at 400 South Street, designed to rival the original Southernmost House's claim to the title. Strabel's little house has been replaced by a much more elaborate one. The original Southernmost House, one block north, continues to claim the title.

Richard Wilbur

The opposite of riot: A bunch of people being quiet.

Why isn't all poetry this much fun? Wilbur has won a slew of awards, including the 1957 Pulitzer Prize for a collection called *Things of the World* and, in 1989, another Pulitzer for *New and Collected Poems*. Wilbur has twice served as Poet Laureate of the United States. His poems show up all over the place—in the *Atlantic Monthly*, in the *New Yorker*. In 1995, *Moliere's Comedies*, a Broadway hit, was translated from French by Wilbur. Richard Wilbur lives with his wife Charlee in a famous writer's compound on Windsor Lane. Generous with his time and talent, Wilbur performs one or two readings of his poetry every winter in the public library's auditorium. Call the library for a schedule of events, and get there early if you want to get a seat.

William Wright

He lives on Love Lane, close enough to the public library on Fleming Street to put his portable telephone in his pocket and go next door to work in the icy air conditioned comfort of the chilly archives. Among his biographies are *Lillian Hellman: The Image, the Woman*; *All the Pain that Money Can Buy*; *The Life of Christina Onassis*; and *The Von Bulow Affair*. Though the subjects of William Wright's biographies are often doomed, the author is upbeat and very dear.

Bookstores

Flaming Maggie's
830 Fleming Street ✹ 294-3931
Local authors are well represented here, as well as the literature of alternative lifestyles. Flaming Maggie, named for its location at the junction of Fleming and Margaret, is tucked into this historic building where local legend has it Ernest Hemingway ate his breakfast when "Mrs. Baker's Electric Kitchen" operated here. Back in the early 1930s Mrs. Rhonda Baker, who Hemingway dubbed "Mrs. Rutabaga," scrambled Papa's eggs on the island's first electric stove.

At booksignings, proprietor Paul Hause becomes Flaming Maggie, in an elegant black dress, fetching rhinestone brooch, and a wide-brimmed, ostrich-feather trimmed hat. Book signers are superstars like nationally syndicated gay columnist Deb Price, novelist Larry Shames, and cat lover Leigh Rutledge.

Key West Island Bookstore
513 Fleming Street ✹ 294-2904
It's the Key West authors' bookshop, hosting signings by people like Jimmy Buffett, James Hall, and Alan Maltz. The best-selling author here is, and has always been, Ernest Hemingway. You can find, rare, first-edition and autographed copies of books. If you have a special need or request or question, ask John, owner, or Liz Lear, his right hand.

Bargain Books
1028 Truman Avenue ✹ 294-7446
A large, well-stocked bookstore full of books to buy, sell or trade. It also offers local interest books, and a well-informed bookseller to answer questions about them. Also hundreds of paperbacks, videos, collectibles, as well as newspapers and magazines are also available. Behind the counter: a bona fide Key West character. Opens at 7 a.m. daily.

Blue Heron Books
1014 Truman Avenue ✶ 296-3508
Can two long-time Key West career ladies, Pat, a bartender, and Dawn, a real estate broker, find happiness in the bookstore business? When former owners Georgia and Stan put the shop on the market in the summer of '98, partners Pat and Dawn scooped it up. It's a fine collection of local interest books, alternative lifestyle fact and fiction, classics and pretty cards. As in all island book stores, the clerks themselves are often the kind of characters you meet in novels. Some of the books still smell like Georgia's incense...

Great Key West Anthologies

Once Upon An Island and *Beyond Paradise*. By the Key West Author's Co-op. Absorbing collections of short fiction, non-fiction, and poetry, from Key West's best up-and-coming writers.

The Key West Reader, the Best of Key West's Writers 1830–1990. Edited by George Murphy. Literature, poems and letters about Key West by John James Audubon, John Malcolm Brinnin, Philip Caputo, Jim Harrison, Ernest Hemingway, Wallace Stephens, Tennessee Williams, Hunter Thompson.

Upstart Crow Bookstore
218 Whitehead Street ✶ 293-0709
An upstart crow, explains bookseller Joan Roethler, can change the color of its feathers. Joan says she had to change the color of her feathers when she was one of 40,000 laid off from AT&T in 1995.

"I found I related to the upstart crow," she says.

After the lay-off, Joan looked for work that would utilize her education and her love of books. The outcome of her search was the move to Key West and the establishment of the Upstart Crow Bookstore.

Upstart Crow carries books that appeal to people on vacation. Joan has learned that books by local authors, about Florida and Key West, are big sellers, so you'll find plenty of those here. Joan is also interested in New Age books, so she keeps a good selection of those handy, too.

Upstart Crow features seminars, workshops and poetry readings. The Key West Poetry Guild meets here at 8 p.m. on the first Sunday of the month. Writers and listeners are invited.

Waldenbooks
2212 N. Roosevelt Boulevard ❧ 294-5419
One of the spunkiest clerks behind the counter is Jill Caputo, former wife of Pulitzer Prize-winning author Phil Caputo. As all local bookstores do, the people at Waldenbooks maintain a well-stocked collection of books on local topics, as well as a wall of magazines, a children's section, and lots of bargain tables. There are even occasional book signings, and the bargain counters really do contain bargains.

Valladares and Son
1200 Duval Street ❧ 296-5032
Key West's oldest newspaper stand opened in 1927, when current owner Arthur Valladares was two years old. Today Arthur carries an impressive selection of over 3,500 titles of out-of-town and foreign newspapers, paperbacks and magazines.

Arthur tells the story of the first time he met Ernest Hemingway. The writer, clad in his favorite baggy cut-off shorts and rope belt, reportedly wandered into the recently opened Valladares store in 1932. Arthur said to his father, in Spanish, "Look at the bum." Hemingway introduced himself to the boy, and demonstrated that he spoke excellent Spanish. The store ended up selling Hemingway's books. They got an extra dollar for autographed copies.

Hemingway once asked Arthur's dad to arrange for him to receive the *New York Times* via the Valladares stand. The older Valladares told Hemingway that Arthur was so new to the business, he didn't even know how to order the *New York Times*. So Hemingway made the arrangements himself. Not only did Hemingway have the *Times* delivered from New York, albeit two days late, but he also ordered *The New York Mirror*, *The World-Telegram* and the *Herald Tribune*, which all came in by train.

Valladares' customers would reserve their Sunday *New York Times* by paying for them in advance. There were always a few extras ordered for tourists, and those went fast. Every week Tennessee Williams wanted a Sunday *Times*, but refused to pay for it up front. Several times he stomped out of the store, enraged, when Valladares was sold out of the *Times* and refused to give him an already-paid-for paper, reserved for another customer.

Poetry In Paradise

The past few years in Key West have spawned a fresh crop of new poets and, perhaps more significantly, a resurgence of interest in poetry. Poetry raves and slams have been happening regularly around town. Nowadays you can count on finding at least one good slam every month. At the best slams you'll see impassioned readings by members of Key West's winning slam team. The New-Agers show up, Generation X is represented, and the late blooming baby boomers are there, too—wailing, bewildered, and still braless at 50. But that's O.K. They're poets! Honest-to-God poets, whose words sizzle in your brain long after everybody's gone home, and you're settled in your bed, listening to the singular drama of your own heart beating.

Blue Heaven Outback, at 729 Thomas Street, sponsors slams on the third Friday of the month. Call 296-8666 for information on that. The Green Parrot Bar sponsors poetry slams, too. Between 50 and 75 people gather at 8 p.m. to read original works and to bark at the moon. Usually the event turns rowdy. Anyone who wants to, can read. Anyone who can, does. It gets messy and sloppy and if you're serious about your poetry, it seems you wait a long time for a few minutes of glory.

The Key West Poetry Guild meets on the first Sunday of each month at the Upstart Crow Bookstore. Poets and journalists and songwriters are all invited to present their stuff. This is a good group of dedicated writers, nothing like the crazy crowds that meet in the bars. Meetings are wonderful, almost holy.

Hemingway in Key West

☾

In 1935, one of Key West's biggest tourist attractions
was a drink called a Papa Doble, which was promoted
as Ernest Hemingway's favorite drink:

Two-and-a-half jiggers of white Bacardi rum,
Juice of two fresh limes,
Juice of ½ grapefruit,
Six drops of maraschino juice.
Mix in an electric blender.

The better you treat a man and the
more you show him you love him,
the quicker he gets tired of you.

– FROM *To Have And Have Not*, PUBLISHED IN 1936,
HEMINGWAY'S ONLY NOVEL SET IN KEY WEST

A FEW WEEKS AFTER I arrived in Key West, I begged my new island
boyfriend to accompany me on a tour of the Hemingway House. The
house is magnificent, much more spacious than most on the island,
and in those long ago days of the mid-1970s, not at all crowded the way
it is today. Back then you wandered freely about the place, taking your
time, dreaming your dreams, imagining your imaginings. When I saw
Hemingway's bedroom, I threw myself onto the bed.

"What are you doing?" Miguel asked incredulously.

"I'm lying in his bed," I answered, waving my arms and legs in the king-sized bed. "I'm seeing what he saw, feeling what he felt. I'm going to bed with Hemingway's ghost!"

In the many years that followed that day, I've learned that the great Ernest Hemingway was nothing at all like I imagined he was. (Neither was Miguel, for that matter.)

There's no getting away from Ernest Hemingway in this town. Nothing has promoted our earthy, end-of-the-road machismo image like America's first celebrity writer and Key West's biggest big deal. Stick around for a while and you feel you are sharing the place with his ghost, and indeed, you are. The Hemingway legacy is very much alive and well.

The Key West Years

Hemingway arrived in Key West in April, 1928 after seven years in Paris. He traveled with his newest wife, his second, a small-boned, dark-haired woman named Pauline. Pauline Pfeiffer had befriended Hadley (the first Mrs. Hemingway) and Ernest in Paris. She'd dined with them. Socialized with them. Traveled with them. And somewhere along the way, she'd stolen Mr. Hemingway's heart. A time of terrible suffering followed. Ernest couldn't quite decide how to handle the situation. He sent letters to his guy friends, describing the hell of being involved in a romantic triangle. He loved them both, he said. Finally poor Hadley, who'd stood by her husband through the lean Paris years and donated her small fortune to the family's upkeep, faced the sad reality of the situation and sent Ernest packing, freeing him to marry Pauline.

Pauline was a devout Catholic, the daughter of a wealthy Arkansas family. She was also the cherished niece of perfume king Gus Pfeiffer. As a wedding gift, Uncle Gus bought the Hemingways a new car and later a grand Key West house as well, the first one Ernest had owned. When Hemingway got restless, good old Uncle Gus financed a very expensive African safari, at the height of the Great Depression.

When Ernest and Pauline arrived in Key West, Ernest was 29 years old and as handsome and healthy as he ever would be. He fit right in to Key West's crazy assortment of characters. Mornings he worked on his novel *A Farewell to Arms*. Afternoons he hung around with tough guys who drank, fished and admired Hemingway's worldly bravado. He began wearing a rope around his waist to hold up his cut-off pants. He gave his new friends nicknames and encouraged them to call him Old Master, although he was the newcomer to deep-sea fishing and island living. Hemingway loved fishing excursions that carried him far into the ocean. He liked roughing it—living on Bermuda onions, (the bio's all say these onions were a staple of his diet), fresh fish, conch salad and booze. Always lots of booze.

Prohibition didn't cramp anyone's drinking style in Key West. Bars continued operating, their liquor and beer supplied by rumrunners who easily and often made the roundtrip between Key West and Havana, located just ninety miles away. Rumrunner Joe Russell, one of Hemingway's buddies, was the original owner of Sloppy Joe's Bar, located today at 201 Duval Street. Charles Thompson was another of Hemingway's Key West friends. Thompson lived for many years after Hemingway died. In the last years of his life Thompson became a favorite interviewee of Hemingway biographers digging for information on Papa's Key West years.

There are many stories of Hemingway's terrible need to out-fish, out-shoot and out-box anyone who challenged him, and even those who did not. His competitiveness sometimes put a damper on things. But mostly, because there was so much about him that was fun, his friends just put up with it. Writer John Dos Passos, a member of Hemingway's Key West mob, wrote: "Hem was the greatest fellow in the world to go around with—when everything went right."

Rich, sporty and devoted, Pauline Hemingway was a dutiful wife who often left their two young sons with nannies or relatives to join her husband on fishing and hunting retreats. The Hemingways summered in Wyoming or Europe and wintered in Key West.

For several winters the Hemingways rented homes on the island. Then in 1931 Uncle Gus bought the house at 907 Whitehead Street for $8,000. The house was designed with a European flair, which greatly pleased Pauline, a former fashion writer for *Vogue* magazine. The Civil War-era house, in the middle of an entire acre of gardens, was one of the grandest estates on the island. It still is.

Once the house was theirs, Pauline hurried to Paris to reclaim her French and Spanish antique furniture out of storage and have it shipped to Key West. (Left from Pauline's dowry—a hand-blown Venetian glass chandelier still hanging in the dining room.) Hemingway designed a writing studio on the second story of a carriage house in the back yard. A catwalk was built to connect the studio to the house. Through the years the Hemingways covered the walls and floors of their home with the skins and heads of beasts they themselves had shot on various hunting trips. Servants cared for the children, cleaned the house, did the laundry and the cooking. They were paid $5 a week each, a good wage for the times.

Hemingway was intrigued with costumes and the impressions they created. Sometimes he was taken for a bum in his favorite Key West garb: a dirty shirt, cutoffs and rope belt. In Wyoming he enjoyed decking himself out in boots, cowboy hat, plaid shirt and leather vest. In Africa he wore a brown felt Stetson and a white shirt with rolled sleeves. Sometimes he wore his hair and beard long and affected a wild-man look. No matter what he was wearing, by the time he was 33 years old, he had begun to tell people: "Call me Papa."

In the 1930s the Hemingways never stayed put for long. Papa was a restless fellow, and Pauline did her best to keep up with him on his travels. Clearly, he was not one to be domesticated. Home, he told a friend, is a place to leave from and come back to. Still, he managed to work well during the '30s, which was the most productive decade of his writing career. In Key West he ate breakfast in bed, wrote all morning in the studio, then napped or walked to the ocean for a swim. Then Papa moseyed down to Sloppy Joe's Bar, located then on Greene Street, where Captain Tony's Saloon is today. Sloppy's was a rough place, where fights were common and the alcohol, as well as the talk, was cheap. Papa's drink of choice was scotch and soda. He paid 25¢ a drink (others paid 35¢ for the same drink) and ran a monthly tab of $25-$30, which means he paid for roughly four drinks a day. Yes, he got plastered from time to time, Joe Russell recalled. But certainly not every day. Mostly, Papa liked to sit, watch, listen and soak up the atmosphere.

When the sun set, Papa headed back to his palatial home, where he enjoyed a hearty dinner accompanied always by plenty of good French wine. If there were guests, and often there were because Pauline loved to entertain, drinks were served on the outdoor patio. Usually he was in bed by 10 p.m., where he read for an hour or two. He was an early riser all of his life.

Papa loved to box, and Key West had several very fine young boxers. Papa set up a ring in his back yard and paid local guys fifty cents a round to spar with him. He also refereed at island boxing matches.

Several Key Westers today remember Hemingway quite well from those days. Jeanne Porter, who grew up on Whitehead Street, played with Hemingway's sons when she was a little girl. She recalls one strange incident. The boys kept several raccoons outside in cages and had named them after movie stars. One day they discovered the raccoon named "Greta Garbo" eating another named "Harold Lloyd," whom she had just killed. Although disturbing Papa when he was in his writing studio was strictly forbidden, the children were so horrified they yelled for him to come. Papa surveyed the scene, went inside and came back out with a shotgun. Then he blew the head off Greta Garbo, in full view of the children. Jeanne says she figures Papa shot the raccoon because he feared she might have rabies.

Key Wester Julia Hoffman, now a senior citizen, also remembers Papa. She often swam in the water off the Navy base when she was a girl, and Hemingway liked to swim there, too. One day as she was swimming, she felt something suddenly grab her ankle. She was badly startled, fearing that a barracuda had bitten her foot off. "I almost had a heart attack!" she remembers. But it wasn't a fish at all. It was Ernest Hemingway. When they got to the dock, Julia scolded him for frightening her. After that, Hemingway never forgot her; every time the two saw each other, Hemingway would say, "Have you forgiven me yet?"

"He was a very sweet man," Julia adds.

Besides boxing, Hemingway was also enthralled with bullfighting, and he traveled to Spain often to hang out with his bullfighting friends. His bullfighting book—*Death in the Afternoon*—was written during his Key West years. He also wrote frequent short stories and grandiose accounts of his fishing expeditions in the Gulf Stream, which he sold to grateful magazine editors in New York.

In 1933, friend Charles Thompson, Papa and Pauline set out for Africa. They bid their children and their home goodbye and did not see them again for nine months. Uncle Gus underwrote the excursion with a

Hemingway's writing studio

gift of $25,000. When they returned to Key West, Hemingway wrote *The Green Hills of Africa* and one of his best-known stories, *The Short Happy Life of Francis Macomber.*

In 1935 a tourist guidebook published by the City of Key West featured a fold-out map highlighting forty-eight local tourist attractions. Number eighteen on the list was Hemingway's home at 907 Whitehead Street. Hemingway was furious. It galled him that he couldn't walk around his own yard without being approached by tourists. So he hired Toby Bruce, a friend of Pauline's from Arkansas, to come to Key West and build the red brick wall that surrounds the house to this day.

Hemingway's Key West was, in many ways, a much wilder place than it is today. The law was lax then. The town was full of rough sailors, northerners on the lam, out-of-work drifters, and other victims of the Depression. Most of the town's people were on relief. Only the bars and the whorehouses flourished, and they were reputedly the best in the country, prompting someone to say, "If you can't get it in Key West, it hasn't been invented yet."

But with the advent of tourism, in 1935, the town began to attract rich Americans who sometimes arrived by yacht and sat in the harbor, insulated from the real world, while Key West citizens were surviving on fish and grits. Papa's reaction to the contrast between the rich and the poor here became fodder for his novel *To Have and Have Not*, the only Hemingway novel set in the United States.

Then one day in December 1936, Hemingway's third wife showed up at Sloppy Joe's in a black dress, high heels, and pearls, determined to meet Papa. In short order, she did. Her name was Martha Gellhorn, "Marty," and she was a writer, too, but not for a fashion magazine as Pauline had been. Like Hemingway, Marty was an adventurer. She traveled the world, covering wars and disasters for major American magazines and newspapers. Shortly after their first meeting, Papa and Marty traveled together to Spain to cover the Spanish Civil War.

Just as he had done to his first wife, Hemingway demoralized Pauline by carrying on a none-too-secret affair with Martha for a very long time. He prolonged her agony by continually putting off the eventual dissolution of his marriage. Just as he'd done a dozen years earlier, Papa wrote long letters to friends, describing the pain of his romantic triangle. He even wrote letters to Pauline's mother, assuring her that all would turn out well, "no matter what"—whatever that means. Pauline hoped the affair would run its course. In desperation, she had a swimming pool installed in the garden of their Key West house, hoping that the novelty would bring her husband back home. It was Key West's first pool, and it cost her an astounding $20,000, which, it is noted on Hemingway House tours, is the equivalent of $250,000 in today's market.

For a while Papa shuttled between Pauline in Key West and Marty in Spain. Being with Marty made him miserable with guilt. Being with Pauline made him miserable with longing for Marty. Finally, at Christmastime in 1939, eight years almost to the day since he'd moved into the elegant house on Whitehead Street, he packed up his clothes and officially moved out.

In October 1940, thirteen days after divorcing Pauline in Miami, he married Martha Gellhorn in Wyoming. His new wife affectionately called her new husband "Pig." Their home, however, was in Cuba at the Finca Vigia, located in San Francisco de Paula, a town fifteen miles outside of Havana. The marriage to Marty lasted five years. Today Finca Vigia is a museum, into which visitors may look but not enter.

Meanwhile, Pauline continued to live in the house on Whitehead Street with sons Patrick and Gregory until her death in 1951. In March 1963 the house sold for $80,000. The new owner Bernice Dickson soon discovered that tourists and curiosity seekers made it impossible to live in the house that had once been Hemingway's. On January 1, 1964, Bernice Dickson opened the main house as a museum, known as the Hemingway House. Today it is Key West's number-one tourist attraction.

Through the years the Hemingway House tour has been criticized often, even by Patrick Hemingway, who grew up there. Did Picasso really give Papa that ceramic cat in his bedroom? Patrick says no. Is the furniture in the house today Pauline's cherished French and Spanish antiques? No, Patrick says. Did Pauline really have the kitchen fixtures placed on a raised platform to accommodate her tall husband? Ridiculous, Patrick says. Hemingway was six feet tall, and he was not the kind of guy to putter around in the kitchen. Were there six-toed cats all over the place? No, no, no, says Patrick.

Contrary to the story you'll hear from the Hemingway House tour guide, the porcelain urinal in the back yard was brought home by Pauline. She bought it from Joe Russell, owner of Sloppy Joe's Bar, when he renovated the saloon's men's room. Pauline hoped to make a fish pool out of it. Handyman Toby Bruce piped water into the trough and decorated it with Spanish tile. Today it serves as a water trough for the famous Hemingway cats.

As for Henry Faulkner, the artist who painted the Hemingway House portrait that hangs over the Hemingway bed, he is not the brother of writer William Faulkner, as was said on a recent Hemingway House tour. Henry was no relation at all to William.

Does any of this really matter? To most people it doesn't; it's the ambiance that counts. The writing studio is certainly legit, and so are the gardens, the house's wonderful lines, and that long, red brick wall built by Toby Bruce in 1935. Papa has definitely not left the building!

People whose only previous exposure to Hemingway has been a short story in their junior-high American literature book come to Key West, see his elegant home, hear of his four beautiful wives, his six-toed cats, his rugged sportsmanship, and his long-lasting literary success, and fall easy prey to the super-hyped Hemingway myth. And they really don't mind.

At the height of the season the town hums with tourists hungry for fresh information about the long-dead but ever-provocative Hemingway. Historian Tom Hambright, who runs the Florida history department at the public library, says more people come looking for information on Hemingway than on any other subject. At the Key West Island Bookstore, hardly a day goes by, says owner John Boisonault, when he does not sell at least one book written by, or about, the famous Ernest Hemingway.

A Family Tree

Ernest Hemingway married four times. His first wife was Hadley Richardson, whom he married in 1921. The marriage lasted six years and produced one son, John "Jack" Hadley Nicanor Hemingway, born in 1923. Jack Hemingway had three daughters: Joan, born in 1950; Margaux, born in 1955; and Hadley Mariel, born in 1962.

Pauline Pfeiffer was wife number two. She married Hemingway in 1927 and had two sons: Patrick, born in 1928, and Gregory Hancock, born in 1931. Patrick's only child is Edwina, born in 1960. Gregory's children are Lorian, born in 1951; John Patrick, born in 1960; Maria Ann, born in 1961; Patrick Edward, born in 1966; Sean, born in 1967; Edward Brian, born in 1968; and Vanessa, born in 1970.

There are no children from Ernest Hemingway's third marriage to Martha Gellhorn, 1940–1945. In 1946 Papa married Mary Welsh, who was a devoted companion until the day he died in 1961. They had no children together either.

Vital Statistics

Ernest Hemingway was 6 feet tall. His weighed around 200 pounds, but was capable of gaining his way up to 260. His shoe size was 11½. His eyes and hair were dark brown, in his later years turning white. Ernest Hemingway never went to college. At dawn on July 2, 1961—a Sunday—Ernest Hemingway shot himself in the head with a double-barreled Boss shotgun he'd used for pigeon shooting. He was nineteen days short of his 62nd birthday.

Hemingway Days

It's kind of fun.
It's a chance for an old fat man with a
beard to get some attention.

– RICHARD BARTON,
WINNER OF THE 1995 HEMINGWAY LOOK-ALIKE CONTEST

Every July the Hemingway legend gives the town an annual infusion of tourist dollars and world-wide publicity when we celebrate his birthday with a week-long festival called Hemingway Days. The Hemingway Look-alike Contest, that goes on for three nights at Sloppy Joe's, attracts the biggest crowds and the most photographers. But there's so much more: sporting and literary competitions; parties and events; contests and playoffs designed to pay homage to different aspects of Hemingway's celebrated life. One year, when stamps were only 25 cents, the U.S. Post Office released a Hemingway stamp, amid much pomp and circumstance, on the steps of the Key West post office. Lately, a golf tournament has been added to the agenda, and an arm wrestling competition. The calendar of events has been growing steadily since the festival was founded nearly 20 years ago.

A flock of Hemingway's relatives come, too. They help out by judging a couple of contests, presenting the occasional award, and writing memoirs of their hazy memories of Papa. But mostly they just sit around looking Hemingway-ish. With their high cheekbones and rugged all-American good looks they give the festival an air of irrefutable authenticity.

Tennessee Williams
In Key West

ENNESSEE WILLIAMS was 30 years old when he arrived in Key West for the first time in 1941. He came to the island to write and to swim. These things he did every day. Throughout his life the restless playwright's choices of locales and lodgings often were based on his need to be near a pool or a good swimming beach.

Thomas Lanier Williams was born on March 26, 1911, in Mississippi. His father was a traveling salesman, and his mother really was a southern belle, like the mother in *The Glass Menagerie*—but a self-styled one. She had been born in Ohio and had arrived in the South only after she had married her southern-born husband. Williams claimed that he adopted the name "Tennessee" because his forefathers helped to found that state.

Following the great success of *The Glass Menagerie* in 1945 and Pulitzer Prize-winner *A Streetcar Named Desire* two years later, Williams was finally able to afford to buy a house in Key West. He bought a modest one-and-a-half story Bahamian house at 1431 Duncan Street, which he decorated in old wicker from Havana. The floors he covered in sisal pago pago, a rope-like plant from Mexico. He eventually added a swimming pool, a writing studio, and a guesthouse resembling a small youth hostel, with two narrow, double-decker bunk beds.

Williams, however, did not spend much time in his Key West house. He lived instead in a series of hotels and rented apartments in the U.S. and in Europe.

In her book *Key West Writers and Their Houses*, Lynn Kaufelt recalls that when she was invited to Williams' home for dinner, a friend in the know warned her that she might arrive at Williams' house "to find no Williams, or Williams in a bathrobe, or fifty people drinking champagne." So were the Williams days in Key West.

In January of 1969 Williams was cajoled by his weird brother Dakin into being baptized at the St. Mary Star of the Sea Catholic Church. Don Pinder, a local photographer who captured a number of significant events in Williams' Key West life, was there for the occasion. "He was crocked," Pinder recalls.

During the last decade of his life Tennessee, now in his sixties, decided to take up painting as a softer, easier way of expressing himself. Painting, he said, did not wear him out the way that writing did. Tennessee's painting instructor was the brilliant and bizarre Henry Faulkner, a Kentucky-born orphan who longed to be a famous poet but had to settle, instead, for being a much lauded painter. Faulkner adored Tennessee Williams and was willing to do just about anything to bask in the playwright's golden glory.

Another friend, Viola Veit, daughter of character actor Conrad Veit, modeled for Williams. When he turned a work over to be sold at the Gingerbread Square Gallery, there was sometimes a note turned in with it. When the painting sold, the note instructed, $500 of the proceeds was to go to Viola for modeling services.

So Williams painted his primitive images in dreamy pastels, giving each painting a dreamy name: *Fairy in a Wicker Chair*; *Great Silence of the Storm*; *Many Moons Ago*; *Recognition of Madness*; *Abandoned Chair Occupied Briefly*.

Nobody ever said that Williams was a great painter, but he was indisputably a literary giant. Some critics believed that Williams' paintings and drawings, with the familiar "TW" scrawled in the right-hand corners, were new expressions of his genius and, therefore, significant treasures. His paintings and sketches sold, too, and brought Williams fresh recognition and respect from new sources: art and collectors magazines.

As talented as he was, the fact remains that Key West has never embraced the world's greatest playwright the way it has Ernest Hemingway. And while Tennessee Williams' works, many believe, outshine those of Hemingway's, it is the charismatic Hemingway who steals the spotlight whenever it turns its hot glare on the writers of Key West.

The reason is simple, says Leigh Rutledge, who writes of Williams in his book, *The Gay Book of Lists*. America cherishes Hemingway because he represents all that is desirable in masculinity: power, aggression, daring and courage. Hemingway, after all, boxed, hunted great, wild beasts, and wrestled giant fish in the Gulf Stream. He wrote of bullfights and war and dangerous thugs.

Williams, though, was a timid man, small of stature and somewhat delicate. As a writer he was profoundly aware of the comedic, tragic ruts and twists of human nature. And this eternal balancing act of man's emotions formed the basis of his work. America is proud of men like Hemingway, Rutledge explains, and sort of embarrassed about men like Williams.

Williams and Hemingway met only once. They were introduced in Cuba, at the Floridita, Hemingway's favorite bar. Williams was uneasy before the meeting, having heard of Hemingway's homophobia. "Hemingway usually kicks people like me in the crotch," he said. As it turned out, the two found common ground in their hypochondria. They discussed Hemingway's plane crash injuries and compared liver problems.

Tennessee Williams lived into his seventies. He died in February, 1983 when he accidentally inhaled and choked to death on an eye drop bottle cap. When word of his death reached Key West, *The Rose Tattoo*, the 1955 locally filmed movie based on Williams' happy-ending play, ran all afternoon and all evening at a chic alternative cinema on Duval Street. The theater was packed for every viewing. Williams died in the Hotel Elysee in New York, a place he called the "Easy Lay." He kept an apartment there that had belonged, up until her death, to Tallulah Bankhead.

The house on Duncan Street remained vacant for many years after Williams' death. A group of Key West writers joined forces to try and have the property made into a sort of shrine to the writer, but the memorial was not to be. The property was sold in 1992 and completely refurbished. The re-do included a high, white fence to keep out curiosity seekers, and a large addition to the back of the house. The gazebo, or Jane Bowles summer house, as Williams called it, was moved back several feet, to behind the fence.

Today there is little to be seen of the house Tennessee Williams called home. But here's a small, odd postscript: Not long into the restoration project, a group of bathroom fixtures—a sink, a bathtub, and a commode—appeared in the grass in a side yard. Propped against the commode was a sign: "Free," it said.

Jimmy Buffett

OR LEGIONS OF HIS FANS, the names Key West and Jimmy Buffett are synonymous. Both conjure images of bright sun, blue skies, sandy beaches, agelessness and fun. If that's how it works for you, Jimmy has accomplished his mission, which is to enjoy his life to the max and to help you enjoy yours. Buffett fans, also known as "Parrot Heads," are of all ages and all walks of life. The theme that unites them is their love of Jimmy Buffett and the songwriter/storyteller's wonderful songs and music. Buffett concerts are famously entertaining, and always packed with thrilled audiences who share Buffett's dedication to the ideal of growing older but not up.

"In concert I try to convince people that if they can't go to Paradise I can bring it to them," Jimmy once said.

A Brief Buffett Bio

Jimmy Buffett was born on Christmas Day in 1946 and grew up in Mobile, Alabama, reading adventure stories by Mark Twain and Robert Louis Stevenson. He remembers being greatly influenced by the novel *Treasure Island* and by the hit musical *South Pacific*. During his childhood, the television series *Adventures in Paradise*, about a guy sailing the South Pacific on a 85-foot schooner named the *Tiki*, further fueled little Jimmy's desire for warm waters, white sand, and the exotic promise of the tropics.

Buffett attended Catholic schools all the way through high school graduation. While attending the University of Southern Mississippi at Hattiesburg, he escaped the genteel world of academia often for the sites and sounds of New Orleans, some 80 miles away. There he began his career in music, playing guitar and singing in clubs on Bourbon Street.

In 1969 Buffett finished his education and married a Mobile beauty queen named Margie Washichek. The couple headed for Nashville, where Buffett planned to continue writing and performing his songs. But jobs were scarce for performer/songwriters, and so he settled for a job as a reporter at *Billboard* magazine, which turned out to be an excellent education in the hard realities of the pop music business. During those two years in Nashville, Buffett was turned down by twenty-three record companies.

"I couldn't get nothing recorded in Nashville," Buffett told a reporter, several years later. "Got depressed, got pissed off, got divorced and left. Best move I ever made."

Musician Jerry Jeff Walker, a frequent visitor and sometimes Keys resident in the '60s, is credited with introducing the downhearted but ever hopeful songwriter to Key West around 1972. Buffett's first stop in town was the Chart Room at the Pier House, a celebrated watering hole where Buffett is still spotted occasionally. Legend has it that Buffett made his Keys debut in the Chart Room that day, where he performed an impromptu concert for the appreciative crowd.

What he couldn't do at all in Nashville, Buffett did well in Key West. The decade of the '70s was one of the island's finest for swashbucklers and poets. Marijuana smuggling was a major cottage industry, and drinking was a favorite sport. The living was easy. Rents were cheap. The island had not yet been re-designated a major tourist destination. On the island of Key West Buffett found the characters and the situations for the songs that laid the foundation for his success. It was at this time and at this place that it all came together, creatively speaking, for Jimmy Buffett.

In 1973 Buffett recorded the first in a string of best-selling albums, *A White Sport Coat and a Pink Crustacean*. He was 26 years old. By the time he was 30, he was an established rock star. He'd fronted for the Eagles, hung with President Jimmy Carter and Dolly Parton, and become chief executive of his currently multi-million dollar business called "Jimmy Buffett."

In 1977 *People Magazine* published an article and photographs of Buffett's Aspen, Colorado, wedding to Jane Slagsvol. Buffett called the publicity "the kiss of death"—the end to his relative anonymity. And so it was. When Buffett later bought a house in Aspen, *People Magazine* reported the fact and accused him of deserting Key West, the place where he'd gotten his start. But he hadn't deserted. He'd merely expanded his range of operations, he explained. Buffett still owns a home in Key West.

In 1985 Key West's Margaritaville, a massive cafe, bar and shop, opened at 500 Duval Street. The house has been packed ever since. Caribbean Soul, Buffett's Florida-based clothing line of Margaritaville-mood tropic wear and T-shirts, nets millions of dollars each year. The *Coconut Telegraph*, a newsletter and catalog of Caribbean Soul clothes published six times a year, is distributed to thousands of adoring—and paying ($5 a year)—Parrot Heads who want to keep up with news of Buffett's latest projects, as well as his current concert schedule.

Buffett's lust for the spotlight seems almost as keen as his sharp business sense. His annual income has been estimated to be around $3.5 million.

The charismatic Buffett frequently contributes to fundraising projects by playing at free concerts. He's an ardent environmentalist and an active Democrat, performing with President Clinton at the 1993 inauguration. The President blew sax.

A Parrot Head Tour of Buffett's Key West

Parrot Heads arriving in Key West are likely to head directly to **Margaritaville**, at 500 Duval Street. There fans will find Buffett's shrine to rock 'n roll and free enterprise—a restaurant serving the quintessential "cheeseburger in paradise," endless music played loud and hard, a city-block-long bar, and a retail shop chock full of T-shirts, books, hats, hot sauce, and other merchandise related to the eternal quest for Margaritaville.

Unfortunately, Jimmy Buffett's concert tour does not come to Key West, but Jimmy Buffett himself does stop into Margaritaville from time to time. When he does, he takes out his guitar and plays a few numbers. When that special event happens is anybody's guess.

For much of the '70s, Buffett lived in a second-story apartment at **704 Waddell Street**. Today the house contains several luxurious condominiums that are rented out to up-scale tourists. To envision 704 Waddell in Jimmy's starving-artist days, push the calendar in your imagination back twenty years. Envision the same house (minus the fresh paint) as it was then, battered by the winds from the sea, baked to silver by the tropic sun. Then, picture Buffett, sitting in a front porch swing, strumming his six-string on the wide, airy veranda.

Louie's Backyard, an eatery next door to Buffett's first Key West home, was not the pretty, manicured, high-priced tourist attraction you see today either. But it is on the beach. To see what Buffett and his friends saw, explore the beach to the right of Louie's. In the '70s a gate separated Louie's and Buffett's backyards. Buffett ate at Louie's, often playing for his supper, often signing for meals that were ultimately never paid for.

Buffet's first haunt, **The Chart Room** at the Pier House Resort, 1 Duval Street, still operates in a small, dark room in a hind corner of the resort. Drinks are now expensive in the Chart Room, and the place is usually frequented by people for whom drinking is a favorite pastime. The place doesn't begin to live up to its mythical, somewhat sinister reputation until very, very late at night.

Upstairs, at an opposite corner of the Pier House Resort you'll find the **Havana Docks Bar.** Bright and spacious, it is very much the opposite in atmosphere of the Chart Room. The video version of Buffett's song "Who's the Blond Stranger" was filmed here in the mid-80s. Florida Senator Bob Graham, who was then Governor of Florida, appears in the video. The blond stranger, by the way, was then-Key West model Susan Jones, today a Birmingham Parrot Head, wife, and mother, with a really neat video to show her friends and neighbors.

Another Buffett haunt is the **Caroline Street** seaport. Back in the '70s it was home to the island's shrimp fleet. The other side of Caroline Street was lined with shoddy saloons that served the shrimpers who came in from two-week shrimping trips loaded down with plenty of expendable bucks. Mayhem, and sometimes even murder, went on in those bars. Nonetheless, it was not uncommon in the '70s for Buffett and friends to end up down here at the end of a long night of carousing. It was in one of these bars that Buffett reportedly met up with the lady who inspired the song "Woman Going Crazy on Caroline Street."

Today, Jimmy Buffett still owns a recording studio at the Key West Seaport, but the small, two-story building is currently unmarked (see our Old Town Walking Tour). There are rumors that, with the gentrification of the seaport area, Buffett will turn his anonymous building into a snack bar to sell cheeseburgers as well as T-shirts and shorts from Buffett's clothing line, Caribbean Soul.

Dennis Pharmacy Conch Korner at 1229 Simonton Street is still pretty much as it was in Buffett's early island days. Grilled cheese sandwiches. Milkshakes. Cuban toast. Black beans and rice. Beef stew. Basic island cuisine, at easy prices. Lately a plaque has been posted in the '60s-era-decor eatery to let people know that Jimmy Buffett was once a regular.

Blue Heaven Restaurant at 729 Thomas Street is the place immortalized in the song "Blue Heaven Rendezvous." It's a tiny patch of '70s-era, Key West atmosphere, featuring a wonderful collection of zany and unpredictable characters. Even non-Parrot Heads flock to Blue Heaven. It's a trip. And the food is very, very good. Big, morning-after breakfasts are popular for Margaritaville-seeking revelers.

The Scoop via the Coconut Telegraph
800-262-6835

Can't make it to Key West just now? You can still be a Parrot Head. Call the toll free number and the office Parrot Head will send you Jimmy's official newsletter, the Coconut Telegraph.

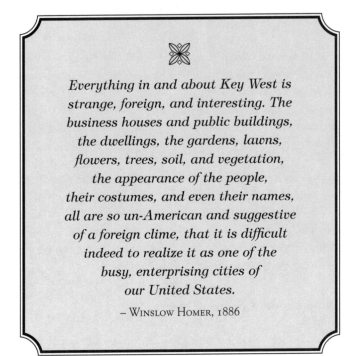

Everything in and about Key West is strange, foreign, and interesting. The business houses and public buildings, the dwellings, the gardens, lawns, flowers, trees, soil, and vegetation, the appearance of the people, their costumes, and even their names, all are so un-American and suggestive of a foreign clime, that it is difficult indeed to realize it as one of the busy, enterprising cities of our United States.

– WINSLOW HOMER, 1886

Some Key West Artists

John James Audubon visited the Florida Keys for the first time in the spring of 1832. He arrived at Indian Key on his 47th birthday and soon witnessed a flock of flamingos, which, according to his journal, was exactly what he hoped to find in the Keys.

In Key West, Audubon was a guest at the home of Captain John Geiger, the city's harbormaster. The Geigers were one of the island's leading families, and, since Audubon was an artist of some renown by the time he arrived here, he was invited to stay, as dignitaries were in those days, at the upscale home. The Geiger house at 205 Whitehead Street has since been extensively restored and is known today as the Audubon House Museum. Several Audubon engravings are on exhibit there.

Audubon visited the Keys with the hope of finding many new species of birds to sketch. And he did. When he discovered a specimen new to him, he killed them. Then he ran wires through the dead birds and arranged them in life-like poses. In a personal account of his visit in Audubon's journal, it is chilling to read of how much the naturalist seemed to relish shooting birds! Because he did not have the time to complete his studies of the flamingo, he had one killed and preserved in rum so that it could be shipped to his studio in Charleston, where he finished the job of sketching the bird.

Audubon's 1838 collection, *Birds of America*, is a four volume set containing 435 plates of over a thousand life-sized portraits of birds. The amazing likenesses were first engraved in copper, then printed on handmade drawing paper, and finally painted with watercolors. Often Audubon himself supervised the application of color. In 1841, copies of Audubon's *Birds of America* sold for $1,000.

Audubon's letters, journals and a book entitled *Ornithological Biography*, is a richly detailed account of how the Florida Keys appeared to the naturalist in the early 1800s.

Katherine Proby's book *Audubon in Florida*, is full of surprising revelations about America's premier naturalist artist.

George Carey remembers being in trouble for drawing in the margins of his school papers back in the first grade. Recognizing his potential when he was 12 years old, George's mother scraped together the money for him to study oil painting. Artist Gerald Leak taught painting classes on the grounds of the Hemingway House, where kindly Pauline Hemingway served cool drinks and cookies to the budding artists. Today Carey's magnificent paintings, realistic portrayals of Key West conch houses and store fronts, are strongly evocative of the island's salty, innocent bygone days.

During a stint as metal shop teacher at Key West High, Carey directed his students in the construction of amazing metal sculptures. The first was an 8-foot conch—the school mascot—in front of Key West High School at 2100 Flagler Avenue; a larger-than-life Bengal tiger in the yard of Glynn Archer School at 1302 White Street; and a towering buccaneer wearing an eye patch, a skull-and-crossbones belt buckle, a conch ring, a sword, and a huge, colonial-looking revolver tucked inside his coat, standing in front of Horace O'Bryant Middle School at 1105 Leon Street.

Henry Faulkner was no relation to the writer William Faulkner, though Henry didn't mind if people mistakenly believed he was. Henry was from a poor, disintegrating Kentucky family. He spent most of his childhood in orphanages and foster homes. Thin and delicate and flighty, he epitomized the word "fairy." And yet he eventually found his way to art schools, and into the important galleries of New York City in the 1960s. New York critics called Henry "the American Chagall."

At the height of his success in the '60s Faulkner came to Key West and bought a house, which he shared with pet goats. Henry is still remembered by those who knew him for his penchant for conversing with his favorite goat, Alice, as if she were fully capable of understanding him. With all his odd habits, Henry, nevertheless, fit in quite well. Reveling in every moment of his existence, he considered life itself to be his art: donning a black dress and wailing the blues at Captain Tony's Saloon; reciting poetry at the top of his voice when the mood struck him. As he rode his bicycle through the streets of Key West, he shouted off-color comments to young men along the way. It was not uncommon for him to be physically assaulted for his outrageous antics.

Among Henry Faulkner's Key West friends were Tennessee Williams and James Leo Herlihy, who wrote the novel *Midnight Cowboy*, which was later made into an Academy Award-winning film. *Midnight Cowboy's* central character, Ratso Rizzo, is modeled after Henry Faulkner.

"He seemed always to be running naked through a cannibal village with a sprig of parsley behind his ear, stirring up the natives and somehow, triumphing over them instead of getting eaten," Herlihy once said of Henry.

In the late '70s, Faulkner was commissioned for $3,000 to create a painting of the Hemingway House. Today this painting still hangs over Hemingway's huge bed in the museum at 907 Whitehead Street.

Although thousands of Faulkner's fantastic paintings survive, they are rarely available for sale. People generally hold on tightly to their Faulkners. The Gingerbread Square Gallery in Key West handled

Faulkner's and Tennessee Williams' works while they were alive, and still do, whenever they become available.

Winslow Homer spent two winters in Key West—1886 and 1904. He came to paint in watercolors, and to escape the cold, snowy winters of his Maine home. Some of his most famous and often reproduced Key West paintings are *Hauling in Anchor, Taking on Provisions, Palms in the Storm,* and *Fishing Boat, Key West.* It is clear from these enduring images that Homer loved painting that very-different-from-today, turn-of-the-century-era Key West.

Anne Irvine says, "My life is all about Key West and has been thus far, a fairy tale story."

In the late '60s Anne Irvine, daughter of parents from a middle-class background, found herself married to an Air Force captain in Tallahassee, bored to desperation by her slack existence. So she packed up her kids and her dreams and came to Key West. She began painting, and has been painting and selling her work ever since. What is most characteristic of Anne's work is its bright humor—Anne's joyfulness shines from every painting. "If somebody in Key West wins the lottery," Anne once said, "we'll fly to Paris to celebrate. If somebody up in America wins the lottery, they'll fly to Key West. But if you live here, there's really no better place to be...except maybe Paris for a day or two."

See Anne's work at the Guild Hall Gallery on Duval Street. Anne's often there, too.

John Kiraly's paintings, for many people are simply irresistible. They see them, they want them. The paintings are filled with fantastic plants, columns, statues, archways, waterfalls, and placid pools, all painted in luxurious greens, deep-hued blues, rich purples, pinks and turquoise. Kiraly's works create a sense of deep and restful tranquility—the same sort of serenity that John Kiraly seeks for himself.

Kiraly's images have broad appeal. Often spotted on the walls of television and movie sets, his work is also popular in Japan.

The son of a concert violinist, Kiraly was born in New York of Hungarian descent. He moved to Miami as a teenager in the '60s and studied art at the University of Miami. He has lived in Key West for nearly 25 years. Kiraly was the life partner of Richard Heyman (1935-1984), who founded the Gingerbread Square Gallery. Kiraly's work is translated into serigraphs (silk-screened prints) and posters by publishers Chalk and Vermillion of New York, and is available at the Gingerbread Square Gallery.

Stanley Papio established his welding studio and home on a lot in Key Largo. He created a fence with old bedsprings and erected odd renditions of men, women, and animals out of abandoned, often pitifully rusted metal. He encouraged people to leave their old cars, rusted refrigerators, car fenders and kitchen sinks on his property for later use in his art. When authorities complained about the unsightly appearance of Papio's yard, the sculptor replied that the heaps of refuse were future works of art. He fought long and hard with his neighbors, who begged him to clean up his yard and get rid of the odd sculptures.

"A bunch of junk is a welder's glory," he said.

Eventually, in response to the controversy he created in Key Largo, Papio renamed his welding shop "Stanley's Art Museum," and charged 25¢ admission. Tour buses full of awed visitors, folk art collectors, and, eventually, serious critics took notice of Papio's works. Three of his sculptures toured Europe in 1981 as part of a traveling exhibit sponsored by the U.S. State Department.

When Papio died suddenly of a heart attack in 1982, his family donated his work to the Key West Art and Historical Society. The Papio Collection, now on display at the East Martello Museum in Key West, includes nearly 100 three-dimensional constructions, composed of painted or chrome-plated ferrous metal, created by Papio during the final decade of his life. In art circles, Papio's sculpture is internationally praised and is said to display extraordinary visual inventiveness and humor—but you don't have to be a serious art critic to love it.

Mario Sanchez is one of America's most eminent and renowned folk artists. Born in Key West to Cuban immigrants in 1908, Sanchez grew up in Gato Village, an area that gets its name from the Cuban factory that employed many in the neighborhood. Sanchez began carving and painting fish in the 1930s. Later he began illustrating scenes of old Key West, thus documenting the colorful citizens, activities and storefronts of the city's bygone days. The shops, churches, saloons, and neighborhoods in Sanchez's works are all historically accurate. Though many of the buildings are gone now, some, like the East Martello Museum and the San Carlos Theater, still stand. It is fascinating to compare Mario's portraits of old Key West to the Key West of today.

Mario, who has been called a national treasure, in Key West is known for his charm and humor. He works for four hours every day in an outdoor studio on Catherine Street. Evenings he sits at the corner of Duval and Catherine, with his brother Perucho, to watch the world going by.

Except in a permanent exhibit of his works in the East Martello Gallery, it is unusual to see an original Mario Sanchez carving. The supply cannot possibly meet the demand. And so there are now posters on the market, many of which are signed.

One of his many fans was actor Cary Grant, who came to Key West in 1961 to film the movie *Operation Petticoat*. Grant was so taken with Mario's work that he bought a couple of the carvings for himself as well as one for his friend Spencer Tracy. At Grant's insistence, two Sanchez carvings appear in a hotel lobby scene in his movie *A Touch of Mink*.

Posters of Mario Sanchez's works are sold at the East Martello Museum and Gallery store.

Some Art Galleries

Island Arts
1128 Duval Street ☞ 292-9909
Twenty Key West and Lower Keys artists show their work here. Prices on prints, paintings, crafts, sculptures and stained glass are very affordable; also, hand-painted greeting cards, boxes, bowls and picture frames; hand-fired tiles and ceramic light-switch covers. All of it has a Caribbean feel. Hours are 10 a.m.–6 p.m. daily. Open later in season.

Baron's Folk Art Gallery
1075 Duval Square ☞ 294-3629
Folk artist Jack Baron's studio is right in the window of his gallery in Duval Square. "People wave at me. I wave back. And then they come in," Jack says. Other artists represented are painters Jo Cooper and Ruth

Lawson; Sculptors Lee Dodez and Gloria Shaw. Baron's unique paintings are bright and unmistakably island-themed. Open daily from 9 a.m.–3 p.m. or by appointment.

Caribbean Gallery
1000 Duval Street ✴ 292-0060

The gallery specializes in art from the Caribbean islands, and is also Key West's only current Cuban art collection, imported directly from Cuba. Prices on Cuban pieces range from $300 to $1,000. The Caribbean is one of five Kennedy galleries on the island. Open 10 a.m.–8 p.m. daily.

East Martello Museum and Gallery
3501 South Roosevelt Boulevard ✴ 296-3913

Several locally created or themed art exhibits are shown here each year. All are fascinating and often coordinate with other cultural activities. The gallery is located in a series of arched rooms in a mid-1800s-era brick fort. On permanent exhibit is a collection of wood carvings by native folk artist Mario Sanchez. In the outdoor garden and upstairs in the second and third levels of the citadel are the magnificent and zany metal sculptures of welder and junk sculptor Stanley Papio. When the Key Largo based sculptor died, his family donated over one hundred pieces of Papio's work to the museum.

The gallery at East Martello is part of a wonderful museum featuring exhibits and relics from Florida Keys history. The gallery and museum are open daily from 9:30 a.m.–5 p.m. Admission is $5 adults; $1 kids, free for kids under 7.

Gingerbread Square Gallery
1207 Duval Street ✴ 296-8900

The oldest gallery in Key West, it was founded by Richard Heyman, America's first gay mayor (at least that's what all the headlines said when he was elected by a landslide vote in the fall of 1983).

The most famous of the artists that show here is John Kiraly, represented by publishers Chalk and Vermillion. Original Kiralys are on display here—rare and very expensive—as well as wonderful serigraphs, and posters that evoke dreamy, hopeful images.

The gallery also features rainforest scenes by Key West native and owner Sal Salinero. Open at 11 a.m. daily and stays open many evenings.

Guild Hall
614 Duval Street ✻ 296-6076
A twenty-year-old, two-tiered artists' cooperative, it has been owned since 1985 by seven women members of the gallery's 21 participating artists. The building was constructed in 1919 and restored in 1975. Stairs and railings are from a dismantled Catholic convent. Floor bricks are salvaged from original Key West streets.

"What we bought when we purchased Guild Hall is job security," says Sonia Robinson, a willowy beauty whose original leather bags and painted clothes are inexpensive and sensational. People who work here are the artists who display here.

Ann Irvine, Sonia Robinson, Judi Bradford, Mally Weaver, Sheila Freeman, Reen Stanhouse, and Cappy Seiler are just some of the artists who show their unique works at the Guild Hall.

Open 9:30 a.m.–11 p.m. daily.

Haitian Art Gallery
600 Frances Street ✻ 296-8932
The doors of this wonderful place opened for the first time in 1980. It's owned and operated by Boris Kravitz and his daughter Ruth. Boris lives in Haiti and buys the oil paintings and sculptures directly from the artists. By eliminating the middleman, the Kravitz's are able to offer original art for very affordable prices and help Haitian artists to survive in their native country. Haitian art, by its very nature, is primitive, sometimes very sweet, and sometimes very shocking! Papier-mache fishes and animals painted in bright acrylics are so much fun. The sculptures are under $50. Paintings start at around $75. Open 10 a.m.–6 p.m. daily.

Harrison Gallery
825 White Street ✻ 294-0609
The gallery's owned and operated by wood sculptor Helen Harrison. Harrison turned to woodwork after she and her husband, musician/writer Ben Harrison, built the 38-foot sailboat that brought them here from

Costa Rica. From scraps of native mahogany, walnut, sea grape and sea hibiscus wood, she creates her richly grained and wood-colored sculptures. Garden metal sculptures by George Carey are featured as well.

The Harrisons live next door to the gallery in a 100 year-old house. Harrison Gallery is open from noon–5:30 p.m. every day but Sunday.

Key West Art Center
301 Front Street ** 294-1241
It was founded originally as an art center by F. Morgan Townsend, who came to Key West to work for President Roosevelt's WPA in 1933. After the Depression, the center became the local Red Cross Building for a while. Then it was abandoned and fell into disrepair.

In 1960 a group of local artists set out to find a place where they wouldn't have to pay rent and therefore could afford to hire a receptionist. Key West Mayor Delio Cobo agreed to let them use the abandoned and condemned Red Cross Building on Front Street, which they then restored and turned into the lovely, little local artist's co-op you see today.

The seventy artists represented here live in the Florida Keys and contribute equally to the upkeep of the building and to the salaries of the staff. Everything you see in the gallery is for sale. Hours are 10 a.m.–5 p.m. daily.

Lucky Street Gallery
1100 White Street ** 294-3973
Dianne Zolotow is on the forefront of an important cultural shift for art galleries and non-T-shirt shops. They're pulling up stakes on expensive and busy Duval Street and moving into a cozy old neighborhood on White Street.

Sign of Sandford
328 Simonton Street ** 296-7493
The owner is the artist, usually busy at work in her shop. Sandford Birdsey paints in watercolors, designing the hand-painted fabrics for bags and luggage, and painting silk scarves and furniture and anything else that will hold paint. Her work—bright and very buoyant—reflects her

joie de vivre. If she's not too busy, have a chat with this world traveler, whose life is art and creativity. This is cottage industry at its most elegant and productive best. Usually open 11 a.m.–5 p.m., Monday–Saturday. Closed Sunday.

Whitehead Street Pottery
1011 Whitehead Street ✱ 294-5067

Potters Chuck Pearson and Tim Roeder restored this old Key West storefront and also the guest cottage next door. They work in an exposed studio. There are raku fired pots with lizard-handled lids, turquoise and pink and purple glazed bowls, large raku vessels, and tiny raku fish pins. In a tiny L-shaped gallery off the main gallery, Chuck Pearson has been showing the earthy photographs he creates with Polaroid image transfer. Hours are 10 a.m.–6 p.m., every day but Tuesday.

Theatre

Cinema

Cinema Shores
Atlantic Shores • 510 South Street • 296-2491

Cinema Shores shows art-house and alternative-culture flicks outdoors at the island's most progressive motel. Like a New Age drive-in, only no cars! Lounge chairs are arranged in a corner section of the parking lot, protected from noise and wind. Films run on two projectors: they're shown against a white wall that used to be part of a racquetball court.

Movies are on every Thursday night at 9 p.m. sharp in the summer, 8 p.m. in the autumn and winter. Admission is $3, the popcorn is free, and cocktails are available from waitrons.

The films are the ones that usually don't make it all the way down to Key West, or blockbusters that you might have missed in the big theaters.

Call for a monthly schedule.

Cinema 6 Movie Theater
Searstown Shopping Plaza • 294-0000

As you may have guessed from the name, they offer six films, which change every Friday. During holiday season and peak tourist weeks, 1 p.m. matinees are offered; otherwise, shows begin around 3:30 p.m. or 4 p.m. Is it because we're at the end of the line down here in Key West that we don't get movies the minute they're released? But we always seem to get plenty of films that appeal to kids—especially at holiday time. Call for a complete listing of movies and times.

Key Encounter Theater & Museum
Clinton Square Market, 291 Front Street • 292-2070

Do take the time to see this wonderful, affordable and gloriously air conditioned nature treat. If you can't or don't want to go near the water, this

is the very next best thing. This multi-image movie of the world of the
Florida Keys living reef, and Keys wildlife is projected onto 3 screens,
each of them 48-feet wide. You'll come away with a fresh enthusiasm for
the natural Keys. The film is around a half-hour long. Admission is $3
for adults and $1 for kids, and fascinating enough to entertain folks aged
9 months to 99 years. Very, very charming. Designed by a group of local
Creationists, the final moments of the film feature well-chosen quotes
from the Bible.

I know people who see this film again and again! It's a lot cheaper
than a snorkeling trip, and you're guaranteed a good look at denizens
of the deep like scorpion fish, parrot fish, puffers, eels, stingrays and
barracuda.

After the film, visit the nature museum where you'll see the famous
22.5-foot snakeskin of the anaconda that reportedly once ate a woman.
Also on display: art, shells, stuffed wildlife and merchandise.

Live Theatre

Eaton Street Theatre
524 Eaton Street ♦ 296-3030
This lovely cabaret theater, located in what was once a Baptist church
attended by President Harry Truman, is dark as we go to press. But we
won't write it out of this edition. We believe in theater, and we are confident the Eaton Street Theatre will revive and survive.

Ghost Tours of Key West
416 Fleming Street ♦ 293-8009
Every night at 8, as dusk descends over historic downtown Key West,
performer/storyteller/ghost tour guide David Sloan begins telling his
haunted tales to his thrill-seeking audiences. The walking tour covers a
little less than a mile, and visits places where eerie apparitions have been
documented by legend, and sometimes even by photographs. David asks
participants to raise their right hands and repeat the following:

I do solemnly swear
To have the time of my life on this ghost tour.

I will not complain that my feet are tired.
And I will not ask the nice tour guide any questions
he doesn't have the answer to.
I will laugh at the tour guide's corny jokes,
And tell him how great he is at the end of the tour.

David holds forth in a Dracula cape, black top-hat, ruffled shirt and black bow tie, black vest, and silver tipped black boots. He might be the ghost of Zorro, or maybe Abraham Lincoln, dandied up for a night on the town.

Ghosts along the way are the scorned wife of a bigamist cigar baron, and, at the Audubon House ("Most of my guests say this place is for the birds," David cracks) a haunted doll, thought to be a replica of a young girl who died of yellow fever 150 years ago.

Big fun for everyone. Reservations are a must. Tickets: $15 for adults; $12 for students; $10 for kids.

The Red Barn Theatre
319 Duval Street (rear) ✹ 296-9911
Before it was used as a theater, the little building that is home to the Red Barn Theatre was a carriage house behind a fine old Key West home. The playhouse was renovated and opened as the Red Barn Theatre in 1980. Since then, 90 shows have been mounted on the theatre's versatile stage. Cocktails are available at the Chicken Coop bar before the show and during intermissions. Milling with the crowd in the open-air lobby is a mood setting treat.

The Red Barn staff does a great job of advertising upcoming presentations. For an annual seasonal brochure or a schedule of plays and musicals, call or write.

San Carlos Institute
516 Duval Street ✹ 294-3887
The first San Carlos was lost to fire; the second to a hurricane. This current structure was built in 1924 in the architectural style of Cuban baroque, similar in appearance to the presidential building in Havana. The foyer features high ceilings, a crystal chandelier and a rounded marble staircase lined with majolican tiles. In the 1980s the San Carlos

was restored to its present nobility. Inside are housed a 400-seat theater, a museum, and a library containing the complete writings of Jose Marti. The museum, where guided pre-arranged tours are available, is open to the public and shows a movie about Cuban-American culture at 1 p.m. and 3 p.m. The San Carlos is open from 11 a.m. to 6 p.m. every day but Monday.

Each January in the theatre, the San Carlos Institute hosts the Key West Literary Seminar. Ballet, opera and theatrical performances are presented here, as well, but no regular program of events is scheduled.

Theatre des Seances
429 Caroline Street • 292-2040

Don't show up at this seance hoping for a chat with your long dead Aunt Edna. Do plan on being amazed by this evening of interactive theater, staged in one of Key West's oldest and most fascinating houses. Tim Glancy is a performer with particular skill in special effects. He spent many summers on the road with Jimmy Buffett tours, warming up crowds with preconcert illusions. As a "parrot trooper," Glancy says he learned a lot about people, and their willingness to be entertained. Recently he combined his fascination and skill in theater and illusion, with his interest in Key West history and came up with the Theatre des Seances.

As a prelude to the seance, Glancy warms up his Key West audiences with a series of psychic parlor games and tricks, designed to put folks into a psychic frame of mind. The parlor is decorated just as it was at the turn of the century. A coffee table is replicates the headstone of William Curry, Florida's first millionaire, and one of Key West's most famous historical citizens. The seance table is the same dining table the house's original owners used 100 years ago.

In spite of many announcements that the production is only for fun and not a serious attempt to contact the other side, there is usually a true-believer in the crowd, convinced of its authenticity. That makes it more fun.

Reservations are a must. The theater accommodates only 13 at a time. Tickets are around $30. Group rates and private parties available.

Tennessee Williams Fine Arts Center
5901 W. College Road ✹ 296-1520
Tennessee Williams promised to make an endowment to the Florida Keys
Community College for the construction of this lovely theater named for
him. When the project was nearly completed, Williams bestowed an
audio tape of himself reading his own poetry. He suggested that money
might be raised by playing the tape for a paying audience.

The Tennessee Williams Fine Arts Center opened with a production
of Williams' play *Will Mr. Merriweather Return From Memphis?* Williams
had written the play in 1969, but it premiered in January 1980 at the
Arts Center named for him. It was not a memorable show and has rarely
been staged again since.

Founders is a group of theater supporters who preview everything pre-
sented there on "Founders Night"—the first night of any presentation.
The theater seats 300; it's a plush, very modern, high-ceiled auditorium.
It is said that there are no bad seats in the Tennessee Williams Fine Arts
Center. Believe it. It's a honey of a theater and is, sadly enough, rarely
crowded.

Waterfront Playhouse
Mallory Square ✹ 294-5015
The Key West Players, Inc., formed in 1940, moved around for a while,
staging shows at various locations around town, until finally settling into
the present-day Waterfront Playhouse on Mallory Square in 1960. The
theater was an important warehouse during Key West's wrecking days.

In addition to a full season of varied performances, the Waterfront
hosts the annual Key West Classics, featuring local celebrities and personalities performing a vaudeville-formatted show.

Attractions and Museums

Key West Aquarium
1 Whitehead Street ❧ 296-2051

In 1934, when Key West set out to turn itself into a tourist town, one of the first things built with the government's Works Projects Administration (WPA) money was this aquarium. Located at the foot of Whitehead Street in Mallory Square on the gulf side of the island, it was the world's first open-air aquarium, and considered to be a modern and fantastic achievement. WPA artists painted several murals of the construction; They are on display in the aquarium still.

The aquarium certainly did what it was supposed to do. Tourists loved the place. The world was much smaller then, and, for many people, this was a first opportunity to see sharks and porcupine fish and sea turtles. For years it was called the City Aquarium and owned by the City of Key West. It's privately owned now, part of the same mega-corporation that owns the Old Town Trolley and the Conch Tour Train. In the early '80s the aquarium was refurbished and enclosed.

In her travel guide for kids, travel writer Susan Moffat rates the aquarium a "3" out of a possible "5." But consider this (you, too, Miss Moffat): there are few great kid-pleasing attractions in the Keys. Among them, the Key West Aquarium is surely at the top of the list. During a 30 minute tour, kids are invited to pet the surprisingly rough hide of a shark, and even watch one eat lunch. Notice how a nurse shark eats a fish: it seems to suck it, like a hungry baby at the nipple, which is how the nurse shark got its name. In a "touch tank," there are conchs, horseshoe crabs, triton's trumpet, and starfish for the curious to pick up and observe.

Marine life on display in the aquarium is caught, tagged and released back into the sea within a year or two. Some specimens have become dependent upon captivity, like Floyd, a giant loggerhead turtle who was found on Smathers Beach after Hurricane Floyd in 1987. In order for Loggerhead Floyd to survive, a substantial part of a rear flipper, gangrenous after an injury, had to be amputated. Floyd's fine now, although he's pretty slow—even for a turtle. He'll probably live at the aquarium for the remainder of his days.

The Key West Aquarium is open from 10 a.m. to 6 p.m. daily. Tours begin at 11, 1, 3, 4:30 p.m., but otherwise you can wander the aquarium on your own. Admission is $7 for adults; $3.50 for kids ages 8 to 15; free for kids 7 and under. Your ticket is good for as many visits as you like on the day you buy it, and on the following day.

Audubon House and Garden
205 Whitehead Street ☎ 294-2116

Captain John Geiger's beautifully restored house is a wonderful example of early 19th-century island architecture. The elegant yet utilitarian furniture typifies the period of John Audubon's first visit Key West in 1832. Captain Geiger was a master wrecker and Key West's first harbor pilot. His house was built with the assistance of shipbuilding carpenters and furnished with items salvaged from the cargoes of wrecked ships.

Upon arriving for a visit to the house everyone is given a portable cassette player, headphones and a taped tour. This way, an attendant told us, visitors can pace themselves and linger as long as they like over exhibits particularly interesting to them. The system works well, providing you and your companions are able to keep your tour tapes synchronized. Otherwise, you might turn to one of your pals, your eyes wide with wonder, to remark upon some surprising revelation to find that they are still contemplating some earlier disclosure.

Your hosts, who are only heard and never seen, are the ghosts of the Geigers themselves. Interestingly, the information on the tapes is taken from actual letters and journals kept by the Geigers.

In the parlor you'll find a gold harp from Dublin, a Chinese tea caddy, and a sewing necessaire in the shape of a globe, decorated with hand-painted signs of the zodiac. Chippendale furniture can be seen throughout the house. A charming children's room, with 19th-century roller skates and an Italian puppet collection and stage, is on the third floor, so as not to disturb the adults, a Geiger daughter explains.

By 1958 the once-elegant home of the prosperous wrecker, Captain John Geiger, was scheduled for the wrecking ball. Mitchell Wolfson, a wealthy businessman and native son, renovated the house where John Audubon slept, and created one of the island's first tourist attractions.

In a garden there are orchids, bromeliads, a lovely herb garden, and papaya, banana and sapodilla trees. The gift shop features bird and garden-themed items. There are canisters of flower seeds and a small collection of books on Keys history. Today, the Audubon House and Gardens is a popular setting for weddings. The Audubon House is open from 9:30 a.m. till 5 p.m. Admission is $7.50 for adults; children 6 to 12, $2. ALA and AARP members get $1 off.

City Cemetery
Margaret and Angela Streets ✹ 292-8177
Key West's 150-year-old cemetery covers 15 acres. Because the cemetery's earliest records are long gone, no one knows exactly how many bodies are buried here, but estimates range as high as 100,000—about four times the city's current population.

The cemetery was created during an era in American history when expansive, landscaped cemeteries were much more popular than grave-yards. They doubled as lush parks, where fanciful tombstones were important expressions of art. It was not uncommon in the 1800s for families to picnic on Sunday afternoons at the tombs of their dead loved ones. The graves of wealthier citizens were marked with elaborate imported stones, into which symbols such as plants, flowers and shells were engraved. Each item has its own meaning. Many graves are marked with brick or tile, representative of the town's Cuban heritage.

Most graves are above ground because during Key West's earlier days there was no mechanical equipment powerful enough to dig into the coral rock that lies just two feet below the island's surface.

Today the City Cemetery remains one of the busy island's most restful and charming retreats. Trees and flowers on this property are some of the most spectacular in town. The cemetery also includes a section for babies and a section for pets.

The tiny streets in the cemetery are named. On the corner of Palm and Magnolia Lanes, an ornate wrought iron fence surrounds a number of white stones that commemorate the men who died in the 1898 sinking of the battleship USS *Maine*, in Havana Harbor. A solitary sailor stands on a pedestal above the white marble markers of those who died. Shading his eyes with his left hand, he searches the horizon for his lost comrades.

Gravestone Symbols

Anchors	*hope*
Calla lily	*majestic beauty*
Clasped hands	*farewell and friendship*
Eye	*divine vision*
Grapes	*fertility and sacrifice*
Ivy	*immortality*
Lamb or cherub	*death of a child*
Laurel	*reward or glory*
Lily of the valley	*bride*
Oak leaves	*strength*
Wreaths	*eternity*
Open book	*divine knowledge*
Pansy	*humility*
Rose	*love*
Shell	*the journey through life*
Lily	*purity, chastity*

Also on Magnolia, there is a white, marble-winged angel, placed as a reminder of a child's early death. Between the Angela Street boundary of the cemetery and Palm Avenue, within the cemetery, there is a slightly smaller than life size sculpture of a naked and bound woman. The eerie statue was placed on the grave of the man who lies within. No one knows why he requested this mysterious marker, and he died with the reason.

Key West's most famous hypochondriac, a waitress named Pearl Roberts who died in 1979 at the age of 50, has the best known marker in the entire cemetery. It says: "I told you I was sick," and people come from far and wide to see it. It has been endlessly photographed.

The State of Florida publishes an excellent self-guided cemetery tour, directing visitors to the cemetery's most elaborate, bizarre or sentimental graves, and giving information about the dead who occupy them. The brochure is free and available in the cemetery sexton's office, which is open from 7 a.m. till 4 p.m. daily. The cemetery is open from 7 till 7 daily. Also there are several cemetery tours available. See Tours for more information.

Curry Mansion
511 Caroline Street ✻ 294-5349

Built by Milton Curry, son of William Curry, Florida's first self-made millionaire, the Curry Mansion is one of the town's most stunning architectural landmarks. The five-story, 22-room Victorian style mansion was modeled after a Newport, Rhode Island cottage. When it was built in 1905, replete with Tiffany glass, splendidly carved woodwork, grand verandas and a widow's walk affording a bird's-eye view of the entire city and miles out to sea, it was the most ornate house on the island.

By day tourists are invited to explore the mansion. Only the guest rooms are off limits. The dining room, its elegant table set for a formal dinner, is a good place to take photographs because you are allowed to sit at the table.

In a cozy library you'll see Hemingway's big game gun on display. (No, it's not the gun that killed him.) There are fascinating historical photographs, and a wonderful collection of books which may well keep you entertained for hours. That's just fine. The owners Al and Edith Amsterdam love it when you find their treasures as glorious as they do.

You will hear a lot about William Curry when you visit Key West's historic downtown area. It was William who built the first house that stood on this property, and his son Milton who tore it down to make way for this stunning mansion. The elder Curry sailed to the Keys from Green Turtle Cay in the Bahamas in 1847. He was a poor boy with a lot of ambition and a pleasing personality when he began working as a clerk in a ship's chandlery. Although he never went near the water, Curry became rich on wrecking. He eventually became owner of the city's largest mercantile business and ship's chandlery. When he died in 1896, seventy carriages accompanied his body to the cemetery.

At the height of his great wealth in 1890, William Curry ordered a set of 18-carat-gold flatware from Tiffany's in New York City. In those tax-free days, a millionaire had more money than he could spend. When the special order was completed, it was displayed in Tiffany's windows before being shipped to Key West. John Jacob Astor, another famous millionaire of the times, happened by Tiffany's, saw the fine flatware, and, not to be outdone, ordered an identical set for himself.

The tour of the Curry Mansion is self-directed. You'll get a brochure highlighting the details you shouldn't miss. The house is open daily from 10 a.m. till 5 p.m. Admission is $5 for adults; $1 for children.

The Custom House
Clinton Square • 296-3913

Under construction now, and a bit tired looking with all the hubbub going on around her, this century-old lady is the queen of the harbor. And she always will be. The State of Florida Division of Historic Preservation has designated the Custom House the best example of Romanesque revival architecture and one of the five most important buildings in Florida. Notice the terra cotta faces which adorn the exterior of the Custom House where the arches connect: a lion, a fox, a ram, a human and a demon. So how come the City of Key West allowed the massive Hilton Hotel to dwarf the once stately queen?

Back in the late 1800s, when Key West was the largest and most important port city in Florida, the U.S. Treasury authorized the construction of the Custom building as a custom house, post office and federal court house. Construction began in 1888 and was completed in 1891, which is where the stunning building gets its local name: "Old '91."

Old '91 was turned over to the Navy in 1932. During World War II it was a center for Naval operations. After the war the building was used for office space and eventually abandoned. For many decades the building was empty, subject to neglect and vandalism. Old '91 went on the National Register of Historic Places in 1973 and was designated a Historic Custom House by the U.S. Custom Service in 1976. That designation saved it from demolition.

Eventually the Key West Art and Historical Society took on the task of restoring the abandoned Custom House and bringing it back into service. A five-million-dollar restoration began in 1992. Upon completion, the structure will house a first-class museum. The modern facility will meet all standards for the exhibition of art and historical objects, providing a new venue for traveling displays currently unavailable to Key West due to lack of modern facilities.

Cayo Hueso Y Habana
Mallory Square

Providing a fascinating glimpse into Key West's colorful Cuban roots, Historic Tours of America has created a modern interpretation of what our island looked like back in the days when Key West cigar factories manufactured a hundred million Cuban cigars a year. At El Meson de Pepe's Casa Cayo Hueso, you can sample some authentic Cuban cuisine or linger over a Cuba Libre at the bar. Inside, visit old Key West as you stroll past excellently rendered recreations of Gato's Cigar Factory, the San Carlos Institute, Sociedad Cuba, El Anon Ice Cream Parlor, Mariano's Barber Shop, Pepito's Cuban Sandwiches, Mi Abuela's Bodega and other scenes of Key West's Cuban neighborhoods, as remembered in the painted wood carvings of Mario Sanchez, Florida's most beloved folk artist and a Key West native.

Historical photographs on the walls tell the stories of Jose Marti, famed liberator of Cuba who visited the island many times in his quest for freedom in his homeland; Key West's baseball players, many of whom left to play in the minor and major leagues of America; local boxers; showgirls from the Havana Madrid Nightclub; and vicious cock fights encircled by feverish gamblers.

It's a fine exhibit, and also a wonderful opportunity to purchase Cuban cultural icons like freshly rolled cigars, Guayabera shirts, Cuban cuisine cookbooks, a set of dominoes or a real, stuffed fighting rooster. It's free, and divinely air-conditioned. Something for everybody!

East Martello Museum and Gallery
3501 South Roosevelt Boulevard ✻ 296-3913

The red brick fort that houses the museum and gallery is across the street from the ocean, in front of the airport. Plenty of parking is available. You can lose yourself for hours wandering through this incredible collection of Keys artifacts and memorabilia. Exhibits are set along the broad, red-bricked corridors of a Civil War-era fort, created for combat that never happened.

One compelling exhibit is an actual raft built by Cubans who used it to escape from Communist Cuba in 1969. It was found ten miles south of Key West, made from saplings lashed together to form a deck, with a hollow hull containing three innertubes. Attached by wire to the stern was a propeller. A small tree trunk made the mast, which was rigged with burlap sails. It is unknown whether the three Cuban exiles who traveled aboard this handmade vessel ever made it to freedom. No one was aboard the raft when it was found by the Coast Guard. However, identification papers belonging to the three individuals were found.

In another exhibit, a carefully handwritten chart, created after the devastating 1935 hurricane that hit in the Upper Keys contains the names of the dead and the locations of their burials or cremations. According to this meticulous account, 423 bodies were discovered in all. Of those, 164 were local residents; 259 were veterans, working at that time on the Overseas Highway. Many other bodies were washed out to sea and never recovered.

During the Civil War, when Key West remained under Union control, a rebellious Confederate citizen named Caroline Lowe risked her life and her safety in 1861 when she hung a Confederate flag from the window of her home at the corner of Duval and Caroline streets. Posters had been displayed around town warning Key West citizens—most of whom were actually Confederate sympathizers—to show no outward signs of support for Confederate causes. Caroline Lowe disregarded those orders. Local lore has it that when Union troops came to her home to remove the flag, she hid it under her skirt. Or, she might have hidden it in the newell post of her home's staircase. Just where she hid her flag is unclear. Both the skirt and the staircase are on exhibit at the museum. You decide.

Located in an underground wing of the citadel is a gallery featuring a regularly changing exhibit of Keys-related art and, on permanent display, works by woodcarver Mario Sanchez, the island's most famous native artist. The East Martello is also the permanent home of a collection of over 100 metal sculptures by Stanley Papio, most of them on the three levels of the tower.

The East Martello Museum and Gallery is operated by the Key West Art and Historical Society. It is open daily from 9:30 a.m.–5 p.m. Closed on Christmas. Admission is $5 adults; $1 kids. Free for kids under 7.

Fort Jefferson
Dry Tortuga National Park ✱ 242-7700

As the majestic fort appears on the horizon, alone and mighty, it seems
at first to be a magnificent mirage, or perhaps Atlantis rising. Massive
and stately, 68 watery miles west of Key West, the red brick hexagonal
construction hearkens back to a very different time in America's history.

Fort Jefferson, named for President Thomas Jefferson, was designed
as part of a coastal defense system built to protect the Gulf and the east
coasts. Construction began in 1846 and continued off and on for thirty
years. During the Civil War the fort stayed in Union hands and helped
enforce the blockade of Confederate shipping. It was also used as a prison
for Union deserters, who worked on fort construction. It was a terrible
place to be incarcerated; conditions were unsanitary, and, with little
hope for escape, prisoners often died from yellow fever.

After the Civil War, Fort Jefferson continued to be a military prison,
America's version of Devil's Island. Dr. Samuel Mudd, who set the
broken leg of President Lincoln's assassin, John Wilkes Booth, spent four
years in a Fort Jefferson dungeon, sometimes tethered in chains and leg
irons. Mudd had been sentenced to life imprisonment at hard labor.
In 1867 Mudd bravely treated inmates and staff during an outbreak of
yellow fever. What did he have to lose? Though the fever killed nearly
half the men stationed at the outpost, the other half lived, thanks to
Mudd's courage and skill. For his valiant efforts, Mudd was pardoned two
years later by President Andrew Johnson. By the time he was pardoned,
he was the only prisoner left at the fort.

The federal government declared the area a wildlife refuge in 1908.
In 1935 the four islands that make up the Dry Tortugas were named Fort
Jefferson National Monument.

Today, after over a century of sun and salt air, the fortress is deterio-
rating badly. Time has taken its toll on the far-flung structure, created
from over 16 million bricks. The National Park Service is patching as
much as it can, restoring the worst spots of crumble but not rebuilding
them. A complete restoration would be prohibitively expensive.

Of the four islands that comprise the Dry Tortugas, Garden Key,
16 acres, is the island upon which Fort Jefferson stands. Loggerhead Key
supports an 1857 lighthouse that functioned until the 1930s. Bush Key
and Long Key are home to rookeries of frigate birds and sooty terns, birds

rarely spotted anywhere else in the United States. More than 300 species of birds migrate through the Dry Tortugas. Although the bird islands are within swimming distance of Garden Key, they are sometimes closed during nesting seasons and migrations. Birdwatchers and photographers from around the world flock to the Tortugas, particularly in the spring.

The only concession at the park is a tiny bookstore; there are no snack bars or gift shops, no T-shirts or postcards for sale. Attractions are what nature provides—clear, shallow water, excellent for snorkeling, and balmy park grounds perfect for picnics. The coral here, protected and healthy thanks to the island's inaccessibility, is alive and teaming with fish—and you may well see a precious and endangered sea turtle.

Camping is free at Fort Jefferson, with ten sites, including charcoal grills and picnic tables, available on a first-come, first-served basis. (Don't worry. Crowds are rare.) You have to take absolutely everything you need with you—including water! You must also take it all back with you when you leave. Thirty days is the maximum stay. The park has bathrooms but no trash cans. There is no running water or food. But—veterans will tell you—nothing in this world quite compares to the stunning beauty of the endless sky, crowded with stars, on a full-moon night. The silence is magic. Shine a flashlight into the moat waters on a moonless night and see barracudas, eels and lobsters. Fishing is permitted in special areas. Nearly 50,000 people visit the Dry Tortugas National Park and Fort Jefferson annually. The park can be reached by daily seaplane service, private boat, or via a ferry service.

Fort Taylor
Truman Annex • 292-6713

When the Civil War began in 1861, Captain James Brannon quietly marched his troops into Fort Taylor, placing Key West in Union hands where it remained throughout the war. The fort became an important Union military post. Its cannons were an impressive deterrent to the Confederate Navy—so impressive that the fort was never attacked. None of Fort Taylor's guns or cannons were ever fired.

Construction on the fort began in 1845. Many of the workers who built it were Key West slaves, rented out by their owners for a dollar a day. Workers faced many perils during the building of the brick fort. Mosquitoes, yellow fever, hurricanes and shortages of materials created multiple hardships. In 1850, President Zachary Taylor died in office, and the fort got its name.

In the late 1960s, a backbreaking excavation of the fort turned up not only the discarded, though intact, Civil War guns, cannons and ammunition, but also a number of personal artifacts left behind by soldiers who had occupied the fort during the Civil War and the Spanish-American War. Today, Fort Taylor has the greatest collection of Civil War armament in the United States. Scale models of the big Civil War guns, one-eighth the size of the actual guns, are on exhibit in Fort Taylor's museum.

There are some dramatic photo opportunities here, like endless arches and strange nooks and staircases. The top of the fort is an excellent place to view the super powerboat races that loop through the harbor each year in November.

Hemingway House and Museum
907 Whitehead Street ✹ 294-1575

Key West's number one tourist attraction, the privately owned Hemingway House and Museum is visited by hundreds of thousands of people each year. The authenticity of the furnishings and the stories of the goings on in the house Hemingway inhabited during the most productive decade of his life is endlessly disputed. Did he really write his best works here? He wrote *The Old Man and the Sea* in Cuba. Did he create his works on that typewriter on his desk, or did he write them in pencil? Did he really love six-toed cats? Or did they arrive after he'd run off with his third wife? Only Papa knows for sure, and he's gone—though not forgotten, by any means. This is another of those Key West tours that is most entertaining when you agree to suspend disbelief. The price of the tour has remained one of the best deals in town for many years. If your guide's version of Hemingway in Key West is convincing and/or entertaining, tip him or her. The guides work very hard for the money. Open 9 a.m.–5 p.m. daily. Admission $6.50 adults; $4 kids.

Heritage House Museum
410 Caroline Street ❡ 296-3573

It was so hot on the summer afternoon when we finally made it down for a visit to the Heritage House Museum, we felt kind of bad waking the guide who was napping on an antique chaise in the parlor. But he jumped right up when we yelled through the open window, and our tour was quickly under way.

Up until she decided to turn the place into a museum, a sixth generation Conch named Jeannie Porter lived in this amazing house. The Caribbean colonial styled house is chock full of original furnishings, rare antiques and unusual sea-faring artifacts, collected by seven generations of this notable family. Our guide amazed us when he noted the dollar value of many of the treasures. Also, the stories behind them. Famous icons of history, Tallulah Bankhead, Tennessee Williams, fan-dancer Sally Rand, and philosopher, John Dewey, socialized in the quaint parlor. The original chairs in which the famous and infamous once sat are still here. And many of the famous guests sent autographed photographs to commemorate their visits. These are now displayed in the entry hall.

On display are musical instruments from around the world, several grandfather clocks, scrimshaw, a pewter tea set, the guide says was made by Paul Revere (worth thousands!!), and a magnificent shell box, said also by the guide to have been created by Dr. Samuel Mudd during his unfortunate incarceration at Fort Jefferson. Somehow, a toreador's jacket and pants, handmade in Spain and presented to Pauline Hemingway by her wandering husband on the occasion of her birthday, have found their way to this museum. The outfit is so tiny! You wonder if even Pauline, who was small of frame, could have wiggled into it. At the Heritage House, it is exhibited quite simply—laid out on a bed as if waiting for the matador to put it on. Its glittery bugle beads and embroidered seams remind one somehow of a stripper's costume… perhaps a stripper named Carmen. The guide said the costume was, of course, worth thousands.

Security is surprisingly lax at the Heritage House, considering the valuable treasures lying about. Perhaps the guide exaggerates a bit. Still, it's fun to imagine Sally Rand, who really did live for a while in Key West, chatting it up with Tallulah Bankhead, who visited often. Imagine Dr. Mudd sending a shell box to his friends, the Porters, in Key West (and did they think he was innocent?).

In August, the Heritage House is stiflingly hot. When your tour finally arrives in the backyard, you will be very, very happy to get there. From the backyard you see the rear end of a little green cottage where poet Robert Frost often stayed in winter months. Our arrival in the courtyard activated a tape of Frost reading his poem "The Road Not Taken." Frost never wrote a poem about Key West, in spite of the fact that he and his wife spent many winters here. At one celebrity dinner party here, Robert Frost was seated across the table from Truman Capote. "I don't think I dig that young man," Frost told his hostess. It's all pretty neat, and whether the furnishings are as valuable as the tour guide keeps claiming, the stuff is fascinating.

The Heritage House is open 10 a.m. till 5 p.m. Admission is $6 adults; $3 students; children under 12 free.

Jackson Square
Monroe County Court House ● 500 Whitehead Street
You've got to make a stop here and have your picture taken at the "End of the Rainbow" sign. U.S. Highway 1 ends right here, 2,209 miles from where it begins in Fort Kent, Maine.

Behind the sign there is a great kapok tree. The fluffy stuff inside the kapok pods was once used to stuff pillows. Often you will find courthouse employees sitting on the benches here, taking smoke breaks. The county jail used to be located here at Jackson Square, but it has moved into a state-of-the-art facility on nearby Stock Island.

Key West Lighthouse Museum
938 Whitehead Street ☛ 294-0012

The first thing visitors to the Lighthouse Museum want to know is, "Can we climb to the top of the lighthouse?"

Yes, you can, and, for the ultimate view of the island of Key West, you should. Make this one of the first stops on your Key West itinerary to get your bearings. From the top of the lighthouse you'll have a memorable, panoramic view of Key West's harbor. Look out to the Atlantic and see ships steaming across the horizon heading for Europe or South America in the warm waters of the Gulf Stream. Watch cruiseships chugging into Key West Harbor to dock at Mallory Pier. Enjoy the island's visual crazy quilt, formed by hundreds of tin roofs, criss-crossing streets, patches of green yards, and blue swimming pools. See bronzed sun worshipers lounging in the courtyard of a nearby guesthouse.

From the top of the lighthouse you'll see why Ripley, author of "Ripley's Believe it or Not," named Duval Street the longest street in the world—because it stretches from the Atlantic Ocean to the Gulf of Mexico. (14 blocks in all.)

This lighthouse, old though it is, is not Key West's original lighthouse. That one was built in 1825 near the Southernmost Point and operated until it was swept into the sea by a hurricane in 1846. Eight islanders who'd sought shelter in the lighthouse were killed—the only loss of life ever in a hurricane in Key West's history. The new lighthouse was built on higher ground in 1848 at the location where it stands today. Active for 121 years, in 1969 the lighthouse was decommissioned and leased to the Key West Art and Historical Society.

The Lighthouse Museum is open from 9:30 a.m.–5 p.m. daily, except on Christmas Day. Admission is $5 for adults; $1 for kids. Kids under 7 free.

Little White House Museum
Truman Annex **⋆** 294-9911

The two-story, wooden frame residence, built in 1890 to house officers on the Navy base, was vacant in 1946 when President Truman was advised by his doctor to seek a stress-free getaway. The president came to Key West and stayed in the handsome residence. Like so many others before and since, President Truman was instantly smitten with Key West's lazy, tropical splendor and vowed to return as often as possible. Because Truman took such a fancy to Key West and its people, the Navy had the officers' quarters redecorated and modernized in a style described by one reporter of the times as "modest but reliably elegant." In 1948, reporters dubbed the newly restored retreat "Truman's Little White House."

"I've a notion to move the capitol to Key West and just stay," the happy President wrote to his wife after the refurbishing.

During his presidency that spanned the years of 1945–1953, Truman and his staff spent eleven working vacations, a total of 175 days, in Key West. It was during one of these working vacations that Truman reportedly made the decision to fire General Douglas MacArthur over the Korean Conflict. Truman was also in Key West when he decided in favor of the Marshall Plan, whereby America contributed to the rehabilitation of Europe after World War II. When President Truman traveled, his advisors traveled with him. A large press corps regularly followed the popular President to the southernmost city as well. The many photographs and newsreels of President Truman's palm-studded retreat introduced Key West to Americans, many of whom had no idea that an island like Key West, and a place like the Florida Keys, even existed in their country.

President Truman enjoyed strolling through Key West, often visiting Cuban coffee shops and Duval Street restaurants to greet the locals gathered there. Sometimes he dropped in, unannounced, at the Navy mess hall to dine with the enlisted men. Always pleasant, always at ease with the common man, President Truman was named "Truman the Human" by adoring reporters.

After the Truman Naval Base was decommissioned in 1974, the Little White House remained vacant for many years. Much of what could be carried from the house—dishes, linens, artwork, and small furniture— was stolen. In 1990, Henry and Mary Drettmann of Detroit, Michigan restored the Little White House with the help of old photographs and meticulously kept Naval records. When the museum opened in April 1991, it looked very much as it did during Truman's presidency.

Truman loved to play the piano and poker, take long walks, swim, and drink bourbon when he was on retreat. The original piano remains, where Truman played his beloved Chopin, as well as the original poker table where the President and his cohorts played penny-ante poker. Also on display is an exact replica of Truman's writing desk, upon which is perched a plaque with the President's famous motto, "The Buck Stops Here."

The Little White House

The Little White House has hosted Presidents Eisenhower and Kennedy, and, during WW I, Thomas Edison. Edison lived in the building for six months when he was developing depth charges for the U.S. Navy. The museum sponsors several annual fundraising events, including an authentic-looking lawn party and croquet tournament, replete with Truman-era white dresses and flannels.

The Little White House is open daily from 9 a.m.–5 p.m. Admission is $7 for adults; half that for students and children. Guided tours only.

Mel Fisher Maritime Heritage Society and Museum
200 Greene Street ✱ 294-2633

This former Navy warehouse is now home to sensational treasures found at sit of the wreck of the 17th century Spanish galleon *Atocha*, which sank in 1622. The booty includes Spanish pieces of eight, gold and silver bars, jewel-studded crosses, and chains of 18-carat gold that visitors are invited to touch. All of this is moderately interesting for most, particularly fascinating for sunken treasure enthusiasts. Young children will find little of interest here.

What is most intriguing at Mel Fisher's museum is the story of Mel Fisher, one of the world's great adventurers and the amazing tale of the treasure of the *Atocha*, that he uncovered on the ocean floor in 1985. The story began when a little boy in California read the book *Treasure Island*. Visions of gold and silver scattered across the ocean floor ignited a passion in little Mel Fisher that still fuels his dreams. In the early 1950s Fisher got together the money and the gumption to move his wife to Florida to hunt for treasure. For years, he and his family lived in a run-down houseboat in Key West. They lived off loans and speculative shares, good for a year, that he sold in the classified section of the *Key West Citizen*. If the treasure came in that year, shareholders were rich. If it didn't, they started all over again with new shares for the next year.

The staff of the Treasure Salvors went unpaid for months. They hunted for the *Atocha* by day and lived in low-rent Key West apartments by night, eating fish and drinking cheap Busch beer. They wore T-shirts that said, "Today's the day," the slogan that kept the whole town watching and waiting in wonder at Fisher's tenacity, as well as his ability to sell the dream to others, the shareholders who literally kept the operation afloat.

After a 16-year search Fisher hit paydirt on July 20, 1985. Ironically, it was on the anniversary of the day, ten years earlier, when Fisher's son and daughter-in-law had drowned in a freak boating accident.

Mel Fisher and his treasure salvors operation have been the subject of several *National Geographic* spreads, two made-for-TV movies, and Mel's appearance on Johnny Carson's *Tonight* show. Carson became so intrigued with treasure hunting that he came to Key West and dove with Fisher on the sight of the *Atocha*, to see for himself the remains of the famous galleon.

The actual value of the *Atocha* probably isn't really worth the $400 million Fisher says it is. His lawyers say its true monetary value is about half that.

Florida is the treasure-hunting capital of the world, and Mel Fisher's Treasure Salvor's, Inc., operating out of Sebastian and Key West, is the world's most famous treasure hunting operation.

The museum is open daily from 9:30 a.m.–5 p.m. Admission: $6 adults; $4 students; $2 kids 6–12.

Our Lady of Lourdes Shrine
St. Mary's Star of the Sea Church ✱ 700 Block of Truman Avenue
Behind and to the right of St. Mary's Star of the Sea Church, stands the Grotto to Our Lady of Lourdes. In 1922, Sister M. Louis Gabriel was inspired to create a grotto as a shrine and outdoor prayer garden. She asked her friends and fellow nuns to help, and together they created the grotto of natural rock gathered on the church grounds.

On the day the shrine was dedicated, Sister Gabriel bestowed this blessing: "For as long as this grotto stands this island will never suffer the full force of a hurricane." The dedication ceremony fell on May 25, 1922, the twenty-fifth anniversary of Sister Gabriel's entry into religious life. Sister Gabriel had come to Key West from Montreal in 1897 to teach music and art at St. Mary's Convent. In 1898, during the Spanish-American War, the convent was turned into a temporary military hospital. Sister Gabriel then worked as a nurse caring for injured soldiers.

At the turn of the century, Sister Gabriel became the convent's bursar, or treasurer. As such, she became acquainted with people throughout the island. The Sister tended to the grotto for the rest of her life. She died in 1948 at the age of 69. Over five hundred people came to the church to see the casket of the beloved Sister buried in the convent's small cemetery, next to the shrine. There is a wrought-iron fence around the Sisters' graves now, but you can still see Sister Gabriel's gravestone.

When hurricanes threaten, it is common to see people paying visits to the shrine where they pray, meditate, and light candles. Sister Gabriel's blessing seems to be protecting us still. Since the dedication of the shrine three quarters of a century ago, Key West has been spared the full fury of a hurricane. There is no charge to visit the shrine.

Reworx
825 Duval Street ✱ 294-0351
In a massive space behind the Pandemonium store, artist Valerie Hoh has installed a recycling museum. Valerie has scoured the world for remarkable examples of recycling and put together an amazing display. Some

recycled goods are for sale. Others are just for display. It's brand new, and for South Florida, very innovative.

Ripley's Believe It or Not! Odditorium
527 Duval Street ● 293-9694

Every kid who sees this seductive facade wants desperately to go on in. "Odditorium" is a good description of this mostly hokey collection of amazing facts, shocking films, and scary exhibits. It's good for a couple of air-conditioned hours of fun. Of course, the exhibits here have little, if anything, to do with local culture or history. One Key West exhibit is a plaque carrying a line from Ripley's cartoon strip. It says: "The longest street in the world. Duval Street, Key West, Florida, runs from the Atlantic to the Gulf of Mexico." And yes, it does. Also, Ernest Hemingway's high-school yearbook picture is on exhibit, too. But that's not what kids care about.

They'll be interested in a tropical rainforest though, and a hall of jungle-themed exhibits, featuring a couple of shrunken heads and a film of tribesmen, who knows where or when, who roast worm-like insects and then eat them. A couple of years ago, someone filched a shrunken head from Ripley's and pawned it at a local shop. The pawnshop owner read an article about the missing artifact in a local paper. Could it be? He called the cops, and, sure enough, the pawned head was Ripley's missing head. Within a week of its disappearance, the Ripley's shrunken head was back in its rightful place, with the bug-eating savages exhibit.

Ripley's shows you hideous pirate tortures, a replica of the world's tallest man, and ancient film clips of assorted weird people doing odd things: a man who smokes cigarettes through his eyes; a guy who drives spikes into his nose with a hammer; a life-sized shark that snaps his bloody, tooth-studded jaws at anyone who steps too close to the end of a little pier (only you don't know you're getting too close until it's too late). During my visit, a little boy was so taken with the shark exhibit he insisted upon pulling me away from the pirate torture room to personally escort me—a perfect stranger—to the edge of the make-believe pier so that he could watch me jump out of my skin when the shark lurched. Ahhhh!

The shark is the most popular exhibit, of course. Second favorite is the tongue-curling mirror. You try to roll your tongue—many people are genetically coded for tongue curling, the great Ripley has discovered— while on the other side of a one-way mirror, people are watching and laughing their heads off at you.

Ripley's is open daily from 10 a.m. to 11 p.m. Admission is $9.95 for everybody older than 12 years old; $6.95 for kids ages 4–12. Kids under 4 free. Audio tours are available in German, French and Spanish translations.

Shipwreck Historeum
1 Whitehead Street ☎ 292-8990

The Shipwreck Historeum celebrates Key West's golden era of wrecking, an industry that made this city the richest city per capita in the country during the mid-1800s. Whether or not your kids understand what wrecking was all about and its significance to this island city's history, they'll enjoy this visit to an earlier century where they'll meet master wrecker Asa Tift. Mr. Tift, who, incidentally, built the handsome home on Whitehead Street that went on to become the famous Hemingway House, will try to recruit them as sailors or divers for his next wrecking venture. "How long can you hold your breath, lad?" he asks. "That long? We can use you." This museum, built at a cost of half a million dollars and opened in 1994, is a wonderfully authentic reproduction of a wrecking warehouse. Exhibits feature actual artifacts salvaged from the 1856 wreck of the *Isaac Allerton* and historically accurate films, featuring actors in 1800s-era garb—dig those crazy, side buttoned pants—portraying early Key West citizens. The film characters, portrayed by Key West actors, describe how the phenomenon of wrecking figured into their lives.

Asa Tift, portrayed by a live actor, will coach you in the yelling of "Wreck a-shore!!" You yell it again and again until you get it right. "Climb to the top of the tower, if you've got the air," Mr. Tift says.

That's the very best part of this adventure, for kids that is. The wrecker's lookout tower is 65 feet high. Once towers like this one were located all over the island, providing bird's-eye views of the harbor and reefs to hopeful wreckers and salvagers.

Open 9:45 a.m.–4:45 p.m. daily. Admittance: $7 for adults; $3.50 for kids ages 4–12; kids under 6 free. Shows begin every 30 minutes.

The Southernmost Point in the Continental United States
Whitehead and South Streets, on the ocean

Albert Kee has been taking care of business at the corner of Whitehead and South streets since before Key West's most popular tourist stop was officially dubbed, "The Southernmost Point." Kee's ancestors have been selling seashells, sponges, conch and other treasures from the sea at the same spot for nearly a century.

Albert Kee's grandfather, a Chinaman, migrated to Cuba in the late 1800's to work in a laundry. There he met his Cuban wife. The couple moved to Key West and made a meager living selling the fish they caught in the waters just beyond the point. They also gathered conch, the tough, tasty mollusk that once served as a staple of the Florida Keys diet.

Today, beneath the same cork tree that once provided shade for Albert's grandmother as she yanked conch meat from their beautiful pink and beige shells, sits a display of straw hats atop an overturned fruit crate.

"One day," Kee remembers, "some people from the City came along and asked us to move our stuff out of the way so they could put up a new sign."

The little sign that said "Southernmost Point in the USA" was promptly stolen. Each time the City replaced it, it was again stolen. The Kees regularly reported the pilfering, but City Hall took so long to replace it each time, that Albert Kee began recreating the sign himself, hand-lettering the words on slabs of driftwood.

Finally, it became clear that souvenir-crazy tourists would never be able to resist the colorful bit of island art, so in 1983 city fathers installed a massive eight-and-a-half-ton cement monument resembling a giant buoy, encircled in black, red and yellow stripes, to designate the continental USA's southernmost point.

"We call this the conch challenge," says one tour driver to his passengers, as the busy clicks of camera shutters fill the air. "Try taking *that* home."

Every ten minutes or so a sight-seeing trolley or tour train comes from one direction or the other, and Albert Kee stops whatever he's doing and blows a mighty blast on a conch shell. The sound is somewhat like the bellow of a tuba. The delighted tourists clap and snap pictures for which Albert Kee is happy to pose.

For quite a few years an Englishman named Robert Lepora, dressed in spiffy nautical whites, took photographs of tourists with their cameras. Lines of folks often formed, waiting for Lepora to snap their pictures.

"Oh, aren't you the lucky one," he might say to a man with two women. And, "Over there, young lady. There you are, dearie."

And then he would suggest that the visitors drop a dollar or two through a slot in a detachable wooden box on the front of the Western Union Cable House, a tiny building the size of a Vermont outhouse. Western Union did own it, once, but of course modern technology made cables obsolete long ago. In 1990, Lepora asked that Western Union deed the useless property to him, and they did. And for five years or so everything went well for Lepora and his "restoration fund." Then some local guys noticed how profitable Lepora's photo-snapping enterprise was and decided they wanted a cut of the action. Then a couple of tourists sued the City of Key West after they fell off the Southernmost Point while posing for Lepora. The City decided that even though Lepora owns the cable house, the City owns the property upon which it is perched.

The ensuing litigation could take years. And meanwhile, Lepora will probably continue his career.

"You know this is a scam, don't you," a local woman said to her parents, as they fumbled for a couple of dollars to push through the slot.

"Maybe so," said her father. "But he's the nicest man we've met since we've been here."

St. Paul's Episcopal Church
401 Duval Street ▪ 296-5142

Key West's first church is named for St. Paul, one of the Bible's most famous shipwreck victims. The original structure was built of coral rock in 1838 and destroyed by a hurricane in 1846. A second wooden frame building was lost to the fire of 1886. A third resurrection was destroyed in the hurricane of 1909. Finally a concrete structure was completed in 1919, and that's the one you see today. But this concrete reincarnation is not without its problems. The cement was apparently mixed with salt water, so the steel beams began to oxidate, requiring a massive project to replace them. Currently, St. Paul's is quite gloriously solid, and visitors are invited to enter the church for a look or a prayer.

John Fleming, one of the town's founding fathers, donated the property for St. Paul's church. He is buried on the grounds, but his tomb is now hidden behind lush foliage. It was once believed that Fleming's ghost regularly wandered the grounds of the church. Then it was discovered that the restless nocturnal wanderer was a white goat, who slept on Fleming's sun-warmed gravestone to stay warm at night.

A heart-breaking scene in the film version of Tennessee William's play *The Rose Tattoo* was filmed at the dramatic exterior of St. Paul's Church.

Wrecker's Museum/Oldest house
322 Duval Street ✱ 294-9502

Here's a real old house, in fact, Key West's oldest. It was built in the late 1820s at the corner of Caroline and Whitehead streets by ship's carpenter and grocer, Richard Coussens. With the aid of mules, logs and manpower, it was moved shortly thereafter to its current location on Duval Street. The city's oldest house was owned and occupied by one of the city's oldest families, the Watlingtons. Captain Frances Watlington, a prominent seaman, wrecker and one-time Key West harbor pilot, spawned nine daughters—all of whom grew up in the little old house. Watlington's descendants occupied the house for many years, thereafter, but were unable to keep up with the maintenance, so in 1973, the century-and-a-half year old house was sold to Rosemary Austin. Austin donated the house to the state for use as an historic landmark.

In a second-story bedroom there is a dollhouse furnished with miniature authentic 19th-century rugs, paintings, and furniture. The dollhouse was created by museum ladies—not the Watlington girls.

In the master bedroom there is an elegantly carved bed, a round mirror inlaid in its elaborate headboard, which stimulates plenty of speculation regarding the marital habits of Captain and Mrs. Watlington and comments like "No wonder they had nine kids." And "Oh! Those kinky Victorians."

The kitchen, or cookhouse, is located in the back yard, as they were in those times, to spare the house and its inhabitants from the heat of the ovens as well as to protect the house in the event of fire. The cooking hearth in the tiny cookhouse is said to be the oldest beehive oven in South Florida. The house is still hot, since there is no air conditioning.

Recently the 167-year-old chimney, fireplace and beehive, understandably acrumble, were given a much-needed restoration. Most of the bricks
you see are from the original construction.

There's also an outhouse with a drooping crescent moon on its door.

Museum volunteers tell some good stories about the wreckers who
inhabited Key West in the 19th-century. You can study a history book to
learn of the intricacies of wrecking, or you can take a tour of the
Wreckers Museum. It's one of the best deals in town.

Aside from an introductory talk about wrecking, and the role wrecking played in Key West's swashbuckling past, you're on your own in the
Wrecker's Museum. However, the volunteer on duty is pleased to answer
your questions. Open daily 10 a.m. to 4 p.m. Admission $4 for adults;
kids, 50¢. It gets very, very warm in there in the summertime. Schedule
your visit for early in the day.

Sunset Celebration
Mallory Pier

The famous sunset celebration is said to have started back in the 1960s,
when a small group of friends gathered daily to share a thermos of marti-
nis and watch the sun slip into the Gulf of Mexico. Folks brought their
own lawn chairs. When the show was over, everybody clapped. Then
they packed up their chairs and their empty thermos, adios-ed each
other, and moved on into the night.

That's how it used to be.

Today, the daily sunset celebration is nothing short of a carnival,
featuring every wonderful, and not so wonderful, attraction you would
expect to find at a carnival.

The action begins a couple of hours before the sun is actually scheduled to drop when a small army of vendors arrives at the pier to set up
their mobile shops. They display their handmade wares on tables or
racks, and even on blankets spread on the ground. The open air marketplace is tended by a colorful band of shopkeepers, many of whom appear
to be trapped in a 1960s-era time warp.

On the other side of the pier, the side closest to the water, performers
begin preparing for showtime on their cement pier stage, with its Gulf of
Mexico and sunset backdrop.

Tourists begin to assemble as the afternoon begins to cool. They buy smoothies, or fresh fruit cups, or popcorn, or slabs of coconut. They fill their cameras with film. They watch as the crowd gets bigger and bigger and bigger.

The carnival acts are many: guitar players, drummers, and bagpipe players in kilts. There are buskers: a mime, a tightrope walker, a sword swallower and a fire-eater. There's a magician and a guy who balances a shopping cart on his nose; trained cats who jump through burning hoops—an act that inflames the sensibilities of animal lovers, who then go home and write angry letters to the mayor of Key West.

Another act is a Houdini wannabe, who invites volunteers from the audience to wrap him in many yards of chains bolted by a fat padlock. He wiggles and writhes until the chains shift, and he can squirm his way out. Sometimes it takes over an hour for him to execute his escape. He drools and sweats and appears to be in terrible trouble. Occasionally someone is sent off to find the dockmaster, who has the key to undo the chains. The escape artist's face is often as red as the sky just after sunset, by the time he finally takes his bows and collects his tips.

That's how the performers get paid. Tips.

Nothing in Key West so titillates visitors like the sunset celebration. This is something everybody has heard of way before they arrive on the island. It is one of the most written about attractions in Key West, and one of our biggest tourist draws. At the height of the tourist season, a traffic jam regularly ensues just after sunset when spectators get into their cars and head out of downtown Key West and back to their hotel rooms.

By day, Mallory Pier is one of three docks for cruiseships. The cruise-ship business is a clean one for Key West; guests arriving by this venue arrive without cars. Ships pour their passengers into the downtown area, where they are met by various tour businesses: the trolley tour, bicycle tours, walking tours. Shoppers hustle off to Cavenaughs or the Cat House, or to Millie's Sundries (everybody's looking for a drugstore and Millie's fills the bill), or for an ice cream at Ben and Jerry's—all within easy walking distance of Mallory Pier. The Cuban Coffee Queen offers bollos and sandwiches in addition to hot, strong Cuban coffee by the shot, or mixed with steamed milk for a cafe con leche. This is as close as anybody's cruise is going to get to Cuba these days. Cruise ships must leave the dock well before sunset because of a state-mandated plan designed way back when the Mallory Dock was turned into a modern cruise ship-docking facility.

The sunset celebration is managed by the Cultural Preservation Society. To become a part of the show, sunset merchants must sell only handmade merchandise; performers must be sanctioned by the CPS. And there is only so much room on the pier. It is not unheard of for performers and merchants to wrangle over the most desirable locations on the dock.

Still, you will envy them their simple lives. These people have managed to duck walls, conventions, taxes, shoes, bras and barbers. Who, at some time, doesn't envy that kind of nerve?

And the sunset celebration is free. Municipal parking adjacent to the pier is available from 8 a.m. until midnight for $1.50 an hour. No parking for campers, RVs, buses or trailers.

Tours by Land

Conch Tour Train
Mallory Square ✹ 294-5161

The Conch Tour Train is composed of a series of canopied cars pulled by a jeep disguised as a locomotive engine. Your kids are going to beg you to take them for a ride on the Conch Train because, as everybody knows, no kid can resist a train. The train chugs (pretend!) around the island, past the beaches, the airport, and down some of our famous, tropical streets lined with historic houses. Halfway through the tour you stop for a shopping break at the Conch Train gift shop. There's ice cream for sale, too, which makes the kids even happier than they are already! The Conch Train has been pulling happy kids and their parents around Key West for over 35 years. It's open every day of the year, unless there's a hurricane.

Tickets for the hour-and-a-half long tours are $18 for adults; $8 for kids. Group and charter rates available.

Island City Strolls & Bike Tours

Sharon Wells, author and publisher of the *Walking and Biking Guide to Historic Key West*, served as the island's State Historian for 17 years before setting out on her own to launch a walking and biking tour company. Sharon's personalized tours take you off the beaten path, past cultural, natural and architectural island landmarks. Sharon, author of several fine books, offers illuminating insights as well as deep love and respect for her subject matter. Tours are $15–$18. Call for schedule of cemetery, literary, architectural, or personalized walking or biking tours.

Key West Nature Bike Tour
Moped Hospital, 601 Truman Avenue • 294-1882 or 296-3344

Don't just see Key West. Smell it and taste it, too. That's what you do on Lloyd Mager's bike tour. A must for nature lovers hearty enough to spend two hours outdoors on a bicycle. Sample native fruits, view local flora and fauna, and meet a true Conch or two on this off-the-beaten path to back lanes and alleys rarely visited by anyone other than locals. Why do we love this place? You'll know better after your environmentalist and long-time island-resident tour guide shows you around. Immensely enjoyable. Very popular. Maybe too popular.

Schedules vary. They're designed around the arrival of the cruise ships. Otherwise, you can go to the Moped Hospital on Truman to begin the tour. But you've got to call and find out when the next one departs.

Cost of the tour is $15 per person. If you don't have bike, you can rent one for $3. "Think of it as an investigative field trip," Magar says.

Old Town Trolley
Mallory Square • 296-6688

A good thing to do when you arrive on the island is to jump on an Old Town Trolley. The trolleys are not true trolleys. They're really gussied-up buses, made to resemble old-time San Francisco cable cars by a national corporation called Historic Tours of America. A trolley tour is a good way to get your bearings on your first day on the island. The ride takes about an hour-and-a-half. You can get off at any of the fourteen or so stops that catch your fancy and climb back on the next trolley that will arrive 30 minutes later. The stopping for new passengers all along the way is a bit of a distraction, so you might opt for the Conch Tour Train. Otherwise, favorite stops are the East Martello Museum and Art Gallery or the elegant lobby and grounds of the Casa Marina Hotel. Don't forget to ask for a reboarding pass. Before you disembark, ask your driver if you

The Conch Tour Train

will be likely to encounter any delays in reboarding because of crowds. This has been known to be a problem, particularly at the height of the season. Best time to take the trolley is first thing in the morning. Trolleys depart at 9:30 a.m. and run every half hour until 4:30 p.m., with returns until 6 p.m. Adults $18; kids $8.

Perfect Pedicab
292-0077
Chauffeured pedicab service available anywhere on the island. If you stroll Duval Street, you will probably be solicited by one of these hard-working bicyclists. You pay by the trip or by the minute. Careful, though. These guys and gals set their own fees. Ask before you board what your fare will be. Dicker. Deal. It's part of the trip.

The Pub Tour
294-WALK (294-9255)
A 2-hour guided walk through 5 infamous Key West bars and pubs. It's o.k. if you don't drink much; you'll still have a good time laughing, touring, and comparing vacation notes with new friends. The tour starts at the Green Parrot Bar, corner of Whitehead and Southard, where you get your souvenir mug, T-shirt, and free drink tickets.

Writers Walk: A Tour of Literary Key West
293-9291

A one-hour tour that passes the homes and haunts of some of the island's favorite literary lights. The tour begins, of course, at the home of Ernest Hemingway. It does not pass by Tennessee Williams' island home, inconveniently located on another side of the island. The walk ends in the courtyard of the apartments on Simonton Street where Hemingway and his pregnant wife Pauline stayed during their first visit to Key West in 1928. The walk is on weekends in the season and every day during Hemingway Days in July and the Literary Seminar in January. Tickets are around $11 for adults and children.

Tennessee Williams' house

Tours By Sea

Dixie Duck Showboat & Casino
909 Caroline Street ✶ 294-3004

A gambling ship. There are usually several operating out of Key West. The boat motors out to sea through Key West harbor, which in and of itself is a great feast for the senses, out to the 3.5 mile limit where you see other similarly sized gambling boats bobbing in the same area. They're all out there to be legal. The *Dixie Duck* shoves off at 7 p.m., returns at 10:30 p.m. nightly, weather permitting. Usually features live entertainment (but not always), dancing, two cash bars. You've got to be 18 years or older to take this cruise. You'll pay around $16 per person.

Key West Excursions
941-263-3900 ✶ 800-650-5397

The *Friendship IV* is a 92-foot, high-speed catamaran sailing daily roundtrip excursions between Naples, Ft. Meyers or Marco Island and Key West. The boat has two Detroit diesel engines and travels at around 27 knots. It's a very big, very new boat, and so long as the weather is mellow, so is the ride. The *Friendship IV* is the fastest cruise vessel in South Florida cruising to Key West.

The *Friendship IV* heads to Key West at 7 a.m. and docks at around noon. Reboarding is at 5:30 p.m.; arrive back at Ft. Meyers at around 11 p.m. Same day roundtrip is $99; $94 for seniors (60 and older). Children's fares are $79, ages 3-14.

Reservations recommended. Phone the toll-free number for information on Gulf ports served. Office hours are 7 a.m. till 6 p.m.

Sunny Days III Fort Jefferson Tour
201 William Street ✶ 296-5556

The 62-foot power catamaran *Sunny Days III* makes a roundtrip excursion to Fort Jefferson on Tuesdays, Thursdays and Sundays. The boat leaves shore at 9 a.m. for the two-and-a-half hour cruise to Fort Jefferson. It docks before noon, and stays for four hours—plenty of time to tour the fort and enjoy the buffet lunch on the beach prepared by the *Sunny Days* crew. You get back to the dock in Key West by 6 p.m. In addition to the

lunch, snorkel gear and unlimited soft drinks are included in the
$85 fare. Kids 16 and under pay $50. It's a long ride. No alcoholic beverages served.

The Yankee Freedom Cruise to Fort Jefferson
294-7009 ✹ 800-634-0939
The 100-foot ferry *Yankee Freedom* was once a whale-watching boat out
of Gloucester, Massachusetts. She departs Key West Harbor at 8 a.m.
Mondays, Wednesdays, Fridays and Saturdays for a three-and-a-half hour
cruise to Ft. Jefferson. A free breakfast of coffee, eggs, sausage and muffins
is served, and a naturalist lectures on marine wildlife and maritime history. He or she will point out the place where Mel Fisher found the wreck
of the Spanish ship *Atocha.* You may see dolphins or sea turtles. And
then, the fort appears on the horizon. There is an other-worldliness to
this moment, a sense of indescribable awe. *How can this be?* your senses
scream.

A short, informative tour of Fort Jefferson led by park rangers intro-
duces visitors to the fort's intriguing features, the history of its on-again,
off-again construction, and its status as an obsolete, though fascinating,
monument to national ambition and determination. You'll see where
Dr. Samuel Mudd was imprisoned, sometimes in chains, for being part of
the conspiracy to kill President Abraham Lincoln...or was he? Following
the tour, passengers have four hours to explore, picnic and snorkel before
the ferry heads back to Key West. This is a long day, and not particularly
exciting for children.

A roundtrip aboard the *Yankee Freedom* is $75 for adults; $65 for
senior citizens, $45 for kids 16 and under.

Parasailing

Parawest Parasailing
700 Front Street, A & B Lobster House Marina ✹ 292-5199
Fly through the air with the greatest of ease, strapped into a seat suspended beneath a parachute connected by cable to a fast boat. The boat
takes off and as it gains speed, the chute inflates and, like magic, you are
lifted high into the air! Very thrilling. You get a panoramic view of up to

25 miles in several directions. But the ride never lasts long enough—only ten minutes.

Parawest has two parasails. The first is $35 for ten minutes; the second is $45. On that one you go higher, for longer, and experience more free-falls and dips. Parawest is open daily from 10 a.m. Boats leave every hour on the hour. Reservations are absolutely necessary.

Fury Flyer Parasailing
Hilton Marina ▪ 245 Front Street ▪ 294-8899 ▪ 800-994-8898
You don't even have to get your feet wet to soar above the Key West Harbor with the Fury Flyer. Their platform wench boats pull you right into the sky, dry. You can wear whatever you want. In some ads for operations like this, couples in tuxedo and white bridal gown are seen sailing in tandem above the harbor just to show you how easy it is to fly high. And if the rest of the wedding party wants to come along, that's certainly possible, too. They'll pay $10 each to sit on the boat and watch.

Parasails are $40. Tandem sails are $80 and a bit tricker to set up. You'll be asked for your weight...sorry.

Girl Captains

Captain Vicki Impallomeni
294-9731
Chartered trips into the backcountry of the Great White Heron National Wildlife Refuge. Captain Vicki grew up in Key West. She knows and loves the area with an inspiring reverence. Full day around $350. Half: $250.

Captain Karen Luknis
292-9403 or 744-8241
Venus Charters is lesbian owned and operated. Captain Karen takes up to six people (of any sexual orientation) snorkeling, lobster diving, fishing, nature touring, dolphin watching. Clothing optional. Snorkeling and fishing gear on board. Standard rates.

Backcountry Tours

Mosquito Coast Wildlife Tours
1107 Duval Street ✹ 294-7178

Dan and Ellie McConnell brought kayaks to the Keys nearly ten years ago. They have been running the tour ever since, geared toward educating the public about the Keys' natural resources.

Mosquito Coast Island Outfitters and Kayak Guides is the only full service sea kayak training and sales company operating in the Keys. Their guided backcountry tours take you into a wonderland of unique and beautiful mangrove islands and crystal-clear water, as you silently glide across the water in the comfort of advance-design sea kayaks.

Before heading out into the backcountry, you study a map which shows exactly where you're going, as well as listen to an enlightening little talk on how the various elements of the backcountry's fragile ecosystem are interdependent.

The mangroves, the trees that anchor the small islands of the Keys to the shallow bottom, are a fascinatingly complex system of natural checks and balances.

On the journey you'll learn to handle, and love, sea kayaks designed precisely for this environment. The water is shallow here, inches deep in some places. It is sad to see the great, yellow slash scars in the sea grass meadows created by powerboat propellers; it can take up to ten years for these wounds to heal.

In the backcountry you can see wading birds, birds on wing, lemon sharks, stingrays, and horseshoe crabs as well as remarkably clear water where the kayak tour anchors for some underwater exploration. With snorkeling equipment, participants see the natural world of the backcountry from beneath the surface of the calm, clear waters.

It's a long, hot day but a rewarding one. The kayaks are not difficult to maneuver, but it does take some muscle power, and you may well feel the effects later that night. But you'll also understand how the delicate environs of the backcountry, so near and yet so far from civilization, are in such peril.

Waverunner Tour
Key West Boat Rental and Watersports Center
617 Front Street ☎ 294-2628

Tour the backcountry on a Waverunner. See the shallow grassy bottom and seaweed meadows of the backcountry and understand how vital these serene shallows are to the Keys marine environment. Mangrove roots are nesting grounds to many species of fish. Their branches are nesting areas for birds, sharks, and rays. As you motor through the delicate beauty, your guide will remind you to create as little disturbance as possible.

Eventually the tour moves on to deep, open water, and you get to find out just what your Waverunner can do: it's a wet and wild ride! Ziplock valuables that you simply must carry along into plastic baggies. Stuff them into the waterproof compartment under your seat And don't forget waterproof sunscreen. You'll don a full-torso life vest and be fully instructed on the operation of the Waverunner. Maneuvering a Waverunner is very simple, but just to be sure you know what you're doing, most rental agents will ask you to sign a form that says you are willing to take responsibility for the vehicle and agree to respect nature and others on the water.

You have to be 18 years of age to rent a Waverunner; 16 years old with parental consent. The two-and-a-half hour backcountry tour leaves daily at 9 a.m. Cost is $100 for one person on a Waverunner; $150 for two people sharing one. Make reservations!

To simply rent a Waverunner you'll pay $60 for an hour; $30 for a half hour. You must agree to stay in a designated area, within view of the rental center.

Glass-bottomed Boats

Discovery
Lands End Village Marina ☎ 293-0099 ☎ 800-262-0099

A 78-foot, three-level boat, with plexiglass windows along the lower deck providing passengers with a close-up view of the underwater world. On the upper deck are seats in the open for sun lovers. Three viewing wells are on the main deck, as well as an air-conditioned seating area where you can enjoy wine, beer, softdrinks and snacks.

The two-hour trip is a nice alternative to snorkeling and a way to show the wonders of the reef to very young children, the elderly, and anyone who doesn't want to get wet. Most of the two hours are spent getting out and back from the Sand Key reef, located about seven miles offshore.

Kids accompanied by adults go for free on the first trip of the day. In season, that first trip is usually at 9:30 a.m. In the summertime, it's at noon. Call ahead to make sure. Regular fares are $18 for adults, $12 for kids under 12, and kids under 3 always go for free.

The final trip of the day is the Champagne Sunset Trip.

The Appledore

The Great White
Hilton Hotel Marina ☙ 245 Front Street ☙ 294-8899

A 65-foot double-decker catamaran cleverly designed to look like a mechanical shark, with pointy, jaws-like teeth, a top fin, and a porthole eye. The *Great White* carries around 100 passengers out to the Sand Key reef, or, when the wind is whipping, into the backcountry for a look at a shallow patch reef. There are seats for forty people at a time to view the reef through the subsea viewing windows. Soft drinks, beer and wine are sold on board.

Two-and-a-half hour excursions are $14 for adults; $7 for kids. Departures are at 11 a.m., 2:30 p.m., and a sunset cruise, where subsea windows are open, too. The *Great White* is equipped with lights for night-time viewing. Fares are $19 for adults; $9.50 for kids. The sunset cruise, the last cruise of the day, with complimentary beer, wine, soda and champagne, costs more. It's $25 for adults; $12 for kids; kids under 6 go free. Reservations strongly recommended.

Party Boats

Schooner Appledore
201 William Street ☙ 296-9992

The 86-foot windjammer sailing ship *Appledore* winters in Key West and summers in Maine. The *Appledore* is a working ship, with a live-aboard crew. The tall wooden schooner has sailed around the world. The attraction here is all American authenticity. Now this is a mighty vessel. You'll probably want to join the crew and sail away. Seriously away.

The *Appledore* makes two trips to the reef daily. The buffet lunch is fresh fruits, veggies and sandwich fixings. Their sunset cruise is very elegant, with hors d'oeuvres, drinks, and plenty of champagne for around $30.

Schooner Western Union
201 William Street ☙ 292-1766

The schooner *Western Union* launched from Key West nearly 60 years ago. The classic frigate is 130 feet long and features 4,800 feet of sail, and Spanish mahogany deck and ribs. The wood was imported from the

Cayman Islands. Cayman Islanders and Key Westers worked together to craft this marvelous beauty. Each rib of the hull is fashioned of wood from the same tree to strengthen the curve of the hull, adding flex, and avoiding breaks at the joints on particularly rough seas.

After a maiden voyage to Nova Scotia in 1939, the *Western Union*, sailed by Captain Dick Steadman, spent the next 35 years laying and maintaining more than 30,000 miles of cable stretching from Key West to Mexico to Venezuela. When cable lines were retired, so was the *Western Union* and her proud captain. Captain Steadman, who died in 1997, enjoyed visiting the *Western Union*. She's as sleek and sturdy today as when she was brand new, he said.

After several misadventures by other owners, the *Western Union* sailed back into Key West, where she is lovingly maintained by Paul and Evalena Worthington.

The *Western Union* sets sail for sunset around 7 p.m. most nights. Sunset cruises are 2 hours long, and feature live music, beer, wine and soft drinks, all included in the $35 price tag. Make reservations and call for information about private parties on this very graceful lady of the high seas.

Tours By Air

Key West International Airport
South Roosevelt Boulevard

The funky terminal, built in the 1950s to accommodate two airlines and 35,000 passengers a year, is currently among the busiest small-town airports in America. A couple of years ago it was decided by the powers that be that the time had come to bring Key West International Airport into the twentieth century. That's when the controversy began. After several years of bickering between politicians and citizens, it has been decided by a majority of the people to simply restore the funky old terminal rather than flatten it entirely to make way for an all-new one.

Now Monroe County commissioners are reviewing five sets of plans, each one more glossy and high tech than the one before it, to fix the aging terminal.

"Leave it the way it is. It's right out of *Casablanca!*" cries one camp. We need air conditioning, more airline counter space, modernization, for Pete's sake," cries the other.

In the 1950s, flights on the Cuban airline Aerovias Q flew passengers between Key West and Havana for $18 roundtrip. Twenty years ago a little airline known as Air Sunshine, or "Air Sometimes" as locals jokingly called it, was the only game in town. Air Sunshine flew DC 3's on hour-long flights to Miami for around $50 roundtrip. In the last twenty years big airlines like Delta, American, and US Air have tripled the number of flights in and out of Key West; ticket prices have tripled too.

In spite of its tiny size and funky old-fashionedness, Key West International Airport does a splendid job of handling thousands of visitors annually. And since there's only one gate for all arrivals or departures, you never have to worry about missing your friend's arrival.

Some folks like to joke that Key West International Airport's name is longer than its runway. Actually the 5,000-foot runway is long enough to handle large jets. For a few years in the early '80s commercial jets did fly into Key West, and they were fast! Seventeen minutes in the air between Key West and Miami. But they made so much noise that citizens complained, and the jets then were banned.

Little Airlines

Cape Air
800-352-0714
Three daily roundtrip flights between Naples or Fort Meyers and Key West. Same-day round-trip travel from Naples is around $150; from Fort Meyers, $170.

Caribbean Air Charters
800-997-8448
Twin engine executive aircraft available for private charter from $50 per person. Seats five and flies from Marathon or Key West Airport to Miami, Naples, Bimini, Palm Beach, Nassau, Orlando, Tampa, Eleuthera, Jacksonville, Tallahassee, and anywhere else within a 1,000-mile range.

Gulfstream International Airlines
800-992-8532
Gulfstream services Florida and the Bahamas and is a co-carrier with United Airlines. Rates for travel within Florida are usually a bargain compared with the big guys.

SeaCoast Airlines
800-742-6278
Flies between Key West and Fort Myers or St. Petersburg, seven days a week (no service to Miami). From Key West there's service to Treasure Cay in the Bahamas. All flights are aboard nine-seater Piper Navajo planes that fly only 500 to 700 feet above the sea. Flights from the mainland down the Keys' coast and into Key West follow Hawk's Channel all the way. Your pilot gives a narrated tour along the way and points out dolphins, manatees, and other visible sea life that might appear. One passenger gets to sit in the co-pilot's seat. An added bonus with SeaCoast Airlines is free ground service into the downtown area of Key West—that's worth a few bucks.

Call and ask about Key West vacation packages and the frequent-flyer fun club. Roundtrip service from Fort Meyers to Key West is around

$140, less on weekends. Between St. Petersburg and Key West $180, less on weekends.

Island Aeroplane Tours
Key West International Airport
294-8687
Conch pilot Freddy Cabanas started Island Aeroplane Tours in 1987. In March 1991 Cabanas intercepted a Cuban MIG jet while flying over Key West in his Pitts Special, while the Navy failed to spot the Cuban jet in U.S. airspace. Cabanas says he averages 5,000 tours a year in his Waco planes and has accumulated over 10,000 air hours in his career. Of 600 Wacos built, only about 100 are still flying. The Waco biplanes carry two passengers each and feature open cockpits. The Pitts biplane is strictly for aerobatic rides and instruction. Pilots looking to learn the delicate art of the loop-to-loop learn how at Island Aeroplane. Occasionally, Freddy Cabanas takes the Pitts up just before sunset to perform a dazzling demonstration for astonished tourists. He climbs, he falls, he loops, he spins as gracefully as a bird. The dare-devilish Cabanas clearly loves flying.

Island tours of around eight to fifteen minutes cost $50–$90. There are three combination reef and island tours, twenty minutes to an hour long, costing $120–$200. And if you're very brave, ask about Freddy's daredevil aerobatic flights, guaranteed to turn your belly upside down.

Seaplanes of Key West
Key West Airport ● 294-0709 ● 800-950-2359
Daily flights to Fort Jefferson, and magnificent Dry Tortugas National Park, 68 sea miles west of Key West. (Read more about Ft. Jefferson on pg. 103). Amphibious planes carry 5 passengers and offer 3 tour options. Half-day trip is $159 per person; Full-day is $275. For campers staying over for one night or for two weeks, airfare is $299. And seaplanes will deliver water and ice from the mainland every day you're out there. They also provide snorkel gear and a cooler of soft drinks for day-trippers.

How to get from Miami Airport to the Keys

Greyhound Bus Airport Shuttle
Key West Airport ✻ 800-410-5397
Direct bus shuttle from Miami International Airport to Key West, or vice versa, is available on a 43-seat Greyhound bus leaving from Miami three times daily; early morning, noon, and late afternoon. One-way to Miami takes around five hours and costs around $32 one way, or $60 round trip. What's annoying about taking the bus is that it stops frequently along the Keys. Greyhound Bus Terminal is now located at the Key West Airport.

Eggs Transport
305-294-0190 ✻ 304-4035
Luxury mini-buses seat 29 and feature TV, VCR, and bathrooms. Also sleek Ford Metro Trans Classics. Lincoln Town cars. Drivers are very good eggs. They'll transport big groups around town, or around South Florida. Airport pick-up, meet and greet in Miami or Key West. If you're coming to vacation with a large family, your gang or wedding party, leave your cars home, call ahead and make arrangements. Competitive rates. Seat belts. Baby seats.

Southernmost Shuttle
293-1811 ✻ 800-390-7176
Television, VCR, video collection, bathrooms and luxury are what you'll find on the 17-seat Southernmost Shuttle bus. Trips between Key West and Miami are $45 one way, and $75 round trip. Group rates available. Charter the whole bus for around $625 round trip.

Annual Events
Paradise Uncovered Month by Month

January

Average temperature: 70°
Average rainfall: 1.9 inches
Sunset: 5:50 p.m.

Old Island Days
Old Island Restoration Foundation
PO Box 689, Key West, FL 33041 ✽ 294-9501

A series of events scheduled from mid-January till late March, designed to celebrate Key West's island roots. Many old Key West families are descended from Bahamian wreckers and shipbuilders, and those bygone days are celebrated with Bahama Village night. Food festivals featuring island cuisine, and a nationally renowned, juried sidewalk art show. In the midst of all these celebrations is the Conch Shell Blowing Contest, which garners the most attention. Journalists come from all over to meet the strong-lipped competitors of the contest, which, as far as anybody knows, is the world's one and only competition of its kind.

Old Island Restoration Foundation House and Garden Tours
294-9501

Buy a ticket, board a Conch Tour Train, and visit five private residences. Or take a self-guided tour to the five homes, finding your way with a map. This is the OIRF's big fundraiser of the year, and it's popular indeed. You want to go into the homes of Key West's rich and famous? Here's your chance. There are three House and Garden Tour weekends: the first is the last weekend of January; the second two are middle and final weekends of February. Write or call for a full schedule of all events.

Island Food & Music Festival
Bayview Park, Key West ✺ 294-2587

Sponsored by the Key West Rotary Club for a weekend in mid-January, the fundraiser offers rides for the kids and good food for everybody. Lots of performances by local celebrities, which makes the admission fee worth your while. A great opportunity to experience a sampling of what Key West has to offer musically. Some rumblings were heard, after the 1996 festival, about high prices on kids' rides. If you've got a big family, you might find this afternoon kind of pricey. Remember, it's a fundraiser, and the Rotary raises a lot of funds for a lot of good causes.

Race Week in Key West
401-849-4644

Sailboat races sponsored by *Yachting Magazine* and Mount Gay Rum. Up to 4,000 yacht people party, attend sailing seminars, and compete for awards presented each night of the week—usually the second week in January. All kinds of fun for the yachting set and boater groupies. For information, call or subscribe to *Yachting Magazine*.

Key West Craft Show
Key West Players ✺ 294-5015

Nearly 100 crafters and artists display their works for sale on Whitehead Street between Greene and Caroline streets. Sponsored by the Key West Players, there is no admission fee, but there is a registration fee for artists.

Key West Literary Seminar
419 Petronia Street ✺ 293-9291

Second week in January. Stands with America's greatest literary fests. Themes like poetry, travel writing, journalism, and literary superstars like Hemingway and Tennessee Williams discussed by world famous writers, scholars and critics. Social events mix attendees with presenters, real writers with wannabes, but the really famous people are often disappointingly shy or last-minute no-shows. Kurt Vonnegut, for example, changed his mind only twenty-four hours before he was to be the cornerstone speaker in a panel on Literature and Film. Several tours and writers workshops augment the three-day affair. The Writer's Walk goes on three

times a day during this event. Newest director of Literary Seminar is
Miles Frieden, a world traveler. Call the Literary Seminar office and ask
to be on the mailing list—you'll be well informed.

February

Average temperature: 71°
Average rainfall: 1.6 inches
Sunset: 6:16 p.m.

Wesley House Valentine's Party
The Curry Mansion ❧ 511 Caroline Street ❧ 296-8964
Held every year at Al and Edith Amsterdam's house, the regal Curry
Mansion. Up to 1,000 people dress in romantic red in honor of the day
of hearts and love. Magnificent trays of food are donated by local restau-
rants. A busy bar. Always there is a hot band and a fabulous raffle. Prizes
are getaways, bicycles, jewelry, sailing trips and meals at area restaurants.
It's a great party. Admission is around $20 per person or $35 for a couple.
If you don't have a sweetheart on Valentine's Day, this would be a good
place to find one. Proceeds from this big bash benefit Wesley House
Daycare Center.

Gordon Ross and Friends
296-6196
A stellar cast of local singers, musicians and other performers put
together an evening of truly great entertainment. All proceeds from
ticket sales benefit local people with AIDS. If you're in town for this,
don't miss this annual February production.

Monroe County Fair
296-2202
A traveling fair usually makes a stop in Key West some time in the
second half of February. Fair features are the usual rides, exhibits, cotton
candy and displays by local civic organizations. Strangely, it seems to
always rain on fair week.

Key West Women's Flag Football Tournament
293-9315

The largest women's flag football tournament in the United States goes on at Wickers Field in mid to late February.

Old Island Days Art Festival
Key West Art Center ✹ 294-1241

Last weekend in February (or first in March). The juried art show is sponsored and organized by the Key West Art Center. At least 100 artists, representing all mediums and all regions of the country, are selected from several hundred applicants to appear in the show and compete for $10,000 in merit and purchase awards. Participants must apply with slides and an application to be in the show. Space is limited. (Call for an application.)

The exhibits sprawl from the corner of Whitehead and Caroline Streets, the Presidential Gates, on into the Truman Annex. Show hours are 10 a.m.–5 p.m. Although an estimated crowd of 20,000 people wander through the booths of art, artist friends who have appeared in the show a few times say very little actual selling goes on.

Civil War Days
Fort Zachary Taylor ✹ 292-6713

A weekend, usually toward the end of February, of living history at this authentic fort, now a National Historic Landmark. The celebration of Key West's fortunately under-utilized military might feature reenactments, skills demonstrations and a sea skirmish. Participants are invited to wear 1800s-era costumes, just like the actors do. Every year at least one couple marries in antique wedding finery. See what life was like in 1861 when Union troops occupied the fort. Highlight of the affair is a dinner party on Saturday night followed by the firing of the cannon that was never fired in wartime.

Sponsored by the Florida Park Service and the Friends of Fort Taylor.

March

Average temperature: 73°
Average rainfall: 1.5 inches
Sunset: 6:31 p.m.

Spring Break

Although some downtown merchants welcome spring breakers, many
locals don't like it at all when the town is wall-to-wall students hell-bent
on having a good time. Spring breakers rent mopeds and drive through
the streets at all hours, beeping their horns and yelling to each other.
They're noisy, and that seems to be everyone's chief complaint. It's not
the kids individually, it's their number. Too many!

Many hotels and reservations services turn away spring breakers.
Nonetheless, they seem to find a way to rent rooms and vacation homes
anyway. In the last decade, since spring breakers discovered the Keys,
tourism during the month of March has dwindled alarmingly.
Meanwhile, townspeople are noticing a visible decrease in the number
of students showing up for spring break in the last year or so. Nobody
likes being where they're not wanted. New spring break destinations like
Pensacola Beach, which is more easily accessible to many students, and
Mexico, which is much cheaper than Key West, are coming into vogue.

Conch Shell Blowing Contest
Ocean Key House Sunset Pier ✷ 294-9501
Usually held on the last weekend in March, on the waterfront. A funny
little contest that has grown into a world famous annual event. Once
contestants tried merely to blow a suspended honk on the conch shell.
Now, melodies and all sorts of amazing feats are performed by people of
all ages. Something free and fun to watch.

April

Average temperature: 77°
Average rainfall: 1.7 inches
Sunset: 7:44 p.m.

Seven Mile Bridge Run
PO Box 500110, Marathon, FL 33050 ✶ 800-262-7284

On a Saturday morning, mid to late April. The bridge closes and the starting gun fires at 7 a.m. Two hours later, traffic is backed up many miles in both directions as a bus drives over the bridge to pick up anyone who hasn't made it to the finish line. Then, the bridge reopens while contestants are massaged by volunteer therapists set up at the finish line. Free de-kinking mini massages are for bridge runners only! Only 1500 runners allowed. Many more runners attempt to participate in the run than the bridge can actually handle. If you think you're ready for the challenge, here's how to get in: Send a self-addressed, stamped envelope and request an application. They're sent out about a month before the event. The minute you get yours, fill it out, write the check, and mail it back in. Immediately! Competition to just get in is vicious!

Conch Republic Independence Days & Celebration
296-0213

The Conch Republic was born on April 23, 1982, in response to a United States Border Patrol blockade of the road where the Florida Keys meet the mainland near Florida City. Border guards searched every car entering or exiting the Keys for illegal aliens and drugs, as if the Keys were another country. They created a border where there was none. Traffic was backed up for nineteen miles, and many hours. Word got out quickly, and would-be visitors headed away from the Keys. Tourism is the lifeblood of the Keys economy. It was a very bad scene all around.

Furious over the intrusion, and stung by being treated by the federal government as a separate country rather than part of the United States, Key West Mayor Dennis Wardlow and a group of businessmen staged a secession ceremony at Mallory Square, the center of Old Town Key West. A single shot was fired, and heard by media around the world. Key West and the Florida Keys seceded from the union, declared war, surrendered, and then demanded foreign aid.

The border blockade was abandoned, and a stream of reporters swarmed into the Conch Republic to witness the coup. Small fortunes were made in Conch Republic T-shirts, arm bands and hats. Uncle Sam was embarrassed internationally while the rowdy denizens of the Conch Republic celebrated one of their most glorious chapters.

Today the Conch Republic includes all of Monroe County. There are Conch Republic passports that have reportedly been recognized by immigration officers in thirteen Caribbean countries, Sweden, Russia, France, Spain, Ireland, and Germany. In 1994, I witnessed my husband convincing a very nice, and moderately suspicious, Canadian border guard in Calais, New Brunswick, to stamp his Conch Republic passport, but not until after he'd run our names through an Interpol computer, and we'd suffered a half hour of incredulous stares.

There is an official Conch Republic flag, too. We have ministers, ambassadors, commodores and secretaries. Each April there is a parade. There are kick-off parties, nasty natives parties, and funky beach parties. There are pedicab races. A Pirates' Ball. A pig roast. A car show. Lectures. Poetry slams. And all manner of frolic. Each year organizers come up with new wild and wacky events to commemorate our independence.

To order your passport contact the office of the Secretary General, 296-0213 or 296-8803. Long live the Conch Republic!

May

Average temperature: 80°
Average rainfall: 2.7 inches
Sunset: 7:58 p.m.

Harry S Truman's Birthday Party
Little White House Museum ✹ 292-6718
The b-day is May 6. A benefit staged on the Little White House
Grounds. Celebrate America's 33rd president's birthday with the showing
of newsreels, dinner dancing, bridge, and a game of poker on the same
table where the prez played.

Queen Mother Pageant
David Thomas ✹ 296-0079
A mid-May spoof on beauty pageants featuring a line-up of island boys
dressed like girls in a hilariously funny, and eminently campy affair that
sells out each year. The costumes and performances make this a spectacularly entertaining event, and money raised goes to AIDS Help. The 1994
queen, Helen Bed, brought the house down when, for the talent program,
she played "Lady of Spain" on an accordion with a wicker headboard
strapped to her back, wearing a red sequined dress, with a rose between
her teeth. The Queen Mother wins a list of local prizes like manicures,
massages, gift certificates at the fabric and glitter store, lunches and dinners, and, of course, the crown, which she gets to wear for one year.
During her reign she sponsors at least two fundraisers for AIDS Help.

    The pageant is held in various venues around town. The producer is
a truly marvelous and remarkably inventive drag queen and performer
named DDT.

Survivors Party
La Te Da ✹ 296-6706
Memorial Day Weekend—usually held at La Te Da on Duval Street.
The first Survivors Party went on in the now defunct Monster Bar on
Memorial Day, 1975. Conceived and produced by Key Wester John "Ma"
Evans, the annual costume (if you like) party celebrates late May's tradi-

tional tourist lull, a time when locals take back the town. Always a fundraiser, for the last eight years for AIDS Help, the party features a glorious buffet contributed by the island's restaurants; local comedy; musical and variety acts; drag queens; performance art; and a campy survivors award ceremony. Admittance is usually around $20, which, considering the food and the entertainment, is a real value. The people at Survivors Parties are the island's creative core, the movers and the shakers united for two common goals: good times and AIDS Help. T-shirts from this party are collector's items. A heartfelt party: fun for locals and visitors, straights and gays.

American Super Boat Racing Series
296-8963

May's super powerboat race week kicks off the American Super Boat Racing series, a seven-month series of races that begins here in May and ends with the world championships in November.

Key West's deep harbor creates a natural marine amphitheater for watching super and open class boats complete thirteen 10-mile laps around the island. Harborfront hotels stage plenty of gulfside dining and/or drinking specials, so you can party and view at the same time. Serious boat race fans will want to buy a comprehensive pass to all activities in the dry and wet pits, and the viewing area on Truman Annex.

Annual National Historic Preservation Week
Mel Fisher Maritime Heritage Society and Museum ● 294-2633

Celebrated in mid-May in the Maritime Heritage Society Museum Theater with a series of lectures. Activities change each year. This is a good week for history buffs, but then, every week is a good week for history buffs in Key West.

June

Average temperature: 82°
Average rainfall: 4.4 inches
Sunset: 8:15 p.m.

June 1: Hurricane season begins

That's right. There are no big events in June. This is a low-key month in the Florida Keys, and a very nice time to come for a quiet visit.

July

Average temperature: 84.5°
Average rainfall: 3.6 inches
Sunset: 8:22 p.m.

Annual Swim Around the Island
745-1331

Usually in July, but sometimes in June, according to tide schedules. Anna Fugina started this tradition on July 4, 1977, when she swam around the island of Key West in eight hours flat. In 1978, after she'd learned to use the tides to her advantage, she made the swim in six hours and twenty-five minutes. The following year, a couple of Anna's friends went along on the swim to keep Anna company. The next year swimmers began bringing along coaches in boats to row along beside them. One boat for each swimmer. The Fourth of July swim around the island has been going on every year since.

Organizers traditionally aim to hold the swim on the July 4th week-end, but actually schedule for a time when the tides and currents are easiest for swimmers. Call for this year's date.

Underwater Music Festival
Looe Key Reef ✻ 872-9100

Usually held on the first Saturday in July. One of America's most unusual musical events, and one of the Keys most publicized happenings. The spin-doctors love this story! The scenic coral reefs of the Looe Key National Marine Sanctuary, six miles off Big Pine Key, is the setting for this underwater concert, founded by WWUS Radio News Director Bill Becker twelve years ago. Music is blasted over the coral reef for an underwater audience of up to 800 snorkelers and divers. For six hours, music—reggae, new age, and jazz—is played over eight Lubell underwater speakers suspended from dive boats. The broadcast features a commercial-free program designed to highlight and augment the underwater experience. The event is for fun, but also to reinforce reef conservation.

To participate in the festival, divers and snorkelers book rides aboard area dive and charter boats in the Lower Keys.

In 1995, the hit of the festival was a group from the local Elvis fan club. The Snorkeling Elvises (yes, that's really the name of the club!), descended 25 feet, in scuba gear, white jumpsuits and black Elvis wigs, with guitars, to entertain fellow divers. The music festival is followed by a seafood festival (on land) in the little town of Big Pine Key.

Big Pine Seafood Festival
872-2411 ● 800-872-3722
Follows the Underwater Music Festival. Visitors are invited to sample conch fritters and chowders, and visit arts and crafts booths.

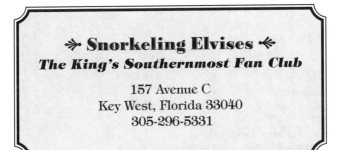

➤ **Snorkeling Elvises** ◄
The King's Southernmost Fan Club

157 Avenue C
Key West, Florida 33040
305-296-5331

Minimal Regatta
Schooner Wharf Bar ✆ 292-9520

July 4th weekend. Any excuse for a party, this one is "the only boat race you can view from start to finish from shore." A major challenge is staying afloat for the length of the race. Schooner Wharf Bar, at the foot of William Street, sponsors this annual, all-day party event. Competing vessels are built of:

- one sheet of 4x8' ¼" plywood
- two 2x4x8' lumber
- one pound of fasteners
- one roll of 2"x60 yard duct tape
- no caulking or adhesives

Painting of boat is optional. The winning vessel becomes the property of Schooner Wharf, where it goes on display.

July 4th Hospice Picnic
Casa Marina Resort ✆ 294-8812

Staged on the lawn and beach of the historic Casa Marina Resort, this is the fundraiser of the year for Monroe County's Hospice program. A beachside picnic with an endless supply of hot dogs, hamburgers, salads and watermelon. An afternoon of entertainment provided by local celebrities. Lots of activities for kids. Hot fun. A raffle with great, donated prizes, like a framed serigraph by world-famous artist John Kiraly, who lives and paints in Key West. The entire town turns out for this. Tickets are $14 for adults (2 for $25), and $7 for kids.

July 4th Fireworks

They set them off from the White Street Pier but you can see them all over the island. Best view is from the top of the La Concha Hotel, at 430 Duval Street.

Hemingway Days Festival
P.O. Box 4045, Key West, FL 33041 ✆ 294-4440

Sixteen major events celebrated during the week of July 21, which is the day of Ernest Hemingway's birthday (born in 1899). Members of the Hemingway family, scholars, and thousands of participants make it to this

annual event, Key West's very hottest. Begun in 1981 as tribute to
Hemingway, the week-long celebration includes a short story contest,
story-telling competition, and macho sporting challenges like a 5K run
and arm wrestling championship and golf and fishing tourneys. Also
walking tours of Hemingway's Key West, and poetry readings. A Writers'
Workshop and Conference opens with a gala on the lush grounds of the
Hemingway House. The Hemingway Look-alike contest, which attracts
over 100 big-bellied, white-bearded men, goes on for three nights at
Sloppy Joe's Bar.

In 1997 the festival was nearly canceled due to a dispute with
Hemingway's sons over the licensing of Papa's image. The issue was
resolved, the festival goes on, and anytime anybody buys a Hemingway
T-shirt or anything else evoking the image or name of Ernest Hemingway, his sons get a cut of the action.

Reef Awareness Week
Contact: DeeVon Quirolo ✽ 294-3100
Week-long event, usually second half of July, to increase awareness and
support for the world's third longest coral barrier reef. On Children's Day
kids are led on guided tours and free excursions to the coral reef on a
glass bottomed boat. Local television airs a Reef Awareness Film Fest.
Speakers, poetry readings, an art auction and reception, annual membership meeting, diver first aid courses, a mooring buoy splicing party and
lots more activities all relating to the reef go on throughout the week.

Reef Relief is a grassroots organization founded in 1986, to protect the
endangered Florida reef.

Mini-Lobster Season
July 24–25 ✽ 800-DIAL-MFP
The last week in July, the mini-season is a 48-hour open season on
Florida spiny lobster for sport divers. Thousands of people descend upon
the Florida Keys to participate in this event. After a four-month closed
season, divers get their first shot at the lobsters before commercial fishermen begin setting their traps for the regular commercial season, which
begins August 6 and runs through March 31. A valid saltwater fishing
license and a current crawfish stamp, available at tackle and dive shops,

is required. Bag limit is six lobsters per diver per day. The Florida Marine Patrol hands out information and pays close attention to make sure the divers don't violate the rules or bring home illegal lobsters. No night diving for lobster allowed. John Pennekamp Coral Reef State Park in Key Largo is closed to lobster harvest during the mini-season.

Many hotels and guesthouses jack up prices and require two or three-day minimum stays during the two-day event.

August

Average temperature: 84°
Average rainfall: 4.6 inches
Sunset: 8:11 p.m.

Coral Reef Spawning

America's newest and perhaps weirdest spectator sport is a night dive with the hope of showing up on the reef in time to watch the annual, simultaneous release of eggs and sperm by billions of coral polyps. The egg bundles look like bb's or pearls. Those who have seen this other-worldly event say the sight is spectacular and worth all the trouble it takes to get there at the very instant it all begins. Spawning has gone on forever, of course, but it is a recently discovered phenomenon on U.S. reefs. It was first observed in 1990, at the Flower Gardens Reef Bank, 100 miles off the Texas coast. The phenomenon occurs each year, usually five to eight days after the August full moon, and every dive shop and promoter in the Florida Keys knows all about it. Just ask them for details.

Call the Florida Keys National Marine Sanctuary, 305-743-2437 for more information.

George Bush Bonefish Tournament
Contact: Julia Perrin ✱ 664-4651 or 800-327-2888
Fish with George Bush! Call Julia Perrin for details.

September

Average temperature: 83°
Average rainfall: 6.4 inches
Sunset: 7:45 p.m.

Womenfest Key West
296-4238 ✽ 800-535-7797

Usually right at the beginning of September. A week of wine tasting, tea dancing, gallery browsing, sunset cruising, and a sisters-for-brothers blood drive, empowerment seminars, guided bike tours, film festival, theater, lesbian comedy, street fair, tennis tournament, golf tournament, and backcountry kayak tours. Wet T-shirt contest is infamous! Promoters say they expect to host over 4,000 women. September is a nice, quiet time in the Keys, and this is a terrific get-together.

Florida Keys Poker Run
Horne's Motorcycle Specialties ✽ 294-3032

Third weekend in September. Sponsored by the Sunrise Rotory Club of the Florida Keys. Bikers drive down the Keys in a charity event for children. Yes, their bikes make big noise, but those bikers raise a lot of money for good causes like the local hospital's infant nursery.

The poker run starts in Miami, and includes five stops throughout the Florida Keys. At each stop participants draw a card. At the end of the route, which is Key West, the highest hand wins a cash prize and often other fabulous prizes. Each September, 13,000–20,000 motorcycle enthusiasts converge in downtown Key West to congregate outside Sloppy Joe's Bar on Duval for one wild Saturday night. Mike Horne founded this annual fundraiser in 1972. He and wife Debbie handle all the publicity through Mike's motorcycle shop.

Call for details and a schedule.

October

Average temperature: 79°
Average rainfall: 5.4 inches
Sunset: 7:13 p.m.

Key West Theatre Festival
292-3725

Still in its infancy, the Key West Theatre Festival is slowly building its reputation. Scripts considered for inclusion in the festival are solicited from agents, other theater festivals, and new, up-and-coming dramatists. Local scripts get top priority.

Some plays are read; some are actually staged. Readings are free; plays are around $10 or a show package of five for around $40. A playwrights workshop and an evening of poetry and jazz are usually on the program as well. Ticket stubs work as meet-the-playwright party admissions. They're good parties, too.

For information about plays, actors, directors and theaters involved in this year's festival, or for information on submitting material for next year's festival, call.

Fantasy Fest
296-1817

Key West's answer to Mardi Gras. An annual ten day island-wide festival climaxing in the famous Twilight Fantasy Parade held on the last Saturday in October. Theme of the fest, which changes from year to year, is reflected all over town—in costumes, shop window displays, and restaurant decors. 50,000 people from all over the world converge on the island for this party.

Make your plans early. Visitors who come for the Fest year after year book the best rooms, months or even a year in advance, in spite of the prices. Hotels and guesthouses hike their prices to the max. The airlines are packed—make reservations as soon as you possibly can.

The Fantasy Fest party moves from neighborhood to street block, from restaurant to bar, from club to hotel. The fun, glitz and glitter never stop. It simply changes locations, adjusts attitude, and moves to a new scene from time to time. Follow the crowds and you won't miss any of the action.

Fantasy Fest launches with the Goombay Festival, a traditional street fair in Bahama Village. This is a locals' favorite. Everyone turns out to dance with their neighbors, eat something authentically African or Cuban, and wander among the pretty displays of African-American fashions.

The Pet Masquerade and Parade on the great lawn of the Marriott's Casa Marina Hotel is always a crowd pleaser and attracts some pretty bizarre pet/owner look-alikes.

The Pier House Pretenders in Paradise, also known as the World's Most Outrageous Costume Contest, is a gala centerpiece to the Fantasy Fest celebration. Prizes, including cash prizes worth $10,000, are awarded in various categories appropriate to the theme.

One of the rowdier events of Fantasy Fest, Sloppy's Toga Party, is fueled by live, smoking rock 'n roll. There are plenty of prizes for the best togas.

At sunset, on the Friday before the big parade, party animals don Caribbean marching clothes and costumes (What kind of costume? Let your your conscience be your guide) and join the Masquerade March through Old Town. The group gathers at the City Cemetery. The merry band is led by fifes and drums through the winding streets of downtown Key West, picking up many more carousers along the way. The crowd finally spills into the Tea Dance in the street, at the 801 Bar at 801 Duval.

And then, the climax: the Twilight Fantasy Parade. The streets are packed. The mood is frenzied! This is the parade the whole world watches. Floats, imprecision marching groups, all kinds of bands playing all kinds of music, and thousands of masqueraders from every corner of the world come to Key West for the parade.

On the morning after, Children's Day at Bayview Park is on from noon to 5 p.m. (information: 292-8611). Families turn out for Children's Day, and that's why this event attracts local political candidates. They're out glad-handing, kissing babies and supporting Moms and apple pie. Great fun, particularly if you don't have to vote for one of these shameless panderers.

Call for a brochure and schedule of events.

November

Average temperature: 74°
Average rainfall: 2.45 inches
Sunset: 5:47 p.m.
Hurricane season ends November 30

Offshore Powerboat Race Week
Contact: John Carbonell ✱ 296-8963

Early-to-mid-November more than 50,000 powerboat fans crowd into Key West's waterfront hotels and beaches to watch the races. Annually it's the biggest collection of high-performance ocean racing boats assembled anywhere in the world.

Powerboats with four 1,000-plus horsepower engines, cost over one million dollars, and cost another million to campaign over the racing season. The powerboat racers follow a circuit of national races. Key West is considered the powerboat capital of the United States. The powerboat race season ends each year with this week-long event in Key West, where the world's champs are crowned. Catamarans, or twin hulled powerboats, race against traditional deep-vee hulls and reach speeds of 125–150 mph! The harbor water is generally calm, but once the boats get out in the Atlantic, the rough part of the course, the waves can be up to four to six feet high, making for a hazardous race.

Best viewing spots are harbor-front hotels—the Hilton, Hyatt, Pier House, and Ocean Key House. And oh! The parties!

December

Average temperature: 71°
Average rainfall: 1.8 inches
Sunset: 5:38 p.m.

Images by the Sea
East Martello Museum ✱ 296-3913

Presented in the early weeks of December. A Christmas fundraiser and fine arts exhibit, all created by artists and craftspeople from the Florida

Keys. Exhibitors pay to display their creations in the show, and shoppers pay to see them. That's how they raise money. This is always a sensational show, worth all the hype it gets in local publications. Never disappointing and always a good centerpiece for an evening out. Also, great opportunity for major Christmas shopping. Features seasonal decorations, home furnishings, ceramics, canvas floor clothes; hand-painted furniture, screens, photographs, ironworks, and anything else this subtropical culture's artists and craftspeople can imagine. Funds raised by this annual show have benefited AIDS Help, and the Wesley House childcare center. Not to be missed!

International Gay Arts Festival
800-535-7797
Sponsored by the Key West Business Guild. Seventh annual is scheduled for December 1997. The festival focuses on all aspects of the arts and talents of gay and lesbian craftsmen, authors, artists, and actors. Attracts some of the most notable gay artists on the international scene. Performance art, gallery shows, a gay artists and writers tour, theater, concert and television productions, book signings, and a house and garden tour of gay-owned residences.

For information write: GAF, 714-B Passover Lane, Key West, Florida 33040.

Key West Women's Club Christmas Party
319 Duval Street ⚏ 294-2039
It has become a local tradition for the Women's Club to kick off the Christmas season with this annual tree-lighting party on the first Sunday in December. This is a free party, open to all. Always lots to eat and drink. Entertainment, too.

Christmas by the Sea
Chamber of Commerce ⚏ 294-2587 ⚏ 800-352-5397
The Sleigh Ride, a fundraising progressive cocktail party, costs $25 per person. Also, a truly beautiful and unique lighted boat parade, parties, parties, parties, many of them terrific bashes with inexpensive entrance fees. La Te Da, for example, puts on a big show with dozens of local entertainers, a buffet, and dancing in the street. The city blocks off the street for La Te Da

parties, and they're a blast. A recent Christmas party was a fundraiser for the Family Resource Center. Tickets were $15. Quite a deal for a night of live entertainment with a wonderful, giving local crowd. Events and activities vary from year to year, but look for a full slate of events.

Season rates in hotels and guesthouses usually kick in around December 20. The first few weeks of December are particularly peaceful. It's a very nice time to plan a visit.

St Paul's Christmas Concert
401 Duval Street ✷ 296-5142
Mid-December. Make a joyful noise unto the Lord! This seasonal high point is our island's bright Christmas star. It's performed only once each year and goes on in stately and venerable St. Paul's Church. Stained glass, seasonal decorations, and a musical program featuring a parade of the island's most creative people. A spellbinding concert that you wish would last throughout the season. Good vibes! If this doesn't get your Christmas spirit pumping, nothing will. Usually around $10 a ticket. But buy your tickets early—or you'll have to sit on the steps of the church.

Kwanzaa
Bahama Conch Community ✷ Laura Butler ✷ 296-4177
Yes, Virginia, there is a Kwanzaa celebration in Key West. Kwanzaa is a 30-year-old holiday, designed and celebrated by African-Americans for the first time following the devastating Watts riots in California in 1966. From December 26 to January 1, each day is dedicated to a different principle. Several churches and community organizations sponsor local events appropriate to the theme or principle of the day. Principles celebrated are unity, cooperative economics, collective work and responsibility, faith, creativity, self-determination and purpose.

Christmas Lights Tour
December, all month
Any cabbie you ask will probably cut you a good deal on a motor tour around the island to visit some spectacular light displays. Call any cab company for information, or ask at your hotel or guesthouse for help with arrangements.

Little Island, Big Fun

Snorkel

If you can swim you can probably snorkel. A snorkel trip to the reef aboard a catamaran, schooner or power boat will cost anywhere from $25 to $45 per person. On some boats the snorkeling equipment rental fee is included in ticket price. Most snorkel trips out of Key West will take you to the area of the Sand Key Lighthouse reef. When shopping for a trip you should ask how many others will be going on the same trip and how many crew members will be along to assist. It's kind of like the teacher-student ratio. You don't want to find yourself in a huge group.

Certain Keys weather plays havoc with the reef, limiting visibility beneath the water, and creating some serious chop on the surface. If it is possible, avoid going to the reef when the weather is lousy. Don't expect the booking agent to discourage you from going out, however. On the contrary. They want you on that boat! No matter how choppy the sea.

Most snorkel boats offer a daily sunset cruise as their last trip of the day, sometimes in combination with a snorkel trip. The "combo" is a good way to squeeze all the gusto you can out of one afternoon on the water.

Dive Charters

The Fury
Hilton Marina ⚓ 245 Front Street ⚓ 294-8899 ⚓ 800-994-8898
Three-hour snorkeling trips leave twice a day at 9:30 a.m. and 1:00 p.m. The *Fury* is a 65-foot catamaran with a shaded lounge and spacious sun decks. The reef trip includes snorkeling equipment and professional instruction, as well as free beer, wine and sodas. There is also a combo snorkeling/sunset sail that leaves at 4:00 p.m. in the winter and 5:00 p.m. in the summer. On this trip free champagne is also offered. All snorkel trips are $38. Kids ages 7–12 are half-price. Kids 6 and under go free.

The Sebago
201 William Street ✱ 294-5687

Three-and-a-half hour snorkel trips to the living reef, all equipment and instruction included, are at 9 a.m. and 1 p.m. daily. The *Sebago* and the *Sebago 2* are 60-foot catamarans with freshwater showers, and free soft drinks. After the snorkeling, the crew breaks out the complimentary wine and beer. The *Sebago* also offers a combo snorkel and sunset cruise, featuring all of the above plus a magnificent view of the sunset on the way back into port on the last trip in the afternoon.

All snorkel trips are $38. The two-hour sunset cruise with unlimited beer, wine and champagne is $28. Children go on all *Sebago* trips for half price.

Scuba

If you have a PADI Certification card, the universal diver's license, be sure to bring it with you to the Keys. There are several charter dive boats catering exclusively to scuba divers, and many boats that take both snorkel and scuba divers to the reef. But they will all require you to show your certification card.

A 3-day PADI Certification course is available locally, as well as the popular resort course, so called because it is designed to give vacationers with limited time the chance to dive the reef with a minimum of on shore instruction. Resort course divers learn about scuba equipment in the morning and dive at two coral reef locations in the afternoon, all for a set price. They are accompanied constantly, on the reef, by a dive instructor, and are not qualified to dive alone. Nor are they certified to scuba dive.

Dive Schools and Charters

Captain's Corner
0 Duval Street ✱ Ocean Key House ✱ 296-8865

Scuba divers interested in deep dives on less frequented reefs will appreciate the *Sea Hawk's* daily dive trips designed for advanced scuba divers. Advanced dives are $30 for two tank, two location trips. Equipment rental is $30. Combination scuba and snorkel dive trips are offered twice daily. Cost is $30 for scuba; $30 for snorkel. Snorkel equipment is included; scuba gear is an additional $30.

The Captain's Corner is a five star rated facility, offering PADI accredited instruction up to Assistant Diver and the popular Resort Course. The three or four day PADI accreditation course is $300 plus tax. The Resort Course is $100. And—in the summertime there are twilight wreck and night (scuba) dives. All instruction is available in Japanese, German, Spanish, French, Italian.

Southpoint Divers
714 Duval Street and 535 Duval Street
305-292-9778 or 800-891-DIVE

Southpoint Divers caters exclusively to scuba divers. Reef trips depart twice daily aboard 42-foot jet drive dive boats that comfortably accommodate 15 divers. All crew members are PADI instructors. Certified divers using their own gear pay $54 for a two tank dive. The same dive with all equipment is $70. If room permits, snorkelers accompanying scuba diving companions are welcome, but the dive destinations are suited to scuba, and not snorkel, diving.

The Resort Course at Southpoint Divers is $100. The three day certification course is $400.

Fishing

The waters of the Florida Keys contain over 600 varieties of edible fish, and plenty of them. A day of fishing off Key West is one of America's great tourist bargains. When you are in Key West, you are 130 miles out to sea already, mere minutes from the world's greatest fishing.

Who Needs A Fishing License?

Non-Florida residents must have saltwater fishing licenses when fishing from either a boat or land. Licenses are available at the County Court House, 500 Whitehead Street, and also from tackle shops and marinas. A seven day license for non-Florida residents costs under $20; An annual license is around $32. On most charter fishing boats the license is provided by the boat.

Call the Florida Marine Patrol at 800-342-5367 for further information, but don't be surprised if they take a while to answer.

Charter Boat Row
Garrison Bight Marina • Palm Avenue and U.S. 1
Thirty-five members of Key West's charter fishing boats are docked at the Garrison Bight on the Amberjack Pier. A visit to charter boat row is lots of fun, particularly in the afternoon when boats are returning to port. Sometimes there are fish being made ready for the frying pan on cleaning stations along the wharf. Huge, hungry sea birds hover over the pier, waiting for their share of the feast. On a visit to the bight you'll see the fishing boats and meet the captains and crews who run them.

Party Boats
To experience the salty thrills of offshore fishing, without spending a fortune to hire a private charter, sign on for a fishing trip aboard a party boat, where up to 50 anglers share the fun of dropping lines and waiting for the bottom fish to bite. You'll pay around $25–$30 for a trip out to

Yellowfin tuna

the deep blue sea, and that price includes your license, tackle and bait. They'll even give you a pill to ward off seasickness. On party boats there are mates to teach you the intricacies of offshore fishing. You'll find party boats from Key Largo to Key West at commercial piers.

Charter Sport Fishing

Sportfishing boats carry up to six anglers 15 or 20 miles out to sea to do battle with leaping monster fish like marlin and sailfish. It costs plenty to fish with a knowledgeable captain who knows where the fish are. A day

Blue marlin

on a charterboat can cost up to $625, but that fee can be split between passengers, if you don't mind sharing the boat. Arrange your trip directly with the captain. Ticket booth vendors on the sidewalks promise to arrange for anything, and they will—it's just that the arrangements they're making are often hit and miss. Usually the charter boat captain supplies everything but your food and drinks.

To find a private charter visit charter boat row, any marina, or call ahead to the Chamber of Commerce for a list of all types of fishing charters. Phone 800-FLA-KEYS.

Flats Fishing

Flats or shallow-bottom fishing is nothing like charter boat and party boat fishing. Flats fisherman must have sharp eyes, good instincts, lots of patience and sunscreen. Shallow fishing excursions travel on open skiffs, with shallow draughts and nothing above the deck to interfere with fly casting. They reach the mangrove islands at dawn. There are frigate birds, and great white herons swooping low as fish become visible in the clear shallow water. Here are tarpon, bonefish and permit, the wily creatures flats anglers are looking to hook. None of them are edible. The trick to fly-fishing is to convince the feeding fish that your hook is a tasty morsel of crab. But it's hard to fool these fish. They are wary, and very cautious. After you catch them, you measure them, photograph them and deliver them back into their crystalline world. Fishing in the backcountry is as much about enjoying the surroundings as it is about catching fish.

Saltwater Angler
219 Simonton Street ✴ 294-3248
A complete booking service for backcountry guides is available at the Saltwater Angler store. Also, equipment and supplies for flats fishing enthusiasts.

Golf

Key West Resort Golf Course
Junior College Road, Stock Island ✴ 294-5232
A Rees Jones designed 18-hole championship golf course with a full house of dog-legs, water hazards and mangroves, located on one of the largest areas of greenery in Key West. A lake behind hole number ten is a sanctuary for rare birds.

Pro shop is open from 6:45 a.m. till 6 p.m. daily. Play 18 holes for $65, including the cart. Clubs rent for $21.50 a day.

Tennis

Bayview Park
Truman Avenue, 1300 block
Recently refurbished courts at Bayview Park are looking pretty spiffy lately. Here are the rules: Time limit for play is 45 minutes or one set, whichever comes first. There is no system for reserving court time, and

you can't reserve a court if your partner is not yet present. The park is open from 7 a.m. till 11 p.m. No dogs allowed. No charge to use these public courts.

Casa Marina Court
Reynolds Street at the Beach ☎ 294-4436
These are also city-owned courts, free to the public. A small parking lot is for tennis players only. To schedule call ahead. Time limit here is 30 minutes or one set, whichever comes first.

Swimming

The Martin Luther King Jr. Community Pool
300 Catherine Street ☎ 292-8248
One of the island's best kept secrets is this big, beautiful pool in Bahama Village. Also, there's a baby pool, picnic tables, and basketball courts. There are swimming lessons in the summertime, and water exercise classes year-round. The pool is open from 10 a.m.–6 p.m., opens at 8 a.m. for lap swimming, summer months, but those lap swimming times are subject to change around quite a bit. Call for the current schedule.

The pool is surrounded by a cement skirt, where you will see people tanning on beach towels. The place is full of kids during summer months, but weekdays in the wintertime it's very quiet and a wonderful retreat from crowded beaches and hotel pools.

Bocce Ball

Southernmost Bocce Ball
Bocce ball is serious fun for the local crowd that gathers at the six red clay courts at Sonny McCoy Indigenous Park, White Street and Atlantic Boulevard. You'll find here a crowd of Key West professionals: journalists, historians, politicians, executives, attorneys, and even judges, all very friendly natives. Tag along to the bar scene after and make some new friends. Games begin at 6:30 p.m., just as the sun is fading and the cool breezes of the Gulf Stream begin to blow over the land.

Gyms & Fitness Clubs

Caribbean Spa
Pier House Resort, 1 Duval Street ✻ 296-4600
Free to guests of the Pier House, it's also open to hard-bodies with the money to afford a chi chi gym. In addition to state-of-the-art fitness equipment, the spa has exercise classes and a full-service beauty center, featuring massage, facials, manicures, pedicures, and most other forms of beauty pampering, and the pamperers do a terrific job. The gym is small but luckily, rarely crowded. Appointments are necessary for services at this stunningly pristine spa.

Club Body Tech
1075 Duval Street, Duval Square ✻ 292-9683
Air-conditioned, very modern gym with pounding, high-tech music to match. Hours are 6 a.m.–10 p.m. weekdays; 8 a.m.–9 p.m. Saturday; 9 a.m.–9 p.m. Sunday. Join for a day ($12) or a week ($39) or a month ($79) or a year ($459). Prices are subject to change.

Shape U. Family Fitness Center
2740 N. Roosevelt Boulevard in Overseas Market ✻ 294-9193
Tourists welcome. Child-care on the premises. Yoga classes. Massage. Treadmills. Nautilus. Many girls at this gym wear full makeup when they work out. On Stairmasters, you might hear arguments over what programs to watch, when the talk show crowd clashes with the soap opera devotees.

Pro Fitness Center
1111 12th Street ✻ 294-1865
Not as expensive as the others, probably because of its weird location in the basement of the Professional Building, behind K-Mart. This place smells more like a gym than any other gym on the island.

Yoga College of India
812 Southard Street (Upstairs) ✴ 292-1854

Inexpensive, 90-minute classes of stretching and strengthening. Classes daily Monday thru Friday, at 10 a.m. and 6 p.m., and an early-morning class at 8 a.m. during the winter season. Weekends 10 a.m. only. A very challenging workout, amazing body shaper! Newcomers welcome. If you can't take big heat—stay out of this yoga class. Room temperature is kept oven-like with electric heaters to aid muscle flexibility.

The Reach Body Shop
1435 Simonton Street ✴ 296-5000

A dandy little gym. If you get a pass from your guesthouse to use the facilities at the Reach, you'll be happy to know that access to this gym is one of your privileges.

Coffee Mill Cultural Center
916 Polhaski Street ✴ 296-9982

Stop by and pick up a schedule or ask them to FAX it to you. Aerobics, stretch and relaxation classes, karate, African dance. Newcomers always welcome. Sweat and shape up on a great, bouncy floor.

Kidstuff

Kids Discover Key West
P.O. Box 5892 ▪ Key West, FL 33040 ▪ (305) 304 1600

Maybe you don't consider petting a live shark, being tickled by a horse-shoe crab, or meeting a sea turtle up close to be a very big deal, but your kids probably will. Kid-size adventures are available for kids ages 6 to 12 years old through Jonathan and Lisa Weinshank, a couple of island saints in the business of showing kids a good time in Key West. Morning, after-noon or evening sessions are three hours worth of local adventures. Cost is $35 for one session; $63 for a whole day of adventures.

The Weinshanks are certified in CPR and first aid; their business is fully licensed and insured. Jonathan is a part-time family counselor, and they are parents to their three children ages 17, 15, and 3. The Weinshanks also manage and cater birthday parties and babysit. So they've had lots of practice at keeping kids happy.

The kids travel in a 15-seat passenger van in which they can be picked up and dropped off at your hotel. The Weinshanks carry a cellular phone with them at all times, so you can contact them to check on your kids whenever you want to. Group rates are available.

Discovery Underseas Tours
Lands End Marina/Foot of Margaret Street
293-0099 ▪ 800-262-0099

A great trip out to the reef where kids get a big kick out of the huge, slanted plexiglass windows on the bottom of the boat that open up for viewing the mysteries of the reef seven miles off shore.

Kids three and under go free on all trips. Kids under twelve go for free on the first trip of the day, providing there are seats left over after the paying customers are aboard. In the summer, the first trip is around noon; in the winter, usually at 9:30 a.m. Kids must be accompanied by an adult. Call for information and reservations.

Mom's Baby Stuff Rentals
P.O. Box 1844, Key West, FL 33041 ✴ 294-8645

Everything you need for baby is for rent here. Cribs, portable cribs, strollers, highchairs, Swing-o-matics, and jogging strollers rent for around $25 a week each. Walkers, backpacks, baby gates, and umbrella strollers are slightly less. Rent a rocking chair for $5 a day or $35 a week. If you call or write and put in your order, your baby stuff will be at your hotel or guesthouse when you arrive.

Monroe County Library
700 Fleming Street ✴ 292-3595

Every Saturday the county library hosts a children's hour at 10:30 a.m. Kids do arts and crafts and watch a movie. During the summer months, children's librarian Karen Jensen hosts children's hours four days a week. For a schedule of programs tailored to specific age groups, phone the library and ask for the children's events schedule. Children of all ages are welcome throughout the year.

Martin Luther King Memorial Pool
Catherine Street ✴ 292-8248

A terrific pool beside a shallow kiddie pool around which local mothers congregate on hot days to put their babies and their feet in the water. Older kids are kicked out of the pool for lane swimming hour and water aerobic classes, but these activities are usually scheduled for very early in the morning, and later in the afternoon. The pool is open from 8 a.m. until 6 p.m. daily. There is no admission charge.

Charter Boat Row
Garrison Bight Marina ✴ Palm and North Roosevelt Boulevard

Around 4 p.m. the charter fishing boats come back to port after a day of deep sea fishing, usually with fish to be cleaned. As the captains or mates clean the fish, they toss scraps to a flock of very appreciative pelicans who gobble them quick as lightening. Kids love watching this. It's truly amazing how much a pelican can swallow, and how flexible are the throats of long-necked sea birds.

Some kids, at least five and up, love going out to sea and fishing with their parents on a party boat. Deep sea fishing on a party boat is a surprisingly inexpensive and wonderfully entertaining way to enjoy the Keys. On party boats, kids ages 5–12 go for half price, which is around $13.

Artstamps of Key West
507 Southard Street ✒ 296-2201

Your glass is half full, right? So decorate it with a hibiscus or an owl or a lizard artstamp. There are over 500 affordable stamp designs in this little shop of feel-good art. There are ink pads, too, and 108 colors of watercolor markers. Who couldn't use a little more art in their life? A must-see for little artists on vacation.

Paint-A-Pot Glazing Studio
208 Telegraph Lane (Near Captain Tony's) ✒ 292-3322

Make your own souvenir. Choose from 400 ready to glaze pieces. You paint them. They glaze them. You pick up your finished work the next day. Kid's pieces start at $6. Plates are $16. Vases $20. What a great gift for Granny! A morning or afternoon of family fun and art. Staff members are helpful, patient and personable.

Lazer Challenge
416 Eaton Street ✒ 292-2330

Lazer tag arena, game room, and those weird video games that your kids love. Buy them an all-day pass or a 3-day pass, which the best deal of all. All-day passes get bracelets that allow them in and out. Hours: Noon till midnight, daily.

Beaches

EOPLE PROBABLY ASSUME that Key West must have some pretty amazing beaches, being at the end of a string of tropical islands and all.
Well, our beaches are amazing, but not for their looks. Our beaches are not the extra-fine sanded, coffee ice cream colored stretches people imagine when they think "Florida beach." Like many things southernmost, the beaches here are rough, battered and kind of seedy. Lots of character, but not all that pretty—not in the traditional sense anyway.

The locals' favorite beach is at **Fort Taylor,** an 87-acre state park with a pre-Civil-War-era brick fort, several acres of Australian pine trees, spacious parking areas, a scattering of picnic tables, and a few grimy charcoal grills for whoever claims them at the beginning of each new day.

The track of pine-needle forest that separates the parking lot from the bluff and the beach below it is always a few degrees cooler than the rest of the island. The forest floor is sheltered from the sun by the pines and cooled by breezes from the deep, rough channel where the Atlantic Ocean and the Gulf of Mexico collide in an endless tumult.

Bring along a beach chair, or a tough hide, to lie on the rocky (you can hardly call it sand) Fort Taylor Beach. Swimmers will find water deep enough here for a good workout not too far from the stony shore, but those stones are really hard on the feet. In fact, they're downright obnoxious. For playing, wear rubber sandals or sneakers into the water.

For swimming, wade out into the water with your sneakers on, then toss them back onto the beach until you get back from your swim.

Walk the beach all the way to the right toward a jetty of rocks. They're steep-sided, slippery and dangerous, just as the sign says. Climb up onto the path that winds along the bluff above the beach and continue on around the point. You'll come to another long string of huge gray, sharply planed boulders. The water beyond the rocks is very rough, full of currents, and absolutely no good for swimming. Find a perch on the rocks and wait for sunset. It is glorious from this location.

This is the sunset setting for many windy weddings. Sometimes you will see two or more wedding ceremonies going on at once. And a

funeral. By now, so many of the ashes of former Key West people have
been tossed into the wild winds that blow into a fury as the day draws to
a close, that the locals have named this part of the shoreline **Ash Beach**.

The Park has a few rules to remember. Thong-style bathing suits are
not allowed on this beach, nor is topless sunbathing. Rangers will give
you a plastic bag when you enter the park so you can take your trash back
out with you. Few garbage cans are available in this area, to cut back on
costs. The park recycles aluminum cans and makes compost. Cigarette
butts go into ashtrays donated by the R.J. Reynolds Tobacco Company.
Warning: get out of Fort Taylor Park by dusk or risk being locked behind
its very high, barbed-wire laced security fence. This really did happen to
people I know, and they had a hellish time climbing over the gate in the
dark.

You enter Fort Taylor through Truman Annex, at Southard Street.
Follow the signs to the ticket booth where you'll pay $2.50 for a car with
one person, $5 for a car with two and fifty cents for each additional
person. Buy an annual pass for $69.50. Good for up to eight people at all
Florida state parks.

South Beach is located at the very end of Duval Street, on the
Atlantic Ocean. A concrete pier extending fifty feet beyond the last
block of Duval Street provides a good sunning and people-watching area,
as well as entry via a ladder into water deep enough for a swim. A
recently constructed black wrought-iron fence closes off the pier to the
public from 11 p.m. until 7 a.m. each day. The beach, and the beach
restaurant, are closed during those hours, too.

A thin layer of pebbly sand covers South Beach. There are plenty of
sheltering palms for shade. This was for many years very much a locals'
beach. Tennessee Williams sunned here, as well as a number of other
local celebrities who appreciated the relative peace and calm of this
often-overlooked public beach.

Today, South Beach is frequented by locals and tourists alike who
gather here to take in the sun and the Key West color, in a place with
easy access to refreshments and bathrooms. Because the water is relatively shallow, and almost the entire area is enclosed by fences, it's a
particularly user-friendly beach for small children and babies still inno-

cent enough to get amusement from a plastic bucket and shovel at the edge of water so calm it barely moves.

On South Beach, dedicated explorers will find the occasional nature treat stranded in the shallow pools on the craggy surfaces of the long, slippery, green, sea-slime covered rocks along the shoreline. They might see a hermit crab, no bigger than a thumbnail, or tiny, wiggling shrimp, barely discernible to the naked eye, or a rare, delicately whorled sea shell.

You swim at your own risk off South Beach because there are no life-guards. Dogs, alcohol and glass containers are all prohibited. You use the bathrooms, rustic but clean, in the city-owned restaurant.

When you've had enough of the great outdoors, you can go inside and order breakfast, lunch, or dinner, while you watch the beach and the sky from a canopied deck, built of rough square beams painted blue and, somehow, evocative of a funky New England beachside resort. There is a full bar inside the restaurant.

Another public beach downtown is **Simonton Street Beach,** where Simonton Street ends at the Gulf of Mexico. Tucked between two giant resorts, the Pier House and the Hyatt, you'll find a tiny, gritty square of beach with public bathrooms and a few metered parking places.

The crowd that tends to congregate here is pretty rough as are the waters beyond the pier. Many nicer places are available on the island to go for a swim or to sunbathe.

To take your dog for a dip, or to view another local beach scene, take South Street over to Vernon Avenue, turn right, and head to the end of the block. **Dog Beach** is straight ahead. This tiny, public beach is next to Louie's Backyard, a restaurant at the corner of Vernon and Waddell. The beach is sandy with tiny waves here, but the shoreline is rocky and slip-pery.

Jimmy Buffett's first Key West home is next door to Louie's, at 711 Waddell Street. Like the others on this side of the block, the house was recently restored to its original seaside splendor by the Coconut Beach Resort. Today it is a much spiffier place indeed than the shabby, salt-and-wind-battered rental house where Buffet composed "Margaritaville"—*Strumming my six-string, on my front porch swing…*

Key West
...

Another beach dear to locals for its off-the-beaten-path charm is located below the white concrete pier at the corner of Vernon and Seminole streets. On either side of the pier, you can swim at the tiny, sandy strips of beach.

Twenty years ago it was called **Broken Glass Beach**. My neighbor, an artist named George Lee, once created a beautiful mosaic fish on his backyard fence with glue and bits of sea-worn colored glass he had collected during daily swims off the tiny beach. People also take their dogs swimming here. It is also called "Casa Marina Beach," although it is public and not part of the Casa Marina Resort on the same block.

The waters here are perfect for beginning snorkelers. The scenery beneath the calm surface is good, and the water is shallow. I have spotted quite large stingrays gliding along the sandy bottom in this area and plenty of fish hanging around the aging Casa Marina pier, just to the left of the beach.

Monroe County Beach, at the foot of Reynolds Street, is a wide sandy cove beside a long, wooden pier officially named the Reynolds Street Pier, but known locally by a variety of names like the Dick Dock, the Queer Pier, or Gay Bay. You get the picture. Not so many years ago this wooden pier was a favorite sunning place for bronzed beauties from the island's gay population. Gay tourists, perhaps having heard about the Queer Pier from an older brother—or sister—or returning to the island for the first time in many years with fond memories of sun-baked afternoons on the Queer Pier in the pre-AIDS era, will still find their way to this popular sunbathing wharf. But the "Dick Dock" is no longer what it used to be. By now, many of the local beauties have moved on or decided to take better care of their skin and sworn off sun-bathing, or found new roosts on the more cosmopolitan Fort Taylor Beach. Today, the Queer Pier is pretty hetero.

Monroe County Beach is broad and sandy, studded with palms and a few Australian pines. A series of concrete-surfaced pathways converge at a spacious gazebo, right in the center of the beach. There is plenty of parking here, a very funky concrete bathhouse, sheltered picnic tables, swings, a jungle gym, and a snack bar. Astro City is a small, usually busy playground, featuring a whirly-gig, a great jungle gym, swings, monkey bars, and a sandbox. At the back of the playground you can eat at a

[172]

couple of picnic tables beneath a roof; this is a favorite birthday spot for kiddies.

Beach chairs, sailboats, and rubber rafts are available for rent from a concession on the beach.

On the opposite side of the beach from the Reynolds Street Pier sits the West Martello Tower, surrounded by a high, curving wall of red brick. For a cozy hideout from the wind on blustery, cool days, settle yourself down in the soft sand at the foot of the West Martello Tower's sheltering brick wall. Recently restored and renamed is the **C.B. Harvey Rest Beach Park**. Cornelius Bradford Harvey, nicknamed C.B., served two years as a city commissioner and eight years as mayor of Key West. The park is accessible to the handicapped, with wheelchair pathways that lead to the water's edge. There are erosion-fighting dunes, sea oats and other vegetation, foot bridges, and a bike path. The brand-new picnic tables are rarely in use.

Smathers Beach, on the southern side of the island, is a half-mile-long stretch of quite wide, man-made beach. Because of the reef, there is no pounding surf on any of Key West's beaches. The natural process of erosion that grinds giant boulders down into tiny grains of sand does not occur here (there's no surfing here). The sand on this beach is imported from the Bahamas in huge barges. Last time they re-sanded the beach it cost the city $150,000 for two barges of Caribbean sand. It all blows away eventually, so every few years, the renourishment process beings all over again.

At any time of the year you're likely to see vans and campers parked along the curb of South Roosevelt Boulevard, which winds along the side of the beach, or across the street on a very bumpy, very dusty strip of earth with the unlikely name of the "Bridle Path." Unlikely, because no one rides horses around Key West. There are lots of cars here, as generally parking is easier at Smathers than at downtown public beaches. There are no meters here yet, so you park free. There are bathhouses and a few picnic tables but no lifeguards.

The crowd at this beach is active. It's a good place for fun-seeking, sun-loving tourists to find each other. There are beachcombers wandering along the water's edge, spirited volleyball games, frisbee tosses, and watersport rental concerns. For a fee, you can try parasailing, windsurfing or jet skiing.

Burgers, snowcones, soft drinks, smoothies and all manner of refreshments are offered from the many snack trucks which arrive bright and early each morning to claim a spot in the heart of the action. Be prepared to pay for the cup if you ask for ice or water.

A wide, flat concrete promenade/bicycle/skate path begins at the foot of the beach at the corner of Bertha and South Roosevelt and continues for the entire length of Smathers and well beyond. The parade of bodies in motion on the bike path goes on all day long.

Dogs are not allowed on this beach. It is also illegal for women to sunbathe topless here.

Gardens and Green Space

Bayview Park
1400 Truman Avenue

In the past year a lovely lush carpet of fresh green grass has been installed in Bayview Park, and dogs have been banned from the place. The Bayview's bathrooms, ball fields and tennis courts have been refurbished. Even the old bandstand, that has showcased hundreds of concerts and events since the park was created in 1923, has undergone repairs and received a fresh coat of white paint. Today the park looks as inviting as it did back in the 1920s.

The tract of land that is Bayview Park was once the yard and garden of a wealthy cigar manufacturer, Eduardo Gato. The millionaire's mansion stood in the middle. When Gato sold the property to the City, his house was moved to 1206 Virginia Street and turned into a charity hospital known as Casa del Pobre. Today Gato's house is an upscale complex of condominiums. According to local legend, Casa del Pobre has long been haunted by the ghost of a nurse who occasionally materializes to take midnight pulses.

In the fall, the Key West High School's cheerleading squad practices in one corner of the park. On weekends there are picnics and birthday parties. The park is studded with magnificent tropical hardwood trees. On either side of the bandstand there are lignumvitae trees. You'll recognize them from their stature, they're shorter than other trees, and more shrub-like. In the spring they are covered with delicate blue blossoms.

In the area behind the bandstand there are several important monuments that memorialize Key West boys who served in Viet Nam, a local man killed at Desert Storm, soldiers of the Confederacy, and Jose Marti, a Cuban poet and leader of the Cuban Revolution.

Nancy Forrester's Secret Garden
1 Free School Lane (off the 500 block of Simonton Street)
294-0015

It has taken Nancy Forrester twenty-five years to bring this magnificent mini-rainforest to its current state of grandeur, and now she's sharing her marvelous 16,000-square-foot gallery of tropical plants and fruit trees with the world. Commune with a spectacular collection of sumptuous

Hibiscus

tropical flowers, fruit trees, giant hardwood trees, and butterflies. This garden of flora is located in an unlikely place, and though it's in the very heart of Old Town Key West, it's difficult to find. And there's no parking area. But none of that will matter once you enter the place. You're welcome to stay in the garden for as long as you like. Picnic. Or rest.

In the middle of the property there is screened conch-style cottage, available for rent ($750/week). It is a favorite honeymoon retreat for couples staging their weddings in the garden. When you marry here, an orchid will be named and dedicated to mark the event. Then you can come back everytime you're in town and see how it's doing.

Open 10 a.m. to 5 p.m. Admission $6; off the 500 block of Simonton Street.

Key West Botanical Garden
College Road, Stock Island • 294-5426

This was a Federal Emergency Relief Administration project. The Botanical Garden was planted with eighty different species of plants when it was founded in 1935. Today the gardens feature both native and exotic plants, and the last remaining specimens of Stock Island tree snail. Environmentalists say that if Florida holly continues to choke out native hardwoods, prospects are pretty grim for the snail. See them here, while you still can.

The garden is operated on a non-profit basis by the Key West Botanical Garden Society. Within the gardens there are benches and resting places, and brochures that lead visitors on self-guided tours. Often the brochure racks are empty. Still, it's free, and interesting in an other-worldly sort of way.

Little Hamaca Park and the Salt Ponds
Government Road (off 1500 block of Flagler Avenue) • 294-2116

When you turn onto Government Road on your way to the boardwalk and trail through Little Hamaca Park ⅔ mile away, you'll pass Key West's Salt Ponds. Look to your right to see these shallow tidal pools that are home to many species of fish, and a variety of birds, including the rare roseate spoonbill.

These tidal pools were once part of an important island industry, salt gathering. Large, flat, evaporating pans were laid out in the very shallow pools. Salt water flowed into them during the spring and summer months. When the tidal pools receded during the dry months, the moisture evaporated, leaving 340 acres of crystallized salt dried on the pans.

Also on your right is the runway of the Key West International Airport. Watching planes arriving and departing is fun, and enormously entertaining for kids.

Little Hamaca City Park has a picnic area, a parking area, a bicycle stand (this whole trip is best experienced on a bike), and a boardwalk. Information plaques tell the story of these transitional wetlands. The three main species of mangroves are well-represented here. The red mangroves grow up, and then bend back into the water to plant new roots. Black mangroves shoot straight up out of the mud. Buttonwood trees grow along the shoreline—they line the sides of the Overseas Highway in some areas of the Keys—and emit salt on the underside of their leaves. Taste one and see for yourself.

The trail through Little Hamaca Park is ⅓ mile long. Two boardwalks lead through the marshes and lowlands. Between the two is an area of hardwood hammock. There are endangered species of animals living here: the Key West raccoon, the red rat snake, and the white crowned pigeon—so named by John Audubon in 1832. The discovery of these special inhabitants on this property saved it from being turned into a concrete suburb of Key West.

Little Hamaca Park is open from daylight until sundown, daily. There is no admission fee.

Charles "Sonny" McCoy Indigenous Park
Atlantic Boulevard at White Street ☎ 292-8157

The Indigenous Park is named after the Key West mayor who served the longest time in office: five two-year terms. Mayor McCoy, who was an architect and a world-class water-skier, went down in the history books when he water-skied to Cuba in the early '70s.

The native tree park is planted with a great sampling of indigenous trees including several endangered species. There is no charge to explore the grounds. Many trees are marked with their common as well as Latin names. You'll see lots of island trees like silver buttonwood, gumbo limbo, geiger tree, wild dilly, autograph tree and satinwood. Also an amazing ficus tree. Sometimes there is a printed guide to the trees available at the entrance. Often there is not.

Doves, mockingbirds, butterflies, as well as a multitude of chickens, are in evidence. It's very quiet. There's rarely a crowd. Every summer, a small army of boy scouts spend a weekend camping on the grounds.

The park is open Monday through Friday from 7 a.m. till 4 p.m. There is parking and restrooms. Also a pavilion for picnicking.

Wellspring Medicine Garden
800 Amelia Street ✹ 292-2022

It's not marked and it never has been, so you've got to look for this jungle garden sanctuary dedicated to spirituality, higher consciousness, and healing. Peaceful folks are invited to commune with nature, join a meditation circle or put in some solitary time at the koi pond. The goldfish are large and happy. Everywhere you look you'll see something wonderful—small snakes curled around thin tree trunks, a grassy walk, Buddhas smiling benevolently from odd perches, and thick chunks of crystal. The garden is shaded with exotic hardwoods. Wednesday nights at 8 p.m. tapes on spiritual subjects and/or guest speakers are on hand. Thursdays there is a silent meditation circle beginning at 8 p.m. No special training is required and all are welcome. Chi-netics, a special form of Tai Chi, is practiced in the garden. Healing massage available.

The garden is open during daylight hours. There is no fee to enter.

West Martello Towers
Atlantic Boulevard and White Street ✹ 294-3210

The Joe Allen Garden Center (named after beloved local son, Joe Allen, who served as state representative in Tallahassee) is housed here. The West Martello is one of a trio of forts built on the islands' coasts in the 1800's. Both the East and West Martello Towers were built mostly by slaves, and completed in 1862, just one year before the Emancipation Proclamation outlawed slavery. In 1890, the U.S. Navy used the West Martello Tower for target practice, which is why it looks as if it barely survived the Civil War. In fact, none of Key West's three forts ever was involved in battle.

The Key West Garden Club maintains this lovely ruin turned flourishing tropical garden. Admission is free, but you must be wearing shoes and a shirt, not a bathing suit. Children are to be accompanied by adults, and no dogs are allowed. When you enter you will be greeted and told all about the fort's marvelous history. (Probably they'll leave the part about the slaves out.) There is much to see, and long lists of plants to search out. There are marvelous photo opportunities against the backdrop of cool, red bricks, crumbling fireplaces and 135-year-old arches. You'll find the base of a tower that was blown away by gunfire, as well as many well-placed benches for peaceful times. On a jungley knoll there is a gazebo, popular for weddings.

Orchids are much cherished here. The Garden Club sponsors frequent lectures and discussions on growing their beloved orchids—the more exotic, the better. Club members bring their own orchids into the garden on a Saturday in mid-May and compete for prizes for best species and best hybrid. At an annual plant ramble, plants are offered for sale, and refreshments are served. The event, a local favorite, is open to everyone, and everyone comes. Magic! Call for a schedule of events.

The West Martello Tower and Garden Center is open Tuesdays through Saturday, from 9:30 a.m. till 3:30 p.m. During the winter months the center is open on Sundays, too.

Accommodations

WHILE I WAS DOING RESEARCH for this guide, I was driving through the Keys with my 17-year-old son. I was pointing out various hotels and guesthouses, telling him what I knew about them, how popular they were and so forth. Then I asked him where he would choose to stay were he a tourist coming to the Keys for a visit. Funky and old-fashioned? Or sleek and new?

"It would depend on who I was with," my wise Capricorn said.

It really does depend on who you're with. Kids, for example, will be happiest staying in a motel or hotel with a pool. Their parents will, no doubt, appreciate this feature as well. Some properties have hot tubs but no pools. If you tell a reservationist that you want to be near a beach, and the answer is that the beach is nearby, ask how nearby?—how many blocks? And then check a map. But the island is, after all, a small place and easily negotiated.

It is important to check on features such as telephones and televisions in rooms. In some guesthouses, the main phones are not answered after business hours. If you need to be accessible, you should check on this point. You can count on air conditioning and, in most places, islandy ceiling fans. Breakfast isn't always part of the deal in a guesthouse, and so-called cocktail hours often feature no cocktails at all, but wine or punch instead.

Parking is at a premium here. An inn, especially a downtown inn, won't necessarily have a parking lot. And though most places in Key West are within walking distance of downtown, several fine, family-oriented places are located on the south side, also considered to be the quiet side of the island, and definitely a car ride from Duval Street and the tourist attractions.

Pets are usually not welcome, and when they are, they'll cost up to $10 per day extra. Many guesthouses discourage children, and some prohibit children all together.

Gay guesthouses are sometimes exclusively for gay men. Or gay men and gay women. Or gay women only. If you're timid around the subject or the presence of homosexuality, state that to the reservationist. If you're extremely sensitive, you should know that Key West is a gay-friendly destination, and up to 20% of our population is gay.

It is difficult to nail down rates in the thumbnail sketches that follow. This list is merely a sample, an overview, of what is available. Often a hotel has four seasonal rates. During Fantasy Fest week, the week that ends on the last Saturday night of October, rates are the highest of all. The other peak week is the one between Christmas and New Year's Day. You will also probably be asked to commit to a minimum number of nights during these times.

Rates also shoot up on 3-day-holiday and special-events weekends. The Lobster mini-season in July, for example, is a local event that hikes prices. Check our chapter called "Annual Events" for a schedule of special events.

Some summer weekends offer low rates, and fall is also a time when great values can be found. Early December has traditionally been a grindingly slow time for tourism—which makes it a wonderful time to visit. No lines and no humidity. Many folks enjoy Key West at this time of the year; many come annually to Christmas shop and enjoy a pre-holiday R & R in Paradise.

Key West's hotel rates generally though are some of the highest in the country. You will find better deals thirty or fifty or one hundred miles up the Keys, but, if you definitely want to stay in Key West, you'll pay plenty. And don't forget to add in the local, state, and tourist taxes, for a total of 11.5% on all accommodations.

Renting a house of your own for a week or two is a popular alternative to staying in hotels and inns. If you have a good-sized family or group, you might investigate this possibility. Many wonderful houses can be rented for short terms, and usually the amenities include a pool, a washing machine and dryer and a telephone—everything exactly as if you were in your own home. Maid service is usually available, also.

Reservations Services

Once you've scheduled your visit, you can call ahead to a reservation service. They'll find you what you want and make the reservation for you. They collect their fee from the place, not from you. Reservation services are highly competitive in the Keys. The ones listed here have free 800 numbers. Call around and chat with various reservationists until you find one you really like. Then, get down to business. A good reservation service can save you a lot of time and hassles—particularly if you are the mad-cap, spur-of-the-moment type.

Florida Keys Reservations
800-352-5397

Florida Keys and Key West Reservations
800-889-2457

Florida Keys Visitors Bureau
800-648-6269 ✹ 800-352-5397

Key West Innkeepers Association
800-358-6307

Key West Travel/Condo Vacations
800-544-9016

We Love Florida Keys Visitor Center
800-403-2154

Information Services

Key West Chamber of Commerce
800-648-6269

Gay Chamber of Commerce
Key West Business Guild ✹ 800-535-7797

Hotels and Motels

Banyan Resort
323 Whitehead Street ❥ 296-7786 ❥ 800-225-0639
The Banyan Resort features thirty-eight individually designed timeshare
units (available for rent to the public), in eight renovated Victorian
houses, five of which are on the National Register of Historic Places. The
entire compound takes up roughly half a city block, with lush gardens,
swimming pools, a jacuzzi, a bar, and a fish pond. There is no ocean view,
but Fort Taylor State Park beach is nearby, and it's a good one.

The place gets its name from the spectacular banyan trees in the front
yards of the Cosgrove house, at 321 Whitehead Street, and the Delaney
house, at 323. Here are fine examples of how one banyan tree can cover
literally acres of ground. In India, several families can live in the thick
roots and branches of one banyan tree. The banyan's aerial roots drop
from the upper part of the tree and take root in the ground beneath,
forming new trunks wherever they may land. The banyans on this property are some of the finest anywhere.

The units of the Banyan are available to the public for around $250
per night, sometimes less, occasionally more—depending upon the time
of year. Unit number #702 is most spectacular, with three stories of windows overlooking the garden and the majestic banyan tree that gives the
place its name. All units have full kitchens and private patios.

Best Western Key Ambassador Resort Inn
3755 S. Roosevelt Boulevard ❥ 296-3500 ❥ 800-432-4315
One hundred rooms on seven nicely landscaped acres, directly across
the street from the Atlantic ocean. From the pool deck, elevated to take
advantage of ocean breezes, you look out across the blue sea. Located
on what employees like to call "the quiet side of the island," the Key
Ambassador makes the most of its location with large, clean, quiet
rooms, ocean views, and a congenial atmosphere.

The employees here are particularly gracious and seem genuinely concerned with your happiness. The resort has been owned and operated by
the same family that built it in 1958. Every two years, the family says, the

property gets a face-lift. And, sure enough, the place looks brand-new, and even smells new.

A substantial complimentary continental breakfast is served in a bright breakfast room from 7 a.m. till 10 a.m. daily, and coffee is always available in the lobby. The guest laundry is a great convenience. And though it's difficult to imagine why you might need one of these on vacation in the Florida Keys, there are ironing boards in every room! Also screen-enclosed balconies come with every room. Outdoors, in a chickee hut, there is a fitness center challenging enough for a real workout; a poolside bar and burger grill; and several nice picnic-table groupings and barbeque grills are available to guests.

It's a great place to stay when you want to be away from the downtown tourist crowd, although downtown is only ten minutes away by taxi. Or bring a car; there is plenty of parking. The airport is close, but since large jets are prohibited from landing on the island, the noise is not offensive. There are several restaurants within a mile radius, and a spectacular oceanside promenade that runs for a two-mile strip along the beach on the southern edge of the island.

Rooms are oceanview, poolview, harborview or gardenview. Summer rates in range from $85 to $120. "The harbor," by the way, probably refers to the salt ponds, or mud flats, behind the motel. The same rooms in the high season are $155 to $195. Additional persons are $10 each.

Casa Marina Resort (Marriott)
Reynolds Street on the Ocean ☞ 296-3535 ☞ 800-874-4118

Although he did not live to see it completed, railroad baron Henry Flagler planned the Casa Marina, a glittering southernmost layover for his affluent Overseas Railroad customers traveling to Cuba. (Passengers trained to Key West, then steamshipped to Cuba, ninety miles away.) The hotel opened on New Year's Eve, 1921. In the pre-Depression splendor of the 1920s, Casa Marina guests fished, sailed, shot traps, played tennis and croquet, and danced beneath the stars on a seaside courtyard.

To imagine how glamorous an evening at the Casa might have been back then, read the party scenes in F. Scott Fitzgerald's *The Great Gatsby*. Sit in a wicker chair on the hotel's veranda and sip something cool. Time this reverie for one of those magical evenings when the full moon is on the rise even before the sun has set.

The Casa Marina started out with two hundred small guest rooms. Each contained a sink with running water; half had private baths. When it opened, the Casa's rates were very high for that time, from $8–$12 a day, and $84 a week on the American Plan—all meals included. During the Casa Marina's reign as the island's premier luxury hotel, the Astors and the Vanderbilts were frequent guests, as well as showbiz notables like Gregory Peck, Gene Tierney, Rita Hayworth, Ethel Merman, and Al Jolson. Guy Lombardo's band played, and Sally Rand, the fan dancer who lived for a while on the island, taught local kids tap dancing on the grand ballroom's polished hardwood floor.

In spite of its glittering clientele, the Casa Marina, like Flagler's railroad, was apparently ahead of its time—or perhaps in the wrong place at the wrong time. The hotel's elegance stood out conspicuously in an otherwise shabby town. By the end of the '30s, the hotel, unable to fill its 200 guest rooms, shut down.

The completely restored Marriott's Casa Marina reopened in 1979. Today the hotel has over 300 rooms of varying degrees of quality and dimensions. Loft suites contain two bedrooms, full kitchens, and spectacular views of the Atlantic. The grounds of the Casa are meticulously maintained, terraced, and dotted with the same coconut palms, Bermuda grass and 500 foot-long beachfront enjoyed by America's most "rich and famous" back in the Gatsby days. You don't have to stay at the Casa to marvel at its Spanish Renaissance architecture, giant arched doorways, and polished hardwood floors. Stop in to the lobby for a look. Or go out to the beach for a drink.

Ask about the many vacation packages offered here. Nightly rates are around $180 to $300 on non-oceanview rooms; $295 to $415 for oceanview suites.

Duval Suites Guest Accommodations
724 Duval Street ✷ 293-6600 ✷ 800-648-3780

The beauty of these units is their location: right on Duval street, which is, of course, "party central." The drawback is that there is no pool. The closest beaches are about five blocks in either direction. The noise from Duval Street is a constant reminder to guests that they are indeed, in the center of Key West's tourist universe. Four rooms contain queen-sized beds (one to a room), full kitchens, and balconies overlooking Duval.

Two other units overlook a garden and have abbreviated kitchenettes. All have the usual amenities and a communal jacuzzi. Off-season rates are $80 for the rooms with kitchenettes and garden views; $90 for rooms with full kitchens and Duval Street views. Season rates: $120; $110.

Eden House
1015 Fleming Street ✶ 296-6868 ✶ 800-533-KEYS

There once was a starving artist, a friend of mine, here in the tropics. About ten years ago he got a break and moved to New York City. (I hear you saying "That's a break?") There he became a big success. Nowadays, when he comes to Key West with his wife of the moment (he's had a couple), where does he stay? That's right: the Eden House. Nowadays, of course, he demands a room with a private bath.

And there you are. The Eden House has the kind of character that appeals to writers, like my old friend. Europeans particularly like it, too. There's an interesting ambiance, a history; and iron beds just like in your grandparents' house.

In 1990, the Eden House was roughed up for a filming to look like it did back in the 1960s. In real life it looked like a movie set. But in the resulting film, a stinker called *Criss Cross*, which must be Goldie Hawn's only bomb, the hotel looked legitimately funky. Before they left, the movie people put the place back together again, just as it had been before they arrived. This hotel has been through some changes!

The Eden House opened as the Gibson Hotel in 1924. Local legend has it that gangster Al Capone liked staying here, where he spent his days rocking in a favorite chair on the veranda. The rooms are small and efficient, clean and affordable. With some rooms you hang out near the pool, or on the sun deck or the veranda, or in a hammock beneath the cool shade of an enormous ficus tree in the backyard.

The pool is nice, with lots of decking, and a nearby private sun deck allows topless sunbathing. Breakfast and lunch are sometimes served, sometimes not. It depends on how rattled the German chef is that season. But you can always count on a very good dinner, served in the outdoor dining area, where authentic German food is served, as well as the standard American stuff—all of it outstanding.

Suites are $135–$250. Private rooms with private baths are $80–$135. Semi-private (share a bath with one other room), is $65–$95. Several

European rooms that share a hall bathroom and shower are $55–$80.
During weekdays, in the summertime, you can get an even better deal.
Ask about a European room and you might just find the very best deal
in town.

Hilton Resort and Marina
245 Front Street ✻ 294-4000 ✻ 800-HILTONS

Brand-spanking-new hotel that developers claim they designed with an
"historic flavor." In fact, it feels futuristic. Before the Hilton, it used to be
that the best part of cruising out of Key West Harbor was the postcard-
perfect view of the harborfront with its grand centerpiece, the 1891 red
brick Custom House. Now, from the water, you've got to search the horizon for a tiny tip of red brick to know it's still there. The Hilton Resort
has wrapped its 178 rooms around the poor little Custom House and
nearly hidden it entirely. There's also a 400-car parking garage where
nothing used to be.

The Harborside Hilton offers plenty of amenities: a private gym; private balconies in all rooms; a marina filled with plenty of charter boats
for cruising or diving; and a free boat shuttle from the marina to Sunset
Key, a tiny offshore island upon which an astonishing number of condominiums are being erected. On a spot of sandy shore the Hilton has set
up a private beach for their guests.

Harbor-front dining is lovely, but not at lunchtime because of the
heat. On the second floor, the deck bar has a sunset happy hour with live
music.

But wait, there's more: a couple of yacht slips, and a harborwalk that
connects the hotel to Mallory Square, the very heart of the downtown
tourist area. The resort hopes to attract important business people with
plenty of executive meeting rooms with computers and high-tech communication gadgets that business people need, even when they're getting
away from it all. Rooms have big beds, wall safes, two phones, hair dryers,
and ironing boards for really, really fastidious guests. Oceanfront rooms
start at $245 a night. Kids stay free with their rich parents.

Otherwise, a variety of rooms, views, minimum stay requirements, and
local holiday and events price-hikes must all be figured into the formula
to find what rate you'll pay for a room. Too many variations and possibili-

ties to list here. Use the 800 number and check for yourself. Happy hunting.

Island City House Hotel
411 William Street ✹ 294-5702 ✹ 800-634-8230

It's actually three guesthouses—circa 1889—in one compound, with private tropical gardens, a huge deck, jacuzzi and pool, all connected by a meandering red brick path. You can get lost in the Island City House's lush grounds and gardens. That is, I can, and I have. The Arch house, one of Key West's only remaining carriage houses, built in the 1880s, contains six suites, all with full kitchens, private baths, air conditioning and phones. All of the buildings have three-story wraparound porches that guests adore.

Nice features are hammocks on small porches of some units, many cats, and an excellent pool, nearly invisible because of the proliferation of lush plants.

Continental breakfast is served in the courtyard patio. Heavenly! Kids under 12 stay free. Make sure you know how to find your way to breakfast before you go to bed. No pets, no Spring Breakers, no parking available on premises. Rates are $165–$275 winter; $95–$175 summer.

Key Lime Inn
725 Truman Avenue ✹ 800-642-4753

Key West's first motel. They called them motor courts in the 1930s, when a retired circus performer, gruff but lovable Joe Zorsky, cleared away most of the trees that remained of Key West Mayor Walter C. Maloney's one-time tropical fruit grove. The grove covered an entire square block, and right in the middle of it was the mayor's house. After Maloney's death the house stood abandoned, and appeared so foreboding it was rumored among neighborhood kids to be haunted.

Joe Zorsky built 18 tiny cottages on his cleared land and founded the Cactus Terrace Motor Court. Zorsky, perhaps more tolerant of freaks than most due to his background in the circus, befriended necrophiliac Dr. Count von Cosel after he was arrested and charged with "not burying a body." (See von Cosel's story on page 276). When an army of reporters arrived on the island, Zorsky helped set up von Cosel's interview on the grounds of the Cactus Terrace.

*A night-blooming
cereus cactus*

In the 1950s Zorsky, who sometimes juggled for his guests, bought one of the island's very first televisions and set it up outdoors for community viewing. Zorsky's neighbors were invited to join his guests in watching the amazing invention. In 1971 Zorsky was shot to death in a burglary. New owners bought the place, installed air conditioning, a pool, and renamed it Key Lime Village.

A reconfigured and reorganized Key Lime Inn re-opened in January, 1999, by the historical property's newest owner Julia Fondriest. Fondriest has done a masterful restoration of the original Maloney house and has rearranged the property to provide for plenty of parking. There are still 37 rooms, cottages and bungalows, but they've been substantially upgraded. The gardens, once a lush grove of fruit trees, is being restored also.

Prices are midrange.

Nancy's William Street Guesthouse
329 William Street ✶ 292-3334 ✶ 800-71NANCY

It's difficult to classify Nancy's place. It's not a B & B because it doesn't serve breakfast. It's not an apartment complex, because these are transient rental units. It's much more personal than a hotel; cozier than a motel. It's not elegant; it's funky. Staying at Nancy's feels like sub-letting the apartment of a friend with a well-equipped kitchen, recycled furniture, eclectic tastes, and a deep love of paperbacks and magazines. The apartments, each one different from the next, but all of them railroad flats, have one bedroom, private bath and pull-out couches. There are three floors, each of them with two units. Nancy collects antique patchwork quilts and the cheeriest flowered sheets you've ever seen. The decor is kitschy Florida Keys secondhand. Refrigerators are festooned with magnets holding up brochures and postcards. Very bright. Televisions and telephones in every unit, and lots of privacy on back decks. Both units on the first floor have private entrances to the pool and garden deck area. The pool and garden are the only community areas. Guests are welcome to use Nancy's grills.

In the attic there are two dormer rooms, one of them with an old-fashioned scuttle. The attic rooms have small refrigerators and no kitchens. They share a bath, and are a good value—especially in the slow season. And like all the beds at Nancy's, these are dressed in homey sheets and quilts.

Nancy's is located in the historic district, a few blocks walk from Duval and just about everywhere else you want to get to in Old Town. No off-street parking. Rates are figured for double occupancy. Additional guests in the same apartment are $15 a day more. Prices range from $69–$195, based on size of the unit and time of year.

The Southern Cross Hotel
326 Duval Street ✶ 294-3200 ✶ 800-533-4891

Key West's answer to NY City's Chelsea Hotel. Twenty-seven rooms on three floors; some private baths; some shared. A hodge podge of arrangements and possibilities: twins, doubles, queens and kings. All with phones. Air conditioning. No TVs!

"Nobody comes to Key West to sit and watch TV," says David Axtell, owner since 1996.

The Southern Cross is madly popular for Fantasy Fest. It's funky, gloriously real Key West, and downtown. The balcony that stretches grandly across the building's exterior is a perfect place for watching the parade on Duval Street, on Fantasy Fest Eve and on any other night of the year. There's a fine garden out back. Hotel corridors feature magnificent murals of island greenery, flowers, roosters, cats and lizards painted by wonder artist, Rick Worth.

Prices $58 to $125 in the off season, around 20% higher during high season, special events and holidays. Kids welcome. Pets $25 extra.

La Concha Hotel
430 Duval Street ▪ 296-2991 ▪ 800-745-2191
The San Sebastian Troubadours of Spain performed at the grand opening when the seven-story La Concha Hotel opened in January, 1926. Advertised as "the only absolute fireproof hotel in Key West," the La Concha was patronized by high society until the Depression years. The demise of the Overseas Railroad in 1935 spelled disaster for this one, and the Casa Marina hotel. Like many downtown buildings, the La Concha, located right in the center of Duval Street, was closed for several years. On the hotel's roof, the Top, a seedy bar with tall windows offering its customers panoramic views of the island, continued to do business. Customers reached the Top via two ancient elevators that carried them through the decaying hotel, up to the roof.

The Holiday Inn gave the place a $20 million renovation in 1987 and ran it until 1996, when the Remington Hotel Corporation took over. Today the La Concha is very elegant indeed; the lobby and dining room are ultra-chic, cool, and subdued. Rooms are small but sweet, decorated with Victorian-era furniture and ceiling fans. The swimming pool is disappointing—very shallow, and the pool area is kind of crowded—but it's up a few stories, which means it gets a good breeze and uninterrupted sunshine.

The elevator still transports folks to the roof for one of the best bird's-eye views of the island. (The other great view is from the top of the Key West Lighthouse—but that's 88 steps up, with no elevator. And it costs $5 to get in.)

Over the years several people have made suicidal leaps from the top of the La Concha. The most famous suicide was local attorney Fred Butner, one-time president of the Monroe County Democratic Committee, who set up an elaborate scheme to make his suicide look like a murder. He jumped early on a clear, autumn morning. When he was found, several of his pockets were stuffed with cash, and in another pocket, a tape recorder that had apparently continued recording while he jumped. In his last minutes, Fred spoke as if he were defending himself against his black-mailer, ostensibly in conversation with his former secretary. "Hello, Susan. I got your note. Here's the hush money you demanded in your letter. What do you mean, this isn't enough? You've upped the price? I don't have that kind of money!! Wait! No! NO!" Then, the thud, as he landed on a carport roof, six stories down. In his office, investigators found copies of blackmail notes supposedly signed by the secretary, obviously forged by Butner. Within hours, the lawyer's evil plot unraveled when it was learned that the former secretary had been nowhere near the La Concha that morning and that Butner was in some trouble so sinister he chose to kill himself rather than face the scandal that was sure to follow. What was it? No one knows—except his psychiatrist. And he's not talking.

The news crews from *Hard Copy*, and the writers from the *National Enquirer* are all gone now, so all's quiet and subdued once again at the La Concha Hotel. Cocktail time at sunset at the Top is still glorious. Don't miss the view; And take advantage of the lovely photo opportunities on top of Key West's highest building; Pose on the western side of the roof with the Key West Harbor in the background, and possibly a cruise ship or two behind you. A strange anachronism, indeed.

The La Concha has 160 rooms and suites. The Hemingway and the Tennessee are two-bedroom suites, with king-sized beds, which they rent for $300 off season, and $450 in season. "Junior suites" are around $200 off season; $300 in season. Standard rooms with twin double beds, or a queen bed, are $150 off season; $200 in season.

Pier House
1 Duval Street ❧ 296-4600 ❧ 800-327-8340

When it was built in 1965, the Pier House Resort, gulfside at the foot of Duval Street, was the first of the modern, upscale resorts on the island, and for many years enjoyed a reputation of being the place to stay. (Now there are literally dozens of choices.) The complex of low-rise, box-like buildings is greatly enhanced by spectacular gardens and maze-like tile walkways. There are several bars and bistros, all of them quite pricey, but also top-shelf quality. You might expect the rooms to be much more extravagant then they are. But guests are treated well at the Pier House, and that's part of what they come here for. Employees, beautiful and haughty, appear to have been recruited from *Melrose Place*; apparently they are hired for their looks and their attitudes.

An army of rich and famous have stayed here, or at least hung out at the bars or eaten in the restaurant. John Travolta. Liz Taylor. Margaux Hemingway. Jimmy Buffett. Truman Capote. Tennessee Williams. Big-time drug smugglers. And lots of Miami nouveau riche.

The tiny beach feels very European. Women take their tops off. Guys with big bellies talk on cellular phones and puff cigars. Children play at the water's edge. The pool is pristine and still inviting, in spite of its advanced age. The Caribbean Health and Beauty Spa on the property is a great plus, too. You'll think you're in Switzerland! At night, huge tarpon swarm around an underwater spotlight beneath the pier—a oddly hypnotizing sight. Late in the evening the after-theater crowd gathers at the Wine Galley where Bobby Nesbitt is the piano man at the piano bar. Sunset at the Havana Docks, where One World performs, is memorable, too.

A brand-spanking-new, five-story building with suites as well as rooms opens in early 1997. Meanwhile, rooms are available at a variety of rates, from $195 to $300 in the off season; $275 to $400 in season. Rooms in the new building with views of the Gulf of Mexico will be considerably more expensive.

The Reach Hotel (Marriott)
1435 Simonton Street ❧ 296-5000 ❧ 800-874-4118

The last time I lunched at the Reach Hotel, the waiter told my companions and me that Maria Shriver was scheduled to arrive a half hour hence with a party of eight. We ate slowly and were having our coffee when Maria arrived with her entourage: her three children, one of whom was a brand-new baby; the baby's nurse; the other children's nanny; and two bodyguards. Maria looked our way and flashed us a somewhat beleaguered, though friendly, smile.

"She's incredibly nice," the waiter confirmed a few minutes later, somewhat disappointed.

That happened before the Marriott Corporation took over the Reach Resort and sucked the character out of the place—just when it was beginning to have some. The Reach is still quite beautiful in its own way. But a shabbiness and a pedestrian atmosphere have creeped into a property that was, in its day, quite spectacular. Gone are the little things that made it special, like the spiffy little gourmet deli, the superb croissants and desserts created by the house baker, and The Library Bar, where retired editor and movie producer Frank Taylor held court in a bar created just for him. The lobby bathrooms, however, are still some of the most spectacular on the island.

The dining room looks a lot better after dark than it does by day, when sunlight pours through French doors. The once-tiled floors are now covered with a nondescript-colored carpet. In summertime, the oceanside dining room and deck open only for dinner, and, until sunset, the only bar open is the beachside bar.

The Reach beach, a white, natural-sand bay, is one of the nicest on the island. That's why it's so crowded. Not everyone you see sunning here is staying here. Reach guests share the pool, and the waterfront, and a small third-floor gym with guests from nearby guesthouses and B & Bs, who all receive passes to the Reach facilities. The crowds can get pretty thick. And forget about swimming laps in the pool; it's small and always busy!

Rates on rooms with ocean views begin at $162 in the off season and go up to $305 during the week between Christmas and New Year's, the most expensive week of the year. Oceanview suites begin at $272 and go up to $490 during Christmas week. Call the Marriott Reservation Center at 800-228-9290, or call the hotel directly for rates.

The Marquesa Hotel
600 Fleming Street ✱ 292-1919 ✱ 800-869-4631

Here's the extra feature that makes the Marquesa Hotel just a tad different, some might say finer, than every other resort in town: in every closet, next to the fluffy, white waffle-weave cotton guest robes, there is an umbrella, emblazoned with the Marquesa's elegant emblem. The umbrellas don't get much use. It rarely rains in Key West. But the fact that they're there, at the ready in every room, is an indication of how the Marquesa pampers its guests.

The Marquesa has been showered with awards since opening its magnificently renovated doors in 1988. Of particular note is the Zagat Survey, which recently named the Marquesa 17th best hotel in the U.S.! The management works hard to keep the accolades coming with charming features like live orchids in every room, twice-daily maid service, Godiva chocolates at turndown, and room service available for breakfast and dinner. Parking is plentiful and free. All rooms have telephones, voice mail, TV, AC, and security safes. Grounds feature two pools in a meticulously tended split level garden.

The Marquesa, located on a block in the center of old town, is well over 100 years old. The main building was built in 1884 as a single family home. Later the house was converted to commercial use and was, at different times, a haberdashery, the original Fausto's Food Palace, and a bicycle shop. In 1901, the rear of the house was partitioned into 21 sleeping spaces with two decrepit bathrooms. The house was inherited by a daughter, who was a Catholic nun. For many years the place was owned and operated from afar by an order of nuns in New York. Current owners bought the building from them in 1987, did a massive 9-month-long restoration, and opened the first version of the Marquesa Hotel, 15 elegant units. In 1993, they purchased two neighboring historic buildings transformed them into 12 additional guest rooms.

In the Marquesa's cool, bright lobby there are amazing photographs of the Conch-Victorian buildings that are the Marquesa, as they were many years ago, as they are today, and as they appeared throughout the multi-million dollar restoration, for which the Marquesa has also garnered awards.

Like everywhere on the island, room rates are highest in winter and holiday weekends, from $225 for a standard room to $340 for a junior suite. Summer mid-week rates are lowest, from $145 to $220. No kids under 12; no pets.

Sheraton Suites
2001 South Roosevelt Boulevard ✻ 292-9800 ✻ 800-45BEACH

This gigantic complex of nearly identical suites, all 184 of them decorated in turquoise, gray, pink and peach, is a frightening glimpse of the future of Key West and the Florida Keys—if the developers and hotel chains have their way with the islands. If you're looking for a homogenized version of coral island-architecture and ambiance, you'll like it here. The hotel is not four years old yet, so it is still glowing with newness, and still devoid of any character.

Bathrooms here are elaborate. Each commode is in its own private little room; king bed suites have jacuzzi bathtubs; twin double-bed suites don't. That's the only difference. Every suite has many mirrors and drawers to tuck away your stuff (everybody brings too much), an ironing board, a wet bar, a microwave oven and a coffeemaker. The refrigerator is stocked with items like Evian Water, the 8-ounce size, for $3.25. Sunglasses with the Sheraton logo cost guests $12. Coffee, which you make with hot water and instant granules, is free.

Across Highway A1A is Smathers Beach. Some rooms have an ocean view; others overlook the pool and garden courtyard. Less expensive rooms face other hotel buildings. All come with different rates. In the brochure, the Sheraton calls this location "on the sunrise side of the island," which is apt: there is a majestic sunrise here, and a lovely oceanside walking and bicycling path. A couple of good restaurants—Martha's and Benihana—are a very pleasant mile walk from the Sheraton. This is a favorite promenade for locals, and a very busy beach during the height of tourist season. You don't want to be here during Spring Break, when college kids turn the place into a modern-day *Where The Boys Are*.

There is parking, but you'll hunt for a while to find a space. The historic district and Old Town Key West are just a little too far to walk to and from each day, even if you do get up with the sunrise. The free trolley shuttle service is convenient, but you'll need a taxi if you're staying downtown to party till the wee hours.

The Sheraton offers many packages and deals throughout the year. Rates in season are $319–$395; off season: $220–$300. But often you can get a better deal. The national reservation desk is open 24 hours a day at 800-325-3535.

Southernmost Motel
1319 Duval Street ✱ 296-6577 ✱ 800-354-4455
Aside from the standard amenities, there's nothing out of the ordinary here. This is a garden variety resort destination motel. At a desk in the motel lobby you can rent bikes or mopeds or hook up with tours, snorkeling trips, and sunset cruises. Location is dandy, right on Duval—but what location in downtown Key West isn't great? You'll find a parking place in the Southernmost's big lot, although you won't need your car, just some comfortable walking shoes.

There's a nice pool, and if you want sand, a beach. South Beach, owned by the City of Key West and frequented by a motley group of locals and tourists, is about a block from the motel. There's an eatery, a bar and a raw bar on the beach. Waitresses come around and take your drink orders so you can sun and imbibe at once. It's a good beach for kids, too—sandy and shallow. Guests of the Southernmost are also invited to enjoy the pool and sun pier at Southernmost Motel's nearby cousin, the South Beach Oceanfront Motel.

Summer rates (lowest) for a double occupancy room run from $82 to $130. Children under 18 stay free with parents. You'll pay $10 for an extra person in the room. Winter rates are from $125–$195.

South Beach Oceanfront Motel
508 South Street ✱ 296-5611 ✱ 800-354-4455
This oceanside motel's most important feature is its proximity to the Atlantic. You'll find the standard amenities here, as well as a gate that leads you to South Beach, the public beach right next to the motel. There is also an olympic-sized pool and a sun pier.

Parallel to the South Beach Motel pier is the Atlantic Shores, and their wild and wonderful pool and sun pier where guests are invited to bare their souls, and their bodies. The area is the daytime hangout of bartenders, dancers, and other beautiful people of the night. The G-string crowd is clearly visible there, and clearly unbothered by it.

Prices here are jumpy. They rise and fall according to what traffic will allow. Lowest rates are between May and early December when, for around $100 to $140, you can rent a room for two; in-season rates are between $160–$200 and up.

Traveler's Palm Garden Cottages
815 Catherine Street ❋ 294-9560

Seven cottages surrounding a communal pool and garden, all secluded behind a high, flower-covered fence, and connected by red brick walkways, this private compound takes up nearly a full city block. This is the place Charles Kuralt rhapsodized about in his best seller *Charles Kuralt's America*. His bungalow was the very best one in the place—two bedrooms and a private pool with a fence of its own inside the compound fence.

"Is this the pool where Charles Kuralt swam naked?" I asked.

"So he says," laughed a personable young lady with an English accent. "Everyone wants to know about that! Yes, this is where he stayed. But we don't know what he did here, of course. There's a privacy fence."

The Charles Kuralt Cottage, as it has come to be known, is $325 a night during season, and $250 in the off season.

The Old Town neighborhood is kind of iffy in an overgrown, many-cats sort of way, but it's well on its way to gentrification. It's certainly safe, and it's colorful. The busy downtown area, Duval Street and all its thrills, is a short hike away—maybe farther than out-of-shape folks, or people not accustomed to the humidity, might want to walk. A nearby Cuban restaurant, El Siboney, is considered by many islanders to be the best one in town. (If Charles Kuralt dined at El Siboney, he didn't mention it in his book.)

The Traveler's has off-street parking, kitchens in most units, jacuzzis, barbecues, and, thanks to that high wall and many palms and flowers, a wonderful sense of separation from the rest of the busy world. Studios, one-bedroom apartments and private rooms have various prices, from $95 for a studio in the off season to $135 for the same unit during season.

The inn's owners, Clyde Hensley and wife Brigit, confessed to Kuralt that, though they'd enjoyed creating the Travelers Palm, they were growing restless and anxious to rid themselves of all their earthly possessions. But when Kuralt's book came out, with its glowing description of the Hensley's, their kids, and their dog, people began flocking to the place for a Kuralt kind of experience.

"We're having too much fun to leave now," Hensley says.

Bed and Breakfasts

Center Court Historic Inn and Cottages
916 Center Street ✹ 296-9292 ✹ 800-797-8787

Just a half block from Duval Street, Center Court is a compound of cigar-maker's cottages nicely renovated by beautiful and bright Naomi Van Steelandt. After its completion in 1994, Center Court received several awards for historic preservation. Center Court features tropical gardens surrounding a small but lovely pool and jacuzzi. There's an exercise pavilion and a private European sun deck where you may sunbathe naked, but you've got to put your suit back on to venture into the common area for a swim in the pool. Breakfast is expanded continental, which means muffins, fruit juices, coffees and teas. Center Court has become a favorite stay for models working on location for one of many international fashion catalogs shot in Key West during balmy winter months. They love that exercise room. And because it's new, everything in the place is in good working order, and very clean.

Almost everything you'll want to see in Key West is within walking distance, or rent a bike at the bicycle rental shop on the corner. Center Court is located on two-block-long Center Street, that runs through an old Key West neighborhood. Bordering blocks are a marginal blend of old and new. The guesthouse property, however, seems blissfully private and separate from the neighborhoods that surround it. The area is very safe as well as convenient, too.

Center Court has four double rooms in a main guesthouse, one efficiency cottage, a one-bedroom cottage, and two two-bedroom cottages. Children are welcome in cottages, and so are small pets. All rooms have private baths, phones, TVs, air conditioning and ceiling fans. You can put your jewelry in a safe, and every unit gets its own hair dryer.

Rates are $78–$238 out of season; $118–$298 in. Expect to pay in-season rates on holidays and special events weekends.

Courtney's Place
720 Whitmarsh Lane ✽ 294-3480 ✽ 800-869-4639

Kid friendly. Pet friendly. Baby boomer friendly. Hey, it's friendly!
Courtney's, named after the daughter of your hosts, Nashville songwriter
Chuck Krumel and his wife Linda, is a tiny enclave of renovated conch
cottages located between Simonton and Elizabeth streets on Whitmarsh
Lane. Chief cook and bottle washer is one of Captain Tony's thirteen
children, also named Toni.

The first time you wind your way through Old Town neighborhoods
to find this little corner of the world, you'll wonder if you'll ever find your
way back out again! You will, but you won't necessarily want to. Much of
the island once looked like this—innocent and slow; now, it's a vanish-
ing scene.

No two units are alike at Courtney's. Cottages have three, two or
one bedroom, all with complete kitchens. Linda Krumel is the archi-
tect/designer, her work clever and spirited. And durable. You'll probably
want to take her home with you to do over your kitchen or playroom.

Banana tree

Courtney's offers standard amenities, big breakfasts, and an informal ambiance. Park your car in Courtney's free lot. When you check in you'll get a pass for the Reach Beach Club and Spa. It's part of the deal.

Courtney's rates don't rise and fall all over the calendar. There are winter rates. There are summer rates. Period. Courtney's is booked way in advance by people who come year after year. Rooms are $59–$89 in the off season, June through early December, and $79–$109 in the on. Cottages are $109–$129 in summer, $159–$179 in season. Rates are for two-person occupancy only. Extra adults are $20, $10 for ages 12–18, and free if they're under 12.

Curry Mansion Inn
511 Caroline Street ☞ 294-5349 ☞ 800-253-3466

An astute travel writer once described the experience of staying at the Curry Mansion as being much like visiting a rich, eccentric aunt. You might compare it to time-traveling back 100 years and staying in the home of one of Key West's wealthiest families.

Amenities are standard—private baths, phones, mini-refrigerators, TVs, and breakfast by the pool. But the hospitality here, like this century-old mansion, is polished and old-world. Guests are welcome to roam the mansion as they please. Favorite activities include snapping photos in the formal 19th-century-era dining room, whiling away an afternoon in the well-stocked library, and chatting with hosts Al and Edith Amsterdam at cocktail hour by the pool, where excellent live entertainment is provided by pianist/composer Bill Lorraine.

Several older types of rooms and suites are available in the house, while some newer rooms were added on more recently. You may well prefer staying in one of the exterior units. Since the Curry Mansion is a museum, too, (see the Museums chapter of this book for details) paying sight-seers wander in and out of the museum all day. They won't enter your room, of course, but you will hear them milling in the halls. If privacy is of prime importance to you, if your ideal vacation is lying on a chaise and reading trashy novels by a quiet pool, this probably is not be the right place for you.

Rates are between $175 and $225 off season; $240–$275 in season, and higher during special events and holidays. Some parking is available, but from this location you really don't need a car to get to the best places on the island.

Duval Gardens
1012 Duval Street ✻ 292-3379 ✻ 800-867-1234

There's no pool at this recently renovated wooden house, and the style is more Florida house than conch house, but there is a jacuzzi, and all guests receive passes to the exquisite Reach Beach Club and Spa. That's worth a lot. Also, the location of Duval Gardens, at the corner of Duval Street and Truman Avenue, is super. Not everybody wants to be this close to the coursing river of humanity ever-surging up and down this famous tropical thoroughfare, but if you're one to stay up all night, this is definitely the place for you.

Rooms are light, bright, airy and private, each with its own private entrance. Hosts Andrea and Bryan lay out a big, hot breakfast, featuring bracing main courses like a sausage-and-cheese casserole, or French toast. The place accommodates up to twelve guests at a time. An hour before sunset, a spiked tropical punch and snacks are served on the front balcony. Rooms are equipped with usual amenities, including refrigerators and telephone answering machines.

Guests get discounts on bicycle rentals at the Moped Hospital less than a block away, and there's a safe bicycle storage locker at the inn. Parking is available for $1 per day. Rates run between $85 and $170 in the off season; $120 and $260 in the on.

Duval House
815 Duval Street ✻ 294-1666 ✻ 800-223-8825

Considering Duval House's location on the island's busiest street, it should encourage you to know that the place has been named "one of the ten special, secluded, romantic inns in the USA" by *Vacations Magazine*. Many of the town's B & B's and guesthouses are new, but not this one. This is an old, long-established inn, with no unnecessary pretense. It's weathered, but in the very best sense.

Twenty-nine rooms, all different, are located in two buildings. Between them, lie a spacious garden, a pool, and a gazebo. Hibiscus is the house flower; they're everywhere. Many rooms have skylights, and some have balconies or terraces. Parking is plentiful. And here's a new twist on the morning news: in the breakfast room each morning all current guests' hometown temperatures are posted.

Children over 12 are welcome. Manager Renner James is a sweetie, and knows absolutely everything there is to know about Key West.

Summer rates run between $75 and $150. Winter, $130–$250.

Eaton Lodge
511 Eaton Street ✱ 292-2170 ✱ 800-294-2170

Carolyn West's great-grandfather, Harry M. Stevens, invented the baseball scorecard as well as the drinking straw, an item originally used in baseball parks. Today, his innovative spirit lives on in his enthusiastic and capable granddaughter—proprietress of the Eaton Lodge.

Carolyn says she has found what she describes as "liberty in tranquility" in Key West. She's mad about the island, and her passion shows in everything she says and does. Carolyn and her husband Steve bought the house at the foot of Eaton Street a couple of years ago. Built in 1832, the Eaton Lodge is one of the oldest wooden structures on the island. The Wests lovingly restored the house and brought it up to its current state of authentic, 19th-century wooden-house magnificence. Today the Wests host sixteen units, in three houses. The place is full of nooks, unexpected pockets of serenity that particularly appeal to writers and artists and other reflective souls. All rooms have private baths, televisions, telephones for free local calls, four-poster, carved-mahogany or brass beds. And many antiques.

Throughout their numerous travels, Carolyn and Steve have been collecting curious antiques, beautiful foreign objects like a mirrored Thai spirit house, and countless other pieces of fine art. Now they have a showplace for their unusual treasures. The living room is so full of things to see it feels like a museum. Carolyn calls it "a feast for the eyes."

Carolyn bakes lots of mango and guava breads and other treats for her guests, and invites them to feel at home in her spacious kitchen. Breakfast is served out in the garden, a lush tropical oasis planted with palms and a jungle of bougainvillea encircling a pool. Each evening, seven chatty parrots oversee the sunset cocktail hour, with a complete, self-serve bar in the garden as well.

Other amenities include off-street parking, bicycle rentals, and a library of books that Carolyn keeps current. There's a three-bedroom, two-bath house next door with a dining room, a jacuzzi, and even a widow's walk. It rents for around $275 in the off season, or $375 in season. Guests there enjoy all amenities next door in the main house.

For rent are a couple of suites, each with two rooms and a kitchen, for around $135 off season, and $180 in season. The simplest accommodations—private rooms with baths—rent for $115 and up. Length of stay and time of year are all factors in what you'll ultimately pay.

"Some people don't get this lifestyle at all," Carolyn says. "But for the rest of us, it's Paradise."

Frances Street Bottle Inn
535 Frances Street ▪ 294-8530 ▪ 800-294-8530

Historical Preservation Society winner and favorite Key West guesthouse in *Travel & Leisure* magazine; nautical decor, high ceilings, hardwood floors, wooden doors and roomy porches in a lovely Old Town neighborhood; very Southern ambiance and laid-back atmosphere; breakfast on the porch. There's even a dog and a couple of kids.

Back in 1987 when Bob Elkins first arrived in town, this place was a notch away from being a bona fide flophouse. But it was cheap, and Bob was on a budget, so he rented a room here. Now, Bob's fortunes are reversed, and he and his wife own the place and still live here. The bottles you see everywhere are all part of a priceless collection that Bob has mined from the bottom of the sea in frequent Keys diving expeditions. Located on the corner of Frances and Southard streets, it is a nice walk away from Duval Street. Originally the building housed a corner grocery store and a boarding house. Recently it was used as the set of the *Meteor* newspaper office in the short-lived Fox TV series *Key West*.

Six air-conditioned rooms with private baths are furnished with queen-sized beds. A jacuzzi is in the brick backyard. No phones in the rooms. Children welcome. No pets. $85–$115 winter. $70–$100 summer. A bargain. No off-street parking.

Gardens Hotel
526 Angela Street ✱ 294-2661 ✱ 800-526-2664

The extensive gardens that cover nearly a quarter of a city block were designed in the 1930s by a wealthy botanical enthusiast named Peggy Mills. Peggy devoted years to collecting the exotic flora you see here and created this jungle-like garden of palms, sub-tropical plants and flowers. She paved the grounds with red bricks. The brick walkways are still intact, as are many of the fountains and wrought iron furniture groupings. Peggy Mills' famous tinajones, huge earthenware jars for rain collecting designed in Cuba in the 1800s, weigh over a ton each! Peggy Mills is gone now to that "great garden in the sky," but her splendorous earthly garden still thrives. Current Gardens Hotel owners consider this soft, green haven in the center of Old Town as one of the island's greatest treasures. It is a private place, however. To wander these palatial grounds, you've got to rent a room.

The property has evolved to its present state of opulence through the dedicated ministrations of Bill and Corinna Hettinger. After extensive refurbishing, the Hettingers opened the Gardens Hotel in 1993. The main house was built in the 1870s and is listed on the National Register of Historic Places. There's a pool, a full private bar, and Nina Ricci toiletries in every white marble bathroom. Each room and suite is different from the rest. Guests here enjoy the luxurious details and extras you'd expect to find only in a large resort. The Gardens' elegant (complimentary) breakfast buffet is described as "expanded continental" in their promotional literature. Think of it, instead, as "intensified continental." It's quite beautiful, all the more so because of the bright, white breakfast porch where it's served. An employee told me that he has to jog three miles a day to stay in shape after his daily morning repast of granola, cheese, sourdough bread, French pastries, fresh berries, and yogurt. None of this should come as any surprise—the Gardens Hotel is, after all, a member of the Small Luxury Hotels of the World.

Children, but not pets, are welcome at the Gardens. Rates are steep: $200–$575 in summer; $225–$625 in winter.

Key West Bed and Breakfast
415 William Street ✽ 296-7274 ✽ 800-438-6155

Built in 1898, this attractive guesthouse is full of works by many of the island's most fantastic artists—some of them still living, many of them not. Works of artists like sculptor Jim Rache, and painters Craig Biondi, Ron Clemons, Van Eno, and hostess Jodie Carlson are represented here.

Throughout the house you'll find high ceilings, hardwood floors and natural Dade County pine walls. Eight guest rooms are all fitted with queen-sized beds, but have no televisions or telephones in the rooms, and air conditioning is in guest rooms only. Four rooms on the second floor share two bathrooms. If you must share bathrooms, these—with lots of tile and high-gloss-painted surfaces, are as nice as they can be. A porch at one end of the second-floor hallway is very comfortable, with a large hammock and an old-fashioned porch swing. In the downstairs common areas there is a piano for anyone who can play it, a good library, and more great porches. The kitchen is spacious, utilitarian, and unstoppably cheery.

Breakfast is fresh fruit. There's a juicer and lots of oranges, so if you want fresh-squeezed, go for it. Baked goods are cooked on the premises each evening, in time for breakfast the next morning.

In the back you'll find a dry sauna, an outdoor shower, and a large jacuzzi. Orchids are everywhere because Jodie loves them.

La Mer Hotel and Dewey House
504 and 506 South Street ✽ 296-5611

Surprisingly, in Key West there is only one guesthouse with an ocean view, and this duo of turn-of-the-century houses is it. The Dewey House, one of the places where philosopher John Dewey stayed on some of his many visits to the island, has recently been redesigned and incorporated into the La Mer complex. These are upgraded guesthouses, appealing to honeymooners and others seeking the upscale romance of an oceanside retreat. The rooms, all with private baths and several with ocean views, are decorated in an elegant, contemporary motif.

An extended continental breakfast, featuring hot and cold dishes, fruit, and fresh pastries, adds to the drama, and so does the palm-strewn beach located just behind the houses. Bathrooms in the Dewey House feature bathtub jacuzzis; all rooms have televisions and telephones. The

Dewey House is a totally smoke-free environment. Kids under 18 are unwelcome at both houses.

The La Mer, with eleven rooms, and Dewey House, with eight rooms, are part of the Old Town Resort complex that includes South Beach Oceanfront Motel and the Southernmost Motel, located in the same neighborhood. Guests at all facilities are welcome to use pools at the motels, parking, and a guest reservation office at the Southernmost. The South Beach Motel's breezy sunning pier that juts out into the Atlantic is a favorite place.

On South Beach behind both guesthouses, cocktails are served from the South Beach Raw Bar and Seafood Restaurant, located right on the beach. This is a public beach, a lot less elegant than the nearby guest-houses. You can find nicer beaches on the island, but it's convenient, and it's not a bad place to have lunch or dinner.

Rooms at the La Mer are $145–$160 in the off season; $225–$270 in the on. At the Dewey House, $175 off; $280 on. These are prices for rooms with ocean views; rooms without the view are less.

La Pensione Inn
809 Truman Avenue ✦ 292-9923 ✦ 800-893-1193
A renovated Victorian mansion built in 1891 and restored a hundred years later, La Pensione is listed on the National Historic Register. It has only seven rooms, all of them spacious, with private baths, furnished with king-sized beds. No television, no telephones. Breakfast waffles, muffins, fresh fruit, and endless coffee are served on a massive, carved-mahogany dining-room table. There's a private pool, lovely trees and, very nearby, the elegant, double-steepled St. Mary's Star of the Sea Catholic Church. There's off-street parking and one wheelchair-accessible room. Rates are on a par with comparable properties. Management is always on the premises. The location is sensational—a few blocks from all the best restaurants and museums. Summer rates are $78–$98. Winter $138–$158. No pets. No kids. This is a place to luxuriate. Relax, for heaven's sake!

Merlinn Inn
811 Simonton Street ✻ 296-3336 ✻ 800-642-4753

Since taking the place over in 1997, the Merlinn Inn's newest owner has made plenty of changes and upgrades. It used to be that you couldn't see the Merlinn Inn for the thick hedge of aurelia that marked the front boundary. That's gone now, so from the street you see the building's wide veranda and the inviting rocking chairs on it. You can also look in to see a sea hibiscus tree, coconut palms, mango and sapodilla trees, and a pool in a central courtyard.

Property pets are two parrots and a cat. Yours are not welcome. One room is handicapped accessible. All units are non-smoking. There are 10 standard rooms, 5 king suites, and 5 cottages with separate bedrooms and living rooms. All are fitted with bathrooms, air conditioning, TV. No phones, but there is a phone booth outside. Six off-street parking places. Children in cottages only. Breakfast is a nice expanded continental (*i.e.* fresh baked goods; there are a number of fine bakers on the island these days) and served by the lily pond.

Rates: $70–$120 summer; $90–$150 in season.

The Mermaid and the Alligator
729 Truman Avenue ✻ 294-1894 ✻ 800-773-1894

The classic Queen Anne-style building that is now home to the Mermaid and the Alligator guesthouse was built in 1904, a year before the stunning St. Mary's Star of the Sea Catholic Church, directly across the street. The Mermaid is owned, operated and occupied since January, 1997, by Dean Carlson and Paul Hayes. The team lived in Hawaii for five years, prior to arriving in Key West. They live here now, they say, because in addition to a fabulous tropical climate, our island has a wonderful, cozy sense of community that works well with their sense of tradition.

"We consider our place to be a traditional bed and breakfast," explains Dean, "because we live here, too. It's our home and we share it with our guests."

Wine and beer is served at happy hour. A grand breakfast is served in the gardens, in view of the elegant pool and Wilbur Thomas' sculpture of the mermaid and the alligator. (The sculpture, by the way, inspired the original developers to name the place after the piece, rather than the other way around.)

There are no TVs or phones in the island-elegant rooms, but there are private baths. Five rooms in all, each very different from the other. The Caribbean Queen Room, featuring a gargantuan Roman soaking tub, is most dramatic of all. The living room is cushiony and inviting. Dean says he's delighted when he finds a guest asleep on the couch in front of the TV, because then he knows he's accomplished his goal of providing an intimate and comfortable getaway for his clients.

Off-street parking! No smoking indoors. No pets. No children under 16. Room rates range from $95 in the off-season, up to $218 in the on, holidays and event weekends.

Papa's Hideaway
309 Louisa Street ✹ 294-7709 ✹ 800-714-7709

Papa's is a small, homey operation, just two blocks from the Southern-most Point, and one block from Duval Street. Papa's offers small, adequate studios, 4 in all, each with a king-sized bed and pullout futon. Units have private baths, kitchenettes, patios and porch. A shared pool and jacuzzi are within the enclosed compound. Bread and muffin continental breakfast daily. Rent one of these units for $79 to $89 a day off-season, depending upon the length of your stay; $115–$125 during special events, holidays, and season.

Owner Ellen Nowlin, who has been running the house since 1994 with partner Pat McGee, says: "Our guests never feel crowded. We have plenty of room here." No pets. Well-behaved kids welcome. Off-street parking!

William Anthony House
613 Caroline Street ✹ 294-2887 ✹ 800-613-2276

This beautifully renovated historic inn is the winner of two awards: preservation and new construction. It's comprised of four luxury suites and two guest rooms, all with private baths. Located just a block and half from Duval Street, where the action is, it's also near the sunset celebration at Mallory Dock, and that's something to see at least once. Units here have kitchenettes with microwave ovens, coffeemakers, refrigerators—and all have queen beds, TVs, phones, air conditioning and heat (God forbid you should need it). The decor is sweet and frilly. Two of the

suites have sitting and dining areas. The covered porches are wonderful, particularly during a rare tropical shower; the Continental breakfast is efficient. Wine is served at the evening happy hour. No pool, jacuzzi only.
Summer rates, $79–$150, winter $125–$245.

The William House
1317 Duval Street ☞ 294-8233 ☞ 800-848-1317
This fine house has had a long and colorful past. Built in 1902 by a Cuban physician, the Cuban Club Hotel was a meeting place for the local Cuban Club. Later it was converted by the same doctor into St. Joseph's Hospital. During the golden years of the middle 1920s it was the elegant Oceanview Hotel. It closed during the Depression, and reopened as the Casa Blanca Boarding House in 1952. The cheap, comfortable house was a beloved winter retreat for many, some of whom returned year after year to soak up a month or two of soft winter sun.

The house was restored and transformed into a more upscale bed and breakfast in 1992. New owners in 1998 are steadily fine-tuning. All 10 rooms have phones, voice mail, private baths, queen-sized beds, TV, AC, and a fridge. No pool; jacuzzi. Lovely gardens. Jacuzzi. On-site managers are Gert and Diba, from Sweden and Denmark, who run the place with old world skill and charm. Breakfast is served on a wide deck with a view the Atlantic. It's on the quiet end of Duval Street. Some parking. Prices are quite reasonable: Winter/Spring: $129–$170. Summer/Fall: $69–$135.

Some Gay Guesthouses and Hotels

Alexanders
1118 Fleming Street ✹ 294-9919 ✹ 800-654-9919

The three houses that make up Alexanders contain sixteen rooms, and because these are turn-of-the century buildings adapted in 1981 to guesthouse style, no two rooms are alike. In fact, each room or suite is very different from the next, all appointed in a casual, tropical island style. Third floor treehouse rooms with skylights and stained glass windows are particularly appealing. Some rooms have private decks and verandas.

Although this is a predominantly gay guesthouse, everyone is welcome—except children and pets; 70% of guests are men: 30% women. The swimming pool is open 24 hours a day. The grounds are private, and nude sunbathing is permitted on two of the decks. Items on the expanded continental breakfast change daily as does a daily cocktail hour, each day with a different theme, and featuring hors d'oeuvres and spirits. All rooms and suites are equipped with telephones, TVs, and refrigerators; several have wet bars.

Basic rooms rent for $80–$140. Deluxe rooms are $115–$250.

Coconut Grove
817 Fleming Street ✹ 296-5107 ✹ 800-262-6055

This isn't the fanciest guesthouse, but it's the friendliest. There are twenty-two units here in three buildings, two on one side, and one on the other, of Fleming Street. The Coconut Grove has an interesting feature—a sun deck located above the third story of the main building, affording guests a beautiful and private panoramic view of the island.

Another feature at Coconut Grove is six complete apartments, with living rooms, bedrooms, kitchens, and decks. The apartments are fully equipped and are an excellent value.

The pool and jacuzzi (clothing optional) are open 24 hours a day. A full continental breakfast is served daily, and there's a happy hour in the common room every day but Sunday. Every room has a television and all but two have private baths; these two rooms share one bath.

Women are welcome, but 99% of the guests are men. Many of them are regulars. No pets, no off-street parking. Summer rates range from $55–$120; winter: $85–$200.

The Equator Resort
818 Fleming Street ✳ **294-7775** ✳ **800-278-4552**
Back in the 1970's Bill Galchutt, of Miami, and John Kosik and Steve Bass, of Chattanooga, vacationed frequently in the balmy, friendly, old-fashioned laid-back town that was once Key West. Twenty-five years later, older, wiser, and with lots more resources, the trio decided to open their own gay guesthouse in tribute to those wonderful, carefree days of old.

"The Equator is a guesthouse for yesterday, today and tomorrow," explains Galchutt. "We try to capture what was wonderful about Key West then, and we try to make it what we feel a modern guesthouse should be today."

Toward that end, the Equator features data ports on every phone so that guests can plug in laptop computers. There's voice mail on room phones, a definite step into the new millennium. (Many guesthouses don't answer their phones 24 hours a day, so if you need to contact someone in them, you may well be out of luck.)

Opened for nearly a year now, the Equator is a meticulous restoration of an ancient enclave of dilapidated buildings. Men only. Very upscale. Sexual temperature: moderate.

Every newly created room features a private bath, TV, complimentary robes and snacks. Pocket kitchens in some; just a fridge in others. The rooms are painted and tiled in Mediterranean tones; light and bright. Queen or king sized beds. A couple of extra-long full beds. Also one handicapped accessible suite. All rooms are non-smoking.

Full, hot breakfast. Happy hour. Clothing optional around the heated pool and whirlpool. There's always somebody around on concierge duty. Like many guesthouses on Fleming Street, this one has no off-street parking. But why bother to bring a car? You can easily walk to wherever you need to go, or cab.

Curry House
806 Fleming Street ✱ 294-6777 ✱ 800-633-7439

This is the oldest, exclusively male guesthouse in the city. The atmosphere is subdued and rather reserved, which works well in this grand 1890 Victorian house. The house's nine rooms—seven of which have private baths and two share a bath—are furnished with period antiques. Rooms are also equipped with phones, refrigerators, clock radios, and French doors that open out onto long, wraparound verandas. (There's a communal television in the communal area.) Located in the center of Old Town, the Curry House is convenient to all the great restaurants, saloons and attractions. A pool and jacuzzi in the clothing-optional patio area make it unnecessary for guests to leave the premises if sun and relaxation is all they're looking for. A hot breakfast and afternoon wine are served daily. No off-street parking, but you'll find parking on the street, although you don't really need a car. Rates: three separate rates: summer $75–$95, with a discount for a full week. Fall and spring: $100–$125. Winter season $130–$160.

Lighthouse Court
902 Whitehead Street ✱ 294-9588

This is Key West's largest hotel for men, with forty-two suites, rooms and cottages. The compound, surrounded by very high privacy walls, is directly across the street from the Hemingway House and next door to the Key West Lighthouse, a 92-foot tower from where nosy tourists strong enough to climb to the top can see right into the clothing-optional grounds. Sexual temperature here is reputedly quite warm—one employee told me that the Lighthouse Court is like Fire Island used to be in the 1980s.

Breakfast and lunch are served daily until 4 p.m. at the courtyard cafe and bar. There is no complimentary breakfast or cocktail hour here. The gym is much more than adequate, which means lots of bodybuilders stay here. All rooms are newly redecorated and have phones, televisions, and mini-refrigerators. Many have private baths; some rooms share baths.

The Lighthouse Court is a block from Duval Street and a short walk from several fun beaches. Summer rates are $60–$150 per night. Winter rates are $90–$250.

Oasis Guest House
823 Fleming Street ✹ 296-2131 ✹ 800-362-7477

and

The Coral Tree Inn
822 Fleming Street ✹ 296-2131

This is actually one property on two sides of the street, each house with its own name. Your host Victor manages to be in both places at once. This is an upscale property; the Coral Tree Inn was recently totally refurbished and is particularly new and shiny.

Both houses have large heated pools and, at the Oasis a 24-man jacuzzi! Clothing is optional around pools and decks. The daily continental breakfast is sumptuous and, in addition to a standard 6 o'clock wine and hors d'oeuvres, Victor serves afternoon pina coladas at the pool.

Although this is an exclusively gay-men operation, the sexual temperature here is tepid, Victor told me. You'll find much hotter houses nearby. The Coral Tree is more couple-oriented.

Guests in each house have keys to the other, since the houses share amenities. All rooms have televisions, VCRs, phones, refrigerators and private baths. Bicycles are available for rent. A comprehensive library gives information on the sights and restaurants on the island. Parking is available on the street.

At the Oasis there are two rooms that share one bath and these are least expensive rooms on the property. Rates at the Oasis are $80–$125 in summer; $109–$179 in winter. Rates at the Coral Tree range from $105–$125 in summer and $155–$185 in winter.

The Rainbow House
525 United Street ✹ 292-1450 ✹ 800-749-6696

Since Marian Serelis bought the lovely Pines Guest House and incorporated it into her wildly popular resort, the Old Town inn has become the world's largest hotel exclusively for women, and added a new page to its distinctively unique history. Not only was the Pines the Keys' first gay guest house, it was also the first inn to offer private baths in every room. Built originally as a boarding house for Cuban cigar factory workers, it was an apartment house before finally being converted into a guest house reserved exclusively for gay men and women. The original Rainbow House was a boarding house.

Now the men have been 86'ed altogether, and the Rainbow House features 38 rooms and suites, every last one of them with a private bathroom. With the new expansion comes another chi chi pool, an additional deck, and a second hot tub. Continental breakfast is served in a pavilion in the garden area, between the pool areas.

Units are also outfitted with telephones, televisions, and sometimes, refrigerators. All rooms, from standard to deluxe, have queen beds, tropical decor, air conditioning and Bahama fans.

Location is wonderful. At the Rainbow House you won't need a car at all, since you're in the heart of the downtown, just off Duval Street, and yet on a quiet, safe street that's easy to wander back to late at night. The beach is a 5-minute walk away and the area is studded with great saloons and bistros.

When you call for reservations Marion Serelis herself will take you on an audio tour over the phone while you're on hold, if you're on hold. It's such a great rap—and all true, by the way—you may want to come right away. Once you do arrive, a well-connected full-time concierge will arrange for snorkeling, scuba, kayaking, dolphin watches, parasailing, jet ski, bike trails, mopeds, beaches and women-only cruises.

The Rainbow House is a well-managed operation, with a growing reputation. If you're interested in staying here, book early. And remember, it is a lesbian-owned and operated establishment. No men, children or pets.

Rates in season are around $100–$200. Off season, $70–$140.

Sea Isle Resort
915 Windsor Lane ✻ 294-5188 ✻ 800-995-4786

Sun-worshippers will be happy to know that this small resort boasts more sun decks and more sun per room than any other guesthouse in Key West. And you can take your sun on any one of three levels, or, work your way to the very top, where clothing is optional and sunbathing is very serious business. There's a hot tub on the third-level deck, too. If you've had enough sun, wait for nightfall—the hot tub is open 'round the clock.

Rooms at the Sea Isle feature queen-size beds, mini-fridges, and private baths. You'll find a good little gym to work out in, with lots of free weights and Nautilus machines. Off-street parking is plentiful. Pets are

welcome—for an extra $10 per day. The resort is well-located on a rela-
tively quiet street, yet well within easy walking distance of the best
restaurants and shops. Rates in summer are $75–$115. Winter,
$110–$160.

Travel Information for Gay Tourists

Key West Business Guild
424 Fleming Street ✱ 294-4603 ✱ 800-GAY-9759

Travelers considering Key West can write or call for specific information
as well as a free guide to the city. The Key West Map & Directory is a
complete listing of gay accommodations, businesses and attractions.
Information packets are sent to all callers. Tourists are invited to visit
the office and browse through literature supplied by guild members.

The guild was formed in 1978 by a group of business leaders from the
gay community to promote Key West to the gay market. Members represent gay-owned and gay-friendly businesses.

The travel industry publication *Recommend Magazine* estimates that
more than 20% of all tourists visiting Key West annually are gay or lesbian. The gay consumer usually spends more on the average than other
tourists.

Dining

HERE SHOULD YOU EAT? The possibilities are staggering. Is it atmosphere you're looking for? Impeccable service? A good view? Ethnic cuisine? Gourmet food? It's all here—somewhere. The fun part is finding it. Investigate carefully; there are hundreds of eateries to choose from, and you probably don't have hundreds of evenings for experimentation.

In Key West, a tropical island with an ever-changing population and work force, few things remain the same for long. That's especially true in the restaurant business. The eatery your friends loved when they vacationed here last fall may have undergone some changes since then—perhaps a new chef is training or new management has taken over or the place is completely gone. That is not to say, if it's still there, that it won't be just as good as your friends remember it, maybe even better. That's what makes Key West dining, and life, such an adventure: nothing is ever the same way twice.

Keep in mind, too, that Key West's newspapers publish many glowing restaurant reviews throughout the year. The "restaurant critics" who write them, encouraged by free meals and spirits and royal treatment, can make even mundane places sound fantastic. But don't be fooled! No real restaurant critic exists in this town. These reviews often depend on the amount of money spent on advertising: more bucks, more kudos.

A good restaurant review should be specific and up-to-date. But, since claims of greatness actually are not monitored by the "restaurant police," you can't believe everything you read about Key West restaurants (except in this book, of course).

Remember, too, when you do make reservations, that the height of the dinner rush in island restaurants is 8 p.m. Therefore, it's unwise to make reservations for dinner at eight, although, certainly, no one will say you can't. Even fifteen minutes earlier or later can make your wait shorter.

All that said, be assured that fine dining and great food do await you here. Try the seafood: dolphin and yellowtail, conch steaks and fritters; they're all surely unlike anything you'll find elsewhere.

The Cuban food here, too is unique, and addictive, but fortunately very affordable. That's why, at the height of tourist season, Cuban restaurants are packed to capacity. This is the cuisine you'll find yourself craving when you get back home—it's that good. (And don't forget to pick up a cook book while you're on the island.)

Something else to consider: not all restaurants have children's menus, while some have very good ones. In a few restaurants you will be asked to go elsewhere if there are children in your party. If you have special needs for highchairs or children's seats, or handicap access, it is wise to call ahead and make arrangements, instead of simply showing up, fussy kids in tow, for dinner at eight (not eight!).

The following restaurants are only some of those you might like to visit while in Key West. Their brief descriptions will, it is hoped, answer the most frequently asked questions about food, service, ambiance, prices, parking, and special accommodations.

Some Restaurants

7 Fish
632 Olivia Street ✺ 296-2777
The very conchy neighborhood at the corner of Olivia and Elizabeth has such heart and charm it has the power to lift your spirits. It's the real thing, and so is this charming and very popular bistro. From the moment the doors opened to this recycled and newly-owned cafe (once it was the trendy Pancho and Lefty's), it has been jumping, though elegantly jumping.

There's more than fish here, but the fish really is the star of this show. Sauces are perfect. Also stonecrab cakes. Vegetable egg foo yung. Even a traditional meatloaf. Don't skip dessert! Open 7 nights from 6 p.m.–11 p.m.

Antonia's
615 Duval Street ✹ 294-6565

Sicilian and classical Italian cuisine. Two beautiful Italian women founded this place, Antonia and her childhood best friend, Claudia, who grew up in Rome together. Later Antonia came to Key West to start a restaurant with her husband, Chef Phillip Smith. Claudia, working for TWA in New York City, came for a weekend visit just around the time that Antonia and Phillip were running perilously low on set-up funds. Claudia invested her nest egg and became a partner. The partners are often the hostesses, while a tall, all-American blond named Tiffany tends the beer and wine bar.

Service is elegant but not fast. The tone is European, very laid back. If you're in a hurry, dine elsewhere. Same advice if you don't have lots of money. If, on the other hand, money and time are both plentiful, and you're looking for a romantic dinner that unfolds like a long-awaited love letter, make reservations at Antonia's. Menu is a la carte. Servings are small, but the food is so rich, you'll find your appetite satisfied very quickly. Save room for desserts, though; they're delicate and truly memorable. No parking, but municipal parking is located behind the restaurant off Simonton Street, next door to City Hall. Dinner only, from 6 p.m. Note: Antonia's contributes to AIDS Help with an annual and always well attended $125 a plate annual banquet. If you're in town for one of these, go. You'll meet some of the best people on the island, enjoy a fantastic meal, and contribute to AIDS Help.

Duffy's Steak and Lobster House
Simonton Street at Truman Avenue ✹ 296-4900

Duffy's no-nonsense lunch and dinner menus attract many locals as well as visitors to the island looking for great seafood. The dining room is a bright, split-level room lined with lacquered, blond wood booths. Seafood here is very fresh and nicely, not fussily, prepared. No fancy names or descriptions. Straight food. Beef is top quality, and everything is fairly priced. Dinner entrees prices start at $11.95 for a 9 oz. prime rib and top out at $26 for surf and turf. Portions are satisfyingly robust and come with salad, fresh baked bread, potatoes or vegetables. Service is fast and friendly.

Lunchtime fish sandwich ($6.95) is one of the best on the island. Bet you can't eat the whole thing! Lunchtime chicken or shrimp or chef salad plates are $7.95–$9.95. Soup and salad, $5.25. Steaks and seafood available all day. Duffy's is a consistently fine family restaurant with the ambiance of a bustling tourist town favorite, which is exactly what it very competently is. Full bar. Highchairs. Excellent kid's menu. Open daily from 11:30 a.m. till 11 p.m. They won't take reservations, so you might find yourself waiting a bit on really busy nights. Wait if you must. It's worth it.

Bagatelle Restaurant
115 Duval Street ● 296-6609

Remember when Jackie Gleason on *The Honeymooners*, used to say "a mere bag of shells...," which was Ralph Kramden's bastardization of the phrase, "a mere bagatelle"? Well here you are: A mere bagatelle, Key West style. The big draw here is the wrap-around veranda. It's so damned inviting, although the view has been much compromised by new construction on a parking lot directly across the street. Not only did they pave Paradise, they put a brick addition onto the bank and blocked what was once a pretty view. Too bad.

Dining on the veranda is still lots of fun, though. The flow of humanity down at this end of Duval is thick and colorful. Bagatelle has good food, but not great food. And it's a little pricey for not-great food. That whiff of pretentiousness comes from the kitchen, not your server. Sandwich prices are around $7; salads around $8. Bagatelle's excellent seafood chowder is $3.95 or $5.25. Dinner entrees are around $20. Portebello mushroom with polenta is $14.95, and Jamaican chicken is $17.95. Lobster and stone crab dinners are the most expensive. Bagatelle opens for lunch at 11:30 daily. Dinner from 6 p.m.–10 p.m.

Banana Cafe
1211 Duval Street ● 294-7227

Mario Sanchez, woodcarver whose folkish images of old Key West are nationally renowned, was born in this house in 1907. (See a collection of Sanchez works at East Martello Tower Gallery.) Danielle Dahon and her son Christopher Collect came to Key West for a short vacation in June of 1992, and ended up signing the lease for the Banana Cafe two weeks later. They've been here ever since, serving fine food, beer and wine with a French-street-cafe flair ever since. Bacon, lettuce and tomato sandwiches are slathered with homemade mayonnaise on fresh-baked French bread; crepes stuffed with goat cheese and walnuts, or Norwegian salmon and sour cream and onions. Service is good. Entrees range from $6–$10. Breakfast and lunch only, during summer months. Eggs with toast and bacon cost twice as much as you'd pay in a diner for the same thing—and they don't butter the toast! But hey, that's the French way. Beginning in mid-October, several dinners nightly at prix-fixe of $25. Also, live jazz at dinnertime. No off-street parking, but parking is usually available on side streets in the neighborhood. Hours: around 7 a.m. to around 10:30 p.m. October–April.

Johnson's Cafe
302 Petronia Street ✶ 292-2286
Walk-up and takeout kitchen featuring a spicy Bahama Village version of soul food. Pork chops, fried chicken and shrimp, made to order. Conch salad is delectable. Dine on the outdoor deck. At Johnson's you get lots to eat and more. It's an experience! 7:30 a.m.–7:30 p.m. Closed Sundays.

Blue Heaven
729 Thomas Street ✶ 296-8666
The Blue Heaven is is a terrific place for breakfast, lunch or dinner, but the word is out and tourists have made the restaurant a must-see stop on their Key West itineraries. The lines have become legendary. Come early. Sundays are impossible. Summertime is a good time, if you can bear the heat. No reservations. No off-street parking. Lots of shade from huge, ancient trees. Chickens, dogs and cats are commonplace, but usually well-behaved. The food is wonderful.

But it's not just a restaurant; it's art galleries and shops, too. The building has wonderful history: There used to be a boxing ring that was used by several local sparring partners of Ernest Hemingway. And cockfights were there, too. Even a rooster graveyard, complete with tiny tombstones, remains in one corner of the property. Ask to see the gambling wall, once a blackboard listing scores and odds of various sports. Also a water tower that once stood on Little Torch Key and provided water for the crews building the Overseas Railroad in the early 1900s was later taken down and reassembled at Blue Heaven where it stands today. Still later, the Blue Heaven was a "house of ill repute." The tiny rooms in which prostitutes practiced their ancient trade are still there.

In little shops and galleries in the compound, paintings, carvings, jewelry, photography, painted rocks and coconuts are for sale. There's even a a bead business with a plucky entrepreneur who will braid a bead strand into your hair that will last up to six months and guarantee to turn heads back home.

In his best selling book, *Charles Kuralt's America,* Kuralt says "Their sauce could make cardboard taste good!" A remark that will forever be included in ad copy promoting the Blue Heaven. But it's true! Somehow, the informality of the outdoor dining room stretches back into the kitchen as well as into the attitudes of the waitrons.

The Blue Heaven is open from 8 a.m.–3 p.m., and from 6 p.m.–10 p.m. Closes for a summer vacation, but vacation dates vary.

B.O.'s Fish Wagon
801 Caroline Street ✶ 294-9272

Home of the Square Grouper Sandwich. After a long battle over zoning, B.O. (Conch Buddy Owen) has moved his tiny, old-fashioned take-out fish wagon from Duval Street to its current location at the corner of William and Caroline streets. B.O.'s is always crowded with happy customers. They sip beer and wine and chow down on fried fish sandwiches, terrific hand-cut French fries, conch fritters and chowder. Lunch specials feature generous helpings of picadillo with rice or meatloaf and mashed potatoes, with prices starting at $5. Real funky. Real fun. Picnic tables and friendly fellow diners. B.O. says his place is "the only native Key West restaurant on the island." Friday evening happy hour from 6 p.m. till 9 p.m., features boogie woogie piano lunatic Barry Cuda and his Sharks.

Cafe des Artistes
1007 Simonton Street ✶ 294-7100

Reservations are absolutely necessary. Award-winning French/Caribbean cuisine served in an outdoor garden or indoor dining room, as elegant as

Florida lobster

it gets in the Keys. The elegance is established in a big way by the haughty attitude of the servers. They do a hell of a job. In spite of the big prices, fancy dishes, and imperious ambiance, people show up in T-shirts and shorts and nobody at Cafe des Artistes minds, as long as they have the $100 it will cost for two to dine here on excellent, but small, portions of beautifully prepared gourmet food. Duck is famous. Fish is prepared with reverence. Everything tastes wonderful! A local's special-occasion place. Many say this is Key West's finest restaurant, but they don't say it as often as they used to. Dinner only 6 p.m.–11 p.m. No off-street parking.

Cafe Marquesa
600 Fleming Street ☎ 292-1244

Make reservations. You will definitely need them. "Food of the Americas" theme lends itself to a terrific variety of interpretations by celebrity chef, Susan Ferry, a protege of Norman Van Aken. Seafood intensive with Caribbean flair, of course. Signature dishes include grilled sea scallops with roasted red pepper coulis and pineapple salsa, and rack of lamb with roasted bananas and papaya compote. Post-modern dining room, with white columns, trompe l'oeil murals and open kitchen, seats only fifty diners at a time, so service is uniformly exceptional. Cost of a meal here averages about $50 per person. Chef will accomodate special dietary needs. Dinner only, 6 p.m.–11 p.m.

Camille's
703 Duval Street ✷ 296-4811

The line can stretch around the corner in the morning at Camille's. But if you're a person who doesn't mind a half hour or so wait, go for it. You'll probably agree it's worth it. Camille's serves the heartiest breakfast in town—thick homemade bread and toast, banana and fruit muffins, three-egg omelettes full of lusty goodies like cream cheese, asparagus, and salmon, and coffee any way you like; every herbal tea known to man. Lunch fare is stick-to-the-ribs stuff like thick soups, stuffed sandwiches you can barely fit your mouth around, and the best grilled cheese-and-tomato sandwich you've ever imagined. Breakfast and lunch are kind of pricey, but well worth the extra dollar or two; the dinner is an even better deal. Trim waitresses (they have to be trim to squeeze their way through the tight spaces between the tables) wear real island-girl fashions—short shorts, backless shirts, clogs or sandals, and remind you of a Key West version of Frank Zappa valley girls.

Owners Michael and Denise Chelekis have owned and operated the restaurant since 1991. Michael used to be an entertainment director at a casino in Atlantic City. Denise was Donald Trump's director of catering. When she left him, Trump said: "I know you will succeed because you've watched and learned from me." You don't want to believe a guy with that kind of an ego, but you've got to admit, he was right. Denise and Michael have done an excellent job here.

There's rich local color, and the place is always packed. Many of its patrons are locals. They know you'll *never* get a bad meal at Camille's. Open seven days. No dinners Sunday or Monday nights.

Captain Bob's Grill
2200 N. Roosevelt Boulevard ✷ 294-6433

Steak and seafood, mainly; lunch sandwiches with salads are $6–$7. Dinners start at $7.50, and can cost all the way up to $28.95 for Alaskan king crab legs. House speciality, and it's a good one, is surf and turf: prime rib and Maine lobster for $15.95. Look for daily specials like fresh-caught dolphin, or snapper dinners for around $16. Order from the lunch or dinner menu any time. Food is hearty and crowd-pleasing. Big, funky nautical-themed dining room. Highchairs are available.

This is one of the places frequented by busloads of tourists on sightseeing tours. When that happens, you get a dining room full of hungry diners all at once. The service is good, nonetheless, if you see a bus parked in its big parking lot, you'd best move on and save this dining experience for a quieter time. Kid's and senior citizens' menus. Open 11 to 11 daily.

Chico's Cantina
5230 Overseas Highway ☙ Stock Island ☙ 296-4714

About five miles from downtown Key West, Chico's is a favorite stop for Mexican food—not that the food is so spectacular, though it is just fine—but because the whole operation is spectacular. Dad's in the kitchen, Mom and the kids wait on tables. They're always nice and efficient. Choose standard Mexican fare from the menu, like tacos and burritos, fajitas, quesadilla and guacamole, or from the huge blackboard of specials that change nightly. Usually there's one or two fishes, steak, and chicken, all enhanced with chipotle sauce or green chilies. Prices are reasonable—and there is a parking lot! When you leave downtown, you find these perks. Combination platters are served with beans and rice. The salsa is fantastic and you can get it to go. Chico's sells gallons of this stuff to locals. If you sit by the door, you'll watch them coming in and out all evening for pints of salsa.

Chico's opens for lunch and dinner; from 11:30 a.m. till 9:30 p.m. Wine and beer only. No reservations. Lines do form during the season. Closed Mondays.

The Deli Restaurant
531 Truman Avenue ☙ 294-1464

Family owned and operated since 1950, this funky and old-timey restaurant is a locals' favorite. Fried chicken (served with your choice of two home-cooked veggies, $7.50) is the best in town. Veggie platter is four vegetables for $5. Our teenaged son recommends the open-faced roast

beef sandwich, French fries and gravy, $6.50. Order breakfast all day.
Yummy home made cakes and pies are on display. This is where cops and
ambulance drivers eat, and it's packed during the season. Good service.
Smoking and non-smoking areas. Air-conditioned. A few parking places
out front and in a tiny lot at the back.

Delivery Service
293-0078
If one day you find that vacationing has worn you ragged and you simply
cannot budge from your bed, even to eat, call the delivery service. Let
someone else do the schlepping. Order in. Just about every restaurant in
town will happily pack up your meal to go. For a fee (based on zones),
someone will go for your food, booze, cigarettes, lottery tickets, or anything else you might desire. Open 3 p.m.–11 p.m. Closed on major
holidays.

Dennis Pharmacy Conch Korner
Simonton and United Streets ✎ **294-1890**
Since 1962. Jimmy Buffett ate here in the mid '70s when he was a starving rock-and-roller. Locals know that when they need a grilled cheese
sandwich like Mom used to make, or chili with lots of ground beef, or a
bowl of white bean soup and toasted Cuban bread, there's only one place
to go: the Conch Korner at Dennis Pharmacy. It's great for breakfast, best
for lunch, closes way too early for dinner. Prices are very fair. Wander
through the drugstore while you wait for your lunch. This is one of the
Florida Keys' last remaining independent pharmacies. Celebrate with
an old-fashioned milkshake. The Conch Korner is open every day but
Sunday, 7:30 a.m. till 6:30 p.m.

Dynasty
918 Duval Street ✎ **294-2943**
Probably the best and most consistently satisfying Szechuan and
Cantonese food on the island. Definitely the best prices and service.
Lunch 11:30–2 p.m., specials from $5.25. Dinner 5:30 p.m.–10:30 p.m.;
dinner specials from $7.95. Sometimes there's a TV on at lunchtime; you
can watch that or sit at the table next to the window and watch the

Duval Street parade go by. Early evenings, Mrs. Chow brings her children, a little girl and a baby boy, around to see their daddy, who owns and manages the place with shy, Eastern charm. Take out. Reservations. Outdoor or AC indoor dining.

Finnegan's Wake
Corner Green and James Streets ✻ 293-0222
Key West's only Irish pub and restaurant with live, real live Irish entertainment. Guinness, Harp, Bass and Murphy's Stout are on tap. Save this place for when you're tired of seafood. Entrees run between starters like potato leek soup, Irish brown bread, and potato pancakes, and main courses like Irish stew, corned beef and cabbage, and a wonderful shepherd's pie, just like your Irish waitress' Mommy used to make. Opens at 11 a.m. for lunch, daily. Late-night menu after midnight. Full, busy bar. Happy hour 4 p.m.–7 p.m., Monday thru Friday; it's always packed.

Gato Gordo Cafe
404 Southard Street ✻ 294-0888
Tex-Mex. A courtyard dining room with a full bar, including twenty-four brands of tequila. Happy Hour 3 p.m.–7 p.m. and 11 p.m.–1 a.m. Half off all appetizers during Happy Hours. Saturday and Sunday brunch. No parking.

Half Shell Raw Bar
Land End Village, foot of Margaret Street ✻ 294-7496
Famous "eat it raw" T-shirts. Except for raw bar items like oysters, clams and shrimp, the food here is mediocre and served entirely in paper and plastic. Even plastic utensils! Fast, friendly and efficient servers can't help you from feeling cattled. You share long picnic tables with backless benches. The view of the busy harbor is exciting, but sadly, the food isn't, especially for the price. It ain't cheap—in spite of money they save on a dishwasher. If you must have a hot meal, stick with fried fish—it's reliably good. The bar is fun, especially if you're working on your clam-and-oyster-shucking technique: These guys are the best.

Hard Rock Cafe
313 Duval Street ✹ 293-0230
Hamburgers, T-shirts and celebrity guitars in an 11,000-square-foot,
3-story Victorian mansion that was once a shell shop, then a restaurant
and club, now the 57th link on the Hard Rock Cafe chain. Dine indoors
or out. Visit the gift shop for T-shirts and hats.

Kelly's Restaurant
303 Whitehead Street ✹ 293-8484
Many people want to eat here simply because it belongs to film star Kelly
McGillis. But this building is interesting for other reasons too. The building, home of the first office of AeroMarine Airways, once stood on the
waterfront, a couple of blocks away. It was later moved to its present
location and Aero Marine Airways became Pan American Airlines.
That's why the sign out front claims this to be the company's birthplace.
Pan Am started the first passenger service to Havana from this building
in 1927. Flights were twice weekly between Havana and Key West, on a
tiny fleet of three planes called the Nina, the Pinta and the Santa Maria.

Along with a much-needed facelift to the exterior of this very old and
historically significant building, Kelly has added a brewery, an aeronauti-
cal museum and a local writers library. The bar is an airplane wing. In a
brick-floored garden in the back, Kelly has built an outdoor stage that is
quite dramatic on full moon nights. A variety of events, from poetry
under the stars to jazz singer Melody Cooper's stunning one woman
shows, go on here.

Lunches are good, servers are nice. The thing is, nothing ever tastes
the same twice, and you get the feeling that this place is only a front or
an excuse for something really big going on elsewhere, behind the scenes.
Maybe it's a micro brewery. But prices are fair, so have a mound of fried
onions; great! a full bar, happy hour 4 p.m.–7 p.m. Buffalo wings. Cheap
drink prices. No parking.

Café Solé
1029 Southard Street ✹ 294-0230

Chef and owner John Correa is the son of a restaurateur and has worked in the business all of his young life. John has trained in the culinary arts in the Provence, Normandy, and Bordeaux regions of France, as well as in Venice, Italy. Ads for Café Solé describe the experience as "a meal in Provence" and that's a very fair description. Exquisitely fresh ingredients and sumptuous sauces make the food here quite remarkable. Chef John, though interestingly innovative, never wanders too far from tried and true tradition. His Italian and Caribbean-inspired flourishes are right on target.

Fresh fish dominates the menu. Duck, chicken, lamb, pork, beef, are also available most nights. Prices are upscale: Appetizers from $5–$8. Entrees $18–$23, with a good selection of wines fitting the same price range.

The food is very special, the atmosphere understatedly elegant, the service impeccable. But don't take any of it all too seriously. It's a fun place, too. Charming Chef John enjoys journeying out of the kitchen to visit with his appreciative guests. There's even a highchair. Dine indoors or in the garden beneath a lush breadfruit tree.

Dinner from 6 p.m. till 10 p.m. Closed Wednesdays. Make reservations.

La Trattoria Venezia
524 Duval Street ✹ 296-1075

"La Trat" as it is called locally, is one of the island's most often recommended eateries. Cream-colored stucco walls, dark wooden beams, white lace curtains and tablecloths and tiny, faintly flickering candles create a dreamy, romantic atmosphere that most people find irresistible. A little slice of Europe in the heart of Old Town Key West.

La Trattoria is a family operation, founded nearly fifteen years ago by Sicilian brothers Carmelo and Costantino Vitale. The brothers speak English, French and Italian, which attracts an international crowd.

The menu features traditional dishes from Southern, Middle and Northern Italy. The Vitales are also influenced by classic French cuisine.

The steak au poivre at La Trat is legendary, and so are the crepes and pastas. There's a full bar and lovely wine list.

Around mid-December La Trat begins opening for lunch, which is a great value—after-dark sauces at lunchtime prices. Off season, the place opens for dinner only, from 6 p.m.–11 p.m. daily.

Cafe Blue
1202 Simonton Street ✻ 296-7500

In Key West the name Gail Brockway is synonymous with great food. Twenty-two years ago she founded Las Palmas, then Tux, then the Lighthouse Cafe, and now Cafe Blue. Creating spectacular eateries, and the fantastic food served in them, is Gail's remarkable genius. The artist's newest canvas is Cafe Blue.

The menu at Cafe Blue pays homage to the low-fat and high-flavor cuisine influenced by Gail's travels in the places that rim the Mediterranean Sea. Italy. Greece. Spain. Turkey. Africa. Mediterranean cuisine takes from the very best of all these. Pasta. Paella. Lamb shish ke-bob. Cous cous. Fish. Also an excellent selection of fine wines. Outdoor, or air-conditioned indoor dining available. Also a great bar and party room.

Cafe Blue is open nightly from 6 p.m.–11p.m., and for lunch weekdays.

Louie's Backyard
700 Waddell Avenue ✻ 294-1061

Name any restaurant award given in South Florida and chances are you'll find it on the trophy shelf at Louie's Backyard. Long considered to be Key West's very finest restaurant, noted for it's ambiance as well as it's unique menu, Louie's is an island tradition, and a perennial favorite of tourists and locals alike.

Louie's is first and foremost a visual extravaganza. You enter the 1909 classic revival building through a broad, wide-board floored veranda, equipped with several inviting rocking chairs reminiscent of Key West's slow-moving, bygone days. Immediately to the left of the entrance, a tiny, elegant bar is tucked away, almost out of sight. Decorated with rows of chic cocktail glasses and every imaginable variety of spirits, Louie's cozy inside bar is usually peopled by at least two or three shy souls.

You step up several steps into the indoor dining room, and then, through wide French doors into the outdoors again where you'll see several tiers of tables. You descend, a few steps at a time, until finally you arrive at the Afterdeck Bar, a chic little cocktail den beneath a canvas awning, as lovely and alluring as any you'll find on the French Riviera.

Jimmy Buffett once lived in the house right next door to Louie's Backyard and even penned his big hit "Margaritaville" there. From his front porch swing, where he claims to have composed his ode to wasting away, Buffett would have been able to view patrons coming and going in and out of Louie's on their way to the Afterdeck.

Louie's is perched on the Atlantic Ocean on the south side of the island, so you'll hear and see the tiniest waves lapping at the beach here. On full-moon nights, you won't find a more breathtaking view of the ocean anywhere.

The food can be some of the best you've ever tasted. Then again, it can be so mundane the price will seem well beyond the value. Who knows why? That's just the way it goes. It's a hit or miss place, but when they hit —and more often than not they do hit–oh! Appetizers are finely prepared goodies like cracked conch with ginger pepper jelly and adzuki bean relish and spicy seafood chowder with big, fat shrimp, tasty mussels, and sweet corn muffins. Look for marinated salmon, spinach, shiitake mushrooms and kelp salad. The menu changes frequently.

Lunch is served from 11:30 a.m. to 3 p.m. every day. Dinner is from 6 p.m. to 10:30 p.m. Dress is casual to dressy, and most people dress a bit when spending $50 on lunch or $100 on dinner. You absolutely must make reservations. You're going to ask for a table on the outside terrace, right? So is everyone else, so be prepared to be disappointed.

Smoking is permitted in outside dining areas only, and there are no highchairs for babies, and no children's menu. Parking is difficult because Louie's is in a residential neighborhood.

Mangoes
700 Duval Street ＊ 292-4606
Dining in a brick courtyard overlooking the wild and wonderful scene that is Duval Street is the kind of experience people come to the Florida Keys to have for themselves. Entrees feature plenty of Caribbean island goodies like coconut, passion fruit, mangoes, yucca, mojo and jerk spices.

The same chef who owns and runs the kitchen at Antonia's owns and runs this place. The house specialty is tiny pizzas cooked in wood-burning brick ovens. From the dining area, guests are able to view the age-old process of the pizza man throwing the delicate dough. Toppings are unlike any you may have had before: goat cheese, capers, salmon, shrimp, and slivered onions and peppers are just some.

Lunchtime is not so exotic. Sandwiches and salads are often unremarkable. Service has a slap dash feeling. Still, it's a fun and comfortable spot as long as it's not too hot and you sit under an umbrella to protect you from the sun. The open-air bar is a favorite watering hole, and Chuck, the daytime bartender, is everybody's favorite madman.

Margaritaville Cafe (Jimmy Buffett's)
500 Duval Street ✻ 292-1435

Open 11 a.m. for lunch and dinner. Food is tasty, simple and well-spiced, 'cause that's the way Jimmy likes it. Pretty good fish sandwich. Yummy beans and rice. Blackened hot dog. Conch chowder and fritters. Nice veggies. A terrific "Cheeseburger in Paradise," served just like the song says "with lettuce and tomato, Heinz 57 and French fried potatoes." A dish called Couch Potatoes is fantastic: twice-cooked French fries smothered in chili, cheddar cheese, and sour cream. To die for! Come to think of it, you could die from eating too much of this, it's soooo bad for you. Desserts unremarkable. Young, valley girl and boy servers. Funky, oilcloth covered tables and straight-back chairs. At lunchtime, this place is flooded with locals—lots of judges, politicians, and civil servants, since it's located halfway between City Hall and the County Courthouse. Afternoons are busy, as Duval Street shoppers duck in for happy hour margaritas, and at night, Parrot Head tourists keep the place jumping. After 10:30 p.m. loud music is provided by a wide assortment of road bands who appear for a week or two at a time. A long, fully stocked bar. No off-street parking. Air conditioned. Yes, Jimmy does make surprise visits!

Martha's Steak and Seafood
S. Roosevelt Boulevard (A1A) ☎ 294-3466
Right on the Atlantic Ocean on the "quiet side of the island," Martha's is a long-time favorite of tourists who like to stay here. An ocean view from just about every table; piano music every night from 6:30 p.m. till 10 p.m. Dinner only from 5:30 p.m. till 10 p.m. Service is wonderful. Fresh, nicely prepared seafood and steak entrees priced from $12.95 to $34.95. Most expensive is the twin lobster tails. Most dinners are around $20.

Show up in time for the early-bird special and from 5:30 p.m.–6 p.m. take $5 off every entree. People are generally waiting outside for the door to open at 5:30 p.m. No lunch. Lots of parking. Large, nicely dim dining room. Open seven days. Make reservations for large parties.

Martin's Cafe Restaurant
1015 Fleming Street ☎ 296-1183
It's behind the Eden House Hotel. The owner is a German native, Martin Busam, who is also the chef. Busam prepares German and island cuisine and serves it in a quaint, open-air dining area that can be pretty warm in the summer. The Eden House Hotel is where Goldie Hawn's least memorable film, *Criss Cross*, was filmed. Martin's food is kind of expensive, but it's good, and the German dishes are authentic. Sunday brunch 8 a.m.–3 p.m. Closed on Monday. Open for dinner 6 p.m.–11p.m., Tuesday–Sunday. Brunch prices $5 to $10.50. Dinners $11.50–$19.50. Wiener Schnitzel, spatzle, and red cabbage, $14.50. Saurbraten $13.50. Shrimp Teresa Delight $19.50. Great and exotic selection of German beers and wine. Parties of six or more should definitely make reservations.

Mo's Restaurant and Take Out
1116 White Street ☎ 296-8955
Mo is the host, the waiter, and the guy the place is named for. He's funny. Efficient. Entertaining. And the food is terrific. Mo's sister Rena is the chef. Together the brother and sister from Montreal prepare some of the finest French-inspired cuisine on the island in an intimate, thirty-seat bistro in an old Cuban neighborhood. They use Cuban bread from the bakery next door and play Spanish music from Havana on a radio in the kitchen. Mo serves beer and wine only. Too bad Mo won't consider hiring

an additional server for busier nights, because he could definitely use the help.

Daily blackboard specials are pork stew, vegetable casserole, fresh soups, pies and the like. Favorite dishes at Mo's are rock cornish hen, seafood lasagna and stuffed leg of lamb—all under $10! The lamb, a special one day, was so well received, Mo had to put it on the regular menu. The lunch menu features salads and sandwiches of cold lamb, liver pate, shrimp salad, and smoked ham—the majority of which cost around $5.

If fast service is important to you, you will want to avoid Mo's at the height of the season, as well as during the ever-present 8 o'clock rush on any night of the year. Mo and Rena take a ten-week break every summer, reopen in October. Closed Sunday and Monday. No reservations. No credit cards. No bad vibes. Mo is a happy Frenchman, and he wants you to be happy, too.

Pepe's Cafe
806 Caroline Street ☛ 294-7192

Founded in 1909, a year when a thousand or so local citizens were employed in cigar making, several terrible hurricanes hit the Keys, and out in the Southwest, Geronimo, the famous Indian chief, died as a prisoner of war. Read about these and other fascinating historical tidbits while you wait for your food. The menu is pure entertainment, and it includes recipes, too. Like Pepe's red beans? Copy the recipe right off the menu. Thursday is Thanksgiving dinner day—roasted turkey with all the trimmings for $14. Get there early before they run out of bird, or stuffing. Barbecue dinners on Sundays. The grilled cheese sandwich at lunch is the best in the world. Meatloaf is very good, too. Breakfasts are very hearty. Go early to get a seat beneath the world's biggest ceiling fan, built of a washing machine motor and five-foot-long wooden blades. Booths are very private. Sit in a corner and no one will find you. Free pickles for pregnant women. Busy locals' bar out back.

Plenty of parking in the area. No reservations. Pepe's is a little pricey, but hey, this kind of authentic, Old Town Key West atmosphere doesn't come cheap.

Perry's
3800 N. Roosevelt Boulevard ♥ 294-8472

Early-bird specials served daily from 4 p.m.–6 p.m, and all day Sunday,
are a good deal. Dinners include generous portions of soup or salad,
potato and veggie. From $6.95–$10.95. Handy for big families. Kids like
the aquarium. Seafood and steaks, pasta and Greek dishes. More reliable
than remarkable. Bread basket is the best part. Full bar. Good service.
This is one of three locations in the Keys. Lots of parking.

Pier House Bars & Restaurants
1 Duval Street ♥ 296-4600

The Pier House is one of the oldest resorts on the island and still one
of the most glamorous, in spite of lots of new competition. In addition
to the main dining room, which is the fanciest and most expensive of all
the dining and drinking places in the Pier House Resort complex, there
is a Harbour View Cafe for outdoor, gulfside dining, and the Pier House
Market and Bistro on busy Front Street. The Chart Room Bar, tiny, dark
and chic, and a popular spot for dedicated drinkers, serves the least
expensive cocktails in the house.

The Pier House is a venerable institution. Everything you buy here—
a drink, a room, or a basket of conch fritters—will cost more than
anywhere else. The Pier House is devoted to quality service, and the food
is always great. The wonder of being on a tropical island isn't lost for a
single second by anyone around here. Bring money, throw caution to the
wind, be demanding—they expect it here.

PT's Late Night Bar and Grill
902 Caroline Street ♥ 296-4245

PT's claim to fame is his hours. You can eat here anytime from 11a.m.
until 4 a.m. Daily specials start at $4.95. Sandwiches, fish and chips,
burgers, jerk chicken, and home-style specials like meatloaf or roast beef
with mashed potatoes. Seafood. Eight TVs! Satellite sports all day and all
night. Busy pool table. Icy air conditioning. No windows, so you never
know what time it is.

Locals count on this place for supper after hours. The entire menu is written on a blackboard. Full bar with two happy hours daily, early and late.

The Pavilion
Corner Duval and Southard Streets ❧ **296-9977**

East meets West and less is more in this tiny, but unerringly elegant split-level eatery evocative of some chic side street bistro in Greenwich Village. Decor features earthy mosaic tiles; cream colored tent-like window and door treatments. Sturdy wrought iron and wicker chairs, at once beautiful and comfortable. The Pavilion accommodates no more than 40 guests at a time, but the space is so artfully appointed, the ambiance remains beautifully intact in any event.

The menu at the Pavilion is tiny, too, and ala carte, but every item is perfectly prepared and gloriously presented. Choose from daily specials, and items like greens with goat cheese in pistachio nuts ($8), curried tuna tartar ($9.50) or baked crab cake ($8.50). Entrees feature lamb shank with rataouille ($17), pesto cous-cous cake with grilled vegetables ($14.50) and filet mignon in pink peppercorn sauce ($21.95).

The Pavilion does dinner only, from 7 p.m. till midnight. Beer and wine. Fabulous Sunday brunch in season. No off-street parking. Do make reservations.

Rusty Anchor
Fifth Avenue, Stock Island ❧ **294-5369**

"Where can we get fresh local seafood?" Right here. This is the place. The Rusty Anchor wholesale business delivers fresh fish to most of the restaurants of Key West every day. So the fish you'll eat in this restaurant is the freshest of all, just off the boat. Fish and chips for $5. (Maybe the very best deal in the Keys, so I wonder if it will last.) The most tender fried conch in the world. Great local art and photography in a very spacious, cement-floored, two-leveled place, with lots of fast waitresses, thick chowders and fried fish. You'll usually find a few gritty fishermen sitting around the bar in their white rubber boots. The photographs on the walls are black-and-white studies of famous Key West people and scenes, so naturally Ernest Hemingway is in evidence. Don Pinder, the

guy who shot most of the photos, and even painted some of the paintings, is often at the bar. He likes to talk about the old days when he was
a photographer for the *Key West Citizen* newspaper.

That huge, abandoned building 50 yards or so across the street and to
the left is the old dog track. It's closed now, and up for sale. Across the
street to the right is a brand new public park and playground. The Rusty
Anchor is open 11 a.m. till 10 p.m., closed Sundays. Lunchtime is always
packed with local workers who know they can get in and out in a hurry.
Plenty of parking. Big fun.

Siam House
829 Simonton Street ✺ 292-0302
The building that houses the Siam House is one of the oldest in continuous use on the island. It's built of unpainted and beautifully weathered
Dade County pine. La Bodega grocery store operated here for over a century. New owners have given both the facade and the interior a massive
upgrade. Buffet lunch is a good value at $7 per person. Sunset dinners
include soup, entree and dessert for around $12. Service is flawless.
What's missing is atmosphere—a sense of place. You could be in any
good Thai restaurant, anywhere in the world. It's cookie cutter Thai,
well-executed and consistently satisfying. and the cook grows his peppers,
herbs and spices in a backyard garden.

South Beach Seafood and Raw Bar
1405 Duval Street ✺ 294-2727
Raw bar. Liquor bar. Breakfast, lunch and dinner. The food is not great,
but what is lacking in quality is replaced by quantity; portions are gigantic. Servers are friendly, though bedraggled somehow. The best thing
about this place is that it's located on a beach. And there's a bar. Lately
the City of Key West, who owns South Beach, and the lessee, who wishes
to make lots of money did battle over whether or not cocktails could be
legally served to customers lounging on the beach. The conflict was
finally resolved in favor of bigger and better profits, and so around
11:30 a.m., waitresses begin to roam the beach in search of drink orders.
This works well for certain combinations of companions, some of whom
want to sunbathe with the ghosts of Tennessee Williams and his beloved

grandfather, Reverend Dakin (they sunned on this beach in the 1940s), while others wish to commune with more earthly spirits. The restaurant opens for breakfast at 7 a.m. and serves food throughout the day, until 10 p.m.

Square One Restaurant
Duval Square ✹ 296-4300

The bartender at this popular with locals bar is Patrick Hayes, who stars in the restaurant's hilarious television ads and enters drink-design contests, which he often wins. A couple of Hayes's award-winning cocktails are *Monkey Nuts* and *Godiva Mint Mist.* Hayes's happy hour customers are a wonderful mix of locally colorful characters. He keeps them entertained with wacky antics and skillful barkeeping.

The food at Square One is American cuisine, with plenty of seafood dishes. Service shoots for the top. Michael Stuart, the handsome and gracious host, is also Square One's owner. Ambiance is what makes this place great.

Pianist Joe Lowe, a Conch and an accomplished musician, takes this restaurant a few steps above the crowd of restaurants vying for your business. Open for dinner nightly at 6 p.m.

Thai Cuisine
513 Greene Street ✹ 294-9424

A favorite place to call for to-go. Fast, free delivery in the downtown area. The food is terrific, authentic, and inexpensive, and all portions are generous. The restaurant occupies half of a refurbished auto body shop, but in the other half of the building, there still is an auto body shop. Across the street is Key West's handsome Old City Hall, which makes this an important neighborhood, historically. Also, right down the street on the corner of Duval and Greene, is Sloppy Joe's Bar. When you dine here, inside or out, you won't lose sight of the fact that you're in downtown Old Town Key West. Prices are very affordable, nevertheless.

Yo Sake
722 Duval Street ● 294-2288

Sushi bar. Tatami rooms. Japanese cuisine. Indoor and outdoor dining. Indoors is black and white. Tables are very close to each other. High tech. The whole place feels a little like New York City. Tiny garden tables are charming, and the garden is well cared for. But a bar next door shares a back wall with the garden, and the booming music can be jarring, especially in such delicate surroundings. You'll pay $50 for a modest dinner for two in this award-winning restaurant, but it will be very, very good. You'll seldom find an empty stool at the sushi bar, and everybody sitting there is sleek and healthy, the way people who live on raw fish tend to be. Service is excellent. Reservations absolutely recommended. During the height of the season, you can't get near this place.

Jeni's On Petronia
Between Duval and Whitehead Streets ● 295-2827

This wee bistro is strangely located, like a lonely little petunia in an onion patch, on a funky, edgy block of Bahama Village. But don't let location deter you. From the day it opened in the spring of 1998, Jeni's has been, without a doubt, among the island's finest eateries.

Jeni and Rick Alterman, your hosts, aim for quality dining, not a large quantity of customers. There are only 10 tables, and if they're all seated just once during an evening, that's just fine with the Altermans. Rick cooks. Jeni serves. You don't ever need to rush, and your check will never, ever be served with dessert and coffee.

Already famous specialities at Jeni's are the vichyssoise, French onion soup, pistachio encrusted grouper or snapper, Caribbean Queen jerk Cornish game hen, boneless, glazed duck breast. Steaks are a 14-oz Delmonico and a 20-oz porterhouse. Desserts are as carefully planned and prepared as the entrees, with palate pleasers like mousse with chocolate truffle and raspberry sauce.

Call for reservations and take this in on a night when you're willing to let the food, and hospitality, hold center stage. Wine and beer only. No parking. Dinner 6 p.m. to 10 p.m.

Captain Cliff's
Fool-proof Boiled Shrimp

Select a pot large enough so that the shrimp will be under water. Add estimated amount of water to cover the shrimp. Put pot and water on burner. Add Louisiana Shrimp Boil to water (1 oz per pound of shrimp). Bring to a rolling boil. Add shrimp. Water will stop boiling. It will take a few minutes to boil again. Watch pot closely and at the first bubble that comes from the bottom of the pot, or the very first indication of starting to boil, remove the shrimp from the burner and pour enough water off to leave the shrimp barely covered. Add 6 to 10 ice cubes (not to chill; just to stop the cooking). Shrimp will be crunchy and not tough.

Grunts & Grits

Split fresh-caught, cleaned grunts and dip in flour seasoned with salt and pepper. Fry well on both sides. Serve with hot buttered grits.

Fresh Seafood Available on Keys Menus

Conch—Imported from the Bahamas, but they are the same as conch in local waters. There are just plenty more available there. Ours are endangered. Be warned that conch is tough but interestingly different from anything else you've tasted.

Dolphin or Mahi Mahi—The fish, not the mammal! Throughout the tourist season, many restaurants will offer dolphin fish as their catch of the day. It's plentiful and easy to clean, to cook, and to serve. With very little fuss, dolphin fish can easily be turned into an elegant and tasty dish. In some places dolphin fish is referred to as mahi mahi, so as to avoid confusing it with the aquatic mammal thought by some scientists to be more intelligent than man.

"I wish I had a nickel for every time one of my customers accused me of killing Flipper and serving him up for dinner," a veteran Duval Street waiter once said.

Dolphin comparisons: the fish (foreground) and the mammal (porpoise, background)

Florida or Spiny lobster—Although the lobsters, or bugs, you get from Florida waters are quite different from their northern cousins—they're tougher, and they're clawless—a skillful cook can make a nice bug sing. The trick is to cook them very briefly. Lobster season runs from August through the end of March. If you order lobster at other times of the year, you'll eat frozen.

Grouper—If you like cod or haddock or scrod, you'll love grouper. It's lean, chunky, firmer and flakier than dolphin and, most people believe, has more flavor.

Grunts—A staple and longtime local favorite feast, good for breakfast, lunch or dinner. You will rarely see grunt fish listed on any restaurant's daily special board, however. In Depression-era Key West, grunts and grits was a regular meal for Conch families. It combined resourcefulness (anyone can catch a grunt!) with inexpensive grits. The grits were handed out, free of charge, along with flour, sugar, butter and milk at the WPA project office on Whitehead Street, where the Green Parrot Bar stands today. An average-sized grunt weighs about a pound and is easily caught off any bridge or pier. Grunts are a staple catch on party boats, and yes, they're called grunts because of the noise they make when you catch them.

Maybe the Tourist Development Council should come up with a new name for them to bring them back into vogue.

Scallops—They're not indigenous to the Keys but in such demand that you will see them offered on many menus. They're imported, most likely frozen, but they are certainly not objectionable, since they freeze well. But fishes from local waters are delicious, and as fresh as you could ever hope for. Therefore, we recommend that you pass up the scallops and go for the local fishes.

Shark—You will see shark on "specials" menus, but not often. Some people like it just fine and say it tastes similar to swordfish. Some folks deal with it by squeezing lots of fresh lemon on it. An old South Florida trick for preparing shark for eating is to soak it in salt water in the refrigerator for a few hours. Then, generally, shark is grilled. Some adventurous types do order shark when it's offered, and they'll probably tell you it tastes pretty good. But a shark is a huge, oily muscle of a fish. So many others are so much sweeter, in disposition and in flavor.

Snapper—Yellowtail, red, mangrove or grey. There are many kinds in the Keys, and any one of them is as good as the next. Snapper would probably be most people's choice for the most delicious fish caught in local waters. Snapper is so delicious that once you are initiated, you will find yourself searching and hoping for more. Yellowtail is the snapper you see most often on menus.

Shrimp—In 1984, one windy winter evening, my husband threw his cast net off the end of the White Street pier. Minutes later he pulled in a half pound of pink shrimp. Again and again he tossed the net into the water, filling it each time with shrimp. He caught around 30 pounds! Now, every time we walk or drive near the White Street pier, Michael retells the story of that magical night when the wind was just right and 30 pounds of pink gold swam into his net.

Shrimp is America's most widely eaten seafood, and certainly a staple of most Keys restaurants. Shrimp is a huge local harvest. Although there are many varieties of shrimp available on the market, Tortuga pink shrimp, taken from the shrimp beds located some 70 miles west of Key West, are considered superior to all.

There are countless ways to enjoy fresh shrimp. Our favorite is boiled, in Old Bay Seasoning, then peeled and dipped in cocktail sauce laced with lots of horseradish and key lime juice. Very simple to prepare!

Stone Crab—Of the thousands of edible species of crab in the world, the heavenly stone crab is the main one indigenous to this area. Stone crab legs are harvested from October 15 through May 15. Only one leg is taken from a single crab. The creature, returned to the water, regenerates another. Compare the taste of a stone crab to that of a Maine lobster claw. Very delicate, and many shellfish connoisseurs believe it's the finest-tasting crab on the planet.

Tuna—A grilled tuna steak tastes something like the very best steak you ever had. Odd, huh? There's nothing better than fresh tuna. There's nothing worse than not fresh tuna. You may be offered black fin, blue fin, or yellow fin. Have it. Eat it rare! Eat it raw! Tuna is a favorite of sushi chefs.

Wahoo—O.K., so they have parasitic worms called wahoo worms in their guts. The worms won't hurt you! If I hadn't told you, you would never have known. Unless, of course, you pulled one out of the water and pre-pared it for supper. In that case, you'd be glad I told you.

Wahoo is the largest member of the mackerel family. Mackerel is a somewhat oiler fish. November and December are Wahoo months here. Wahoo is a very tough guy to catch and is usually caught by anglers look-ing for a fight with marlin, dolphin or tuna.

Stone crab

Conch Cuban Cuisine

THE BEST DINING-OUT or taking-out deals in Key West are found in the Cuban restaurants, but beware: Cuban cuisine is addictive. Dining in a Cuban eatery is an adventure unique to Southern Florida. The people who work in Cuban restaurants don't take themselves, or their customers, too seriously. Cuban servers, often an entire family in each restaurant, are warm, easy-going and friendly. They won't mind if you practice your Spanish when you order, so go ahead.

What makes Cuban food taste so good is the heavy-handed use of fat. Lard is the first ingredient listed on the Cuban bread wrapper, followed by white flour, sugar, and salt. Cafe con leche (coffee with milk) is sometimes made with evaporated milk and sugar. Flan, a sweet custard dessert served floating in golden sugar syrup, is made of condensed milk and many eggs. The low-fat revolution hasn't caught up with Keys Cubans yet. Cuban bean soups are studded with chunks of pork, stewed to mouth-watering tenderness. Only black beans, a Cuban staple, are cooked meat-free.

Some of the mouthwatering and quirky sounding favorites on most Cuban menus are Italian style liver: strips of beef liver, onion, peppers and garlic, seasoned and sauteed in oil; fried pork chunks: first roasted, then deep-fried chunks of fatty pork; piccadillo: ground beef fried with onions, peppers, tomato sauce, cumin, olives and raisins; and ropa vieha (translation: old clothes): shredded flank steak boiled, then stewed in tomato sauce. With every Cuban meal, local restaurants serve buttered and toasted Cuban bread, a substantial scoop of rice, fried plantains, and a cup of black beans. You dump the beans on the rice.

"White or yellow rice?" the waitress will ask. This is an aesthetic call; either color tastes the same.

French fries and salads are served as an alternate choice to beans and rice. But go for the beans and rice. You can eat French fries and iceberg lettuce salad anytime.

A bowl of white bean or lima bean or chicken soup, with a side of toasted bread, makes a substantial meal. Rice and beans, with a side order of plantains, makes a meal, too.

Service in a Cuban restaurant is fast, efficient and never fussy. You can ask for your waitrons to describe a dish, and they will—if they speak English.

Cafe Con Leche

Visiting any Cuban coffee stand takes me back to my earliest days on the island when I fell into the habit of visiting the nearest shop first thing every morning for a large cafe con leche and Cuban toast. At Cuban coffee shops, girls like me—and there were lots of us—were called "hippas," the feminine version of hippies, long after the decade of love was over.

It is not unusual for newcomers to find themselves hooked on Cuban coffee. The island's sultry, balmy calm induces most people to start nodding around mid-afternoon. That's when a blast of sweet, Cuban coffee works magic.

Cuban coffee, which isn't actually Cuban at all—there are no Cuban food products in America, there's an embargo on—is rumored to be considerably stronger than the regular Colombian or Peruvian stuff Americans are used to. But actually, it probably isn't stronger at all. It's espresso coffee, so the beans are roasted longer, and darker, but that doesn't necessarily mean it's any higher in caffeine than what you've been drinking at home. What hooks you, what kicks you in the head every time, is that jolt of concentrated caffeine along with two teaspoons of sugar. Ask them to cut down on the sugar.

Cubans are an earthy people and very big on charm. Visiting the Cuban coffee stand is guaranteed to hike your enthusiasm—no matter what you drink there.

Some Cuban Restaurants
and Coffee Stands

El Siboney Restaurant
900 Catherine Street ✱ 296-4184

In Key West, the people's choice of the best Cuban restaurant is an ever-changing thing. Every place seems to have its years of glory, its turn at the top. Today, many people will tell you El Siboney is the best.

The same family has owned and operated El Siboney for eleven years. El Siboney serves breakfast, lunch and dinner. The waitresses wear red shirts and black pants. El Siboney takes no credit cards—cash only. During season people wait on line to get in. There's a counter, and plenty of tables in smoking and non-smoking sections. Photographs of Cuban scenes are on the walls.

El Siboney is open from 7 a.m. until 9 p.m., Monday through Saturday. They're closed on Sundays and holidays.

La Lechonera
3100 Flagler Avenue ✱ 292-3700

La Lechonera in English means "the pig" and this restaurant pays homage to pork with every imaginable poster, knick knack, postcard and symbol gracing the walls and shelves of the cafe's huge interior, even a life-sized painted piggie out front that kids love to ride, and adults love to and have their pictures taken next to.

Open daily from 8 a.m. till 10 p.m.

Five Brothers
930 Southard Street ✱ 296-5205

The best bollos (pronounced "boy-ohs"), ground black-eyed peas, seasoned with garlic, salt and pepper, deep-fried and served in greasy, little brown bags. Also Cuban-style sandwiches and cheeseburgers on Cuban bread are memorable, and coffee made to order. Everything is made to go—outside you can sit and eat on a couple of benches. It's a small store, packed with nifty machines like the ones you need to make authentic cafe con leche, canned chorizo sausages packed in lard, and castille soap.

Busy at lunchtime. Open 6 a.m. till 6:30 p.m. except Sunday, when they close at 1 p.m.

Jose's Cantina
800 White Street ✹ 296-4366

Jose's is generally nowhere nearly as hectic as El Siboney, Old Town's busiest Cuban restaurant, possibly because the prices are a bit higher at Jose's. Sometimes, folks hungry for Cuban head over to Jose's when the line is too long at El Siboney. Jose's food is every bit as good as you can get anywhere. Jose does a big take-out business; it's fun to order a paella or roast pork dinner to go.

La Dichosa
1206 White Street ✹ 296-6188

If you're lucky, Felix is the counter man when you find your way to La Dichosa. La Dichosa in Spanish means "the chosen." Felix will make your coffee, sell you a guava cheese pastry or peanut butter cookies or bearclaws or small aluminum cups of rice pudding and flan. If you sit at one of the three tables while you sip your cafe con leche, Felix will even entertain you. He's a funny, happy fellow.

The bakers at La Dichosa begin their work in the wee hours of the morning, way before dawn. They bake 3,000 loaves of Cuban bread in two styles. One is deluxe, identified by a decorative cord that runs right down the middle of the loaf; that one sells for $1. The bread without the middle cord is eighty cents. At dawn, bread is being delivered all over town. Five Brothers is La Dichosa's biggest customer, buying 75 loaves of the good stuff every day.

La Dichosa opens before dawn and shuts down for the day around 2 p.m.

Bars

PEOPLE WHO LOVE HANGING IN BARS will be thrilled to discover Key West. The list that follows highlights a few old favorites and/or famous reputations. As wild as these islands are, we still abide by a law that says no booze shall be sold before noon on Sundays, presumably so that no one will get too oiled up to go to church. Some restaurants feature champagne brunches where they offer complimentary spirits, thus staying legal. No selling, you see.

Some Bars

Afterdeck Bar at Louie's Backyard
700 Waddell Street ❧ 294-1061
Careful now, this is a very treacherous place. Very charming, very seductive. The full moon never looked more brilliant than it does from the Afterdeck. After a few hours and a few drinks, you might find yourself thinking things like "Hey…why don't I just wrap things up at home, move back, and stay for good? I could tend bar. Or wait on tables. Or work in construction. Why not?"

You've been warned…

Atlantic Shores
510 South Street ❧ 296-2491
Not a family place! Not a place for the easily shocked. Certainly not a place for homophobes. (Actually, all of Key West is a bad destination for homophobes!) If you love picnics and cookouts, you'll love having your lunch—tuna sandwich, hot dogs or burgers—at this seaside bar and eatery. A pool and an ocean are here for swimming and sunbathing. Clothing is optional, so count on seeing nudity, as well as near-nudity. Food is ample and cheap. A bar, good service, and the $2 rental on all-day deck chairs make this a great place for uninhibited hedonists. They're here, too. But oh! In the summertime it is so hot, even on cool

days—no wonder everybody is stripped down to near or complete nudity. Limited off-street parking.

Wax (At Cafe Blue)
1202 Simonton Street ✹ **296-7500**

It has become customary lately for the after-hours crowd to gather at Wax, a trendy, late-night club scene behind the Cafe Blue in the building that once housed the infamous Full Moon Saloon. Full bar, cozy arrangements of fat, stuffed sofas and chairs, low tables, plenty of room for dancing, and a crowd-pleasing DJ spinning the records. The regulars are mostly young, attractive straight kids, many of them European, many of them employed in Key West's downtown restaurant industry. That's why the party rarely gets a head on until around 11 p.m. or so. Wax rocks till the wee hours. Closing time is 4 a.m.! Plenty of free parking in the area.

Boston Billie's House of Blues
6 Charles Street ✹ **292-1155**

Jazz in the Key of West. There are very few jazz clubs on the island, so the recently opened Boston Billie's has been welcomed by jazz enthusiasts and the people who entertain them. Boston Billie's is located way downtown in a backstreet garden reminiscent of the Latin Quarter of New Orleans. House band is the Delta Dawgs, who play host to fine local talent like Bill Blue and R. B. Tolar. The music's important here, and so are the grilled steaks. Blues nightly.

Bull & Whistle
280 Duval Street

You can't miss the bull charging through the cinder block wall. I know several couples who met for the first time at "The Bull," as it is known locally, a long-time institution. You don't have to enter the premises to decide whether or not you want to drink here and listen to Michael McCloud's music; get a sneak preview on the sidewalk right outside. It's a good resting spot on Duval Street: Open air. Funky. Live. Relax over a beer, some great, live local music, and consider your next move. The Fabulous Spectrelles perform here, too. Check schedules on a chalk board out front.

Captain Tony's Saloon
428 Greene Street ✶ 294-1838.

Yes, Hemingway really did hang out here in the '30s, when the place was called the Blind Pig, and then Sloppy Joe's. It was operated by Hemingway's good fishing buddy, Joe Russell, who was given the nickname "Sloppy" by Papa himself. (Hemingway was fond of nicknaming.) Martha Gellhorn, who was to become the third Mrs. Hemingway, came to Sloppy Joe's in 1936 looking for Hemingway, and she quickly found him.

Key West's own swashbuckler, Captain Tony, bought the place in 1958 and owned it for several decades. Mayor Emeritus Tarracino (he was mayor from 1989 to 1991) came to Key West from Elizabeth, New Jersey, after a sinister-sounding misunderstanding with a bookie. In Key West he became a charter boat captain, and eventually a barkeep at Captain Tony's, where his craggy fame has grown by leaps and bounds. Charisma is this guy's middle name, and if you haven't read about him in some newspaper, magazine or book somewhere, where have you been? Members of the press love Captain Tony for the free beers he happily dispensed to them at his saloon, and for his outrageous philosophies and opinions.

Captain Tony has thirteen children, born to a half dozen beautiful women. The last son showed up in 1995, having just been told by his mother of his father's identity. Imagine your mom pulling out the latest edition of *People Magazine* and saying, "Son, this man—Captain Tony—is your father." The son journeyed to Key West and showed up just in time for a tear-jerky Christmas reunion with his brothers and sisters, who report that he fit right in with the clan.

Captain Tony sold Sloppy Joe's in the early '90s, and retired. In 1996 the Captain celebrated his 80th birthday.

Conch Flyer Restaurant & Lounge
Key West Airport ✶ 296-6333

This place is pretty much like dated airport lounges everywhere—kind of dark and gloomy, no matter how brilliantly sunny the day, and filled with desperate characters: drab waitresses, people afraid of flying, people hoping for happy reunions, or mourning the departure of lovers, or celebrating the departure of relatives and friends. Through the years this place has been unable to shake its seediness. In fact, they haven't even tried. Opens at 5 a.m. for breakfast and closes by midnight. The menu is sandwiches only, until 7 p.m.

Diva's
711 Duval Street ✶ 292-8500

Some of the island's finest female illusionists perform in this quintessentially Key West club. The doors open at noon, and happy hour is until 8 p.m. At 10 p.m., DJs imported from all over Florida to mix music in this great room, begin blasting dance music.

Showtimes are 9:30 and 11:30, and shows are quite fantastic. If you have never seen female illusion developed into an art form, this is the place for you. You won't believe your eyes! Dana Douglas. Vogue. Randy Roberts, and other great illusionists from around the world.

There's never a cover charge at Diva's. And the staff and crowd is mixed and fun. No attitude, so everyone, gay or straight, feels comfortable here. Diva's has taken the place of the Copa, which reigned as everybody's favorite gay night club until it burned to the ground in August 1995.

This place is a little different from that. A little more modern. Friendlier. Brighter. More mixed and more fun.

Flagler's at the Casa Marina
1500 Reynolds Street ✶ 296-3535

Coffee Butler plays piano here, and he's a local celebrity you must not miss. Old-time visitors might remember him and his ensemble—Coffee Butler and his Cups. These days, it's just Coffee, from 8 a.m. till 12 a.m., Thursday, Friday and Saturday nights.

Sun Sun Beachside Pavilion at the Casa Marina Resort
1500 Reynolds Street ✷ 296-3535

Live entertainment and refreshing tropical drinks add to the flavor of this favorite island retreat.

Full Moon Saloon

It's gone now, but you're probably looking for it anyway. Once it was the local, late-night bar that was home away from home for infamous drug dealers, smugglers, island entrepreneurs, champagne dolls and cocaine whores. That scene is all over now—fodder for the history books. Too bad you missed it. Actually, it's probably better that you did.

Green Parrot
601 Whitehead Street ✷ 294-6133

The first and the last bar on US 1. A longtime locals' bar, busy from the time it opens at 10 a.m. to the seedy wind-down at 4 a.m. Open air, no glass in the windows, just spidery wrought iron to keep out thieves when the place is closed. Unusual artwork and slogans are pasted on the walls. Once this place was called the Brown Derby, and before that it was a morgue, and in the 1930s, it was the place where the WPA handed out food and clothes to broke natives. The building is now listed in the National Register of Historic Places.

You'll find friendly bartenders, pool tables, pinball, darts, and the best jukebox in town. Never a cover; never a minimum. Great live entertainment on weekends. Open-mike poetry slams are raucous and renowned as are best tattoo contests. Plenty of advertising in local papers let you know what's going on. You'll make friends fast in this bar. The sign above the bar says it all: "No Sniveling."

Havana Docks
Pier House (Upstairs) ✷ 296-4600

Everything at the Pier House is done with as much flair as the all-American staff can muster. The bar that stretches across the width of the building facing the sunset is an elegant place to watch the sun go down. Local soca duo One World plays Monday–Friday beginning around 5 p.m., good live music during sunset happy hour. Dancing to live music again starts at 10 p.m. with various acts and themes each night. Check plentiful local listings or phone for today's entertainment.

Hog's Breath Saloon
400 Front Street ✺ 296-4222
A bar inside. A bar outside. Three bars in all, and seven televisions. The great live music starts every afternoon at 1 p.m. sharp. It was originally founded in Fort Walton Beach, Florida, in 1976 by Jerry Dorminy, a native of Birmingham, Alabama, who views drinking as a sport just as important as sailing or fishing. Additional Hog's Breath Saloons are located in the French Quarter of New Orleans and in Cancun, Mexico. The cult of world travelers faithful to the Hog's Breath Saloons are called Hog Heads, a kind of Yuppie Dead Head cult, they say.

Key West's Hog's Breath features a daily happy hour from 5 p.m.–7 p.m., with live entertainment all afternoon and evening, and a busy raw bar and a world-famous T-shirt concession that sells a truly amazing number of shirts. Enjoy light cuisine like sandwiches, conch fritters, raw seafood, Caesar salad and burgers. Their ads claim their drink prices are the lowest on Duval and urge you to remember: "Hog's Breath is better than no breath at all." Open 11:30 a.m.–1:30 a.m. daily.

Key West Bar and Grill
Down Under Sports Bar ✺ 1970 N. Roosevelt Boulevard ✺ 294-1970
This is a two-level operation but all under the same roof (and management). Downstairs is the Down Under Bar, "The bar with balls," the ads say. The Down Under is touted as a sports bar, and indeed, you won't have to worry about losing track of your favorite team's score with three televisions constantly going.

The pool is free here, and so are games of darts and bocce ball. This is Key West's only weatherproof bocce ball court and is the officially sanctioned court for rained-out league games. Bocce is big in Key West, and if you haven't played it before, this is the place to get a friendly local to show you how it's played.

Many true-life, real day-to-day Key Westers hang out at the Down Under. These are working men and women, laborers who come here on rained-out afternoons, and waitrons and bartenders who come here to sit among friends to while away the hours between work shifts. The Down Under has its fair share of characters—it's a locally colorful place.

Upstairs, Friday's features some pretty remarkable snacks: baby back ribs, pot stickers, fish fingers, and nachos, all complimentary to the happy-hour gang.

Schooner Wharf Bar
Filet Mignon Recipe

Take four filets and cook quickly over high heat until medium rare. In a large bowl mix

1 pint Jack Daniel's
1 pint Courvoisier
1 pint vodka
2 tsp. bitters
2 tsp. lemon rind
1 qt. Perrier

Dip filets quickly into the liquid mix.
Remove and pat dry.
Slice filets into small chunks.
Throw to the dogs.
Drink the gravy.

Rick's/Durty Harry's/Rumrunners
202-208 Duval Street ✶ 296-5513

This is a rocking entertainment complex: Big screen TV's. Satellite dishes. Sports forever. Live entertainment. Rock 'N Roll. Late-night karaoke daily, 11 p.m. till closing. Nine bars! Big party spot, noisy, frantic and young. A full bar and live entertainment nightly. Open from 10:30 a.m. to 4 a.m. Monday through Saturday; noon till 4 a.m. Sunday.

Happy hour daily. "Bogey says the best live entertainment and lowest drink prices in the islands...Rick's."

Behind Rick's: Durty Harry's. Live hard rock six nights a week and televised sports delivered via two satellite dishes. Raucous. Young.

Rumrunners, where reggae rules. Upstairs, there is a topless bar.

Schooner Wharf
202 William Street ✹ 292-9520
A salty, dockside bar with a raucous, swashbuckling atmosphere, it's unmatched anywhere in downtown Key West. A big-time favorite, with happy hours, parties, fundraisers. Music begins late afternoon (sixish) and goes on till two.

Sloppy Joe's Bar
201 Duval Street ✹ 294-5717
There's a whole book about Sloppy Joe's illustrious 60-year history, written by local historian Sharon Wells, and you can buy it in the Sloppy Joe's gift shop. Latest news from Sloppy's: air conditioning! Installed in February '96, just in time for the steamy summer months and the Hemingway Look-alike Contest. Bless them. The coolest place of all is at the door, very inviting. Also, world-famous Hemingway shirts in every color of the rainbow: you'll spot them everywhere—from Paris to Halifax to Laguna Beach. Did Hemingway really drink here? Yes!

Live music all day and all night.

Turtle Kraals
Lands End Village ✹ 294-2640
You can wear this T-shirt as a sort of trophy after you prove yourself worthy by drinking your way around the world. From the large selection of beers, drink 21 brands and you get your own "Drink Your Way Around the World" T-shirt. Happy-hour oysters are a quarter apiece; live music nightly. Open-mike nights attract some grueling amateurs, and some great local color—you never know.

Wine Galley at the Pier House
1 Duval Street ✺ 296-4600

The Pier House is simply the most elegant resort on the island, and this flair shows in this chic but cozy piano bar where nightly entertainers include guest talent—some pro's, some amateurs—all having a ball making music with piano man Larry Smith. Smith's wide-ranging repertoire is astonishing and crowd pleasing. His guests are great.

Bobby Nesbitt, the show-tune prince pianist for whom this little treasure of a bar was originally created, has moved on to the Cabaret Room at San Francisco's swank Fairmount Hotel. We miss Bobby, but we love Larry very much, too.

Shops

Antique Shops

You can find a cluster of a half-dozen antique stores—sometimes more, sometimes less—at the crossroads of Simonton and Fleming streets. Keep in mind that antique shops keep odd hours, hours that don't always match those listed on their shop doors. Remember, we're on *manana* time here.

Cuba! Cuba!
814 Duval Street ✶ 295-9442

This shop is probably as close as you'll get, on this trip anyway, to a shopping excursion in Havana. Stop here for Cuban arts and crafts, cigar label art, a large variety of fine cigars, Cuban foods, books, cookbooks and maps. Also pillows, towels and flags in Cuba colors.

Fast Buck Freddie's
500 Duval Street ✶ 294-2007

The windows at Fast Buck Freddie's are not to be missed; each month the windows change, with themed displays featuring merchandise available for sale in the store that month. For example, one Valentine's Day, the display featured Liz Taylor and her eight marriages—but there are only six-and-a-half windows! No problem, because Liz married one husband, Richard Burton, twice. Each of Liz's seven husbands got a window, although Eddie Fisher's was displayed in the window half the size of the others.

Reserve at least an hour to take in this spectacular emporium of glitzy, nutty and beautiful things in the massive space that once housed the Kress Five and Dime. If you're not shopping, explore the place as if it were a museum. In a way, it is because the owners claim it to be Key West's first department store. It certainly is the island's most extravagant superstore. Try on the trendy clothes. Read the glitzy greeting cards. Test the gadgets. Browse slowly through the amazing tabletop accessories. You'll find toys and T-shirts, books, stationery, and fine writing instru-

ments. Zen rock gardens are a big seller. Fast Buck's is open from 11 a.m.–
6 p.m. daily. Tony Falcone and Bill Conkle, a couple of former advertising whiz-bangs from New York City, founded Fast Buck's in 1979.

Flamingo Crossing
1107 Duval ✺ 296-6124

The Florida Keys' only agricultural export today is mangrove honey,
which tastes best when sampled in combination with walnuts, cream and
ice in a cone at Flamingo Crossing, where fresh ice cream is made daily.
If this isn't the best ice cream you've ever tasted...well, it is. It just is.
And if that weren't enough, it's less expensive than the factory-made
stuff at the other places.

Key West Aloe
524 Front Street, 540 Greene Street ✺ 294-5592

In 1967, New Yorker Frank Romano came to Key West for a visit and got
himself a terrible sunburn. A local friend recommended that, for relief,
he try a time-honored local solution: gel of the aloe plant. Romano was
amazed at the instant relief; his sunburn healed without blisters and
without peeling. As a result, Romano became deeply interested in the
magical healing properties of aloe. He researched tropical aloe for two
years; then he moved to Key West with master perfumer Joe Liszka, and
the two founded Key West Aloe, the first company in America to manu-
facture its own skin-care and beauty products using aloe gel.

Twenty-five years later Key West Aloe now employs eighty-five people
and distributes more than one hundred skin care products all over the
world. At the factory outlet, store visitors can watch the manufacturing
process and pick up discounted merchandise.

The showroom at 524 Front Street is open from 9 a.m. until 8 p.m.
daily; hours are shorter in the summertime. The factory outlet shop and
lab at 540 Greene Street is open from 9 a.m. until 6 p.m. To take the free
tour, just ask!

Key West Cigar Factory
3 Pirates Alley (at Front Street) ▪ 294-3470

Lately, the cigar industry is enjoying a sudden rebound. Cigars again have become chic, just as they were in the 1800s, before the proliferation of cigarettes helped to wipe out the once-thriving cigar industry. Nowadays it is much more hip to sport a fat, fragrant Cuban cigar than a lowly cigarette. Cigar connoisseurs are buying glitzy magazines with names like *Smoke, The Magazine of Cigars, Pipes and Life's Other Burning Desires*, and *Cigar Aficionado*. And they are visiting places like the Key West Cigar Factory, where they can watch cigars being hand made on a cigar rolling table that appears to have been in use since the industry peak in the 1880s. Key West was once a cigar boomtown, producing 100 million cigars annually. Eventually, politics, union strikes, hurricanes, better working conditions in Tampa, and the popularity of cigarettes began the industry's demise. Seventy-five years later only six small factories remained on the island, and by 1963, only one was left; the Key West Cigar Factory is the era's sole survivor.

Now that cigars are again in vogue, the shop's cigar rollers are busy keeping up with the demand. The cigar rollers listen to a Havana radio station and roll tobacco grown in Africa, Brazil, and Colombia. They make cigars called "El Hemingway" and "Cuban Split."

Thirty percent of all cigars smoked in America, a clerk in the shop told me, are smuggled into the country from Cuba. The newest craze for people who have everything—a $30 smuggled Cuban cigar.

The Cigar Factory is open daily from 9 a.m. till 9 p.m. And smoking is not only permitted; it is encouraged.

Key West Hand Print Fabric
201 Simonton Street ▪ 294-9535

During Key West's amazing cigar making era, this brick building was constructed as a warehouse for storing tobacco. During the downtown reconstruction in the 1960s, the building was restored and became home to a factory producing hand-print fabrics.

Designers Suzy dePoo and Lily Pulitzer created the famous turquoise, yellow and pink Key West prints that were made into sports jackets, shorts, shirts and dresses. The fabrics were silk-screened, that is, the paint was stenciled directly onto the fabric in full view of charmed visitors. In the '60s and '70s, it was common to see lots of hand print fabric fashions at all the best parties. Miss Pulitzer has passed on, but Suzy dePoo, who is near 90 years old, still designs fabric in a studio in her Key West home.

The Key West hand-print fabric is no longer printed at the shop. The space that once contained the silk-screening operation is now a showroom. It's full of lovely clothes, constructed of Key West hand-print fabrics; particularly sweet are the children's clothes. All are expensive. Shop hours are 9:30 a.m.–5:30 p.m. every day but Sunday, when the shop is open from 10 a.m.–5 p.m.

Kino Sandal Factory
Kino Plaza ✹ 294-5044
Full of fabulous, very affordable, locally made leather sandals, the factory is in Kino Plaza, corner of Greene and Fitzpatrick. But watch out for those heavy glue fumes! The original Kino sandal, $6, is the best value, and made in a simple, sturdy style. You can't always find your size and color, though, and you can't always find a place to sit down and try on your sandals. But persevere. Kino's are a nearly perfect shoe except for one terrible flaw: on wet pavement they're greased lightening, definitely not the shoes to wear on a rainy day. Otherwise, they're really very cool, unique to the island, and extraordinarily long-wearing. This is another item you'll buy for yourself whenever you get to Key West, or take a pair home to a pal—they're cheaper than T-shirts!

Open Monday through Friday. 8:30 a.m.–5:30 p.m. Sat., 9 a.m. to 5:30 p.m. Sun., 10 a.m.–1 p.m.

From the Ruins
219 Whitehead Street ✹ 293-0897
Amazing assortment of one-of-a-kind garments, handcrafted accessories, and exquisite objects d'art. This is where you'll find the exorbitantly expensive dress that you'll wear for the rest of your life. Over 250 museum-quality garments, designed by artists from around the world, are featured. When you try on these clothes you realize that they've been created by sensual designers who appreciate the womanly form.

The shop's name refers to the timelessness of fashion, and the ancient methods of dying and weaving used in the creation of this collection of wearable art. Kim Harriss, a spectacularly chic woman with a sunny disposition and lust for life, is the proprietress and stylist. Kim will make you beautiful.

There's a mirror propped on a palm tree in the front yard so you can see the clothes in natural light. Kim minds her shop in $2,000 outfits and bare feet. Open 10 a.m.–6 p.m. every day but Sunday.

Pandemonium
825 Duval Street ✺ 294-0351
Artist and proprietress Valerie Hoh grew up in Hong Kong, studied art in London, and came to Key West to be an artist. She's frequently behind the scenes creating new merchandise. But whether she's present or not, Valerie's sunny personality is always in the house. Pandemonium's saleswomen are perfectly suited to this extraordinary emporium. It will take you a long time to see everything there is to see.

Recently Valerie created a recycling museum at the back of the shop. Recycling scientists, engineers and artists from around the world are represented in this eye-opening peek at the future.

Except on "Gone fishing days," which occur spontaneously, and Christmas, Pandemonium is open from 10 a.m. to 10 p.m. daily.

Paradise Tattoo
Stock Island ✺ 292-9110
People who have been thinking for a long time about getting a tattoo often find their courage at an all-time high right here, while on vacation in Key West. Tattoos have now come into their own as a popular island souvenir. For around $100 or so, you can buy yourself a lifelong reminder of Paradise—a dolphin, a sun, a sunset or a moon. Hearts and flowers are ever in demand, and you'd be surprised how often people ask to have a name tattooed onto themselves. The tattoo artists at Paradise will discourage you from this drastic measure, however.

Body piercing is also big lately. The most frequently pierced body part here in bikini land is the bellybutton.

Paradise Tattoo is open daily from noon till 8 p.m.

Perkins & Sons Chandlery
901 Fleming Street ❧ 294-7635

Part museum, part store, part somebody's funky island sitting room. A sleepy dog lies stretched out on the floor. For sale: rough and tumble boater's clothes, books about the sea. Nobody minds if it takes you a couple of hours to make your way through this magical chandlery, and it will.

Enjoy the reproduction glass buoys, ship's wheels, blocks, propellers, and synthetic ivory scrimshaw, brass clocks and barometers, ships in bottles and every other imaginable nautical-themed item for island homes and Florida Keys wannabes. And it has the best windows in town done by Carol Perkins, also the designer of the Shipwreck Historeum down by the harbor. They're so entertaining that you won't mind if the place is closed—it's still worth a visit just to window-shop. Weekdays, 9 a.m.–5 p.m. Saturdays, 10 a.m.–2 p.m. Sundays, closed.

The Sea Store
614 Greene Street ❧ 294-3438

It's difficult to say exactly what the hours of operation truly are in this tiny, antiquish, nautical-themed shop, but keep checking until you find Bill Ford in. The shop is wonderful and is headquarters for the Florida Keys Chapter of the Audubon Society. Ford's telephone answering machine not only takes messages, it gives a rundown of bird sightings for the week. And the machine is always on.

Sponge Market
Mallory Square ❧ 294-2555

Who better than C.B. McHugh, a fifth generation sponger born in Key West in 1923, to tell you all about sponging in the Florida Keys? C.B.'s been sponge fishing since he was eight years old, and he knows sponges. At the Sponge Market, C.B. demonstrates, through the miracle of modern videography, the process of gathering sponges and preparing them for market. You'll get a kick out of C.B.'s old-timey and very subjective narration.

"All sponges that grow in the ocean are called saltwater marine sea fossils," explains the Sponge King. "They're not animals. They're not vegetables. And they're not plants. I don't care what they say, they're nothing but common saltwater marine sea fossils. And I'll argue with anybody about that."

Sheepswool sponge is used throughout the world as bath sponges for racehorses, as dandy carwash sponges, and by tile-layers who use it to wipe the grout off tiles. During World War II sheepswool was used as oiled packing for gun barrels. But best of all, the sheepswool sponge is a luxurious addition to a hot, soapy bath. At the Sponge Market you can buy a high-grade sheepswool sponge for $20 to $30, depending on the size, or a less-stellar sponge for considerably less.

The Sponge Market is open daily from 10 a.m. till 9 p.m., except on cruise ship days, when they open at 8:30 a.m.

Victoria Lesser Inc.
1102 Truman Avenue ✺ 292-0101

Bill Crosby calls designer Victoria Lesser his "pajama mama" because she designed all the pj's he wore on *The Cosby Show*. Cosby still buys his shirts from her. Others who love Victoria's special creations are Barbara Mandrell, Sophia Loren and Goldie Hawn. Victoria offers her clients a special kind of personalized service. At the drop of a hem, she will hop a jet and join them for fittings for a new outfit. She has recently begun a unique service. A client can fly down to Key West for a secret getaway. Victoria will arrange for a house, pool and staff if necessary—along with private showings and fittings.

A new Truman Avenue store "for people who have everything, but can have anything." Huh? Expensive, classically-styled garments.

Wings of Imagination
1108-C Duval Street ✺ 296-2988

Did you know the life expectancy of a butterfly is only ten days? Learn why, and much more at artist/naturalist Sam Trophia's butterfly gallery. Enhanced with soft, silky music, the gallery features artwork using these "flowers of the sky" raised on butterfly farms in South America, Africa, and Southeast Asia. It's amazing and wonderful, and kind of eerie, what Trophia does with these jewels of nature. Trophia's art puts a whole new spin on "Live fast. Die young."

Second Hand Rows

Cheap Chic, Inc.
927 Eaton Street

Consigning Adults
802 Whitehead Street

Dress For Less Consignment Boutique
1021 White Street

Hideaway Thrift and Consignment
3201 Flagler Avenue

Knot So New Consignment & Resale Shop
1102 White Street

Salvation Army
1924 Flagler Avenue

St. Peter's Episcopalian Church Parish Hall Thrift Shop
800 Center Street

The Perfect T

S YOU WALK DOWN DUVAL STREET, you will notice an overwhelming number of T-shirt shops. Some of them pay people to stand out front and offer you coupons for discounts within. T-shirts has become a big business here in Key West. Yes, we know we have far too many T-shirt shops, but our elected officials can do nothing about that since this is America, when you try to impose restrictions on what merchants can and cannot sell on Duval Street, you invite lawsuits and bigger and more expensive lawyers than this city can afford to fight.

There are several reasons why, from an economic standpoint, the T-shirt business is so successful in this tourist town. First, marketing surveys indicate that the most frequently purchased item that visitors take home from Key West is a T-shirt. Second, unlike many trends and fads, T-shirts don't go out of style And, third, they're cheap to produce. In many shops they're not even imprinted until someone buys them and chooses an image they want from a staggering selection displayed on shop walls. A T-shirt shop's main inventory is inexpensive plain white T-shirts. Thus, you may find T-shirts being sold for $5, or 2 for $20, or any other combination that will bring in the money to pay the rent that day.

There are, however, unscrupulous T-shirt merchants on Duval Street, who advertise T-shirts for one price and then charge considerably more for the finished product after the customer has been invited to choose whatever images he wants imprinted on the shirt. Plenty of people have complained, particularly non-English-speaking tourists. It's a dirty trick, to be sure, and it's been perpetrated often enough that City Hall has imposed laws to protect tourists from these bait-and-switch tactics.

Today, T-shirt shops are required to post a list of prices on all shirts within a shop, but be sure to confirm the total price *before* the purchase. If you're going to order a shirt with many slogans or designs on it, ask for an itemized bill before the printing begins, so that you can decide if the price is in line with what you expected to pay. **If you think you were**

overcharged, contact the City of Key West Code Enforcement office at
292-8191.

Some favorite T-shirt designs are the **Hog's Breath Saloon, Sloppy
Joe's,** which features Ernest Hemingway's face, and the **Half Shell Raw
Bar**, sporting a saucy babe in a bikini, inviting one and all to "Eat it
Raw" at the Half Shell Raw Bar.

At **Captain Tony's Saloon,** which Captain Tony sold some years
back, T-shirts are sold in a shop adjacent to the Greene Street bar.
Business is always brisk.

Jimmy Buffett's Margaritaville Gift Shop sells thousands of shirts
each week and so does the Wyland gift shop on Front Street. Those local
classics will cost you about $15–$20.

Last Flight Out, 706 Duval, sells a great selection of T-shirts with a
sort of getting-away-from-it-all motif. "I'll see you in C.u.b.a." is an old
classic available here, as well as the blue plane winging its way into the
sky on the last flight out. We all have a Last Flight Out within us....
I love this place, and these shirts.

Carpenters working for the **Kinky Construction Company** wear
kinky T-shirts. Designed ten years ago by local artist and sailor David
Wegman, the shirt design features a pile of naked people who appear to
be engaging in a round of kinky, group sex. Michael Skoglund, contrac-
tor/architect and owner of Kinky Construction, says that whenever he
wears his shirt out to a bar or restaurant, he is approached by people
interested in having their own Kinky Construction T. The shirts in blue
or yellow, say: "Get kinky with a local. Kinky Construction, Key West."
Yes, they're 100% cotton. Michael Skoglund is not in the T-shirt business, but sometimes, if you ask him just right, he'll figure out a way to get
you one. Write to him at 522 Elizabeth St., Key West 33040, or phone
him at 296-2632.

The **Mel Fisher** "Today's the Day" T-shirts were worn hopefully for
years by those who hunted daily for the massive treasure. The day finally
arrived for Mel Fisher's Treasure Salvors on July 20, 1985. Shirts featuring
the treasure hunting themes are still sold at the Maritime Heritage
museum gift shop.

Local character and Key West Fire Chief **Bum Farto** disappeared in
1976, just days before he was to be sentenced for selling cocaine. "Where

is Bum Farto?" asked one of the most popular T-shirts of the '70s. Alas, old Bum is still among the missing.

Old Island T-Shirts, at 914 A Kennedy Drive, 296-3329, sells shirts by the pound. If you've got ten friends, or, God help you, ten kids waiting back at home for their Key West souvenirs, this is the place to go. The shirts are inexpensive because they're irregular over-runs from other jobs, possibly flawed in some small, Key West-chic way. Maybe the print is crooked or letters are missing or something like that. Whatever. Most are 100% cotton; buy them for $7.50 a pound. Are T-shirts supposed to be perfect? Nah! You'll find all kinds of interesting designs here, so take your time to hunt through all the bins and piles, and chances are you'll find something for even the most discerning collector. Open from 10 a.m. till 5 p.m.; closed on Sunday. Blank shirts are also available for $7.50 a pound in lots of neat colors.

Another place for interesting T-shirts, many of them designed by local artists, is the **T-Shirt Factory** at 316 Simonton Street. As elegant as T-shirts can be, these are hand-printed in an open-air factory, which you can watch. Prices are around a third less than the same shirts sold in fancy Duval Street shops even though the factory is only a block off Duval. Kids' and adults' sizes all the way up to XXXL. Also sweatshirts. Open daily from 10 a.m. till 6 p.m.

T-shirts are designed also to commemorate just about every local event. Often money raised from shirt sales benefits some group or organization. The Annual Memorial Day Survivor's Party T-shirts, sold at the party and afterwards until they run out, benefit **AIDS Help, Inc.**

Some political campaigns, like **Captain Tony's** when he ran and was elected mayor, sell T-shirts to raise campaign funds. These are found for years after in the chic collections of T-shirt hobbyists everywhere.

An exhibit of Key West T-shirts, which we've never had, certainly would be a fascinating way to tell the story of this island's fascinating history. And imagine the swapping that might go on! Collect wisely and save your Key West T's for this future possibility.

Endless Love

Weddings

T IS SURPRISINGLY, some might say frighteningly, easy to acquire a license to marry in the Florida Keys. Both members of the couple must appear when the application is applied for and issued, but neither of them needs to produce any kind of identification. The marriage license form will ask for names, ages, birthplaces, and information on just how past marriages, if any, were concluded. There is no blood test required. After you finish the paperwork and pay the clerk $88.50, you must wait 3 days. Then, you're legally ready for matrimony. If you're in a big hurry, you can be married by a clerk at the courthouse. If you're in a big hurry, you can be married by a clerk at the courthouse. The charge is $20, about as cheap as you can get in Monroe County unless you know someone who is a notary public.

Roughly 200 marriage licenses are issued each month at the Monroe County Court House at 500 Whitehead Street in Key West. Well over half of those are issued to out-of-towners, apparently overwhelmed with the relentlessly rosy romance of an island holiday.

Any legally registered notary public has the power to marry you in Florida. Many of them turn performing weddings into a business. You will see their brochures at the Chamber of Commerce and their ads in the Yellow Pages, as many types of services and ceremonies as there are marriage licenses. The more outrageous, it seems, the better.

Last minute nuptials pose no problem for local wedding planners and teams. One phone call will fix you up with everything you need, from location to custom services to photographs, from the very simplest to the most glorious ceremony imaginable. No challenge is too great for local wedding brokers.

Many resorts, like the Marriott and Holiday Inn Resort & Marina in Key Largo and the Pier House in Key West, actually employ wedding consultants who are a phone call away.

Church weddings for out-of-towners are generally more difficult to arrange in a hurry. Many churches require a counseling session before a clergyman will perform a wedding ceremony. Determination and sincerity may win you the support of a local clergyman willing to tie your knot. Lots of churches are listed in the Yellow Pages. If a church wedding is what you must have, chances are you can find a way to have one. One way is to do the mandatory preparatory groundwork with your hometown clergy and bring certification to present to the local branch of your church here in Key West. The following is a short, and by no means complete, list of possibilities.

Marrying Sam
296-3640
Marrying Sam advertises discounts to pregnant brides, locals and members of the military, with no charge for renewing vows at any point in the marriage. A longtime local character, Marrying Sam wears a safari hat, and drives a moped. Between vows, she'll snap a couple of photos of the happy pair. This is your basic, no frills deal.

Reverend Debra Benedict
296-7439
If appearances are important to you, and you are hoping for a more dressy and refined sort of affair, you might call on the Reverend Debra, for whom fashion holds a high spot on her long list of avocations. If need be, Reverend Debra will dress the entire wedding party. As an interfaith minister, she performs services of appropriate simplicity or economical grandeur. Like all wedding officials, Debra will perform on the very shortest of notice, and offers assistance in planning of location, transportation, accommodation, entertainment, photography, and video documentation. She's also a real-estate person, so, should you become really enamored with Key West, you might press her into even further service.

Captain Orin Opperman
294-6674
The captain will marry couples underwater in scuba gear, just as long as they are certified divers; he'll even help you arrange for scuba certification if you really want it in time for the wedding. Or he will marry you on land or aboard a boat. Furthermore, although such weddings are not

legally sanctioned as of this writing, he'll perform same-sex weddings for couples wishing, nonetheless, to celebrate their commitment with a ceremony. Captain Opperman also will perform simple weddings on the beach, or a 2-hour cruise with marital vows. Naturally, he offers packages that include photographs and videos.

Greg Scorzafave
Goldsmith Jewelers ✶ 294-1243

Greg is fluent in sign language, and will happily perform weddings in sign for non-hearing people.

Schooner Wolf
296-9653

Any number of sailboats will take you and your wedding party out to sea for a wedding; just ask. The Conch Republic Navy's flagship, the *Schooner Wolf*, loves weddings. You bring the license and Captain Finbar Gittelman will perform the ceremony. Dressed in smart captain's whites, he will read your vows at whatever time of the day you desire. Most of the over 500 weddings he has performed, Captain Finbar says, were done at sunset. The *Wolf* provides food, drinks, music and photography. After the vows, you cruise the waters and watch the sun set into the Gulf of Mexico. Somebody blows a peal on a conch shell, the Conch Republic cannon is fired, and—you're married!

Chapel by the Sea
292-5177 ✶ 800-603-2088

A wedding coordinator will handle every detail of your wedding. All you have to do is show up! A ceremony next to the fountain in their tropical garden setting, with champagne and photographs for two, costs just under $200. For around $500, you and your intended and an attending party of four can go on a private sunset cruise, sip beer, wine and champagne, marry at sea next to a bouquet of tropical flowers, and pose for photographs.

Your Wedding in Paradise
Tom Netting ❋ 296-3435

Your parents will forgive you for eloping to a tropical island when you present them with an album of wedding photos shot by photographer extrodinaire Tom Netting. Tom will design a perfect wedding to fit your budget. Your wedding in paradise can be anything from the very simplest seaside event to a lavish, traditional affair. Either way, your wedding album will be the envy of your friends. That's why you hired Tom.

Friederike "Ricki" Fischer
713 Whitehead Street ❋ 296-7264

Hochzeit im Paradies. German-born Ricki Fischer, who has lived in the Florida Keys since 1978, is known for her unusual, romantic weddings. She has married couples on sailboats, motorboats, and in airplanes. She's helped twosomes tie the knot on golf courses, on tennis courts, in piano bars and in restaurants; on beaches, at the Hemingway House and in private homes. For those who are already married (to each other), and who succumb to Key West's romantic nights and wish to renew their vows, Ricki will arrange an unforgettable event.

Weird Science:
The Elena Hoyos Story

COUNT VON COSEL, who wasn't a count at all except in his own mind, was an X-ray technologist at Key West's now-defunct Marine Hospital. In the spring of 1930, a sweet but doomed Latin beauty named Elena Hoyos showed up at the hospital for blood tests and X-rays. Tests revealed that tuberculosis would soon kill the pretty 22-year-old. But von Cosel, a small German man who wore clean white suits, a white Panama hat, and a tiny mustache, was smitten with Elena, whom he claimed to recognize from a dream he'd had forty years earlier. He could not bear to accept the reality of his own diagnosis.

Von Cosel determined to save Elena's life by charging her oxygen electrons with his own invention, a bizarre contraption with electrodes that attached to the girl's wasting body. The treatments were hideously painful for Elena, but von Cosel's weird science was oddly reassuring, too. Elena's poor, heartbroken parents welcomed his devotion and ministrations. He kept their hopes for their daughter's survival alive.

As Elena languished in her tiny bedroom, von Cosel brought her gifts of perfume, scarves, jewelry, and exotic fruits and candies. He bought her an elaborate mahogany bed, that barely fit through the door of the family's humble home. It was in that bed that Elena died on October 25, 1931.

Her family buried Elena in Key West's City Cemetery. According to the memories of those who were there, von Cosel sagged with grief as he watched his beloved being lowered into her shallow grave. (You can't dig a deep grave on an island only a few feet above sea level.) The water! The worms! The flimsy casket! How would Elena's delicate beauty survive the tyranny of the damp earth? After two years of regular visits to Elena's grave, von Cosel could bear the image of her demise no longer. One moonless night he dug up her nearly fleshless bones and took them to his laboratory located in the fuselage of a wingless airplane parked on Rest Beach.

Julia Hoffman, then a young woman dating a newspaper reporter from Ohio, went along when her boyfriend interviewed von Cosel in his Quonset hut on the beach well before Elena's body was discovered. Von

Cosel, Julia recalls, seemed so logical, so convinced of the validity of his bizarre experiments and kookie plans—he was building a plane to fly to Heaven—that she was nearly convinced it could be so.

Von Cosel determined to preserve what remained of Elena's sultry charms with a bizarre series of soaks, washes and regular soapy baths. The mad count replaced Elena's rotting flesh with oiled silk, beeswax and balsam. He replaced her eyes with glass ones. He fought an unending battle with insects, who continually found their ways into Elena's nooks and crannies in spite of his painstaking precautions. Eventually, of course, von Cosel's eerie project was discovered. It's difficult to keep a secret in Key West—especially one as odorous as necrophilia.

Elena's body was removed from the wingless plane and taken to a local funeral parlor where an autopsy was performed. It had been seven years since her death. Doctors noted in written reports that Elena's remains had been the receptacle of physical evidence of von Cosel's love. That's right: intercourse.

Talk about a twisted tale....

Von Cosel was arrested. Elena's body was put on exhibit in the lobby of the funeral parlor, and the townspeople were invited to come by and view the eerie spectacle. Almost 7,000 people came to see Elena. Teachers brought their classes. Reporters came from all over the country. Von Cosel's story caught the fancy of just about everyone in America, in spite of the fact that the bit about the intercourse was considered much too shocking to report in the papers.

More than a few Key Westers suggested that Elena's body be sealed in a glass case and put on permanent display. Wouldn't the tourists love that! There was sympathy for the weird, old man, too. What was his real crime after all? Loving too much?

A local innkeeper named Joe Zorsky, perhaps more tolerant of freaks than most people due to his background in the circus, bailed von Cosel out of jail and let him stay in room 23 of his motel lodge (today the place is Key Lime Village). When the world press arrived to interview von Cosel, they gathered around him, in front of a huge night-blooming cactus.

Eventually the courts discovered that there was no Florida law against not burying a body, and the charges against von Cosel were dropped.

"Can I have Elena back now?" von Cosel reportedly asked the judge, oblivious to the horror of the curious on-lookers who had flocked to the court for his sentencing.

"No! No, you can't!" screamed the outraged judge.

Elena was buried in an unmarked grave. Von Cosel left town in 1940 and spent his remaining years in Zephyrhills, Florida, the place where the natural spring water comes from. He died, alone, in 1952. When morticians came to take von Cosel's body away, they found an eerie sight propped in the corner of the little shack: a life-sized replica of Maria Elena Hoyos.

Songwriter/performer Ben Harrison heard the story of creepy, crawly Count Carl von Cosel, Key West's infamous necrophiliac, and Maria Elena Hoyos, the object of his ghoulish ardor, and immediately felt his songwriting juices begin to gush. Harrison began performing his talk/sing horror story, *The Ballad of Maria Elena Hoyos and Count Carl von Cosel*, at gigs around town. Every time he performed the eerie bit, his audience became enthralled.

"Is that a true story?" people asked him incredulously.

"It is," Ben Harrison told them. "It really is. I promise."

Encouraged by his customers' ghoulish enthusiasm for the tale, Harrison eventually wrote a book about it. *Undying Love* explores every mucky detail of the macabre legend and contains unbelievable quotes from von Cosel's own kooky narrative that appeared in *Scientific American Magazine* in 1940. Next time you've got a few hours to kill (you should pardon the expression), pick up Harrison's book. Halloween Eve might be a perfect evening for this gross and engrossing read. You won't be disappointed.

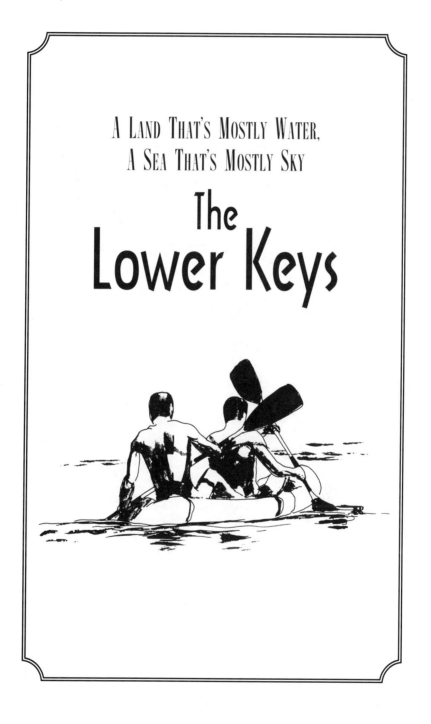

A Land That's Mostly Water,
A Sea That's Mostly Sky

The
Lower Keys

The Lower Keys
· · ·

To Middle Keys

Mile Marker 40

Seven Mile Bridge

Bahia Honda State Park

No Name Key

Big Pine Key

Ramrod Key

Cudjoe Key

1

Sugarloaf Key

Big Coppitt Key

Mile Marker 4

To Key West

A Land That's Mostly Water and A Sea that's Mostly Sky

MANY PEOPLE consider this part of the Overseas Highway, from Boca Chica Naval Air Station at mile marker (MM) 7, to the Seven Mile Bridge at MM 40, to be the most spectacular thirty-three mile stretch in the Keys. The endless expanses are so dazzling that you may find yourself losing the line where the sea ends and the sky begins. It is possible to drive from the urban heart of Key West into some remarkably vast marine flatlands, well within a half hour.

Beyond Key West, development thins out dramatically. With few buildings, no malls, and no fast-food emporiums, but several long, new bridges, many square-miles of mangroves, and lots of water—the Atlantic Ocean on the south side of the highway, the Gulf of Mexico on the north. On this stretch you will find restaurants and accommodations, but not many.

The Boca Chica Naval Air Station, the last major landmark you see as you drive away from Key West, has been here since it was commissioned in 1917. This location was chosen for the air station when Navy research found it to have the most days of perfect flying weather of anywhere in the country. If your car radio is on as you drive past Boca Chica, you will hear a series of little beeps that might make you wonder if your car is being bugged. But no, it's the sky that's being bugged by radar scanning for unwelcome visitors approaching the area by air.

Driving north to Big Coppitt Key, the four-lane highway turns into two lanes. Big Coppitt Key is a predominantly residential community. Many of the residents work at the nearby base; others have moved here to suburbia from Key West to buy affordable homes on the less-glamorous, and certainly less-prestigious, Big Coppitt Key. If you live here, your mailing address is Key West.

The traffic light at MM 17 marks a tiny hub of commerce on the island of Sugarloaf Key. The Bat Tower, a dolphin named Sugar, and a wee airport are all located on Sugarloaf Key.

Cudjoe Key is thought to be named after a guy named Joe who fled the busy city of Key West in the 1880's to homestead on a peaceful island twenty-two miles up the road. Say "Cousin Joe's Key" real fast and you might hear "Cudjoe Key." That's one theory anyway. Another is that Cudjoe Key is named for the joewood tree that grows on the island.

Guarding the sea from a spot high in the air over Cudjoe Key is a 1400-foot-high radar blimp affectionately known as "Fat Albert." The blimp is tethered to a Naval facility on Blimp Road. Fat Albert can be seen from miles away in either direction.

Big Pine Key, eight miles long and roughly two miles wide, is the second-largest in the coral island chain. (Key Largo is largest.) Much of the pineland and hardwood hammocks and mangrove fringe on this island is encompassed in a critical habitat called the Key West Wildlife Refuge for indigenous, threatened and endangered species. The refuge is managed by the U.S. Department of Fish and Wildlife.

Recently the Florida Department of Transportation judged Big Pine Key, the island that begins at MM 29, to be the most congested traffic area in the Keys, triggering an automatic building moratorium. Commercial building is allowed only as long as it does not increase traffic to the island. (How can it not, you might reasonably ask?) The worst time to pass through here is on Saturday mornings between late October and May when the Big Pine Flea Market slows traffic to an inching crawl. All of Big Pine Key, from MM's 29 to 33, is a reduced speed zone— 45 mph by day and 35 mph after dark. Speed limits are strictly enforced.

The beautiful sandy beach that everybody visiting the Keys seems to be looking for is in Bahia Honda State Recreational Area at MM 37, adjacent to Bahia Honda Channel. In this reverently maintained natural preserve are indigenous plants and flowers that, according to park signs, grow almost nowhere else in the world; there's excellent RV and tent camping in the park, too. Many people find the campgrounds in the Lower Keys more relaxed and less restrictive than those to the north.

After the lonely little islands of Ohio, Missouri, and Little Duck Keys, named by Flagler's railroad workers in the early 1900s, comes the majestic and amazing Seven Mile Bridge.

A History Stranger Than Fiction

Sponges and Bats—
Sugarloaf Key's Weird Past

At one point in its history, it looked as if Sugarloaf Key might become
the sponge capital of the world. Charles Chase came to Sugarloaf Key in
1910 to establish the Florida Keys Sponge and Fruit Company. Charles
and his businessman brother (who lived in Chicago) had studied results
of several government-funded experiments in artificial sponge cultivation
and determined that they could make a successful business of raising
sponges in the large, nearly landlocked, shallow sounds at Sugarloaf Key.
The Chase brothers paid $45,000 to buy nearly all of Sugarloaf Key from
J. Vining Harris of Key West.

In an astonishingly short time, land was cleared, living quarters were
built and occupied by workers and their families, and facilities for processing and planting sponges were established. A disk-manufacturing
operation, located in the area of today's Sugarloaf Lodge, constructed

Spongers

thousands of 10-inch round, cement disks upon which sponges would be encouraged to grow. Natural sponges were taken from the ocean floor and cut up into many smaller pieces which were wired onto the disks. The disks and sponge starters were then submerged in shallow water where, presumably, they would mature into uniformly round, sand-free sponges, ready for the already-established, world-wide demand.

When the Overseas Railroad was competed and the first train thundered across Sugarloaf Key in January 1912, the sponge cultivation settlement was a small town with a population of one hundred and a work force of sixty. When the settlement next to the railroad tracks became big enough to require its own post office, it became a town named Chase, after the brothers who'd started it all.

Unfortunately, the earlier experimenters in sponge cultivation had miscalculated on one extremely important point: how many years the sponges would need to grow to commercial size. The Chase brothers had planned on four years; in fact, it was more like six, and so they ran out of money well before their grand scheme yielded a viable harvest.

The brothers solicited money from contacts in their native country of England, and they got it, but before they were able to transfer it back to America, World War I began, and the funds were frozen in English banks.

By the time the Florida Keys Sponge and Fruit Company declared bankruptcy in May 1917, the town of Chase was abandoned. The Chase brothers eventually sold their ghost town and their holdings on Sugarloaf Key to Miamian Richter C. Perky for $200,000.

The Bat Tower

Perky planned to develop the property as a private vacation and fishing retreat. But the future of his planned paradise looked bleak when he realized the severity of the mosquito problem. In an interview years later, a caretaker who worked for Perky recalled that the mosquitoes were so thick that a person could press his hands against a screen and quickly attract so many mosquitoes that, when they pulled away, a clump of hungry mosquitoes in the shape of their hands would remain on the screen.

Perky had heard of an interesting means of mosquito control that had worked successfully in other parts of the country. Following instructions in a book called *Bats, Mosquitoes and Dollars*, Perky built a bat tower on his property. Perky's plan was to rid his island of mosquitoes by filling his tower with mosquito-hungry bats. Then he planned to sell the recycled mosquitoes, in the form of bat poop, as fertilizer; however, the bats never came.

Current tourist literature often makes Perky out to be a crazy man, but scientists say his idea wasn't so outlandish—bats are a natural means of pest control; one bat will eat its weight in insects every night. Obviously, it behooves Floridians to keep their bat populations thriving. Five years ago researchers at the University of Florida in Gainesville built a bat tower similar to Perky's. Today, at least 3,000 bats are living permanently in the gabled stilt house. And recently, more than sixty years after Perky built the 30-foot bat condominium, colonies of bats have been confirmed in the Upper Keys. They are not living in Perky's tower yet, but when they're ready to roost, the bat tower will be ready for them.

Making Charcoal

The Torch Keys were named for torchwood, a small tree that works well in the creation of charcoal because it burns well, even when green. Buttonwood, which grows profusely in the Lower Keys, is another fine wood for charcoal making. Before the use of electricity, and gas or coal stoves, charcoal was the main fuel in Key West. Many settlers in the Lower Keys made their livings creating charcoal, an arduous task. First, trees were chopped down and cut into logs, which were stacked into massive cones and covered with mud or seaweed. Then a fire was started at the center of the tee-pee-shaped construction. The stack of logs was never allowed to burst into flame and burn; instead, the charcoal-maker would keep the interior damp so it would smolder for days. Eventually the wood was reduced to charcoal and transported to Key West, where there was a large and steady demand for the fuel.

Like many Keys and reefs, Ramrod Key got its name from a ship that wrecked near the island in the 1800s. Ramrod, Summerland and Cudjoe Keys were all once centers of charcoal production.

Cudjoe Key

The most famous person ever to live on Cudjoe Key was a trail-blazing woman from Chicago named Lily Lawrence Bow. She came to Cudjoe Key with her husband and their two sons in 1904. But Mr. Bow didn't enjoy the tropical wilderness of the Florida Keys, and soon he returned to the north, leaving his family alone and without means. The Bows, the only white people on Cudjoe Key, grew vegetables and raised chickens; the boys fished. Eventually Ms. Bow, who'd gone to college, became the only schoolteacher for miles, and Keys, around. Her students' parents paid for her services with food so the Bows were able to stay on Cudjoe Key for two years. Finally they moved to Homestead, Florida, another rough and rugged wilderness. With a homestead grant, Lily Bow built a log cabin and planted a citrus grove there. She became active in civic affairs and helped found the area's women's club. Homestead's public library is called the "Lily Lawrence Bow Library" in her memory.

And in the Keys, Bow Channel, that runs between Upper Sugarloaf and Cudjoe Keys, is named after Lily Bow, and today, just like back in 1904, it still takes an enormous amount of courage to survive near the swift waters of Bow Channel.

The Monkey Keys

On Key Lois and Raccoon Key, islands several miles offshore from Summerland Key, two rhesus-monkey habitats are home to thousands of monkeys, who roam freely, consume large quantities of red mangroves, and shriek wildly while they await their turns in the medical research laboratories of Charles Rivers Labs. The monkeys are healthy and free from infections, thanks to their isolation, and that makes them particularly valuable to the researchers.

Although Charles Rivers Laboratories owns the monkey islands, established twenty years ago, they cannot say with any accuracy how many test monkeys live on them. Maybe the number is 1500, they say; maybe it's 3,000. Environmentalists say these monkeys have destroyed significant stands of red mangroves that once ringed the islands. They are concerned, also, about pollution from monkey poop. In addition, Lower Keys residents are concerned that the monkeys might swim to the nearby Keys and invade peaceful neighborhoods. In a hurricane, they suggest, monkeys might be blown into densely populated Key West.

In a spirit of cooperation, the Charles Rivers Lab agreed in 1992 to pen the monkeys in cages of 300 monkeys each, and to cover the remaining mangrove stands in protective mesh. Environmentalists, as a result, charged that caging the creatures was inhumane.

100-acre Key Lois is on the Atlantic side of the Keys; Raccoon Key, a 200-acre island, is on the Gulf side. You cannot see either island from the Overseas Highway, but local kids on Waverunners enjoy riding very close to the shore of the monkey islands for a closer look. "The monkeys are mean-looking," one kid said. "And dirty. You hear them before you can actually see them." It is illegal, of course, to disembark on Key Lois or Raccoon Key. Hey, who'd want to?

Earning a Living on Big Pine Key

The original inhabitants of this area were Indian hunter/gatherers who lived on deer, turtles and fish. Later island dwellers found the soil on Big Pine Key to be very productive. Among the 132 people who lived on this part of the Lower Keys in 1870, more than half were farmers; the rest were seamen. The Bahamian farmers grew cash crops of fruits and vegetables which they transported by schooner to Key West. Settlers augmented their diets with white-crowned pigeons, doves, herons and cormorants, as well as green turtle and conch.

A woman who lived on Big Pine Key as a child in the early 1900s recalls that Key limes were so plentiful her family couldn't use them fast enough. Her father made a tool that squeezed a dozen limes at a time. The Key lime juice was called "old sour" and was a popular marinate for seafood, poultry and fish. Key limes sold for a dime a case in Key West.

By 1900, blacks from the Bahama Islands and freed slaves from the American South outnumbered whites in these Lower Keys two to one. They supported themselves, like everyone else, by making charcoal, sponging, farming, or fishing.

Before the completion of the Overseas Highway in 1938, to reach the Lower Keys by car, it was necessary to make two fourteen-mile ferry crossings. Ferries shuttled cars from Lower Matecumbe Key to Grassy Key, and then from Knight's Key to No Name Key. Operation of the ferries created jobs and several small settlements. Today the remains of a cistern and several coral-rock foundations mark the site of the little town that grew up around the ferry landing on No Name Key.

A shark processing plant was the first major enterprise on Big Pine Key. The shark facility was built in 1923 by Hydenoil Products, a company that butchered sharks for their hides and livers. The hides made a strong, soft leather; shark liver oil is rich in vitamins. The products were

Hammerhead shark

exported from the Keys via the Overseas Railroad, which operated in the Keys from 1912 until 1935.

The company employed sixty men who caught sharks in nets, where they drowned or clubbed them to death. The Hydenoil Company killed up to one hundred sharks a day. The biggest fish they caught was a 1,752-pound mackerel shark. Among the grisly finds made by shark processors when they cut open the sharks' bellies was a human arm still wearing the remnants of a blue serge suit. The material later proved to be from the uniform of a Cuban pilot who'd been on a seaplane that had crashed into the ocean days earlier.

In spite of their seemingly successful operation, the Depression spelled hard times for Hydenoil Company, and the Big Pine Key shark plant closed in 1931.

Mako shark

Lower Keys Chamber of Commerce
MM 31, Oceanside ✸ 872-2411 ✸ 800-872-3722

Outside of the Visitors Center a clean, breezy park has benches, picnic tables, public bathrooms and a spreading poinciana tree in spectacular bloom in early summer. Exhibits by the National Marine Sanctuary program post some surprising information, like the fact that the barrier reef ecosystem of the Florida Keys is the third largest in the world.

Inside you can cool off in fine air conditioning while you stock up on brochures promoting every imaginable local feature, as well as lots of things to see and do in Key West, 30 miles away. Yes, 30 miles farther down the road. Many people are surprised that they're not yet at the end of the road by the time they arrive here. Some people even ask "Are we in the Keys yet?" which is enormously amusing for the people who work here.

Videos describing the reefs, Key deer, and the profoundly luxurious offshore resort of Little Palm Island play fulltime. If you don't like what's playing, change it. The video of Little Palm Island is as close as most people can afford to get to this exorbitantly expensive bastion of splendor.

"Big Pine Key is all about nature," you will be told. "We have nature." And they do. A kayaking tour of the backcountry, a visit to the Blue Hole, and an encounter with a Key deer are all do-able in a day or two visit. Good restaurants are here, too.

What's everyone's first question when they arrive at the Visitor's Center? Where do we go to see Key deer? The Key deer video, popular with schoolteachers from everywhere, chamber personnel say, sells for $12; Key deer T-shirts are $10.

Key Deer

ONE OF THE MOST REMARKABLE CREATURES on the endangered species
list, and perhaps the Keys' most cherished, is the endearingly dimun-
utive Key deer. If you think Bambi was cute, imagine these wee
critters. The very largest Key deer weighs 75 pounds and is two-and-a-
half feet tall. The very smallest is the two- to four-pound infant, who is
born after a 200 day gestation period. At the Museum of Natural History
at Crane Point Hammock, MM 50 in Marathon, a life-like exhibit of a
mama, papa and baby Key deer is on display.

Key deer are mentioned in some of the earliest written accounts of life
in the Keys. At one time Key deer were found all the way from Big Pine
Key down to Key West, thirty miles away. They were eaten by local residents as well as by passing sailors who came ashore to hunt. Through the
years the Key deer population has been thinned through hunting, poach-
ing, and habitat destruction. And yet, the little guys survive.

By the 1940s, when conservation laws were established to save the
Key deer from extinction, there were fewer than 50 of the creatures left
alive. Now there are thought to be 300 Key deer living on Big Pine and
No Name Keys. The species exists nowhere else in the world.

Although the Key deer has done a remarkable job of adapting to
the Keys' limited space and sparse food supply, it is still one of the most
threatened species in the country. The biggest threat to Key deer is cars.
Each day an average of 30,000 vehicles travel the Overseas Highway
during the winter tourist season. Each year the number of deer killed by
cars increases, and the statistics look more grim than the year before. In
1995, the number of recorded deer deaths was eighty-nine; sixty-five of
those were killed by vehicles. The rest drowned, were killed by dogs, or
died of natural or unknown causes. Thirteen of the dead were fawns.

The Overseas Highway now has a reduced speed limit for the length
of Big Pine Key, from Mile Markers 29 through 33: 45 mph by day and
35 mph after dark. The limits are strictly enforced.

In spite of state and federal laws prohibiting people from feeding Key
deer, many people find it difficult to believe that by providing the deer

with food, they are harming them. In fact, deer who are fed may change their behavior, growing overly confident around humans. In addition, unhealthy foods inhibit the deer's ability to reproduce. Laws also prohibit molesting or interfering with the Key deer; violators face $540 state fines and even jail time.

To survive and procreate, Key deer need fresh water and sufficient food sources. They eat red, black and white mangroves, thatch palm berries, and over 150 other species of plants. I have seen Key deer

munching bougainvillea flowers. Accessing their needs becomes more and more difficult.

Roughly one-third of the eleven-square-mile island of Big Pine Key is taken up by the U. S. Fish and Wildlife Key Deer Refuge. Some residents resent the federal government's presence and would like to build an elementary school and other community service buildings on Big Pine Key; progress must go on, they say. Environmentalists argue, however, that overdevelopment of the island has already destroyed wetlands and depleted the fresh water supply. So a bitter environmental controversy rages over the Key deer, which has become a symbol of a community's continuing controversy over land use, and the poster child of the endangered species. Save the Key deer, many believe, and you save the Keys.

And when a hurricane heads our way, how do we protect the Key deer? What will we do with the deer in case of evacuation? It is possible that the entire population of deer could be wiped out by a single powerful hurricane.

Spotting Key Deer

In the novel *Sunburn*, Key West author Larry Shames writes an account of a Key deer-spotting expedition to No Name Key. It's a couple of pages into Chapter 36. No Name Key is described by *Sunburn's* hero as a swampy place with "spiders the size of your fist, leaves that give a rash, alligators that eat Dobermans."

Well, yes, all that's true. But you really do have a good chance of seeing Key deer there. You will be surprised to find how comfortable Key deer seem to be around humans and their vehicles. They don't run away when you show up, but this is not always a good thing. Naturalists say that the more confident a wild animal becomes around humans, the more trouble they are bound to get into.

From around mile marker 31.5 to the beginning of the Spanish Harbor Bridge at mile marker 33, you have a good chance of seeing deer grazing on the gulfside shoulder of the road. Deer seldom travel alone, so if you see one, look around and you will probably see more.

Long Beach Road, which starts at mile marker 33 oceanside, is the eastern border of the Key Deer Refuge. Many times if you simply look down that road from the Overseas Highway, you will spot deer. Drive slowly down Long Beach Road, and you may see good-sized groups of deer.

No Name Key is where the tour buses go with the hope of catching a glimpse of Key deer. To get to No Name Key, you must go over a new cement bridge called the Bogie Channel Bridge. From the bridge you can look over the water and see the Spanish Harbor Bridge out on the Overseas Highway. You can also spot the Bogie Channel Bridge from the Spanish Harbor Bridge.

Before you arrive at the white boulders that mark the end of the road and the ruins of the old ferry town, you will probably see more deer. That's why you must travel very slowly. Follow the road all the way to the end, or simply park on the side and wait. Eventually you are sure to see some deer wandering through the tropical hammock. The creatures blend in very well with the background vegetation, so you've got to keep your eyes peeled. If you get out of the car, beware of poisonwood trees.

It is said that early mornings and late afternoons are the best times to see Key deer, but we have seen them at all times of the day. They are not hiding, you will find, and they are very beautiful; yes, very much like their northern cousins but in miniature.

The Key Deer Protection Alliance
872-3674

Founded in 1989, the goals of the alliance are to help save the Key deer from extinction by creating and distributing accurate and objective information to the public, and by supporting the preservation of the Key deer habitat. The Alliance awards scholarships to students pursuing degrees in biological sciences. They hold regular clean-up days.

Visitors to the islands are invited to attend Alliance meetings at 7:30 p.m. on the second Tuesday of each month, September through May, at St. Francis in the Keys Episcopal Church on Key Deer Boulevard.

Bahia Honda State Park

The Florida Keys' Biggest and Best Beach

Bahia Honda
MM 37, Oceanside ✻ 872-2353

Here is the most beautiful beach in Florida and possibly the whole country. That's what the travel magazines say anyway. What's most thrilling at Bahia Honda Beach are the brilliant colors. The ocean's magnificent arrangement of blue, green, and azure seems to change from day to day, and even hour to hour. What you see is actually a kaleidoscopic light show as the light reflects up from the bottom of the ocean through clear water. Each type of bottom translates to a different color as light bounces off it and back to the water's surface. Grass meadows reflect dark brown or navy blue; sand reflects yellow and beige; corals reflect various shades of blue. As the winds whip and toss the surface of the water, the hues of each color change. A cloudless day or a heavily clouded day will empower or mute the colors. The time of day and the angle of the sun influence your view, too. Beware: The sea is hypnotic.

The blustery sea air here is filled with graceful sea birds, who seem to be having a fine time gliding on the gentle breezes and gusts of the limitless sky. The sand is fine and the color of cafe au lait. You cannot not be dazzled by this glorious arrangement of sea, shore and sky.

The majority of the people you see have come here for the incomparable beach—and that's it. There's another beach on the other side of the park, on Bahia Honda Channel, and it's dramatically beautiful too, but in a different way. The waters of the Bahia Honda Channel are quite deep, by Keys standards, and the currents are swift not far from the sandy shore. Both beaches are the stuff that tourists' dreams are made of. Where's the beach? It's here, baby.

In addition to the main attraction, the beach, Bahia Honda Park's 524 acres also contain several complex biological communities. You will see more subtropical flowers here, particularly in springtime, than anywhere else in the Keys. Sea birds, white-crowned pigeons, herons, egrets, and gulls, are also in abundance.

Exploring the park is great fun. Deep waters begin close enough to the shore to provide exceptional swimming and snorkeling. Campers catch fish right off the shore and docks in front of their campsites on the channel. Kayaks are available for rent by the hour: $10 for a single, and $20 for a double. There are two boat launches and a parking lot for trailers. Snorkeling trips leave the lagoon twice daily. (There's a fee.)

Hike the perimeter of the park to see a tangled jungle of thatch and silver palms, key tiger lily, key spider lily. Sea lavender and bay cedar give way to a beachfront hammock with trees like satinwood and yellow wood. The plants were brought here from the West Indies via the Caribbean Sea by birds, hurricane winds, and ocean waves.

The Bahia Honda campfire circle, which is really an outdoor theater with a movie screen set against the backdrop of the Atlantic Ocean, is certainly the spiffiest campfire circle you'll ever see. Camping has come a long way since Mom and Dad were scouts....

On a map of the world in the park store, you are invited to push a pin into your home town. The areas of the eastern United States, as well as western Europe, are the most well-represented areas on the map.

Plenty of picnic tables and shelters are scattered throughout the park, many of them deliciously private, as well as three camping areas and a concession, where you can rent a boat or sign on for a snorkel trip to the Looe Key Reef.

The park is open from 8 a.m. until sunset every day of the year. Admission is $2.50 per car with one person. $5 for a car with two, and 50¢ for each additional person. Children five and under go free.

Information: Bahia Honda State Park, Route 1, Box 782, Big Pine Key, FL 33040. Phone: 305-872-3897.

The Waters of the Lower Keys

The Backcountry

You might envision an area located at the end of a long, lonely dirt road when you hear the term backcountry. Down here the term refers to expanses of small, uninhabited mangrove islands, scattered, shallow-water seagrass meadows and tidal channels on the north and west of the main island chain. The islands of the backcountry are accessible only by boat.

Because the backcountry is a haven for a wide variety of wildlife, most of the islands are under the jurisdiction of the Everglades National Park, National Key Deer Refuge, Great White Heron National Wildlife Refuge, and Key West National Wildlife Refuge.

Navigating through the sometimes maze-like backcountry can be difficult for newcomers. Tidal channels are not well-marked, and depth perception is difficult for the inexperienced eye. Running aground is a constant possibility in these very shallow flats, and, unfortunately, it is very easy to damage the backcountry's bottom communities with a boat's propeller. Boats crossing the deeper flats at high speed are almost sure to hit bottom at some of the shallower points on the flats. Propeller digs leave cuts in the seagrass beds and cracks that fill with sand and mud. Although sea grasses can withstand some disruption without suffering serious consequences, environmentalists are now concerned that the cumulative effect of increased boating in the backcountry may have lasting negative impact.

To avoid doing harm, keep your boat in the tidal channels, steer clear of the shallower shortcuts, and proceed with respectful caution. It is much easier to back off a flat that you have glided into gently than it is to back away after you've hit hard aground at a high speed. Lightweight, flat bottom kayaks are becoming the preferred vessel for visiting the backcountry. They're easy to operate, and they work for sightseeing, fishing and snorkeling.

Here's some good news about the backcountry for people prone to seasickness: The waters and lakes of the backcountry are usually quite calm, even when it's blowing hard on the oceanside of the Keys.

Looe Key Sanctuary

In March of 1996, Rodale's *Scuba Diving Magazine* readers chose Looe Key Reef as the best one in the United States. Looe Key gets its name from the HMS *Looe*, a 44-gun British frigate that ran aground on the reef during a winter storm in 1744. The reef is still a threatening one for boat traffic; small boats have scraped and damaged corals. Ironically, a large research vessel from the University of Miami caused massive damage when it grounded at Looe Key in 1994.

The 5.3-square-mile reef became a National Marine Sanctuary in 1981 following the success of the Key Largo Sanctuary, created in 1975. On the Looe Key reef, as well as on Key Largo's reef system, concentrations of fish species are spread throughout. The sanctuary designation means that spearfishing, tropical fish collecting and wire fish-traps are banned in the area of the reef. In the fifteen years since Looe Key became a sanctuary, scientists say, reef populations have become significantly more stable than in other unprotected areas.

Water clarity in the sanctuary is excellent, and sea conditions are generally moderate, permitting the reef's many spectacular inhabitants and features to be observed easily. The reef features over 150 species of fish, with descriptive names like yellowtail, jawfish, parrotfish, surgeonfish, barracuda, lizardfish and peacock flounder, swimming gracefully between the coral heads and sea fans and whips. Fifty species of coral are named for the earthly things they resemble: brain, elkhorn, and staghorn, for example. Looe Key Marine Sanctuary's spur and groove formations are the best developed in the Keys; uncommon pillar corals thrive in the intermediate and deep reefs. The seagrass meadows and sand flats provide fascinating views of sea life.

Stuff to Do On the Water

Get Wet Water Sports
MM 24.5 (at Sherman's) ✶ 745-3404

"There are different applications for Waverunners besides going around circles at 90 miles per hour," says Get Wet owner Bob Goetz.

The operation's newest offering is the hydro disk, a 7-foot-wide flat-bottomed circle of a boat that won't flip or negatively impact on the environment. A whole family can tour the backcountry in one of these. If you don't feel comfortable in a big boat, rent one of these babies.

Dolphin Marina Boat Rentals
MM 28.5, Oceanside ✶ 872-2685

The nice thing about the boats you rent at Dolphin Marina is that they're so well equipped. If you're going diving, everything you need—except the dive gear—is on board: ship-to-shore radios, a Bimini top to provide shade, and ice chests.

Boat rents start at around $85 for a half day and $150 for full day. Boat sizes are between sixteen and seventeen feet. Before you leave the marina, someone will go over charts with you to make sure you're headed in the right direction. (You don't have to travel far from shore for some big fun.)

HMS Looe Dives
MM 28.5 Oceanside ✶ 872-1444 ✶ 800-553-0308

The HMS *Looe* is named after the British ship that ran aground here in 1744, which is the same ship that the reef is named after. This namesake is docked at the Dolphin Marina on Little Torch Key. The 60-foot power catamaran is a great, roomy snorkel boat equipped with spacious bathrooms, freshwater showers, a snack bar, and a cash liquor bar. (Best to save your drinking for the return trip; you'll be benched and not allowed to go back into the water as soon as you order your first cocktail.)

The morning snorkel trip heads out to the reef, approximately 30 minutes away, at 10 a.m. and returns at 2 p.m. The afternoon reef trip is an hour shorter, from 2:30 p.m.–5:30 p.m. The fare for either reef trip is $19.95 if you have equipment; add $5 if you need to rent snorkel gear.

HMS Looe Key Sunset Cruise
Dolphin Marina ✺ MM 28.5 Oceanside

As a way of introducing folks to the pleasures of cruising on the spacious HMS *Looe Key* catamaran, they offer a sunset tour Wednesday and Friday evenings. There's live music, free food, and a cash bar on board. The cruise departs Dolphin Marina at 6 p.m. and returns at 9 p.m., all this for $10 a person. Follow signs to Little Palm Island ferry to find Dolphin Marina.

Strike Zone Charters
MM 28.5 Gulfside ✺ 872-9863 ✺ 800-654-9560

Larry Threlkeld, owner of Strike Zone Charters, is frequently called to ultra-posh Little Palm Island to introduce folks like Vice President Gore and family, Rod Stewart and Rachel Hunter, David Copperfield, and Ivana Trump to the joys of diving the Looe Key Reef.

Larry says magician David Copperfield did not make Little Palm Island disappear, in spite of several requests. And those many fashion models he is hired to ferry to the tropical retreat of the rich and famous: "We call them the 'vampire people.' They run from the sun! Their photo shoots start at 5 a.m. and wrap by 10 a.m."

Of course, you don't have to be a star to sign on for one of Strike Zone's many excursions. Through Strike Zone you can snorkel in the Looe Key Marina Sanctuary, tour the backcountry, or fish on assorted package tours, or do it all at once in a popular five-hour excursion designed to enlighten visitors to the natural history of the living coral reef and the Florida Keys, as well as the ecology of several Keys marine systems. Your captain will point out sea birds, marine life, and even help you catch a fish, which you cook and eat on board, too.

The popular trip includes a look at the ocean floor through a glass-bottom boat for small children or other people who are unable, for any reason, to get into the water. You might see a manatee. And if you hear music while you're exploring the reef, don't think you've flipped your lid. Your captain will sometimes lower a big speaker right into the water for an impromptu rock concert.

The five-hour Island Excursion goes out every afternoon from 1:30 p.m. till 6:30 p.m. Cost is $45 per person; kids six—nine years old pay half price; five and under go for free. This is a great family trip out on the water, but take plenty of sunscreen.

A snorkel and scuba dive trip to Looe Key leaves at 9:30 a.m. and 1:30 p.m., daily. Snorkelers pay $25, and $5 more for gear rental. Scuba divers pay $40, and $25 more for gear rental. Kids sixteen and under snorkel for $20, which includes the gear.

Strike Zone also offers a deep-sea fishing charter on a 40-foot or 34-foot sport fisherman. Custom fishing charters are $495 for a full day; $395 for a half day, and that price includes rods, reels, bait, and tackle.

Jig's Bait and Tackle
Family & Snorkeling Center ⚓ **MM 30.5. Gulfside** ⚓ **872-1040**

From the highway, it's easy to find Jig's—just look for the kayak display out front. Not only does Jig's sell block ice, live pinfish, custom rods, tackle, snorkel gear, dive flags, fishing licenses, and just about any other nautical needs, they'll also hook you up with a captain and charter boat to take you out into the ocean for deep-sea fishing, or into the backcountry for flats fishing. Jig's also books kayak tours for Lost World Adventure Tours.

Jig's rents double kayaks for $40 for a half, and $55 for a full day. Single kayaks rent for a bit less. Jig's is open from 7 a.m. till 7 p.m. Monday through Saturday; closes at 5 p.m. on Sunday.

Bahia Honda State Park Concession
MM 38 Oceanside ⚓ **872-3210**

Daily snorkel trips to Looe Key depart Bahia Honda dock at 9 a.m., noon, and 3 p.m. On the dive, snorkelers are assisted in identifying the wonders of the reef by helpful mates. Adults pay $22; kids under 16 pay $18. Snorkel set rental is $5 and, if it's really cold, you can rent a wet suit for $6.

Ask about the sunset eco-tour if you're interested in an hour-long lesson in birds, wildlife, and the reef system. The trip goes out if there are at least eight paying customers. Cost is $18 for all comers.

Lost World Adventures
Big Pine Key ✹ 872-1040

On this Kayak tour of the backcountry you'll learn how mangrove swamps, seagrass beds, rookeries and estuaries are the nurseries for nearly every species of marine life found on the living coral reef. Kayaking is the least invasive way to commune with nature. Marine biologist and photographer Bill Keogh is your reverent and wry wilderness guide. Keogh's fine photography is featured in the book *The Florida Keys, The Natural Wonders of an Island Paradise*.

Saltwater rafting

Osprey

Nature Treats

The Blue Hole
Key Deer Boulevard ✹ MM 30, Big Pine Key

The Blue Hole is an old rock quarry of fresh water that is home to several alligators, many fish, a couple of turtles, and some hawks and herons. It is the largest body of fresh water in the Keys. The alligators swim up to the observation deck to eyeball visitors with their strange, lizardy orbs and seem to think you're going to feed them. Don't do it! When you feed 'gators, you teach them to be unafraid of humans, and brave alligators eat humans, especially small, chubby ones like children. Recently a big 'gator became so tame, so confident about his acceptance by humans, that he begun to snap at tourists. Whoops! He had to be taken away from the Blue Hole.

On Saturdays, a volunteer naturalist spends the day at the Blue Hole, greeting visitors and telling them about the inhabitants of this strange place. Fresh water is crucial to the survival of Key deer, so you will often see them here along with fat raccoons.

To get to the Blue Hole: At the Big Pine traffic light at mile marker 30 turn onto Key Deer Boulevard (gulfside). Go through the intersection of Key Deer and Watson boulevards; then continue for one-and-a-quarter miles farther.

Pinewood Nature Trail
Key Deer Boulevard

A two-thirds-mile-long nature trail is located a quarter-mile past the Blue Hole. The trail winds through an excellent habitat typical of many slash pine and palm hammocks on Little Pine Key. Lots of signs will point the way and tell you what you're seeing.

Key Deer Refuge Headquarters
MM 30, Big Pine Shopping Center ✆ 872-2239

This little office contains a world of information about the unique habitat of Big Pine Key and the wondrous creatures who live here, many of them endangered. Before visiting the Blue Hole, the Big Pine Nature Trail, and No Name Key, stop by the refuge headquarters.

Legal Highs

Fantasy Dan's Airplane Rides
Sugarloaf Airport ✶ 745-2217
Fantasy Dan will fly out to the reef to view Stargazer, a two-hundred-foot-long, seventy-foot-wide 50,000-pound metal sculpture, resting twenty feet below the blue water's surface some five miles northwest of Key West. Stargazer is the world's largest artificial reef. On a full-moon night, when phosphorescent sealife light up Stargazer's form, the sight from the air is breathtaking. Dan charges around $100 for three people to take this special trip.

Dan also does ten minute flights for a closer look at the backcountry or half-hour sight-seeing flights over Key West.

Skydive Key West
Sugarloaf Key ✶ 745-4FUN
At MM 17 there is a blinking yellow light. Turn toward the Gulf there (same side as the Sugarloaf Lodge), and you'll come to the trailer that houses Skydive Key West. Inside there are videos of other people's dives to tempt you to sign up yourself. Cost of the tandem dive, and a video of it, is around $300.

Ultralight Tours
MM 28.5, Barry Avenue ✶ 744-7202
You can't miss the little Ultralight houseboat on the water adjacent to the Sandbar Restaurant. Take an instruction ride, or a ride just for fun aboard an ultralight airplane with Emil Ourednik. It will cost you $50 for 20 minutes, and if you want, Emil will let you fly it yourself. Anybody can fly an ultralight, Emil says. Taking off and landing are the tricky parts, and he handles these parts himself. Open seven days, depending on weather.

From the Ruins

Bahia Honda Bridge
MM 36, Oceanside

Just after you pass over the new Bahia Honda Bridge, heading for Key West, you will see a rough parking area, oceanside. This wild and wonderful place used to be a ramp for the Overseas Railroad and the Bahia Honda Bridge. Hike to the top of the bluff and compare the old railroad bridge, which was the most difficult of all the bridges to build, to the sleek, new bridge next to it.

The original Bahia Honda Bridge is 5,356 feet long, with twenty feet of clearance above the water and a maximum height of sixty-five feet. The trains for which the bridge were originally built in 1907 traveled through the center of the span, protected on either side by high, steel guardrails. But when the bridge was adapted for auto traffic in 1936, it was found to be too narrow to accommodate two lanes of cars. So the roadway was built over the top of the bridge. Imagine driving across that bridge on that road! You can still see the crumbling road surface.

Across the Bahia Honda Channel you can see Bahia Honda recreation area, where great photo opportunities await in this leg-stretching place. Explore the paths and ancient structures. In springtime a profusion of tropical wild flowers bloom on this ground. The wind is wild, always blustery. The waters in the Bahia Honda Channel are the swiftest currents anywhere in the Keys.

A Freaky Nature Treat
Bahia Honda MM 36

During the full moon in late May or early June, tiny palolo worms hatch from the sponges and rocks in the channel under the Bahia Honda Bridge. Tarpon go into a feeding frenzy, gobbling up the poor little worms. From the bridge you see huge schools of silvery tarpon clouding the surface of the water. Call Bahia Honda and ask a park ranger just how the scene is progressing next time you're in the Lower Keys at the end of May.

The Bat Tower
MM 17, Gulfside

Businessman Richter Perky read, many years ago, that a tower built of cypress and baited with food would attract hundreds of bats, which would, in turn, devour the pesky mosquitoes that discouraged anyone from seriously hanging out on Sugarloaf, where Perky had a fishing and gambling lodge. Perky built the tower, but the bats did not come. Now the tower is a historical monument, visited by hundreds of people annually. You might be disappointed when you see it, but it's only five minutes out of your way. And for Sugarloaf Key, it's a major tourist attraction.

The Bat Tower

The Ferry Ruins
No Name Key ❦ Big Pine Key

No Name Key is connected to Big Pine by the Bogie Channel Bridge, a fairly new concrete span that seems to be used more by fisherman than it is by cars. When you cross the bridge, you're on No Name Key, a place with no electricity and no water, either. The people who live on No Name Key get their power from solar units or generators. The houses are located at the end of long driveways with sinister-looking no-trespassing signs that seem to mean business.

Follow the road all the way out to the end, and you'll come to the ruins of a once-thriving ferry town. Park near the large, white limestone boulders that mark the road's end. Beyond them is the sea. This was once the site of a car ferry landing that carried travelers across a fourteen-mile span to or from Knight's Key next to Marathon. A small village with a school and a post office was established here in 1922. The town was a busy one until the Overseas Highway put the ferry out of business in 1938.

Today the ferry landing at No Name Key is unbelievably quiet. The only sounds you hear are the calls of birds in the trees and the whispering of the soft breezes. There are bold raccoons sometimes in the trees and, often, many Key deer. To the right and just beyond the white boulders is a magnificent and unusual clump of seven Canary Island Date Palm trees, their branches heavy and studded with dates. If you want to taste one, make sure you check for bugs first.

Biking

PLENTY OF LONG, SMOOTH, ROADS here are great for biking. On Big Pine Key, Watson Boulevard and Long Beach Road (MM 33) both take you past the Key Deer Sanctuary. As you bike past pinelands, mangroves and tangled jungle, you'll likely spot many deer and ride through pockets of suburbia-like enclaves that feel absurdly out of place. A good bicycle tour and lunch break in these parts could take up an entire afternoon.

On Sugarloaf Key, at mile marker 17, ride Sugarloaf Boulevard all the way to the end and turn right. You'll ride past three-and-a-half miles of dense mangroves on your right and, on the left, the entrances to some elegant estates barely visible from the road. It might cheer you to know that the Beatles traveled this route in 1964 when they were brought back here to visit the estate of Florida state representative Bernie Papy.

Four Star Rentals
MM 30 Gulfside ● 872-2229

If you rent a bike at Four Star Rentals, which is the only place to rent a bike in the area, you'll receive a map directing you to the island's many natural wonders as well as a stop for pizza at the No Name Pub. Bike rentals cost $10 a day or $40 a week.

Accommodations

 IG PINE KEY really is a bedroom community. Plenty of people,
residents and tourists alike, go to sleep each night and wake up each
morning in Big Pine Key but spend their days and evenings in Key
West. You can do the same thing and save yourself some money.

Several waterfront B & Bs are available on Big Pine, rather spectacular ones actually, and, in the Lower Keys, dozens of great campsites—
many of them right on the water in Bahia Honda State Park or in neat,
old fishing camps. Call ahead and the Lower Keys Chamber of Commerce (800-872-3722) will send a complete list of accommodations. It's
a short list, for sure, but you can discover good values and rare finds along
this serene stretch of blue sea, sky and bridge that joins Marathon Key to
the Lower Keys and the fury and bedlam that lies ahead at the very end
of the road on the island of Key West.

By the way, contrary to what you will probably be told or might reasonably surmise on your own, it takes a lot longer than a half hour to
drive from MM 30 to the end of the rainbow; it's more like 45 minutes.

Bahia Honda State Park
MM 37 Oceanside ✶ 872-2353

The beautiful Bahia Honda Park has three excellent camping areas
containing eighty campsites for tents and RVs. Waterfront camping is
available on the Gulf of Mexico, the Atlantic Ocean, and on the Bahia
Honda Channel. The park is excellent for exploring—the beach on the
Atlantic side of the island is often called the best in the Keys, in Florida,
and one of the best in the world.

Bayside camping sites are for tents or pop-up campers only. Camping
units over 6 feet, 8 inches high won't fit through the low underpass you
must take to access the area. There are restrooms near these seven tent
sites, but bathhouses are not so handy. Tent site #80 is the best one here;
it's surrounded by buttonwoods and features an unobstructed view and
access to the Gulf of Mexico.

Many campsites in the Buttonwood camping area face the Bahia
Honda Channel and have great views of the old Bahia Honda bridge and
the new Bahia Honda bridge. It has public phones and a bathhouse. The
shoreline is sandy and jagged, so you're in a fairly private area.

Campsites at Bahia Honda are around $25 a night. Half of them can
be reserved two weeks in advance; half are rented out on a first-come,
first-served basis. Two weeks is the maximum stay.

Bahia Honda Cabins
Bahia Honda State Recreation Area ● MM 37 ● 872-2353

Three cottages on stilts each contain six units that each sleep six people.
You can see the cottages from the highway at mile marker 37; they're on
the gulfside of the Overseas Highway. You have to go through the park
gate to access the cabins as well as an area of rustic campsites. Furnished
cabins are air conditioned, and they have heaters, too. Each unit has two
double beds, two bunk beds, and two cots. There's no television, no telephone, no radio, no microwave, and, although the kitchens are supposed
to be fully equipped, bowls, pots and pans seem frequently to have been
pressed into service as bailing pails and beach buckets. You have to sign
on for two nights minimum and seven days maximum.

The artificial lagoon in front of the cabins is not suitable for swimming, due to some polluted thinking in the early '70s. When the ramp for
the old Bahia Honda bridge was demolished to make room for construction of the new bridge, a ton of metal rods and planks were dumped into
this 35-foot-deep quarry. Recently a park service scuba diver explored the
lagoon and found a veritable garbage dump beneath the quarry's calm
surface. In addition to three junked cars, he found metal barbs and rods
standing upright from the bottom. That's why you see signs prohibiting
swimming. But fishing off the deck of the cabin is fun. Many folks bring
a boat and keep it tied up at their front door. Dining on the deck is
popular, too.

Although many people don't realize that they're available for rent,
the cabins at Bahia Honda are usually very well booked. A doctor from
Miami arrives each August on the opening day of lobster season and
immediately reserves an entire cottage of six units for the same week the
following August. It's a tradition. One year is the longest advance reservation permitted.

Barnacle Bed and Breakfast
Long Beach Drive ✻ 872-3298 ✻ 800-465-9100

The Barnacle Bed and Breakfast is advertised as "barefoot oceanfront living with panache." That's a good description. As you enter the house, a sign on the door reminds you to remove your shoes. You really do go barefoot here.

The house is built in the shape of a star. The rooms are shaped like points. Someone very creative, and a lover of stained glass and bright colors, has done a brilliant job designing these unique spaces. No two rooms are alike. At the middle of the star is an atrium, the communal space where breakfast is served. There's even a stairway to Heaven— well, to the sun deck on the roof. But if you'd rather, you can take your sun on a natural sandy beach and wait till nightfall to climb up to the roof for some stargazing. The sky is amazing out here.

All rooms have queen-sized beds, private baths, refrigerators, beach towels and ice chests. Two guest rooms are off the atrium where the hot tub is located. Two villas, or efficiencies with kitchens, are separate from the main house. If, after checkout time, you'd prefer to lounge on the beach for a few more hours rather than vacate immediately, you are welcome to use an outdoor shower and changing room at no additional charge. It's a nice touch.

No children under 16. No pets. No Smoking. Bikes, paddleboats, hobie cats and BBQ grills are free. Room rates are $115 in season; $105 off season. Efficiencies are $125 and $115.

Big Pine Key Fishing Lodge
MM 33, Oceanside ✻ Long Beach Drive ✻ 872-2351

Beneath the Spanish Harbor Bridge lies a wonderful row of old-timey, oceanside cinder-block cottages, a couple of spanking-new motel units, several rows of RV campsites, and some rustic but very pleasant tent sites. Some RV's spend the warmer months in storage here while their owners summer in the North. Dock your boat on a canal at the back door of your motel for only 15¢ a foot.

The lodge was designed some twenty-five years ago by folks who still live in the area and now operate the Casa Grande B & B on Long Beach Road. From an above-ground pool with a shower and a water fountain, you can gaze out at treetops and enjoy temperate breezes. Downstairs is a lovely clubhouse room with a stage and a bar for private parties.

Prices vary according to type of accommodations—but they're quite reasonable, and that's why guests here are frequently repeaters. Rustic tent sites are directly on the water and look out across the Spanish Harbor to the beautiful Bahia Honda State Park. Take a hike down Long Beach Drive and see Key deer.

A view typical of Big Pine Key guesthouses

Big Pine Motel
MM 30, Gulfside ✺ 872-9090

This motel has surely seen better days. It looks better on the inside than it does on the outside, a clerk in the front office said, and she was right. The motel rooms are clean, moderately sized, and equipped with twin double-beds, televisions, chests of drawers, writing tables, private baths with tubs, air conditioning, and there are phones, with free local calls. Mattress-wise, this is a place for adaptable people with strong, flexible backs.

Rates are posted on a menu board in the front office, which indicates they're subject to frequent changes. They're lowest on weekdays in the off season and highest on weekend nights in the on season. High season rates click in on holidays and special weekends. Motel rooms start around $50, top out around $70. Efficiencies are $70 to $80. This isn't a ritzy place, but it might be a bargain—depending on that menu board. Europeans return year after year. The owners of the Big Pine Motel live in Texas and hire charming local folks to run it.

Casa Grande
Long Beach Road ✺ 872-2878

The Casa Grande is designed for comfort and utility. It's difficult to say whether you're indoors or outdoors at any particular moment at the Casa Grande. Extensive, nearly invisible screening keeps mosquitoes out. A full breakfast is served daily on the patio. Since local building codes call for all homes to be built at an elevation of about one story above sea level, at the breakfast table and in the entire house, you're at eye-level with the coconuts growing in the palm trees rooted on the beach below. And feel those ocean breezes! There's a hot tub and a shade pavilion, too.

Guest rooms, three in all, have louvered doors to let in the breezes and, beyond those, solid doors to keep in air conditioning. There are queen or king-sized bed, fridges, plush private baths, and televisions, though out here you're too far away from the beaten path for cable, and reception is iffy. No private phones either.

Boaters can tie up for free at a dock belonging to the Casa Grande. It's across the street on a canal that takes you through the Coupon Bight and around to the famous Little Palm Island Resort.

The beach out back is small and sandy, outfitted with a hammock and cushioned beach chairs. Key deer wander in and out of the yard all day long. You'll definitely see your fill of them. (You must not touch or feed them, of course.) The water is a bit shallow and rocky for swimming, but the truly persistent will find a way.

Rates are $95 during season; $75 in off season. No credit cards. Personal checks and cash only. Reservations are a must.

Deer Run Bed and Breakfast
Long Beach Drive ❧ 872-2800

A real-estate saleswoman owns and operates this B & B, which is convenient because if you decide to relocate, Sue Abbott will help you find your own house here in Paradise. The Deer Run got its name from its location at the edge of a wildlife sanctuary. Before she built her house, Sue says, she came here often to observe the proliferation of Key deer and raccoons in the area. The Key deer that roam here are docile and beautiful and perfectly at ease around this house that has been here for just over a decade.

There are only three guest units at Deer Run. Two are downstairs behind a screened porch near the water's edge; upstairs in the private suite you can open your door and sleep in sea breezes. This is very much a Florida house, designed to blend gracefully with its surroundings. Amenities include a wide wrap-around porch, outdoor hot tub, and a full American breakfast served on the upstairs porch. All units have private baths, air conditioning and even heaters, though they're rarely needed.

The house is in a hardwood hammock and is next to the Atlantic Ocean. The beach is small and sparse, but it's inviting and certainly handy. In addition to the abundant wildlife, Deer Run is home to a couple of obviously spoiled house cats and some remarkable birds, including macaws, cockatiels, and a talky parrot.

Because of its location, you can be sure that you'll find utter serenity at the Deer Run. More than once, Sue says, people have checked into this quiet place and found it to be *too* quiet. But mostly her guests appreciate the tranquility. For restless tourists, bikes are available. And four miles away, the Bahia Honda Beach and Park.

A few house rules: A 50% deposit is required within ten days of making reservations. No credit cards, no children, no spring breakers, no smoking, and no guests on Fantasy Fest weekend. Rates are $85–$110, depending upon the season.

Little Palm Island
MM 29, Oceanside ✻ 812-2551 ✻ 800-343-8567

It opened nearly a decade ago, and, since then, the world has been heaping awards and accolades upon the Little Palm Island Resort. *Conde Nast Traveler* magazine's reader polls consistently give Little Palm Island high marks for service, rooms, food, location and atmosphere. Splashy publicity keeps locals regularly informed of its status. Last we heard, it was rated the second best hotel in the world. Which, of course, makes us want to know, who's number one? This we know for sure: Little Palm Island is the only four-star-rated hotel in the Keys.

The Florida Keys' penultimate resort is located on tiny, South Sea flavored Munson Island. You must boat to the island, which is probably a big part of its allure. Nestled amid flaming bougainvillea, oleander, hibiscus and palms are thirty one-bedroom suites designed for privacy and seclusion. Located in stilted, thatched cottages, each suite is equipped with a mini-bar, a coffeemaker, ceiling fans, a private sun deck, an outdoor shower and jacuzzi, a hammock, and a wrap-around balcony with views of the ocean. Robert Wagner and Jill St. John honeymooned in the Mockingbird Cottage.

Munson Island, the five-acre island upon which the Little Palm Island Resort is built, was once a fishing camp visited by Presidents Harry Truman and Richard Nixon, among others. It was owned by John Spottswood, a former Florida state senator and a Monroe County sheriff. Spottswood also once owned the magnificent Casa Marina Hotel in Key West. In 1960, *PT 109*, the story of President John F. Kennedy's World War II experiences, was filmed here. The Great House, which still stands today, was built to house film crews. A number of utilities were piped to the island at that time, including electricity and water, transforming Munson Island into the valuable little paradise that is it today.

Daytrippers are welcome to make reservations and skiff over to the island for a sumptuous lunch or dinner, but reservations are absolutely required. The fifteen-minute ferry ride is free. Or just hang around and use the amenities, which include a pool and a sauna, and windsurfers, sailboats, and canoes. Take the launch at MM 28.5 on Little Torch Key.

Dining reservations are strongly recommended. Don't be surprised if you have to wait a few days to get a reservation in the Little Palm Island dining room. Everything here is exorbitantly expensive, I mean, through-the-roof expensive. Call for details.

Looe Key Reef Resort
MM 27.5, Oceanside ☎ 872-2215 ☎ 800-942-5397
If you're coming to the Keys to dive—snorkel or scuba—you might consider staying here at the Looe Key Resort, where you're always thirty minutes away from the Looe Key Reef and on the same premises as a five-star PADI dive center. Looe Key Resort features a pool, sun deck, tiki bar and restaurant. It's inexpensive and very popular. All twenty motel rooms are located on a canal with a boat ramp and dockage. Motel rooms have two double beds, AC, TV and phones.

A 45-foot power catamaran makes two four-hour reef trips daily. Walk out of your room and hop in. Ask about diver and snorkeler packages when you make your reservations. Non-package rates are $60–$90, depending upon the time of year.

Old Wooden Bridge Fishing Camp
Bogie Channel Bridge ☎ 872-2241
The twelve tiny cottages in a row by the bay are painted soft yellow with white trim, and there are palm trees in every yard. Pretty picturesque. Smallest cottages sleep two in single beds. Larger cottages, and they're really very small too, sleep four good friends. The Bogie Channel bridge, which used to be an old wooden fishing bridge, is a holler away. Fish from the bridge and catch your dinner or make a friend of a fellow fisherman. Is this funky or what? You can bring your boat and tie up in the bay. No phones, no TV, no pool, no credit cards, and, for a firm reservation, you need to make a deposit when you book. Room rates are the same year-round. The units for two are $65 per day, $375 per week. The units for four are $90 per day, $500 for a week.

So what is there to do around here? Rest. Take nature walks. Fish. Hang out at nearby No Name Pub. That's about it. You'll need a book and a car.

"We're far away from everything," the manager says.

Sugarloaf Lodge
MM 17, Gulfside ✺ 745-3211

The lodge was built in the '60s and still maintains a '60s feel, physically and spiritually. Surprisingly, there are fifty-five rooms in this motel. Each is appointed in a sedate, sand-colored decor and overlooks mangrove islands on the Gulf of Mexico, which is a breathtaking vista. The pool area is particularly pleasant, though rarely crowded. Most of the time, folks are taking their sun around the lagoon, which is called a dolphin sanctuary. At a tiki bar, drinks and snacks are available.

The restaurant and bar at the Sugarloaf Lodge are both good.

It is not unheard of for Key West couples to honeymoon at the Sugarloaf Lodge, located seventeen miles from the end of the road. Staying at the Lodge is also a wise choice for the budget-minded. You won't get anything quite this nice in Key West for the same money. The drive "into town," as locals call it, is a pleasant twenty-minute hop.

Big Pine Vacation Rentals
MM 29.5, Big Pine Key ✺ 872-9863

Three night minimum stays are required when you lease accommodations from this concern. (The three-night clause is becoming standard practice in the Keys in the past few years, much to the chagrin of tourists.) All homes are on canals with boat dockage and fishing. Rates are deluxe, though still usually less expensive than what you'd pay in Key West for similar luxury.

Some Restaurants

Bobalu's Southern Cafe
MM 10 Bayside ✆ 296-1664

Family-owned and operated. Dad is Bob, Mom is Lu, and the pretty wait-resses are their daughters. The horseshoe bar and restaurant are decorated with antique tavern paraphernalia. There are couple of booths, and a few tables. It's a small place where nothing matches. Gourmands should defi-nitely go elsewhere. Food is just like home-cooked, and reasonably priced. Jamaican dishes are jerked chicken and chicken with cabbage. Southern cuisine includes fried chicken, liver and onions, baked pork chops, with a daily selection of veggie sides (you get two with your entree) like turnip greens, beans, rice, okra, mashed potatoes and fried green tomatoes. Dinners start around $8. A plate of four veggies is $5. Very sweet cobblers and Key lime pie are $2.75. There are no menus, just a blackboard with all the specials propped on a chair by your table. A famous regular at Bobalu's is children's book writer Shel Silverstein. And Jimmy Buffett describes Bobalu's in a scene in his novel, *Where is Joe Merchant*. A long row of newspaper vending machines out front features local papers, and if you get panicky for real news—the *New York Times* and the *Wall Street Journal*. Bobalu's is open from noon to 10 p.m; Sundays 4 p.m. to 10 p.m.

Coco's Cantina
MM 21.5 ✆ 745-1564

The breakfast special is $2.50. Lunch and dinner always features beans and rice. A family-owned and operated Nicaraguan restaurant open from 7 a.m. to 9 p.m. Closed Sundays.

Dippin' Deli
MM 31, Gulfside ✆ 872-3030

How I wish we'd never stopped here. Because now we can't *not* stop here. If you remember root beer floats and coffee milkshakes served with a stainless steel shaker of the stuff on the side, you, too, must stop at the Dippin' Deli. This is a place where teenaged boys order ice cream cones which they eat as slowly as possible, as they sit at the counter to keep their waitress girlfriends company. Ice cream concoctions with names like manatee, manatee junior, rocky shoal, sandy shoal, blowfish. If you're really hungry order a typhoon, a hurricane, or a tropical wave. Submarine sandwiches, and super sub sandwiches and the prices are easy to take.

Thirty miles from Key West. So near. And yet so far! The local folks who frequent the Dippin' Deli are nothing like the Key West locals who suck phony fast food sludge through giant plastic straws and think they're getting something wonderful because that's as wonderful as they've ever gotten. Big Pine still has its innocence. There are no fast-food restaurants here. The ice cream is 100% authentic, full-fat, cream and sugar ice cream. You can also get breakfast, lunch and dinner, and plenty of people do. Open daily at 6:30 a.m. Closes early on Sunday.

Galley Grill
MM 25, Summerland Key ✺ 745-3446
A homestyle restaurant run by Delores Feinberg and her four daughters. Hubby, Ron is the repair and maintenance man. Built in the '50s, the grill is a regular stopping place for lots of local folks. The bar is busy all day and all night. Out back there's a canal where boaters, some of whom live on mangrove islands in the area, tie up their vessels while they come inside to eat or drink. Sunday morning and early afternoon are usually packed with dawdly diners who enjoy reading the papers, and drinking gallons of coffee. Open daily for breakfast, lunch and dinner. Traditional local fare: conch chowder, conch salad, catch of the day, shrimp, fish and sandwiches. And a full bar, chock full of characters.

Geiger Key Marina
MM 10.5, Oceanside ✺ 296-3553
Attractions are drinking, live music, and dining on the dock right next to the canal. Don't bother to dress up for this waterfront hideout frequented by locals and a few lucky tourists who find their way to the place. It's been in business since the '60s, but Geiger Key Marina remains relatively unchanged and undiscovered. Happy hour is every Friday after-

noon from 4 p.m.–6 p.m. and includes free munchies. Good, live music
begins in the afternoon on Fridays, Saturdays and Sundays, and goes on
till 9 p.m. There's barbeque Saturday and Sunday afternoons; sometimes
the main course is ribs; sometimes Jamaican jerk chicken. You buy a meal
voucher from the bartender for around $7, then grab a paper plate, and
plastic fork and knife, and step up to the barbeque grill where the chef
fills your plate. You've heard that food tastes better outdoors? That's true
here. Geiger Key Marina is located in a residential area with lots of
souped-up trailers surrounded by some very lush foliage. The place is
open every day, and serves lunch and dinner, too. Specialities are pizza,
chili, conch chowder, fried fish sandwiches. To find it: Turn toward the
ocean onto Old Boca Chica Road at mile marker 10.5 (there's a Circle K
store there). Geiger Road will appear on your left, after a mile or so. The
marina is on the water, on the right side of the road.

Ice House
MM 31, Gulfside ✴ 872-1215
Finding the Ice House isn't easy, but Italian ices are so refreshing in the
subtropical heat, you really should give it your best shot. Your kids will
love you for it. The Ice House is a take-out window on the northern side
of an auto parts shop. There are signs, but not big ones, so keep your eyes
peeled. There's an outdoor dining area, not fancy—two tables and eight
chairs. At lunchtime, noise from the auto body repair shop out back sub-
sides for an hour or so. Sometimes you'll find the place closed when the
sign says they're supposed to be open. And vice versa. At lunchtime,
local working folks line up for pizza, Philly cheese steaks, subs and hoa-
gies and real homemade Italian ice in eight flavors. Prices are very
reasonable and there's free delivery in the area. They'll create an Italian
platter for your party or picnic. Posted hours are 11 a.m. to 5 p.m.

Island Reef
MM 31.3 Bayside ✴ 8721-2170
A hostess meets you at the door and seats you in the small dining room.
The walls are cedar and the ceiling is very low. Acoustically it seems that
everybody in the place is sitting at one big table, participating in one
great conversation. This does not bother me. I enjoy random snatches of

rhetoric. But if you don't, there is an outdoor dining area, inside a painted courtyard.

Bad acoustics aside, the Island Reef is a wonderful restaurant with a loyal and reverent following. It is not unheard of for tourists staying in Key West to drive up to Big Pine Key to take in a meal at the Island Reef. Many come for the chicken pot pie. It seems foolish to say food is "home-cooked" when in fact it is cooked in a restaurant. But this food really tastes as if someone who loves you has prepared it for you. And the waitresses serve it as if they're Mom and you're a good little girl or boy. If the chicken pot pie, or the seafood Newburg is a special on the day you visit, try it. Same for Philly steak and cheese or Reuben sandwiches. The bread, rolls and puff pastry are fresh and tender.

Closed Sundays. Otherwise lunch served 11 a.m. till 2:30 p.m. Dinners 5 p.m.–9:30 p.m. Homemade daily specials for lunch and dinner.

KD's Steak and Seafood House
MM 30.5 ✹ 872-2314

This longtime family operation was recently passed down to a couple of baby-booming descendants who have turned the Baltimore Oyster House into KD's Steak and Seafood House. Passersby used to stop in for lunch or dinner simply because of its evocative name. Oysters are no longer on the menu, but the place is still decorated in oyster-house decor. That means lots of wood, heavy captains chairs, old-timey booths with banquettes covered in turquoise Naugahyde, and battered life rafts that look as if they did duty at the wreck of the *Titanic*. A nice feature here is that the bar, which serves only beer and wine, is located separate from the main dining room. But if you like the pub scene, you can dine at a table in the bar. The service at KD's is commendable. No slow waitresses here. They're on top of everything and are assisted by busboys. And the food is also served in a reasonable amount of time.

Locals fill KD's at noon. The lunch menu—burgers, fish sandwich, Philly cheese steak and fried-fish platters cost from $5–$7. Many items from the dinner menu are available all day long, so you can have lobster for lunch, or a 16 oz. T-bone steak. The dinner menu features nightly specials, as well as steaks and seafood. Prices for dinner entrees range from $9 for the queen-sized cut of prime rib, to $25 for a very grand version surf and turf. Open daily from 6 a.m. till 10 p.m.

Little Torch Sandbar
MM 28.5, Gulfside ☎ 872-9989

This is a place for drinking, not dining. Food is served as sort of an after-thought. Sometimes the waitress is also the bartender, which means she's overworked, and the customers at tables are under-serviced. Of course nobody is in a hurry here. That's part of the ambiance.

Lunch is standard fare: hamburgers, fried fish or chicken fingers. French fries are a la carte. Chicken jerk salad on a paper plate seems way too skimpy to pass for a $5.95 lunch entree. The forks and knives are plastic.

Everything changes at dinnertime. A chef comes on duty to create culinary theme nights with dishes priced at $8.95, $10.95 and $12.95. Monday is Italian night; Tuesday, Caribbean; Wednesday, gourmet; Thursday, Mexican; Friday, sensuous seafood; Saturday and Sunday, prime rib. Also, when you order a big meal you get real silver and plates. And if you order a burger or fish fingers—lunch at dinnertime in other words—you'll get plastic utensils.

"This is a very casual place," the barmaid explained.

The view of the Pine Channel, which you can see from any seat at the large, rectangular bar, is the big draw here. You can see the highway from the bar. You can see the bar from the highway. And it's pretty damned inviting. Built on stilts above a mangrove-fringed shore, the Sandbar has a pool table and a lot of video games. The bar serves only beer and wine. Hours are 11 a.m. till 11 p.m. Happy hour is 4 p.m.to 6 p.m. daily. To meet locals, stop in to the Sandbar.

Mangrove Mama's
MM 21, Gulfside ☎ 745-3030

Unless someone recommends this place nearly hidden from view by a luxurious cluster of banana plants, you probably wouldn't go in expecting a great lunch or dinner. It looks funky, and it is, but charmingly so. Locals keep it busy year-round. That's a good sign. There's a main dining room, with a library, and a couple of dogs and cats lying around on the cement floor. On the occasional December or January cool night you might find a fire in the fireplace. A series of smaller dining areas extend from the main room, and you'll probably want to dine in one of those. The bar is always packed. An always there sign out front says "music tonight." Well yes.

Who doesn't have music every night? Oh! You were expecting live music. Sorry. That's only on weekends.

The *Miami Herald* once named the Key lime pie at Mangrove Mama's, the best in the Keys. No matter who owns the place, and the ownership has changed a couple of times in the last few years, the Key lime pie recipe is the same. You don't mess with a good thing.

Monte's Restaurant and Fish Market
MM 25, Gulfside ● 745-3731
Fried-fish sandwiches and baskets served unceremoniously by efficient but not very friendly waitresses. During season there are often lines out the door. Although the fish is very fresh, the rest of the food—the rolls, French fries, cole slaw and so forth, is pedestrian. Because it's usually busy, you feel herded rather than served. Wham, bam, thank you sir and ma'am.

No Name Pub
North Watson Boulevard ● Big Pine Key ● 872-9115
Turn onto Watson Boulevard, which is bayside, at the light. This outpost of local color is gaining an ever-larger reputation. Somehow, it's become the place to find when visiting Big Pine Key. You feel you've entered into a time warp here and gone back to the days when bare-footed, beer-drinking expatriate Americans like the ones at this bar, were present at every bar south of Miami. Key West used to be like this twenty years ago. Back then, not owning shoes was a glorious reminder of how far away we were from tradition and adulthood. You'd be surprised to see how tough good soles can become in the right climate.

The beer at the No Name is served in the bottle—no glass. The walls and the ceiling are covered with dollar bills upon which people write their names and the date for posterity. "Do you have any idea how many dollars there are on these walls?" a customer asked a pregnant waitress named Donna. "No, but you're welcome to count 'em," Donna answered.

Once it was a bar used by married men and their girlfriends, certain that no one would ever find them here. Yet, many Keys residents still don't know it's here, since they don't read guidebooks. Lately people from all over the world have been showing up at the No Name Pub to drink in the local color. The pizza, which is renowned, is pretty good. The place is air-conditioned, so it's cool in the summer. Outside, there's a huge beer garden where fundraiser picnics and parties are occasionally held. The entertainment is a jukebox and a pool table. It's out-of-the-way, remote, and believe me, there are no neon signs to help you find it. Open seven days.

To find No Name Pub turn at the light at mile marker 30, and bear to the right onto Wilder Road. Eventually you come to a stop sign, where you'll bear right. This road will take you over a humpback bridge and past a little green sign that says "Access to No Name Key." No Name Pub is on the left side of the road. If you see a fishing camp on your right, you've gone too far.

Old Road Cafe
MM 22 Gulfside ✒ 745-8800

The heady aroma of growing herbs perfumes the air in an outdoor court-yard at the Old Road Cafe. Words hand-printed on a decorative watering can say "From the earth we are formed. To the earth we return. And in between we garden." People are thrilled to see chef/owner Leslie Artique or her sister Lisa Johnson bustle out of the kitchen and into the garden to snip a handfull of lemon basil or dill.

Outdoor dining here is very popular, but indoors is just as interesting. Smoking is forbidden and air conditioning is turned on at the last possi-ble moment; the room is open and balmy—even in summer. A never-ending slide show of images of the Keys of yesteryear is projected onto a wall. The pictures are nostalgic, unbelievable, and provocative. Also, there are photographs mounted beneath a sheet of glass on every table. If you have an interesting old photograph of a Keys scene, or an old menu from a Keys inn, loan it to the house and they'll buy your dinner.

Blue Plate specials are available nightly at $8.95. A favorite is smoked baked pork chops with sweet potatoes, apple slices and onion. Others are country fried steak. Turkey meatloaf. And the freshest fish.

The menu is short and manageable. Presentation is simple. The Old Road Cafe achieves a soft shimmer of Eastern serenity. Dinner only, from 6 p.m.

Raimondo's Ristorante Italiano
MM 21, Oceanside ▪ 745-9999

Turn at the Sheriff's sub-station. Very shortly you will see the sign for Raimondo's on your left. Understandably location is a big, big problem for Carlos and Alex, the brothers who co-chef, and co-own Raimondo's. It's been a big problem for several earlier enterprises that tried, and failed, at the same address.

Raimondo's seats 150 guests, but, judging from the busy night we were there, cannot adequately serve 150 guests. The host is very congenial. The service is friendly, but uneven. Cuisine is traditional Italian fare, described on the menu in mouth-watering detail. Unfortunately the dinners failed to match up to the fanfare. In fact, on the night we were there the food was downright disappointing. The sauce on a rib-eye steak, the special of the evening, could have passed for canned gravy. The pasta was overcooked. The veal was tough. But everyone on the staff was so nice, and the place was so busy, no one in our party had the heart to complain. And from time to time you do hear good things about the place.

On the plus side, the surroundings are splendid. And very clean. Dine indoors or out, on a picturesque canal. A kick is Raimondo's extensive beer selection. Choose from European beers served in their own brand's glasses. One, Caesarus Heller Bock, is said to have been brewed originally for Roman gladiators. An extensive wine list is excellent.

Raimondo's is open daily for lunch and dinner, although you would be well-advised to try Raimondo's on a slow, easy night. Dinner entrees range from around $9 to $21. Reservations are recommended.

Shops

Artists in Paradise Gallery
MM 30, Big Pine Shopping Center ✱ 872-1828

This is a co-op gallery, which means the artists and painters of the Lower Keys are well-represented in person as well as visually. Every day there is at least one artist, or a close relative of one on duty to answer your questions about their work, or about work by any of the other 25 artists represented here. The gallery features mostly tropical art, expressed in watercolors, oils, prints and etchings, embossings, stained glass, sculpture, pottery, weavings and metal wall hangings.

On alternate Friday nights during the winter season a nighttime reception features new work by one of the co-op's artists. Receptions are on from 6 p.m.–9 p.m. and are open to the public. If you're interested in collecting regional art, or just in collecting regional conversation with Keys artists, you should phone the gallery for a schedule of events.

Artists In Paradise Gallery is open daily from 9 a.m. till 6 p.m. in the winter. In the summer the gallery closes on Mondays. Otherwise, hours are 9 a.m. till 7 p.m.

E Fish Co.
MM 22.5 ✱ 745-3887

E Fish will ship shrimp, Florida lobster, stone crab, and their famous seafood sausage to unfortunate people back home who didn't get to come to the Keys with you. Assuage your guilt. Send seafood. They ship anywhere that UPS goes. E Fish is open from 1 p.m. to 7 p.m., daily.

The Nut House
MM 10 ✱ 292-8688

A nut and dried fruit emporium on Big Coppitt Key. Big sellers are Keys Crunch, a bark-like brittle of nuts, seeds and honey, Duval Crawl, spicy Chinese crackers, and bags of golden yellow dried mango. Also hot stuff like Scorned Woman Hot Sauce and Bloody Mary Mix. Shop owner Ann

Labriola is usually in view, wrapping gift trays of gourmet goodies for shipment to Bloomingdales, Saks, and a slew of other fancy food boutiques. As she works, Labriola chats easily, laughs often, and answers many questions. All the while, her hands, ever graceful and sure, are moving.

There is an art to all of this, and in fact, she is an artist. Labriola is a renowned and well-respected sculptor whose monumental works have brought her fame, but not fortune. Making a living in the pricey paradise of the Florida Keys is an ever-constant challenge. She never planned on making money on her sculpture, Labriola says, and she never has. In the twenty years since she arrived in the Keys with a masters degree from the San Francisco Art Institute, she has cleaned houses, maintained yards, waited tables, and developed photographs in a home lab to pay the bills.

She has also created several colossal sculptures, all designed to promote her artistic vision: the union of art, nature and archaeology. Her most notable work, *Stargazer*, is the largest underwater sculpture in the world. It is two hundred feet long, seventy feet wide, ten feet high, and wrought of 50,000 pounds of steel. Holes on *Stargazer*'s surface form patterns of star constellations. Resting on a sandy bottom, in 22 feet of clear, blue water, *Stargazer* is five miles from Key West, and points due southwest toward the Sand Key lighthouse.

The project took three years and $125,000 to complete, Labriola raising most of the money herself. Once she wore knee pads and knelt before one art patron to beg him for money. He wrote her a check for $500.

"I'm used to people looking at me as if I'm crazy," Labriola, a native of Armonk, NY, says, shrugging. "But it takes a lot to give something lasting to the world."

Sherman's Nautical Emporium
MM 24, Oceanside ♥ 745-1748

A warehouse-sized emporium of Florida Keys gifts, goods and gear. You'll find everything at Sherman's from fishing rods and marine charts to Hawaiian shirts and dresses. In the marine Christmas corner there are strings of dolphin and manatee lights, and tiny snow-white sand dollars on gold wires. Buy a real baby shark floating in a jar of water, or a bikini with little foam rubber pads that can be used in the top, if needed, to provide that all important up-lift to your holiday beach scenes. Lousy photographers can buy strips of slides that feature fabulous shots of the Keys' most beautiful sights photographed by hired pros. Slap those slides into your projector and who will know you didn't shoot them yourself? For greater impact, wear your padded bikini top under your T-shirt while you show your vacation slides. Sherman's is open daily from 9 a.m. to 6 p.m.

Second Hand, Fleas and Junk

Big Pine Flea Market
MM 30.5 Ocean ☎ 872-4103
The mother of all Keys flea markets, the Big Pine features 250 vendors every weekend from October until May. Open 8 a.m.–2 p.m. Saturday and Sunday.

Big Pine Methodist Church Flea Market
Key Deer Boulevard ☎ 872-2470
Saturdays only, same hours as the Big Pine Key Flea Market.

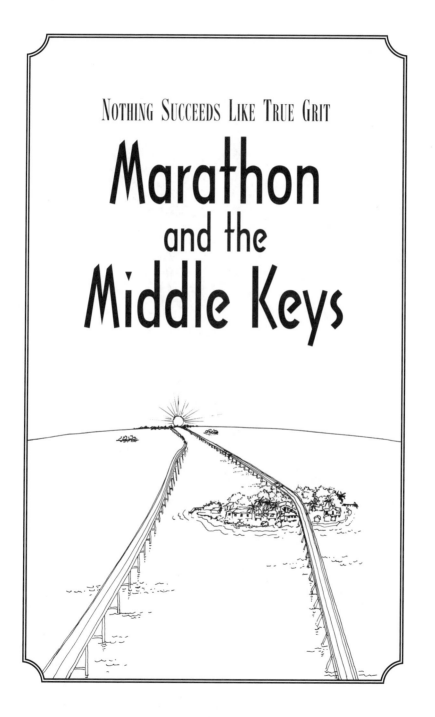

NOTHING SUCCEEDS LIKE TRUE GRIT

Marathon
and the
Middle Keys

To Islamorada

Mile Marker 70

Layton

Long Key

Conch Key

Duck Key

Grassy Key

1

Crawl Key

Key Colony Beach

Vaca Key

Marathon

Sombrero Beach

Seven Mile Bridge

To Lower Keys

Pigeon Key

Mile Marker 40

Marathon & The Middle Keys: Nothing Succeeds Like True Grit

WHILE KEY WEST is ever-polishing and refinishing its surfaces, fast erasing the last traces of the rough and salty exterior that brought tourists there in the first place, Marathon is proud and satisfied to be a last holdout of that indescribable, but-you-know-it-when-you-find-it, Keys island charm.

The citizens of Marathon are proud of the way they've managed to preserve the magic of the Florida Keys and the coral islands' intrinsic seaside languor. "Why hurry? Why gripe?" Marathon's attitude seems to say. "Here it is. Here's what we've got. This is the way we do things." There's the faintest trace of haughtiness in residents' patient responses to your questions as you sample their food, their shops, their resorts. You can't blame them; you're only visiting. These people live here, not just for two weeks, but for every day of their lives, in this hazy paradise of endless summer.

In Marathon, a man wears a shirt that says, "This is as dressed up as I get." Believe it.

Marathon is said to have the largest year-round, live-aboard population at anchor of any place on the east coast: an estimated 100 boats year-round, and up to 300 in the winter when it's too cold for boat-living in the rest of America. The shore is lined with funky marinas that give way to tiny streets of jumbled trailer parks.

Marathon's attractions are limited, and that's part of its allure. It is truly laid-back, a characteristic often described, but seldom actually found anymore in the ever-more-busy Keys. Marathon's charms are subtle; you have to root them out. Make friends with the locals you meet who are tending bar or running the boat rental shops. From the woman who runs a shell and gift shop, I learned that every morning, around 8 a.m., a group of stingrays assembles in the water at the Pigeon Key end of the Old Seven Mile Bridge and seems to greet the folks walking and biking above them. Walking clubs have formed around this phenomenon.

The area of the Middle Keys is a historian's bonanza, much of its magic lying in its remarkable past. The Seven Mile Bridge, built in 1909, remains one of the world's greatest engineering feats. Pigeon Key, the tiny island beneath it, is a shrine to the unlikely heroes who built the bridge and the miracle that was the Overseas Railroad. From Knight's Key, huge steamships once departed for Havana, Cuba, heavy with passengers delivered to Marathon by train from places like Montreal and Boston and New York City.

The Long Key viaduct at mile marker 65.5, no longer used, runs alongside the modern Long Key Bridge. The two-mile bridge is said to have been Henry Flagler's favorite. Since it was built in 1909, it has been one of the most photographed places in the Keys. Long Key, now an attractive State recreational area, was once the location of a posh fishing camp, whose membership list included presidents, writers, and other business and cultural icons of the first part of the 20th century.

The community of Marathon has a private 18-hole championship golf course, a public 9-hole golf course, a children's museum, several dolphin facilities, and a couple of good biking and hiking trails.

Bargains in the Middle Keys include accommodations and food. It's also a terrific central location. For vacationers interested in exploring the Keys, this is the place to be. The brochures all claim that when you're in Marathon, you're only an hour from Key West or Key Largo, but in fact, it's more like an hour-and-a-half. Fly into Marathon's small, spiffy airport, drive a reserved rental car right out of the airport parking lot, and save yourself a few hassles.

The area of the Middle Keys begins around mile marker 70 and ends at the southern end of the Seven Mile Bridge, at mile marker 40. Middle Keys are comprised of Long Key, Conch Key, Duck Key, Grassy Key, Key Colony Beach, Knight's Key and the community of Marathon, which is located on Key Vaca.

Marathon (Key) and The Name Game

A bunch of Marathon business people recently came up with a plan to change the name of the Middle Keys community known as Marathon to Marathon Key, with the hope that the new name would let people know that Marathon is a bona fide part of the Florida Keys, and hence inspire them to book their vacations here. The Monroe County Commission agreed and gave the plan their blessing. But when word of the planned change got around, there was an outcry from citizens opposed to the addition of "Key" to Marathon. After all, they reasoned, Marathon isn't an island or a key at all; it isn't a town or a city—it's a community, on a key, and that key's name is Vaca. But Vaca Key is hardly a romantic name for a tropical island. Marathon Key isn't a lot better…but it beats Vaca, which in Spanish means "cow." And everybody already knows Marathon.

For a while the editorial pages of the local papers were filled with letters on the subject, arguments both pro and con. Finally, just before the matter was to be turned over to the U.S. Board on Geographic Names for a decision, the Marathon Economic Development Council withdrew its name-change petition and the identity crisis was over.

"I've never seen the town come together in such a way to fight a group of big money guys. It's wonderful," said Gail Swanson, a Keys historian and Marathon resident.

History

EY VACA is found on a map of the Keys drawn by Spaniards in the 1500s. Historians believe it was named for the manatees, or sea cows, that thrived in the area's waters. For Keys Indians, manatees were a delicacy reserved for only the most important people in the tribe.

A young Spanish sailor, shipwrecked near Key Vaca in 1575, was captured by prehistoric Indians and lived with them for eighteen years. He was freed by a crew from a passing ship. Back in Spain, Escalante Fontanada wrote an account of his life with the Indians, but historians believe he recorded his memoir nearly thirty years after his captivity. His is the only written account we have of those times. Unfortunately, many of the references are puzzling and do little to broaden our knowledge of the Florida Keys.

In the early 1800s, Key Vaca was settled by Bahamians as well as several fishing families from Mystic, Connecticut. During the 1820s, Key Vaca was a port for a small fleet of wreckers and one of the first three settlements in the Keys; the others were Key West and Indian Key. Bahamian farmers raised limes, guavas, avocados, sugar apples, sapodillas, and sea isle cotton. Eventually these settlers abandoned the area, frightened away by the Indian Key Massacre in 1840. The seafarers from Connecticut moved to Key West, and the Bahamians fled to other islands. In the 1845 election, only nine citizens from Key Vaca were registered to vote. By 1860 only twenty-six people lived on Key Vaca and, of those, twenty-four were of one family. After the Civil War, only two farmers were known to be living in Key Vaca.

When the Overseas Railroad reached Key Vaca, the area became construction headquarters. By 1910 the population was 600; a small town had sprung up. Key Vaca was renamed Marathon by the railroad workers who lived in wooden dormitory buildings on Marathon and adjacent Pigeon Key. From 1909 to 1912, Flagler's railroad operated between Miami and Marathon, which had, by then, become a major depot and administrative center for the railroad. Marathon had wooden sidewalks and a two-story hotel, built in 1908 near the site that is today Marathon Yacht Club.

Knight's Key was the terminus of the Overseas Railroad while the Seven Mile Bridge was under construction. Passengers heading for Key West, Cuba, or the Caribbean got off the train at a wharf on Knight's Key and boarded ferryboats to complete their journeys. In 1912, the train tracks were finished all the way down to Key West.

By 1920 only a few families remained in Marathon, although it was still an important fishing town. The Miami Ice & Fish Company operated hundreds of boats on the waters surrounding Marathon. Fish was iced, loaded onto the trains, and shipped to Miami.

In 1935 the Overseas Railroad which, in its twenty-three years of operation had never turned a profit, was destroyed by the Labor Day Hurricane. In 1938 the Overseas Highway, built atop the remains of the railroad, was completed, linking the Lower Keys to the rest of the country. Marathon became a tourist resort and sport-fishing area.

Hurricane Donna demolished much of Marathon in September 1960. Many people still living in Marathon remember Donna well. Sometimes on the anniversary of the storm, at community get-togethers, survivors describe their memories of the event. Very scary....

A History of Long Key

Long Key was first named Rattlesnake Key by those ever-inventive Spanish explorers. The name refers to the island's shape, historians say, not to rattlesnakes who live there. Yes, the Keys *do* have rattlesnakes.

The Spanish government deeded the unsettled 965-acre island of Long Key to Don Francisco Ferreira, a St. Augustine man in 1814 as a reward for service to the crown. Ferreira sold Long Key to Charles Howe of Indian Key for $1500 in 1827. Around 1838 Howe, then the postmaster at Indian Key, and botanist Dr. Henry Perrine started up a partnership called the Tropical Fruit Company. They began clearing the land for a mulberry tree grove with the hope of starting a silk industry. Unfortunately, Dr. Perrine died in the Indian massacre at Indian Key in 1840, before the plans yielded fruit or profit.

In 1880, a couple of guys bought Long Key and planted it with coconuts. 17,000 coconut palms were growing on Long Key when it was purchased in 1884 by two brothers from New York City. The brothers frequently visited their coconut plantation on their yacht. The entire population of Long Key by 1900 was ten people; twelve when the New Yorkers were in town.

In 1906, Henry Flagler's Overseas Railroad reached Long Key. Flagler thought the coconut grove so beautiful he bought it and created a super deluxe fishing camp, in keeping with his tradition of marking the route of his railroad with spectacular inns and hotels.

Flagler's fishing camp had a clubhouse, a lodge, a post office, and fourteen cottages connected by a boardwalk. Among the Long Key Fishing Club members was Zane Grey, a dentist from Zanesville, Ohio, who was also a novelist. Grey, whose most famous novel is *Riders of the Purple Sage*, is known as the "father of the American Western." Grey served as president of the club from 1917–1920. Presidents Herbert Hoover and Franklin Roosevelt were among the fishing enthusiasts who stayed there.

In September 1935, the Long Key Fishing Club, that magnificent coconut grove, and much of the Overseas Railway were destroyed in the Labor Day Hurricane. The Long Key Fishing Club was reactivated near the camp's original location in 1968. Baseball player Ted Williams was a charter member, as were Jackie Gleason, Arthur Godfrey, Mike Douglas, and President Jimmy Carter, who was not yet president. The club disbanded for the last time when Long Key was turned into a state park.

Long Key State Recreation Area was created by the State Parks Department and opened to the public in 1969. The original Long Key Fishing Club is remembered with a historical marker located around mile marker 66 and with Zane Grey Creek Road, named after the author.

Flagler's Railroad: The Eighth Wonder of the World

When Henry Flagler was 37 years old, he formed a very fortuitous partnership with John D. Rockefeller. That business was the Standard Oil Company, and, in short order, both men were millionaires. There were no income taxes in the United States back then, so Flagler and Rockefeller literally made money faster than they could spend it.

In 1886 Flagler formed the Florida East Coast Railroad, which ran from Jacksonville to Miami by 1896. The train was convenient for folks who traveled to South Florida's tropical paradise with its balmy weather and remarkable environment. Flagler built several fabulous hotels along the Florida coast so that his clients would find not only the country's most marvelous weather but comfortable accommodations as well. Through his hotels, his railroad, and his oil company, Flagler just kept getting richer.

But Flagler's successes only whetted his appetite for more acquisitions and a bigger role in America's economic future. During the Spanish-American War, Flagler noted that the Army shipped supplies to its troops in Cuba via railroad to Tampa, and then by sea, out of Tampa's deep-water harbor. Although Miami is closer to Cuba, its harbor was too shallow for trade. Key West, however, had a magnificent deep-water harbor. Flagler knew Key West's excellent harbor could easily become a valuable gateway to Cuba, the Caribbean, and the Panama Canal.

Building a railroad to Key West, Flagler believed, would open up trade with far-flung ports of the world like China, Japan, and the Far East. He was propelled by visions of cargo moving by rail from America's great northern cities all the way down his Florida East Coast Railroad route, and then on down the East Coast Extension and into Key West.

Key West was the very last in a chain of coral rock islands, overgrown by subtropical jungle, mostly untouched by civilization, and separated by varying spans of ten to thirty-feet-deep ocean water. More than half of the planned railroad would have to traverse water. To most people the idea of building a train over the ocean and through jungle was sheer madness.

When Flagler was asked how he could possibly build a railroad down the Keys, he replied, "It is perfectly simple. All you have to do is to build one concrete arch, and then another, and pretty soon you will find yourself in Key West."

One associate's reply to this was, "Flagler, you need a guardian."

In 1905, in spite of the general consensus among his peers that he was off his rocker, Flagler hired the best engineers his bottomless pit of money could buy and work began. The world called the project "Flagler's Folly."

As the first team of workers, 300 blacks from Florida and the Bahamas, slashed their way through the first thirty miles of jungle between Homestead on the mainland and the thirty-mile-long island of Key Largo, they were bedeviled by merciless heat, mosquitoes, sand flies, alligators and rattlesnakes. Halfway through Key Largo, workers discovered a mile wide inland lake that had been overlooked by surveyors. Appropriately, they named it Lake Surprise.

As construction of the railroad moved down the Keys, a sizable fleet of ocean-going vessels was employed to transport the enormous amounts of gasoline, concrete, dynamite, crushed rock and coal, as well as water, food, medical supplies and goods for a work force that was at times 3,000 to 5,000 men.

Workers lived aboard huge floating houseboats, or quarterboats. When a disastrous hurricane hit the Keys in 1909, one of the quarterboats with 160 men aboard broke from its moorings and was carried out to sea by winds of over 100 miles per hour. Some men, terrified of drowning or of being eaten by sharks, swallowed deadly doses of laudanum from first-aid kits and lay down to die. After the barge broke apart, a few survivors clung to planks and were picked up out of the sea and taken by freighters as far away as Liverpool, England.

In addition to the loss of nearly 130 lives, the hurricane wreaked terrible damage on the railroad and the fleet of boats that carried the equipment and materials. Construction that had been started on the Long Key Viaduct was badly damaged.

Many workers died in dynamite explosions, in hurricanes, in fights and disputes often fueled by alcohol. Keeping workers was an enormous problem for the railroad. The job was simply too challenging for most men. Workers from the Cayman Islands, out in the Caribbean where the weather is similar to the weather in the Keys, did far better than most. Men from places like Norway or Canada might show up from time to time but usually lasted only long enough to collect their first paycheck before heading back to civilization.

Speculation grew that skid-row bums and winos from the streets of New York and Philadelphia had been enlisted to work on the railroad by nefarious methods. But a governmental investigation into Flagler's hiring practices later cleared him of these charges.

Laborers hired from New York were promised $1.25 a day, free room and board, and free hospitalization to work on the railroad. In those days, a man could live well on $2.50 a week, so railroad pay was substantial.

Flagler strictly forbade alcohol in any of the workcamps, which opened opportunities for bootleggers from Key West who arrived with clandestine boatloads of hootch. To counter the damage done by "booze boats," Key West churches sent boatloads of "preacher boats" to camps to hold services.

In spite of the horrific hardships, the Long Key Viaduct was finally completed in 1907, which meant the railroad to Key West was roughly half done. The bridge was built on 186 35-foot reinforced concrete arches, extended over 2.15 miles of water. It required 286,000 barrels of cement, 177,000 cubic yards of crushed rock, 106,000 cubic yards of sand, 612,000 feet of piling, 5,700 tons of reinforcing rods, and 2,600,000 feet of dressed lumber. Imagine the maneuvering required to transport all those materials to their destination.

By 1908 the railroad reached Key Vaca, one of the first two settlements in the Keys. A bustling station on nearby Knight's Key became the train's terminus for the next four years. In Key Vaca, one railroad worker exclaimed, "Building this railroad has become a regular marathon." The name stuck and later became the name of the town that is known today as Marathon.

A busy city grew up on Key Vaca, populated by various employees of the railroad. Regular passenger service began in February 1908. Steamships of the Peninsular & Occidental Steamship Company, also owned by Flagler, met the trains on Knight's Key. The number of passengers and the amount of freight between Florida and Cuba quickly increased.

In January 1909, the first through passenger train between New York City and Knight's Key began regular service every day but Sunday. The train left New York at 2:10 p.m., and arrived at Knight's Key dock at 7:30 a.m. two days later. Passengers slept in Pullman berths, dined in dining cars, and unfortunately missed the most breathtaking scenery, the islands of the Florida Keys, as the train passed over them in the dark. The ferry to Havana then took six hours.

The hurricane in September 1909 severely damaged preliminary work on the Seven Mile Bridge. It took two years to repair the damage. Finally, the Seven Mile Bridge was completed, and the railroad construction continued on, advancing slowly past Little Duck Key, Ohio and Missouri Keys (named by homesick railway workers). Finally, it reached the Bahia Honda channel. Named by Spaniards, the name means "deep bay." The job of bridging the Bahia Honda channel was fraught with terrible difficulties. The deeper the water, the higher the wave; therefore, Bahia Honda's bridge had to be very high. The finished bridge required thirteen

A steam train on the Seven Mile Bridge

spans 128 feet long, thirteen spans 186 feet long, and nine arches of concrete, each one 80 feet long. Just when that bridge was completed, a second mighty hurricane struck in September 1910 and displaced a center span.

When one superintendent was caught in the hurricane, he tied himself to a tree with his belt to avoid being blown or washed out to sea. Only after it was too late and the storm was at the height of its fury, did he realize with horror that he had tied himself to a manchineel, the most poisonous tree in the Keys. As he watched helplessly, the white toxic sap of the tree ran into the wounds torn into his skin by the flying debris. He did not die, but he spent many months in the hospital recovering from the poisoning.

Although the train was scheduled for completion by 1913, the schedule was pushed ahead when it appeared that Flagler, now an old man in failing health, might not live long enough to see his Florida East Coast Extension reach Key West. Workers had luck on their side for the remainder of the construction, and on January 22, 1912, an engine pulling five passenger cars filled with dignitaries and notables, including Flagler himself aboard his private car, arrived in Key West.

On the day that the Overseas Railroad reached Key West, Flagler announced that, in his opinion, "Key West will have a population of over fifty thousand people within ten years from this date."

The governor of Florida, a number of congressmen, and even foreign ambassadors were in Key West to celebrate the arrival of the steam-powered train. The citizens of Key West, always ready for a party, turned out in full force. The mayor spoke and the schools closed; a three-day party celebrated the "Eighth Wonder of the World." Flagler was weak and nearly blind, so he was led from the train, uttering his famous and much quoted statement: "Now I can die in peace."

At that time trains were restricted from crossing any bridge faster than 15 miles per hour and trains did not chance crossing the longer bridges when the wind was blowing faster than 70 miles per hour as measured by wind gauges on bridges. Under the best of circumstances the train's maximum speed was 35 to 45 miles per hour. According to schedules, the train time between Key West and Miami was four-and-a-half hours, but that was seldom the case. It was more like six or seven hours. Trains were often late, sometimes up to twenty-four hours behind schedule.

Flagler's Overseas Railroad made very little money; it never even began to earn the cost of its construction and it didn't even cover the cost of its upkeep.

And yet it was one of the most remarkable and memorable experiences many people had ever had. There are folks still living in the Keys who remember riding through the islands on the train, stopping at tiny stations to drop off mail and ice, and thrilling to the magical sensation of riding suspended over the water. Children were put to bed as the train passed northward through groves of Florida palm trees and awakened the following morning to find themselves rolling past tall oaks and pines.

From the last timetable printed, we know that a roundtrip ticket from Miami to Key West was $4.75; and only $2.50 on Sundays. A round trip from Miami to Havana, via Key West, was $24.

During Prohibition, booze came into the country from Havana, smuggled past customs in trunks and sometimes caskets, taken off ferries and shipped by train to New York. Cuban pineapples were another main cargo. Pineapple harvesting in Cuba was very profitable because of cheap labor available there. Ironically, Flagler's train provided the Cubans with a viable and profitable trade route for their cheaply produced pineapples, and it delivered the final knock-out punch to the staggering pineapple farming business of the Upper Keys.

By the time it was twenty years old, the railroad that had cost Flagler twenty-five million dollars and five hundred railroad workers their lives, and 25,000 more untold suffering, was bankrupt. The railroad was in receivership when the 1935 Labor Day Hurricane destroyed over forty miles of the roadbed. Rather then spending the $1.5 million to rebuild the tracks, which was the estimated cost of the repairs, the receivers decided to sell it. All of the property, the railroad bed and bridges, were sold to the state government for $640,000, which was less than the cost of one of its still-standing bridges. The Overseas Highway was superimposed on the railroad's right-of-ways, across the amazing Long Key Viaduct, the Seven Mile Bridge, and the lofty Bahia Honda Bridge. When the highway was completed in 1938, it became possible to drive a car all the way to Key West, the very end of the coral chain. The link to the mainland would change life in the Keys forever.

Henry Flagler's Doomed Wives

Henry Flagler became a widower for the first time in 1881, when he was only 51 years old. By then he was very, very rich. Unfortunately, his first wife Mary was a sickly woman, usually an invalid never really well enough to share or enjoy her husband's fine fortune.

Henry's second wife, the woman who'd been nurse to his first one, was named Ida Alice Shrouds. Shortly after the marriage, Alice began communicating with a Ouija board and became convinced that she was destined to marry the Czar of Russia. Eventually a doctor friend of Henry's diagnosed Alice as being mentally unstable. She was committed to a sanitarium and eventually judged to be legally incurably insane by the New York Supreme Court.

Meanwhile, Henry had met singer and pianist Mary Lily Kenan. Mary was 24 years old; by then, Henry was 70. Henry and Mary hoped to wed, but what to do about Alice the lunatic? Henry changed his residence to Florida and campaigned friends in the Florida Legislature to draft a law recognizing insanity as grounds for divorce. In 1900, Henry Flagler, with his huge fortune and great visions for Florida, was a powerful and well respected man in the sparsely developed state. In spite of the brewing scandal, the law passed and Henry was finally free to divorce his mentally incompetent wife. He and Mary Lily were wed in 1901.

As a wedding gift, Flagler built the sumptuous Whitehall estate on Palm Beach for Mary Lily. Today, Whitehall is a fantastic museum offering many daily guided tours to a clamoring public. A visit to Whitehall is an amazing glimpse of American wealth at the turn of the century, as well as an intimate portrayal of a winter/spring marriage. In the regal Whitehall ballroom, a secret stairway leads to Henry's bedroom. This stairway enabled Henry, who was never much of a party animal, to exit the festivities when he became tired and leave his young wife in charge.

Flagler died May 20, 1913, in Palm Beach when he was 83 years old. Shortly before his death, he made arrangements for him and Mary to be buried in the resplendent St. Augustine's Memorial Presbyterian Church. Flagler had built the church in memory of his daughter Jennie, who had died in 1889. Henry and Mary Flagler are buried there still.

According to Henry's will, Mary Lily Flagler inherited $108 million when he died. A few years later Mary Lily wed Robert Bingham, a Kentucky politician. Only eight months after the wedding, she died. Bingham had signed a prenuptial agreement foregoing any financial gains he might make in the event of Mary Lily's death. But one month before she died, a codicil had been added to Mary Lily's will stating that Bingham would inherit five million dollars.

Mary Lily's outraged family suspected foul play. They arranged to have her body exhumed and autopsied at New York's Bellevue Hospital. They promised that the results of the autopsy would be made public. But the results were not publicized and the question of exactly what killed Mary Lily was never answered, which gave rise to speculation that she had been a user of laudanum (a form of opium) and had accidentally overdosed. There was also a rumor that Bingham was so furious at Mary Lily's family for interfering in the matter that he threatened to release a story that she had died of syphilis if the family didn't back off.

Bingham's fortune then financed his purchase of the *Louisville Courier* newspaper.

In his will Henry also left his divorced wife Alice with two million dollars for her care. She lived comfortably until 1930, when she died at the age of 82. But for the remainder of her life, it is said, Alice told anyone who would listen about her planned nuptials with the Russian Czar.

The Old Seven Mile Bridge and Pigeon Key

The Queen mother of Florida Keys historic bridges is the Old Seven Mile Bridge, which runs parallel to its replacement, the sleekly modern, and all new Seven Mile Bridge. The new bridge, completed in 1982, was built in three years. It took four years to build the original bridge 75 years earlier.

Once the new bridge, with its wide lanes, sturdy guard walls, and pale gray cement was in place, there was talk of taking down the Old Seven Mile Bridge. But engineers surveyed the structure and deemed it nearly indestructible. The cost of tearing it down, they said, would be prohibitive.

Besides, the citizens of the Florida Keys had grown attached to the old girl. She has survived devastating hurricanes and several million cars. She has starred in a number of feature films, and dozens of television commercials. The black charred areas you see on the bridge are left over

Pigeon Key and the new Seven Mile Bridge

from explosions staged by the makers of *True Lies*, an Arnold Schwarzenegger film.

Every Christmas season someone manages to get to a lone shrub, growing through a crack in the concrete midway across the ancient span, and lace it with strings of white, battery-powered lights. Every night, year-round, the fishing areas at the near and far end of the old bridge are crowded with fishermen. And every day, all day long, you'll see walkers, joggers, bikers and skaters enjoying the sun, the magnificent air, and the spectacular view from the Old Seven Mile Bridge.

She is a marvel, a miracle and a monument to visionary Henry Flagler. The Overseas Railroad, once dubbed the Eighth Wonder of the World, chugged across the bridge thrice daily for 23 years. The Labor Day Hurricane of 1935 that delivered a killing blow to the railroad, spared the Seven Mile Bridge.

Today, the first two miles of the Old Seven Mile Bridge is a recreational site and connects the mainland to Pigeon Key, an historic, 3.2-acre island nestled beneath the bridge. Beginning around 1908, Pigeon Key was a camp for the work crews who built Flagler's railroad. In 1912, once the railroad was complete and underway, Pigeon Key became home to the workers and families of maintenance crews and bridge tenders involved in the operation of the railroad.

Among the permanent work force was a full-time paint crew. The crew worked on the Seven Mile Bridge and the Bahia Honda Bridge. The tracks, plates, girders and even the spikes were painted to preserve them from the salt air. As soon as both bridges were completely painted, it would be time to begin the massive job all over again.

For 25 years Pigeon Key was a small, tidy village with a store, post office, school, and dock. The little island is only four feet above sea level, situated on a shallow reef. From the island's dock it is possible to wade for some distance into the shoal waters abounding with marine life. The children who lived there had a playhouse under the bridge, and a swing hung from a trestle. Imagine what a wonderful place it was to grow up!

A woman who spent her childhood days on Pigeon Key, recalls a huge poinciana tree in the yard by the railroad tracks. When the tree was in bloom, she says, the train would stop so the passengers could take pictures. Pigeon Key is still said to be one of the most photographed places in all of the Florida Keys.

The village of Pigeon Key was abandoned after the train shut down in 1935. For many years it was empty. Later it was leased as a research center to the University of Miami for $1 per year. Environmental researchers and students from around the world ate and slept in the aging white clapboard cottages.

Today, the Pigeon Key Foundation, a non-profit organization dedicated to the restoration the island's historical buildings, operates the island as a park and a research center. Mote Marine Laboratory of

A poinciana tree

Sarasota, Florida, is researching coral culturing on Pigeon Key. Another of Mote's projects is cancer research with sharks, one of the few creatures in the world immune to cancer.

All seven structures surviving from the days of the settlement of Pigeon Key are being restored, one by one, as private funding becomes available. Also in the works are modern restrooms, a children's interactive marine exhibit, and a gift shop. Preservationists promise that Pigeon Key Village will eventually look just as it did at the height of its glory in the 1920s.

Visitors are invited to tour the island and admire the simple, sturdy construction of the buildings. The Bridge Foreman's House is a favorite subject of painters. The Negro Quarters is a stop on Florida's Black

Heritage Trail. The Section Gang's Quarters, the largest structure, was the first to be restored. Pigeon Key's permanent residents are Gertrude the duck and Iggie the iguana. A long deck juts into a flat, shallow bay where snorkeling is likely to turn up artifacts from Pigeon Key's rich past—buttons, bottles, bits of china—as well as a wonderful show of marine life. Pigeon Key's grassy lawns are perfect picnic sites.

For a few weeks in the fall, it is possible to watch the sun sink at the juncture of the old and the new bridges where they meet at the horizon. It is a popular phenomenon, bringing scores of thrillseekers and photographers to the island every year.

Admission to the park is $2. The Pigeon Key Express, a replica train-tram, operates between Pigeon Key and a visitors center on Knight's Key every day but Monday. Hours are 9 a.m. to 5 p.m. A roundtrip ticket is $3.

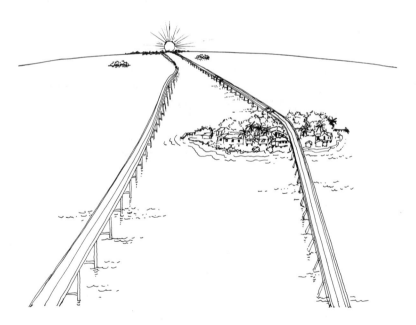

Sunset between the two Seven Mile Bridges

Nuts and Bolts

Marathon Chamber of Commerce
MM 53.5 Gulfside ✴ 743-5417 ✴ 800-262-7284

Anytime you walk into the Chamber of Commerce Visitors Center you are urgently requested to sign the guest book. It seems an important point to the people who work here. But once that detail is out of the way, these folks will chat you up and down again.

Based on information from the guest book, the Marathon Chamber gleans its monthly facts and figures report. Here is information from March, 1996: During that month 6,382 folks signed the book, an increase of 2% over last year's March. Of those visitors, 5,149 were Americans. Canada sent the most foreign visitors, 508; followed by Germany, 222; the United Kingdom, 186; France, 49; and Switzerland, 23. Over half of all those who signed the book stated Key West was their ultimate destination. But many others listed Marathon and the Middle Keys as their primary destination.

The Chamber's carefully tended charts and tables point out that Marathon and the Middle Keys' popularity as a vacation destination is growing. That's understandable—you'll find good bargains in accommodations in the Middle Keys as well as something even rarer than that: several surviving pockets of old-time island styles and attitudes that once prevailed in all of the Keys.

The most often asked question at this chamber, as in all others in the Keys, is "Where's the beach?" These chamber people have good answers: The Middle Keys have beaches; Sombrero Beach is free, rarely crowded, lovely, and nearby; Bahia Honda, called by travel writers one of America's most beautiful beaches, is a twenty-minute drive away.

In some flowery promotional literature, Marathon is described as a sleepy little fishing village. Well...not that sleepy. The local radio station DJs call it "beautiful, downtown Marathon." And though they're probably poking fun, to some people it really is beautiful in a seedy, crumbling kind of small-town way. Every day another weather-beaten layer of local color is scraped away by progress; what's not yet gone is Marathon's honest-to-God character.

George Dolezal Library
MM 48.7, Oceanside ✻ 743-5156

The local library is on a crest between the Sheriff's Station and the Fisherman's Hospital. Slow down or you'll zoom right past the hidden driveway. The library is spacious and user-friendly. The children's room is wonderful and the staff is warm and helpful. You could pass many hours in this cozy, air-conditioned library.

Friends of the Marathon Library sponsor some pretty good coffee-and-discussion hours and presentations Wednesday afternoons during winter months in the library's lovely assembly room. This past winter for the reading of works by Dorothy Parker, the place was packed. The reader, a former Broadway actress now retired in Marathon, was terrific, and she didn't seem to mind, or maybe she didn't notice, when several of the older gentlemen in the crowd began to doze. The coffee and cookies were tasty and plentiful; the crowd was mostly friendly, retired citizens.

A chess club, a computer club and an amateur ham radio club also meet at the library. Their meetings and activities are open to the public, too. Call the library, or stop by for a schedule of meetings and special events. The hours are 10 a.m. till 6 p.m. Monday through Saturday. Late nights—open till 8 p.m.—are Monday and Wednesday.

Marathon Airport
MM 52 ✻ 743-2155

Before very long this airport will probably be almost as busy as Key West International Airport. But not yet because many people don't even know it's here; even travel agents don't know. The airport terminal building has recently undergone a multimillion-dollar upgrade and has won a slew of design awards. With its earthy Spanish tile, fancy restrooms, high ceilings, and works by local artists, the terminal is eminently cool and relaxing.

It's serviced by American Airlines, Gulfstream Airlines, and US Air, so if you're staying anywhere but Key West, you'd be wise to fly into this airport and drive a rental car out.

The Marathon Airport is also a full service facility for private aircraft.

Fort Jefferson by Seaplane
Marathon Airport ✱ 743-5753 or 800-362-440

Fly to Fort Jefferson and the Dry Tortugas National Park on a Cessna
Amphibian. The four-seater departs from Marathon Airport at 8 a.m.,
Wednesday–Saturday. Sometimes your trip will take you down to Key
West, where you might pick up a few more riders. On the way, your pilot
will have lots to say about what you'll see below. The trip out to Fort
Jefferson, a pre-Civil War military outpost located nearly 70 miles west of
Key West, takes about an hour. You'll stay out there for a couple of hours
before heading back. The entire trip takes around five hours and costs
$149 per person.

Air Tours also flies to Everglades City in Everglades National Park.
Schedules on park tours are very flexible, based on demand. Reservations
are necessary. Call ahead; use the 800 number for a firm reservation.

Museums

The Museums of Crane Point Hammock
MM 50 Gulfside ✱ 743-9100

The museum is on Crane Point Hammock, a 63-acre environmental and
archaeological preserve. Displays of several small, natural communities
feature a family of endangered Key deer and a mangrove community of
Keys birds.

There's a photo exhibit of the Florida Keys, shot from space, which
illustrates clearly the ancient coral reef that emerged to form the delicate
and isolated Florida Keys. An exhibit of photographs of the construction
of the Overseas Railroad is a monument to Henry Flagler's vision and
amazing role in history.

During our last visit to the Museum of Natural History, we were
gazing into an aquarium of tiny tropical fish, when suddenly they began
to dart and swim wildly at the surface of the water. We couldn't imagine
what had so agitated them. Then a Cuban fellow named George arrived
with a plate of fresh minced beef liver. George, a butcher who saves
scraps from his other job, feeds the fish three times a week. And those
fish, believe it or not, knew when George is coming with their food.

Imagine how many people come in and out of this room in a week. How do they recognize George?

"Do you always wear the same shirt?" somebody asked. George laughed because he doesn't.

"It's just that fish are a lot smarter than you think," he said.

A self-directed nature trail leads you along a winding path through the unusual and exotic vegetation of the Crane Hammock. Ten endangered plant and animal species live here, as well as 160 native, and fifty exotic plant varieties. Carefully placed plaques tell the story of this rare palm and hardwood hammock. The quarter-mile trail passes a sinkhole or pit, where the top layer of earth has been worn away by a millennium's rainfall, exposing ancient ocean fossils that were once beneath the water's surface. You'll see these same brain corals beneath the water on the living reef.

Another trail leads to the Adderly House, built in 1906 by George Adderly, a black Bahamian immigrant who was a sponger, boatman, and charcoal maker. The house is very simple: one story with a hip roof, in the masonry vernacular, similar to residences built by blacks in the Bahamas during the 19th century. The floors are made of Dade County pine, a wood so resilient that nails can hardly be driven into it. Its walls are two feet thick and were considered to be Indian-and hurricane-proof. Adderly, a lay episcopal minister, lived until 1950 in this house which is listed as a stop on Florida's Black Heritage Trail.

The Crane Point Hammock and its natural history museum are open 9 a.m. to 5 p.m. Monday through Saturday; noon to 5 p.m. on Sundays. Admission to the museum is $7.50 for adults, $6 for senior citizens, $4 for students. Free for children six and under.

Theater

Marathon Community Cinema & Performing Arts Center
MM 51, Marathon ✻ 743-0994

Formerly known as the West Side Cinema, it was purchased in October, 1995, by Marathon Community Theater. This unconventionally laid-out movie theater has a big room with a level floor where eighty seats are grouped around tables, cabaret-style. Movies ($6 adults; $3 kids under twelve) run at 7 p.m. and 9:30 p.m., with weekend matinees at 2 p.m. The plan is that movies will support live theater by the Marathon Community Theater Company.

Florida Keys Renaissance Faire
800-262-7284 ✻ 743-4386

Full contact jousting on horseback; living chess game and "Flight of the Raptor Show" twice daily; belly dancers, minstrels, and jugglers in over sixty shows daily. Plus games, medieval rides, fabulous foods and America's finest Renaissance artisans. Takes place mid-January in Marathon. The big prize is a trip for two to London.

Anyone in my son's eleventh-grade English class at Key West High was awarded 500 extra grade-points (what the hell does that mean?) for wearing a Renaissance-era costume to school on the Friday before the big weekend event. Then local newspaper reporters were invited to the school to photograph the enthusiastic players. Hmmmmm.

There's even a three-day "Renaissance in Paradise Package." It's become popular to renew marital vows beneath the wedding arbor, Renaissance-style, and to remember the event with a personalized "Renewal of Vows" certificate. The Shire Minstrels provide the music. Unless you can't resist those terrific Renaissance costumes—men in armor, damsels in flowery headbands, fluttering with ribbons—you might find the annual Renaissance Faire a tad lackluster. There *are* jousting demonstrations, and that's something you don't see often...still... Admission is $7 per day, but you can get a deal on buying a ticket for all three days of the event, which is, frankly, unimaginable.

Beaches

Coco Plum Beach
Coco Plum Drive, Oceanside ✺ MM 54
Coco Plum is an odd little point of beach, but, since beaches are at such a premium in the Keys and held in such high esteem by travelers, it's been included here. You might call it "Glass Beach" because the place is absolutely spangled with bits of broken glass. One enterprising Keys artist, who creates jewelry out of sea-worn glass, calls her line of designs "Mermaid's Tears." She might stop at this very beach to gather materials where, it appears, mermaids have been absolutely hysterical. Down at the water's edge you'll find a ribbon of shells—the most shells you'll ever see on a Keys beach. A beachcomber with a good pair of protective shoes will find plenty to look at here, including coral, interesting bits of flotsam and jetsam, and weird evidence of sea life, like the snow-white cartilages of man-of-war jellyfish washed ashore. And several tangles of silver drift-wood are poetic, somehow. This is public property, but there are no facilities here. The beach has not been improved or cleaned or touched in any way. Except for that terrazzo floor of glass, the beach is in its nat-ural state. If you're looking for privacy, you can find a comfortable place to sunbathe or meditate or watch the ocean from a shaded place beneath the Australian pines.

To find it, turn onto Coco Plum Road at MM 54 and follow it all the way to the end.

Sombrero Beach
MM 50, Oceanside (Turn onto Sombrero Boulevard)
Follow signs for about a mile to arrive at the Sombrero Beach. The signs that point the way to this family beach are small, so you've got to look for them. The beach has a grassy park and a crescent of rough sand next to the ocean, with picnic tables, grills, restrooms, a volleyball net, a soft-ball diamond and a terrific, kid-pleasing playground. Often you'll see a group of students being instructed in scuba diving technique at the far end of the beach. For the rest of the beach, a wide and deep swimming

area is surrounded by a protective net. Explorers will find lots of crabs and even tinier creatures endlessly washing up on shore in the gentle, barely-there waves of the Keys waters. Pick up a handful of seaweed and shake it. You'll be amazed at what lives in there!

You'll find plenty of free parking here and clean restrooms, often utilized by tour vans. The annual Fourth of July celebration will bring out the whole town to this beach.

On one recent January day we bought an Italian sub and took it to Sombrero Beach. We sat at a picnic table in the sun to eat and watch the action. It was a slow, beautiful day. A grandmother walked her two little grandkids to a water spigot right near our table. She turned the water on and rinsed the sand from the little children's feet. First the girl. Then her squirming little brother. All at once the little girl stopped jumping, stood perfectly still, looked into the sky full of gulls, seemed to shimmy from head to toe, and smiled broadly into the day. It was a shudder of pleasure, a moment of sheer joy, expressed with pure exuberance. A few minutes later, a pair of dolphins way beyond the shore began leaping out of the water, thrilling the people on the beach. The show went on for about ten minutes. Surely those dolphins knew what they were doing.

Long Key State Recreation Area
MM 67.5 ✺ 664-4815

Campsites in this park are popular because of their proximity to the water's edge, a place vacationers in the Florida Keys desperately want to be. The beach is a half mile of natural shoreline from which you can walk way, way out; the water is very shallow and the bottom is sandy. It's a good, fun place for kids and for snorkeling. With roughly one hundred of the park's nine hundred sixty-five acres submerged, you can enjoy many wading bird species and abundant marine life in the shallow waters of Long Key.

When you drive into the park, you choose one way which leads to the boardwalk and the nature walk, or the other, which leads to picnic areas and campsites.

The boardwalk is popular with folks stopping in for a nature hit. The rest area adjacent to the parking lot has clean bathrooms and a couple of showers. A sign at the entrance to the nature walk promises you will see egrets, herons and other shore birds. The boardwalk takes you over extremely dense mangroves and over a tidal lagoon. If you climb the tower with two sets of stairs to take you to the top, you will see a prime exhibit of red and black mangroves. (Red are the ones that curve around and burrow back into the mud below them. Black are the ones that sprout up out of the muck.)

This is not a long walk by any means. If you take your time and read and carefully consider the information plaques along the way, you can stretch the walk out to fifteen minutes. If you walk fast, it will take you only five. Neat campsites along the way make you long for your own cozy, little tent in the mangroves. In addition to the abundant marine and bird life, plenty of mammals live here too. Raccoons are very bold and will help themselves to campers' food if it isn't sealed well, but, in spite of their seeming lack of concern about your presence, it is wise to keep your distance from raccoons. Park rules forbid you to feed or touch any wild animals here.

A few feet from the beginning of the boardwalk you'll find the Golden Orb Weaver Nature Trail named after the spiders that live here. Huge and amazing webs are spun by the red and gold female of the species. These are harmless spiders...still, they look pretty scary. And to help you tell the trees apart, labels identify gumbo limbo, poisonwood, mahogany, and Jamaican dogwood trees in this tropical hammock.

The quiet around you is deafening—spooky if you're used to lots of modern-day noise. All you hear is the rustling of leaves as the wind passes through the canopy above. You'll want to go slow in this serene place.

Choose the other direction at the fork in the road just after the park entrance and find a row of shoreline picnic sites—tables and grills under shelters, right on the water. Get to the park early, though, if you want to set up your party here because these areas are in big demand, and at no extra charge.

Farther down the same road, you'll come to a gate that marks the beginning of the beachside camping sites.

Canoe rentals with a marked, one-and-a-quarter-mile winding canoe trail are popular because you go at your leisure, paying for the canoe by the hour. Bike rentals work the same way and several very pleasant bike paths run within and immediately outside of the park.

Wednesdays, Nov.–Aug., at 9 a.m., rangers lead nature tours; Thursdays at 9 a.m., birding expeditions; Fridays at 8 p.m., campfire chats.

The park is open from 8 a.m. till sundown, year-round. Admission is $3.50 per car, plus fifty cents per person.

Nature Hikes

Layton Nature Trail
MM 68 Bayside
This is sort of tricky to find. Look for the green historical marker for the Long Key Fishing Camp. A tiny sign, close to the ground, marks the beginning of the trail, part of the Long Key Recreational Area which is headquartered on the other side of the street at mile marker 67.5.

This is such a short trail, you could hardly call it a hike. Still, it is an opportunity to guide yourself, at your own pace, through a thick but narrow hammock and out into the clearing that is the Florida Bay, with water very clear and calm. Dried sea grass forms a soft, brown cushion over the rocks. Some trees are labeled: poisonwood, wild coffee, Jamaican dogwood, gumbo limbo, seven year apple, buttonwood, wild dilly and wild lime. If you've hiked anywhere around here, by now you are beginning to recognize some of these indigenous plants. On this trail you'll also see some new ones and a surprise: Spanish moss—the first we've seen in the Keys. From the ancient diary of a Spanish shipwreck victim who lived among the Keys Indians for eighteen years in the 1500s, we know that the native American women of this region fashioned loin clothes, their only garments, of this feathery light material.

Old Seven Mile Bridge
MM 40-47
Walking or riding a bike or roller-blading over the magnificent span that once carried the Overseas Railroad across a seven mile stretch of ocean, is an almost religious experience, particularly around sunrise. Or sunset. The wind whips your hair. The birds swoop and dive into the cobalt-blue water below. The air is clean. The sky stretches endlessly. Your mind expands too, and anything seems possible. The round trip is almost four miles, but there's a nice layover at Pigeon Key. In the early morning it is possible to see tarpon, sharks, and stingrays in the water beneath the

bridge. The big treat is to see an angler, on a boat in the water below the bridge, fighting a tarpon.

As you walk check out the side rails. They're constructed of the old rail ties from the railroad. Imagine. They've been baking in the Keys sun since 1912, when the bridge was completed.

The parking lot is at Marathon end of the bridge.

Crane Point Hammock Nature Trail
Museum of Natural History ✺ MM 50 Gulfside

Crane Point Hammock, a 63.5 acre land tract of rare palm hammock, is one of the most important historical and archaeological sites in the Keys. The area contains evidence of pre-Colombian artifacts, and once was the site of an entire Indian village. You'll have to pay admission to the museum to get to the trail.

Big Fun

Bike Paths

The safe and scenic paths in Marathon provide great opportunities for bicycle rides. Here are some favorites:

Coco Plum Drive
Mile Marker 54

Look for a sign for Coco Plum Drive. Perhaps the loveliest bike route in the area, it's our favorite. You'll bike past a number of stately condominiums, flowering trees, and flat tracks of open land until you arrive at the very end, a natural beach. Sit on the point and watch the boats for a while. It's a wild, windy beach. Chances are good that you won't encounter another vehicle or person on this road.

Key Colony Beach
MM 53.5 Oceanside

The wonderful biking and walking path on this island will take you past lovely homes, stretches of seascapes, and on to a terrific oceanside restaurant and bar called the Beach House.

Marathon Bike Path

Starts at MM 47 (the Marathon end of the Seven Mile Bridge) and runs parallel to the Overseas Highway to MM 54. Lots of local folks regularly use this path as their main means of transportation up and down the island. When the path runs past the Marathon Airport, you can watch the bellies of little planes and jets as they come and go. Just past the airport, on the gulfside of the island, you'll see occasional picnic shelters.

Sombrero Beach Loop

Turn off the bicycle trail at MM 48 and follow the bike path toward the ocean. You'll go to Sombrero Beach and loop around the golf course. It's a nice ride. Sombrero Beach has picnic tables and shelters, showers and clean restrooms.

Bicycle Rentals

The Equipment Locker
MM 53, Gulfside ❧ 289-1670
Bikes rent for $10 for 24 hours/$50 a week. Baby seats available.

Key Colony Beach Marina
MM 53.5 Ocean, on the Causeway ❧ 289-1310
At either one of these rent-a-bike places, you will find yourself in a central location, convenient to Marathon's terrific bike trails. You'll pay $10 for 24 hours/$50 for a week. Only two bikes with baby seats are available.

Golf

Key Colony Beach Golf Course
MM 53.5 (turn at light) ❧ 289-1533
A nine-hole par three course in the truly beautiful island city of Key Colony Beach. Hours on the public course are 7:30 a.m. to 7 p.m. daily. Clubs and pullcarts are available for rent. Year-round rates are $6.50 per person for nine holes.

Sombrero Country Club
Sombrero Boulevard ❧ 743-2551
A full length golf course on 135 acres. The club is strictly private unless you belong to a country club back home. In that case, bring a letter from your country club's golf pro, stating that you are in good standing, and that a Sombrero country club member would be welcome to play on your greens if they showed up at your club.

Guests at Hawk's Cay can pay to be bused to the Sombrero Country Club and play on their greens, but that is the only resort with this arrangement. Fees are $62 for eighteen holes; cart fees are $16. Golf pro is Bob Williams. Summer club memberships—six months—for a single person or a family are around $1,000. Fees are figured on top of that.

Gyms

Marathon Health and Fitness
MM 53, Town Square Mall, Marathon ✱ 743-7618
Good news! You can work out even when you're away from your hometown gym, at this newly remodeled, 3,000-square-foot gym. So much is
available: Free weights. Ten-station Universal machine means never
having to say "Excuse me. Are you almost finished?" Cardiovascular exercise equipment like Stairmasters, treadmills and Schwinn Airdyne bikes.
Also aerobic and step classes on an impact-absorbing floor. A large selection of work-out clothes and accessories; vitamins and New-Age agents
like melatonin, shark cartilage, and phosphagen. Open seven days a
week. Hours vary from day to day. Short-term memberships—a day, a
week, or a month—available for travelers.

Nautilus Fitness Center
MM 49.7 (behind the Marathon Deli) ✱ 743-6350
To visit the Nautilus Fitness Center, you must first contact the Marathon
Deli in person or by calling the number above. A private fitness center
for both men and women, it features Nautilus work-out equipment,
Stairmaster, and a dry sauna. Special summer rates sometimes go as low
as $25 a month. Visitors to the area are welcome to make use of the facil-
ities for $10 a day.

Tennis

City of Key Colony Beach
MM 53.5 Oceanside, at 8th Street ✱ 289-1533
Key Colony Beach Tennis courts are open to the public. Play is $6 per
hour for singles, $8 for doubles. Two lighted courts available daily from
8 a.m. to 9 p.m. at 8th street.

Fishing

IN THE GULF STREAM OFF MARATHON lies an underwater platform rising from depths of 1,000 feet or more, to a peak of 480 feet below sea level, known as the "Marathon Key West Hump." This hump creates a popular feeding ground for gamefish like blue and white marlin, mako shark, blackfin tuna, and amberjack. This area is a favorite stop for private fishing charters, and it's the reason that fishing off Marathon is considered by most serious anglers to be some of the best in the world. Marathon is different from its neighbors to the east (Key Largo and Islamorada), in that the gulfside in the Middle Keys is deeper and more open in this area, giving an extra dimension to local fishing. On a day when it's too rough to fish offshore or on the reef, the Gulf is an excellent alternative, as it's usually calm even in a stiff breeze.

Since 1991, six world record catches have been made by anglers fishing with Marathon guides.

Flats fishing

A True Fish Tale

On June 23, 1912 sport fisherman Charlie Thompson of Marathon, caught a 30,000-pound whale shark (15 tons, 45 feet long) just off the Seven Mile Bridge. It took 36 hours to land the monster, using five harpoons and 151 bullets. The fish was towed to Miami, where it was embalmed and then taken on a railroad tour through America. I am not making this up.

No Fish No Pay, Really

Yes, some charterboat captains do make this promise in their advertising. I was told at the Chamber of Commerce that several charterboats are taking the vow. The catch is: there's always a catch. You are extremely likely to catch something. "No fish" just doesn't happen around here.

Marathon Guides Association
PO Box 500065 ⚓ Marathon, FL 33050-0065

For a complete list of the Middle Keys fishing captains, their specialties, and an informative brochure on fishing off Marathon, write to the Marathon Guides Association (MGA). In the brochure you'll also learn about what fish you can expect to catch at what time of the year, and where you can expect your captain to take you to find them.

Party Boats

Marathon Lady and Marathon Lady III
MM 53, at Vaca Cut Bridge ⚓ 743-5580

These party boats specialize in families with kids. Half day is $22. All day is $37. Rod and reel rental is $3. They advertise themselves as the Middle Keys' only local party boats with thirty-six years fishing these waters. Fish cleaning service is available; also special children's rates.

Departs twice daily for half-day trips, at 8:30 a.m. and 12:30 p.m. (Is anybody besides me wondering what happened to the *Marathon Lady II*?)

Bridge Fishing

It seems that you see more bridge fishing in the Middle Keys than anywhere else in the Keys. Fishing from a bridge is a simple alternative to expensive charterboats. Lots of people say it's the only way to fish because it's such a great way to mix with locals, and what is fishing about after all, if not camaraderie? Excellent fishing can be had from the Long Key Bridge, both the bridges at Toms Harbor, and the east and west ends of the Old Seven Mile Bridge. At night, when you drive over the Seven Mile Bridge, you will see the twinkling lights of fishermen on the old bridge.

Non-Florida residents need a fishing license to fish from the bridges. Numerous bait and tackle shops in the area's marinas have everything you need to get started—including the license.

Some Marinas

Captain Hook's Marina and Dive Center
MM 53 at Vaca Cut ▪ 743-2444 ▪ 800-278-4665

Vaca Cut is a waterway that connects the Gulf of Mexico with the Atlantic Ocean. Captain Hook's isn't a huge marina, tucked against the shore just under the Vaca Cut Bridge, but it's a busy one. Everything to do with watersports is here, in one form or another. You can rent a boat, or a Waverunner, or a parasailer at Rick's Book-a-charter. Walk around the corner and find the *Marathon Lady* charter fishing boat.

Captain Hook's marina store is neat, full of useful stuff. I found featherweight Polaroid sunglasses for $12. Once you've worn featherweights, you won't go back to Foster Grants. Scuba divers: Pick up the wonderful little booklet on the *Thunderbolt*, the area's most famous dive destination. It looks like somebody's term paper and costs around $5. If you're planning to dive the wreck, this information will intrigue you.

At Captain Hook's Marina, you'll see a small, clear lagoon alive with moray eels, stingrays, sharks, and parrotfish. Each day at 4 p.m. the fish are hand-fed in what has become a major attraction. And it's free!

Key Colony Beach Marina
MM 53.5, on the Causeway ▪ 289-1310

Here at one of the area's more upscale marinas, park in the convenient lot and stroll the dock for a look at some fine vessels or to find a charter to your liking. The Landing Restaurant and Bar at the end of the docks overlooks the harbor.

Diving

Y OU CAN EXPLORE fifty dive spot destinations in Marathon waters, according to promotional materials distributed by the Chamber of Commerce. In addition to its beautiful coral reefs, Marathon has numerous artificial reefs in depths ranging from 25–200 feet. Even the shallow waters just offshore offer plenty of marine life habitats to explore. Hard bottom areas support sponges, golf-ball corals, soft corals, lobsters and tropical fish. Sandy bottom areas and grass beds are home to shrimp, crabs, small fish and anemone. The grass beds are also an excellent place to find conch, but remember: it is against the law to disturb conch or coral!

Some Famous Marathon Dives

Sombrero Reef

About four miles offshore, the Sombrero Light Tower marks a stunning spur and groove reef system. At 142 feet, the Sombrero is the tallest light tower in the Keys. You can see the Sombrero Light from shore, and it will take you about thirty minutes to motorboat out there. So far, this is the only reef in the Middle Keys to have mooring buoys, which provide boats with a place to tie up so they don't have to drop their anchors on delicate corals and risk damaging them. The Sombrero Reef is very easy to find and fascinating to dive.

On Sombrero Reef, two fingers of coral meet to create an eight-foot natural coral bridge under which divers enjoy swimming. In the same area, giant brain corals, and mountain star and elkhorn corals, as well as barracuda, French grunts, trumpetfish and yellowtails all make their homes here.

Coffins Patch

The remains of an old lighthouse can be seen scattered along the shallow reef in this area at the east end of Marathon. Snorkelers particularly enjoy this dive because in many places the water is only seven or eight feet deep.

Yellow Rocks
Three-and-a-half miles off Key Colony Beach lies a set of ledges running east and west for more than 200 yards, rising nearly twelve feet from the bottom. Maximum depths are twenty-eight feet, making this a good area for lobsters and plenty of marine life.

Thunderbolt
One of the most famous and most often requested scuba destinations in the Middle Keys is this one-time Navy research vessel sunk in 1986. The *Thunderbolt* sits upright 120 feet below the surface. Stripped of doors, hatches and windows, the interior now features a teeming community of sea life. You are free to enter the vessel to explore the dark hold and swim five floors up into the pilot house. A thrilling dive—for scuba people only.

The Barge
Dive masters adore this 100×30-foot wreck, lying on the ocean floor twenty-two feet below the surface. This is a terrific first-wreck dive, fascinating enough to keep a scuba diver entertained for an hour or so but not terribly skill-challenging. The area is particularly photographable.

Some Dive Charters

Abyss Pro Dive Center
Holiday Inn Marina ❧ MM 53.5 ❧ 743-2126 ❧ 800-457-0134
Volumes could be written describing the wonderful, enthusiastic dive charter people you will meet in Marathon, as well as in all of the Keys. They're so darned nice, I think, because they're blissed out all the time. Whether they're talking about the reef, riding on a boat to the reef, or actually diving the reef, they're deliriously happy. Why not? What's not to be happy about, arranging for people to have one of the finest experiences available on the planet?

Heidi and Bill Ferrell run the Abyss Pro Dive Center, including a full-service dive shop, at the marina of the Holiday Inn. Their operation features a 34-foot boat; reef trips are limited to six divers at a time. A dive trip visits two locations, chosen according to the skill and requests of the people aboard. You get lots of personalized attention from the captain/instructor on Abyss Charters.

A dive package—one night in the Holiday Inn, including breakfast and two dives—is $68 in the summer; $76 during season, per person. A dive trip to the reef is $35 per person, which is the going rate for reef trips in this area.

Never Enough Charters
Sombrero Resort Marina
MM 50, Oceanside, 19 Sombrero Boulevard ✒ 743-7265

Banny Thorne says that diving in the Middle Keys is the best anywhere because the reefs in this area don't get crowded, or "dived to death" like they do in some parts of the Keys. The reefs here are some of the healthiest in the country.

In the Marathon waters, Banny says he knows of thirty or forty great dive spots. Many of them are in 25 feet of water or less. Whatever your skill level, Banny has a place to match it. He loves night diving and will take as few as two people snorkeling or scuba diving, day or night. Banny charges around $35 per person for the trip; equipment is an additional charge.

To the Sea

Skimmers
Kayak Ecotour ✆ 743-0771

Ecotour guide Rick Champlin, a four-year veteran, has such a cool job that people sometimes ask him what he *really* does for a living. It is difficult for them to imagine that paddling around the sunny inlets, coves and lagoons of the Gulf of Mexico and the Atlantic Ocean actually qualifies as a job. "This is my real job," Rick says happily.

Depending upon the weather, what his customers are looking for, and everybody's mood that day, Rick chooses from a variety of sites and destinations for the day's tour. Count on snorkeling in some very clear places, where you'll see stingrays, perfect conchs, and corals. Sometimes there's a stop on a mangrove island, where the only sound you'll hear is the birds and your own breathing. Tours get under way around 9 a.m. and come ashore again around 3 p.m. Cost per person is $50 plus tax; includes a wholesome box lunch.

Ray's Riders, Inc.
MM 54, Oceanside Holiday Inn Marina ✆ 289-0520

Waverunners come in four different sizes suitable for one to three riders. One good thing about Ray's Riders, proprietor Mimi says, is that you can take them anywhere you like. Many folks rent a Waverunner for the day, take it back to their hotel's beach or waterfront and play all day or they stay and cruise the area. It is not uncommon to see customers arriving at Shuckers Restaurant on the 11th Street Marina on Waverunners. Cruise in the Gulf or the Atlantic, go fast or go slow. Rent by the half hour, full hour, half day, or full day. Prices are based on size of the unit and go like this: Half hour, $25–$40; hour, $45–$65; half day, $160–$190; full day, $270–$330.

Rick's Watercraft Rentals
Captain Hook's Marina ✱ 743-5001

Rick rents powerboats, Waverunners, and will hook you up with the parasailing guys. Yamaha Waverunners rent by the hour or half hour. Rick's smallest boat is a 17' Angler, 60 hp, rents for four hours–$70; eight hours–$100; or seven days; $500. The largest boat Rick rents is a 25' Sea Vee, 225 hp, which rents for $175 a day, or $880 a week.

Sunset Boat Rental
Howard Johnson Marina ✱ MM 54, Oceanside ✱ 743-3902

Steve Reese, owner of Sunset Rentals, says that his fleet of mini cigarette speedboats is the only one you'll see anywhere in the Keys, because the company that made them went out of business.

Sleek cigarette boats, about four times the size of these mini models, were once used by local dope smugglers to pick up illegal cargo from Colombian freighters anchored a few miles offshore. The powerful cigarettes easily outran Coast Guard cutters. But those days are over now.

If you've ever experienced the thrill of zipping around a summer lake on a hydroplane, you'll itch for a ride on one of these babies. The mini cigarettes are powered by 40 horsepower motors. With one adult aboard they travel at around 40 miles per hour. Two adults will fit in the boat, but will obviously slow down the ride. Take the boat wherever you like, for as long as you like. This big fun will cost you $29.95 an hour.

Porky's Free Sunset Cruise
MM 47.5 Gulfside ✱ 289-2065

Every night, weather and the boat's engine permitting, Porky's BBQ offers a free sunset cruise on a pontoon boat. It holds only about a dozen people and is usually packed, so make reservations in advance. You cruise out of the lagoon and anchor beneath the Seven Mile Bridge to watch the sun set; then you turn around and come back to shore. You don't even have to buy anything—no gimmicks, no catches. It's really free.

Middle Keys Accommodations

N o B & Bs, but a couple of very nice resorts, and a bunch of really neat, inexpensive motels. (I mean inexpensive by Keys standards.) Waterfront is standard here; in the rest of the Keys you pay big for waterfront. The Middle Keys location is terrific if you have a car and a restless spirit.

Don't forget to check for cost of extra people or kids in your room. Some places don't allow pets. Also, there's an inescapable 11.5% tax on all accommodations. When booking a room, ask lots of questions and get what you want.

The Chamber of Commerce will send you a complete list of RV and commercial camping areas. This list below is by no means complete. Also, there are many more motels and resorts along the way. This selection is actually quite arbitrary, so it's in alphabetical order.

Camping and RVs

KOA Kampground
MM 70 Gulfside, at Long Key ✱ 664-4922 ✱ 800-562-7730
Fiesta Key is a twenty-eight acre island with 309 sites ranging from water, electricity and sewer RV sites to no-hook-up tent sites. A tent village, a round wooden structure with a roof and sides, provides six sheltered, pie-shaped sites with electricity, water and a storage compartment. Also motel units and efficiencies with the expected A/C, TV, showers and double beds. No phones in rooms. Motel rooms require a refundable security deposit of $100, due upon checking in.

Nightly rates for tent camping with no hook-ups are $24.95 off season, $32.95 in season or on holidays. RV sites with water, electricity and sewer begin at $44.95 and go to $67.95 for a waterfront site during season or on any holiday. But they don't consider themselves to be just a "campground." The brochure calls this place a "resort."

The local KOA has some pretty serious rules and regulations about noise, pets, clotheslines (they're strictly forbidden) and the speed limit. Also, quiet time begins at 10 p.m. This is not the place for all-night parties! Amenities include a game room, two hot tubs, an Olympic-sized swimming pool and a basketball court; also a camp store and a full service marina. if this homogenized, by-the-book camping sounds good, write to them for a brochure.

Long Key State Recreation Area
MM 67.5 Ocean ☛ 664-4815

Campsites right on the Atlantic Ocean, with more tents than RVs in a row of sixty narrow sites in a grove of Australian pines (although the ratio is probably different during the mosquito-wild, hot and humid summer months). Each site has a picnic table and grill. Beyond a small bluff and a wide ribbon of brown seaweed, you come to a strip of natural sandy beach on clear, blue ocean water. It's a fun place to snorkel. And plenty of bathhouse restrooms are available. The area, behind a combination-lock gate (only campers know the combination), is pleasant and breezy from the nearby surf, cool and shaded from the pines. At the far end of the camping area is a clearing with benches around a pit for a campfire circle. A large white screen, like a mini drive-in movie screen, is for visual presentations.

Camping sites with electricity are around $26, without electricity, $24. (There are no water and sewer hook-ups.) Half of the sites are reserved up to ninety days in advance; the remaining sites become available on a first-come, first-served basis. The maximum stay in a State Park is two weeks.

On the boardwalk six campsites are reserved for the Boy Scouts. If there are no scouts camping when you're there, you can have a spot on the boardwalk for $3 a night. No electricity or water hook-ups, of course, but the restrooms with cold water outdoor showers are nearby. The drawback is that during daylight hours, when the park is open, you'll be observed by a small army of tourists cruising the boardwalk. Once I was on the boardwalk and heard a camper from within a boardwalk tent snoring very loudly. At 3 p.m.! That's how close you are to them. Campsite #6 on the boardwalk, the last one, is the best one. It's right where the boardwalk ends. You actually have a sliver of waterfront right behind your tent.

Inns, Motels, Resorts

Banana Bay Resort
MM 45.9 Gulfside ✶ 743-3500 ✶ 800-BANANA-1

You want new? Compared to most around here, this seven-year-old place is new. The lushly tropical Banana Bay Resort is on ten secluded acres directly on the Gulf of Mexico. Amenities include one of the Keys largest freshwater pools (olympic size, and that's unusual for the Keys), an outdoor Jacuzzi, two tennis courts, a sandy beach and snorkel area (practice for the reef), conference rooms with full catering facilities, a poolside restaurant and lounge, waterfront tiki bar, and a fifty slip marina. Come in your boat if you like, but make reservations with the dockmaster before you arrive. Dockage for Banana Bay guests is $12 per night.

Vacationers appreciate the on-site charterboats for fishing, sailing and diving. You don't have to wander around looking for a marina.

Guest rooms feature king or two double beds, refrigerators, Bahama fans, TVs, hair dryers, and clock radios, all decorated in Caribbean plantation style. A daily poolside breakfast of seasonal fruit, muffins, bagels, juices and coffee is substantial. Rates range between $95 and $195 during the season; $75 and $145 in the off season, depending on type of room and view. Always ask about packages when you call to book a stay at Banana Bay.

A second Banana Bay resort recently opened in Key West. The attitude at the new Banana Bay is the same—warm and cozy—but the setting is very different.

Bayview Inn Marina
MM 63, on Conch Key ✶ 289-1525 ✶ 800-289-2055

Built originally as a fishing camp, this is the only guest lodging on Conch Key, a sixteen-acre island of lobster traps and lobster fishermen's houses. During the summer season (April—July is the off-season for lobstering), you'll see the traps stacked everywhere. The Bayview Inn's units—nine efficiencies or bedrooms—are clean and cheap. Refrigerators and call-

out-only phones in every unit; tiny kitchens in efficiencies. Free continental breakfast; no pool; no beach. The Bayview offers a little bit of
everything that adventurers come to the Keys to find: Fishing and diving
charters. Dive packages. A dock and boat ramp. Bait and tackle shop.
Boat rentals. Grocery store. Beer. Ice. Proprietors John and Colleen
Williams will hook you up with the area's best fishing captains. Also,
ultralight air tours with a former U.S. Army attack pilot!

The majority of people who stay here, Colleen says, are into fishing
and diving and that's it. "No frills" is just fine for them, so they get lots
of repeat business. In season rates: efficiencies, $75; bedrooms, $65. Off
season rates: efficiencies, $59; bedrooms, $49.

In the marina you can rent a 23-foot Mako speedboat for $195 a day.
Waverunners are $35 for a half hour; $50 for an hour.

Bonefish Bay Motel
MM 53.5 Oceanside ⚓ 289-0565 ⚓ 800-336-0565

Besides the good deals on room rates, the Bonefish Bay offers free use
of their bicycles, and in Marathon you can bike in some terrific places.
(Otherwise, bikes rent in this area for about $10 a day.) Bonefish Bay
is centrally located, and full of lazy charm. The clean and tidy units in
the sixteen-unit motel are located in white stucco cottages with bright,
yellow doors and window frames, with a sort of Jamaican feeling. At a
private beach a mile away at the Cabana Club, Bonefish Motel guests are
welcome for $3 per person. The beach is fantastic, one of the nicest in
the entire Keys, so don't feel ripped-off about the $3. Otherwise, hang
out at the cute pool at the Bonefish; you'll feel part of a little neighborhood here. Often a card game or a barbeque is going on in the yard. At
the boat ramp, there's no additional charge to dock your boat. Rooms
and apartments have the usual amenities, with the addition of a couple of
extra movie stations on the TV. Unit #12 is right on the water; backyard
fishing is popular here. Rates are all over the place, but begin at $39 for a
basic sleeping room during the fall season, and go up to $89 for a one-
bedroom apartment at the height of the winter season. You can bring a
small pet, but it'll cost you an extra $10 a night.

Faro Blanco Marine Resort
MM 48, Gulfside ✹ 743-9018 ✹ 800-759-3276

At Faro Blanco you can sleep in a lighthouse or on a houseboat. The lighthouse apartment is a two-bedroom unit carved into the second level of the gulfside white lighthouse that is the marine resort's logo. Air conditioning blows through ornate vent grates that look like old-fashioned heat vents up north. There's a little gabled room with a single bed, cushioned window seat, and child-sized bathroom, perfect for a romantic little girl, but definitely not for a boy. The adult-sized bedroom also features a window seat, English cottage feel, and windows on the world. In the living room, the couch pulls out to a queen-sized bed. In the fully equipped kitchen, a communal dining table is a wide wooden plank with a bunch of bar-height stools. Easy to imagine a gang of adventurers putting away a few pounds of steamed shrimp and a couple gallons of beer right here. All the ceilings are low; walls are old-fashioned wainscot paneling; the floors are dark and wooden. The living room furniture is modern, and actually, so is the place. But they've done a good job of making it feel old and funky. Two couples or a good-sized family could make use of the additional cots in the walk-in closet and have themselves a fine vacation. It's a unique retreat. Dock the family yacht right out in the harbor, mere seconds away from your door. "You'll either love it or hate it," a woman at the resort's front desk told us, handing us the key. We loved it. The lighthouse apartment rents for $185 during season; $145 in the summer.

Faro Blanco's houseboats are located less than a mile away in a funky marina at the end of 15th Street. It tells the story of Marathon's past, present, and future, all in one weird mesh of old, new and newer. The houseboats are the newest. For people who get only two weeks of salt air a year, this is a wonderful place to breathe in their money's worth.

The Faro Blanco houseboats are tied so firmly to the dock that though they rise and lower with the tide, they barely rock; the water is quite serene. If you're hoping to be lulled to sleep by the action of the sea, you'll find it's not quite as dramatic here as you might have expected. As we hunted for our houseboat in the labyrinth of uniformly gray and white houseboats, young and clear-headed on a bright sunny day, we wondered how it would be to hunt for our lodgings if it was nighttime, and we weren't so clear-headed. So consider this possibility for yourselves if you plan to sleep here. A two-bedroom houseboat rents for $185 in, and $145 out, of season. An efficiency houseboat rents for $119 in, and $99 out, of season.

Flamingo Inn
MM 59.5 ✻ 289-1478

Here's a roadside mom-and-pop motel that looks good enough to eat, like a dainty *petit four*. It's got Triple A's two-diamond rating, and it even landed a small—but important—role in a television series. A few years ago the Fox Television Network came to the Keys to film an ill-fated series called *Key West*. The show, which aired six times before it was banished forever, used a number of Keysy, colorful locations like this one to tell their weak story. So how did the Flamingo fit in?

"It was a Norman Bates kind of scene," says proprietor George Richter.

"How much does it cost to rent a room?" one of the characters asks a weird-looking guy who is supposed to be the innkeeper.

"By the hour? By the day? Or by the week?" the weird innkeeper asks.

"And, of course, he gives these outlandish prices," laughs George.

Besides appearing in *Key West* the Flamingo's adorable facade, painted in pink, white and lime green, also appears in a number of guidebooks, George says. And, by the way, it only rents by the day. Or the week.

Very clean rooms with a '50s-kitsch decor: TV, AC, phones in every room, but if you use them, you pay 50¢ a call. Efficiencies with kitchenettes available. Also a three-room apartment. A freshwater pool encircled by a red brick walkway. No pets, please. There's a boat ramp a hundred yards down the street. Prices start around $50 for a basic motel room in the summer season. (Winter rates and minimum-stay rules may apply during holidays and special events.)

Grassy Key Beach and Yellowtail Inn
MM 58.5 Oceanside, Grassy Key ✻ 743-0533 or 743-8400

The Atlantic Ocean breezes are everywhere in this funky, inexpensive complex of rooms, efficiencies and seaside cottages, located in one of the most mellow and still natural areas in the Keys. Guests make good use of the complimentary rowboats and canoes. A private, natural beachfront runs the length of the property offering sun worshipers and beachcombers many hours of pleasure. The grounds are scattered with plenty of BBQ grills and lounge chairs, and they get lots of action. BBQ is very popular with Grassy Key Beach guests.

Many units are half trailer/half cottage. Sounds a little weird but the blend has been gracefully executed. There's constant repairing and upgrading, so nothing is allowed to run down. The place has an old-fashioned look, but the units are modern, very clean, basic and comfortable. You'll find refrigerators, coffeemakers, TV, AC, and private baths in all units; some units have full kitchens.

The cottage closest to the beach rents for a little over $100 a day. No two units are the same; they're all different, with different evolutionary stories and their own individual charms. Many guests come year after year. Grassy Key is popular with Europeans, particularly in the fall. Rates are lowest from Sept.16–Nov. 14.

Hawk's Cay Resort
MM 61, on Duck Key ❧ 743-7000 ❧ 800-432-2242
Big families and major corporations frequently choose Hawk's Cay as a retreat destination because of its something-for-everyone atmosphere, and its 10,000 square-foot conference center and banquet facilities. And everyone appreciates the free shuttle service to and from the airport.

Built in 1959 by a local contractor, the Hawk's Cay Resort is a self-contained community sitting in the middle of Duck Key, a private, sixty-acre island located between the Atlantic and the Gulf of Mexico. The resort, originally called the Indies Inn, has changed hands several times through the years. Current owners purchased the property in 1983; they refurbished and renamed it. In spite of its many incarnations, or perhaps because of them, the property glows with a lovely patina. There's a vaseline-on-the-lens softness to it. On a busy weekend it feels kind of like an aging Catskills resort in the summertime. Kids are everywhere, and maids wear authentic maid costumes. Uniformed doormen, too.

A children's program provides a seven-hour day of supervised activities for kids ages 5–11. Three times a day trainers feed seven dolphins living in a saltwater lagoon.

There's a quiet, very dignified library, with a remarkable photo display of some people of renown who have stayed here. Most recently, Arnold

Schwarzenegger, his wife Maria Kennedy Schriver, and Jamie Lee Curtis, all in town for the making of the film *True Lies*, partially filmed on the Old Seven Mile Bridge. (The movie stars look so small in these pictures.) There's a mounted 158-pound tarpon caught by Don Johnson. According to a plaque on a bridge that leads to Duck Key's plush residential area, even President Harry Truman once vacationed here—in March, 1964. The library features a fascinating aquarium. Though the room is lavishly appointed, there's nothing stuffy about it. It's comfortable.

There's a beach and a freshwater pool. Jacuzzis. And golfing at nearby Sombrero Country Club. Eight well-tended tennis courts and a fitness center. Green grass lawns. Water activities available at Hawk's Cay Marina—for a fee, of course—include snorkeling, scuba diving, deep sea and backcountry fishing, sunset cruises, sailing, and glassbottom boat trips. A fitness trail is fun, if it isn't too hot.

Breakfast is served daily in the Palm Terrace, a bright rotunda suffused with sunshine filtered through several large skylights. An extravagant breakfast buffet features baked goods and pastries, tropical fruits, made-to-order omelettes. Tables are draped with dusty-rose tablecloths, set with casual elegance.

There are 160 guest rooms and 16 suites in the Hawk's Cay. Daily rates begin at $195 for a standard room and go all the way to $850 for penthouse suites. Off season is May–December, when rates for the same units, respectively, are $140–$600.

Key Colony Beach Motel
MM 53.5, Take the causeway to East Ocean Drive ⚓ 289-0411
If you build a moderately priced motel on the Middle Keys' nicest beach front, the tourists will come. Here it is—a moderately priced motel that backs up to the Atlantic Ocean. The rooms are like motel rooms every-where: two beds, TV, AC. Clean, though a bit shabby, with tiled showers, and carpeting that has been cleaned and fumigated too many times. All rooms have fridges. But who cares what the rooms look like as long as they're comfortable? Four rooms are oceanfront, overlooking the pool (call to reserve them). There's also a good-sized freshwater pool. Key Colony Beach is a very good place to headquarter. Biking, walking, tennis and golf are available nearby. And that white sand beach. Rooms on the beach rent for around $80; off the beach, $70. Summer rates are

lower: $70 and $55 respectively. But the prices are "subject to change." All holidays use winter rates.

Kingsail Resort Motel
MM 50.5 ▪ 743-5246 ▪ 800-423-7474

There must have been a big resort-building boom in Marathon during the 1950s because here comes another resort with charmingly out-dated decor to make you nostalgic for the simpler days of white brick, blond wood paneling, and wrought iron furniture.

What's great about the Kingsail Motel is the staff's dedication to upholding the Keys' balmy reputation. Forget about the rest of the world, put away your city clothes, and head out to the pool. There's a tiki hut if you don't want the sun, or if you need a place for a party. Every day begins with complimentary coffee on the docks.

During the summer many guests arrive by boat. Or arrive with a boat on a trailer. There's a boat launch, and a place to park the boat trailer. Dock at the Kingsail for $10 a night. It's located on an inlet, on the Gulf of Mexico. They've got a laundry facility and a convenience shop.

A charter fishing boat is available at the dock, and when enough people sign up, they'll go out for a day of fishing.

All forty-four units have phones, TV, and air conditioning. Efficiencies have full kitchens; motel rooms don't. Rates on efficiencies are $75 to $125. Motel room rates range from $55–$112. Rates are hiked a bit for special events and holidays, no matter what time of year they occur, but there is no minimum stay requirement.

Lime Tree Resort
MM 68.5, in the City of Layton ▪ 664-4740 ▪ 800-723-4519

The Lime Tree Resort's location is its finest feature: The bay beyond the motel is breathtaking. Many units have tiny decks and chairs for taking in the view. The pool is built on a platform that overlooks the bay; sit in the jacuzzi and marvel at the glory of it all. There are inviting groupings of chairs in the lawn on the bay, and a couple of hammocks as well. It's quite charming. If you stay here, plan to set aside some time for bay watching.

Layton, a two-mile-long city with its own mayor, commissioners, and
police force, is the smallest city in the state. It's a clean, neat place,
founded by a guy who loved fishing and was dedicated to the pursuit of
happiness. At mile marker 68 you're in a good position to find it. You're
close to some of the Keys most interesting sights, restaurants and
beaches. And yet, you can get the feeling of a true retreat here. If your
sole purpose is relaxation, you're in the right place.

Several types of accommodations are available: comfortable waterfront motel rooms, waterfront efficiencies, One-bedroom cottages, and
two-bedroom apartments. Non-smoking rooms are available. Waterfront
efficiencies are $87 in summer; $105 in winter. Apartments begin at $100
and go up to $225. Call for a well-prepared list of unit descriptions and
prices.

Ocean Beach Club Hotel & Resort
MM 53.5 Oceanside, Key Colony Beach
289-0525 ❧ 800-321-7213

Key Colony Beach is located a few minutes from Marathon's fine,
recently updated airport, and yet it feels quite detached from the rest of
Marathon. Key Colony Beach is a tiny city, all on a man-made island,
with only about a thousand citizens. The island is spacious and
windswept, connected to the mainland by a causeway. Many retirees
winter here and rent their condos out to tourists when they're not here.
You'll find a wonderful and well-utilized walking and biking path, and
several very good restaurants.

If you've got to have a beach available twenty-four hours a day right
outside your room, this is the place for you.

The Ocean Beach Club was built on the ocean in the late '50s. Its
thirty-eight units are modest, spotless and roomy. Not luxurious. The
'55-era furniture is a trip. So is the mirror and dark wood paneling. Rent
a room with an ocean view for around $120 in season; $95 out. A room
on the other side of the building—no ocean view, sorry—is $95 in
season; $80 out. One-bedroom suites sleep four comfortably, and rent for
$165 in the season; and $140 out of season. Amenities include complimentary morning coffee in the lobby, an ocean-side pool, heated jacuzzi,
a really neat fishing pier, and a truly wonderful white sand beach. Rates

drop around May 1 for the slower summer season, but they don't drop much. You must sign on for three days or longer.

Rainbow Bend Resort
MM 58. Oceanside, on Grassy Key ☙ 289-1505 ☙ 800-929-1505
The big draw here has always been the free use of a Boston Whaler motorboat. Or you can use the sailboat. Full breakfast is free every morning, too. There are eighteen seaside units, pretty simple, with that good old '50s feel so prevalent in Middle Keys rooms for let. But these rooms are not as well preserved as many in the area. There's a beach and a pool and a jacuzzi.

Rooms, efficiencies, one and two-bedroom suites. Rates from mid-April to mid-December, the off season, range between $110 and $190. In season rates range from $120 to $210, which makes them somewhat high compared to other places in the area. Figure in the cost of renting a boat and that full breakfast and the rates look better.

Seascape Ocean Resort
76th Street Oceanside (turn at MM 50) ☙ 743-6455 ☙ 800-332-SEAS
The Seascape is at the oceanside end of a sedate residential street in Marathon. Sometimes miscalled "the sea escape" by hopeful guests, the

property is a quiet and breezy compound of nine units, well off the beaten path, and yet, conveniently close to it. Spectacular views of the Atlantic from sunrise to sunset are endlessly fascinating. Hypnotic. From a cement jetty on the deep-water marina, the light tower on Sombrero Reef is faintly visible some five miles off shore. Guests are welcome to arrive by boat and dock at the Seascape at no additional charge. (That no additional charge is a deal—usually you pay to dock.)

Monroe County's one-time commissioner of tolls built this lovely seaside villa in the early '50s. In a spacious wing facing the sunrise, he built three apartments for his three adult daughters and their families. New owners eventually chopped the estate into apartments. Finally the Seascape's intrinsic value as a resort was recognized. The apartments were divided into two, creating six units where there originally had been three. Seascape became an inn—but not the snug, blond on white oceanside retreat you see today. It took the artistry and dedication of artist Sara Stites and her photographer husband Bill to bring the Seascape to its current state of bright charm.

Five beautifully landscaped acres feature a freshwater pool on a terraced jut of land with more breathtaking views of sky and sea. A walled garden is one of several serene retreats on the property. Also, a hammock strung between two trees, so close to the water's edge that at high tide you have to wade through water to get to it, looks like a place to reinvent yourself.

A breakfast of fresh-baked muffins, fresh fruits, and gourmet coffee is served in a pleasant, whitewashed community room. A tiny library features books by local authors, including a couple of Bill's sumptuous photography books. Around sunset, complimentary wine and hors d'oeuvres appear.

All units are airy and recently refurbished, some with complete kitchens. No phones. Sara has painted the designs on headboards and the mirror frames. The mattresses, Bill says, are the best that money can buy. And so are the New Age air conditioners...quieter than a whisper.

Rates start around $95 and go up to $135, depending on the type of unit—efficiency or room—and time of year.

Siesta Motel
MM 51 Oceanside ✹ 743-5671

Seven small, neat units so clean that phrases like "neat as a pin" and "clean as a whistle" come to mind. Ancient terrazzo floors you could eat off of. Several units are efficiencies. New mattresses dressed in old, white cotton sheets, worn to dreamy perfection. Ginger Tolle, a proud honorary Conch (ask to see her certificate), opened the La Siesta Motel in September, 1960—the same month Hurricane Donna slashed a swath of destruction right through Marathon. The furniture for the new motel arrived late, which turned out to be a blessing. Had it arrived on time, Ginger says, Donna would have torn it apart. Some of the furniture from that 1960s shipment is still in use in some of the rooms! And some of the guests, or the children of the guests from those days, are still coming, too. There's lots of repeat business, enough to keep Ginger plenty busy.

No pool. No phones. No beach. No remote control on the televisions. No frills. Just clean, comfortable rooms in the heart of the Keys. La Siesta is a good name for the place. Rooms and efficiencies rent for $44–$52 a night, year-round.

Valhalla Beach Resort Motel
MM 56.5, Oceanside ✹ 289-0616

The sheets on your bed in this little motel were dried in sunshine and tropical breezes. That's the way it's done here. There are no clothes dryers. Everything is done as simply and no-fuss as possible. Even the office is stark. The price list is written and hung on a bulletin board on the door. You clang a bell to summon someone when you're ready to check in or out.

Owner Bruce Shofield inherited the Valhalla from his parents, who built the place as a fishing camp in 1951. It's been running continuously since then. Located about a half-mile-lane away from the Overseas Highway, the Valhalla feels quite remote and removed from the rest of the world. Until you see the sign, you might think you're about to become lost in the weeds. The complex includes twelve units located on a tidal lagoon, with water on three sides. There's a very nice sandy beach, with shade if you want it, and great wooden lounging chairs. Hammocks. Picnic tables. Flowers. Palm trees. Birds from the surrounding mangroves fly and squawk happily. Canoes are free to use, and the area is perfect for exploration. Parents with children will find this a comfortable retreat. In the summertime, boaters often arrive pulling their boats. There's a launch on the property and no charge to dock here while you're a guest.

All efficiencies and rooms have AC and TV. Also refrigerators. No phones. That would be obscene. The televisions are bad enough. Efficiencies are $70. Motel rooms are $60, based on double occupancy. Extra people in a unit are $10. Kids are $7. Rates are same year-round. Two night minimum, although there's flexibility on that if you happen to show up when there's an opening. If you want to stay here, make your reservations early. Usually, the place closes for the month of May. The Valhalla does not advertise but is featured in many guidebooks 'cause it is the real thing.

Dining

Barracuda Grill
MM 49.5 Gulfside ▪ 743-3314

The waitresses wear T-shirts and pants, a little informal for such a fancy menu, and arrive at your table saying, "Would you like a bottle of wine with your dinner this evening?" which seems a bit pushy. Then, a long list of wonderful-sounding specials, but no prices. Although the menu says house salads come with all entrees, our waitress asked "would you like a Caesar salad?" pushing the hustle button once again. The Caesar salad costs an additional $3. The house salad turned out to be very nice, particularly with the creamy garlic and peppercorn dressing. An appetizer called Cajun Calamari ($4.95), squid in a creamy hot sauce, was fiery and delicious.

Just when we were beginning to congratulate ourselves on finding a gem of a restaurant, our dinner arrived. The sauce on the seafood pasta with shrimp and scallops was disappointingly bland, although the seafood was certainly fresh. An even blander sauce was the gorganzola cream on the fettucine with sun-dried tomatoes. Yes, there were fragments of sun dried tomato, but mere fragments. It seems disingenuous to mention them at all.

Meanwhile, a man at the table next to ours turned toward us to rhapsodize about his rack of baby lamb. "I think they should charge more for this!" he joked, adding that during his visit to the Keys, he'd been back twice to the Barracuda Grill for the same dish. (Rack of Lamb: $19.95.)

When we didn't rave about our dinners when our waitress asked if we were enjoying our entrees—which, except for the seafood, we'd barely touched—she seemed so miffed we skipped coffee and dessert.

The husband and wife team of Jan and Lance Hill are the chefs at Barracuda Grill, and, according to Michael, the dining room host, they are always the chefs. So we can't think of an excuse for our bland entrees that night. Jan once cooked at the fabulous Little Palm Island. Later, she and Lance ran a place on Cudjoe Key. Now, they're finally doing their own place, the Barracuda Grill. Several Marathon residents suggested this as a local favorite; others told us it was overrated. If you go, plan to spend a minimum of $60 for two, including tip. Dinner only from 6 p.m. to 10 p.m. Closed Mondays. No reservations. And watch out for the barracuda....

Beach House Restaurant
MM 53.5, East Ocean Boulevard • 743-3939

Marathon's beachiest seaside bistro is the noble, and just a bit tattered, Beach House Restaurant, located directly on the Atlantic Ocean. Outdoor dining is on a ballroom-sized deck, protected from direct sunlight by a huge pink awning that bathes diners and servers alike in a soft, flattering glow. Pink cloth napkins and real silverware grace the table. We find this a very romantic place and like to come here for lunch and pretend we're dining in the Riviera (except nobody around here sunbathes topless). A full bar and lounge are separate from the dining area; more dining areas inside, that we know nothing about, appear to be usually closed. Why would anyone sit in there when you can sit outside and dig this view? Wherever you choose to sit in this big place, you see the ocean. At the very edge of the deck are tables for two with bright umbrellas. Just below the restaurant, and on each side, is white, sandy beach with beautiful people sunning, swimming and sand-castle-building. Key Colony Beach has the very finest beachfront in Marathon.

Service at the Beach House is very good. The food is fine and tastes even better because you're eating it on the beach in the salt air. The fish sandwich, grilled or fried, served with French fries, is $6.75 and very, very good. There's also Greek salad and pizza.

The dinner menu features lots of fish, ribs, prime ribs, fried chicken, spaghetti and pizza—the usual crowd pleasers. Prices are moderate, more moderate than you might expect considering the fantastic ambiance. The Beach House Restaurant and Bar close on Sundays, except for special occasions like Mother's Day.

Brian's In Paradise
MM 52, in Marathon • 743-3183

The menu is twelve pages long, and everything on it is good. Honest-to-goodness diner food in an old-fashioned, diner-styled building. Sit in a booth; even the menu is good for the eyes. Regulars keep this place packed. The waitresses at Brian's are a hoot—efficient and wry. Lots of retirees eat here as well as tourists in the know. The menu features salad bar, very good desserts, specials like pot roast (I overhead a customer say to the waitress: "What kind of pot did they roast?"). Entrees on the kids menu are named for places in the area: Grassy Key Eggs, the Vaca Cut Bite, Coco Plum Chicken. Prices are very reasonable. Open every day from 6:30 a.m. till 10 p.m.

Castaway Restaurant
MM 48, 15th Street Oceanside ✺ 743-6247

The ads say this place is hard to find. Believe it! Parking around here is also difficult, with just a small parking lot for the whole place, so it fills quickly. Don't take a chance in a tow-away zone, either, a sign in the Castaway warns. In this marina of shrimp and lobster houses, houseboats and residential trailers, the Castaway fits quite nicely. The dining room is a screened-in side porch. Ceiling fans turn at top speeds to keep the warm air moving since there is no AC. The floor is cement. The chairs don't match, and you might find a shrimp shell, left over from an earlier patron's dinner, under your placemat (we did). The rough-hewn ambiance reminded one guy in our party of his '50s era summer camp back in South Carolina.

You'll be happiest if you get a table with a window on the canal. When the lights of the low-rent neighborhood glitter off the after-dark water, it's quite soothing.

The food at the Castaway is great, of course, (it'd better be, right?) and the crab cakes are the best this crab-cake-lover has ever had. A bargain at around $8, the crab cakes are one of the most popular selections on the menu. They're served with French fries or steamed new potatoes. Other sides are coleslaw, cucumber, or mixed salads in laughably tiny portions.

A small basket of yummy honey buns, two buns per customer, is delivered to your table early; additional buns are 30¢ each.

Other selections include fried or sauteed fish of the day. We had it fried, and at $11.95, it compared to fried fish everywhere in this area, except it cost more. A special that night was broiled swordfish. A woman at the table next to ours, who always visits the Castaway during her family's annual Marathon vacation, raved about it. "We eat here once a year, and we always get lost trying to find the place," she laughed. "It's all part of the tradition with us."

A pound of steamed shrimp is around $12, and you get seconds, on the house. But few people do—have you ever shucked and eaten an entire pound of shrimp? There's also fried shrimp, fried scallops, snapper almondine, fried chicken and steak. Prices on the early summer evening we were there ranged from $7.95 to $18.95.

Beer and wine only. Major credit cards. Dinner is served from 5 p.m.–10 p.m. and never on Sundays.

Cracked Conch Cafe
MM 49.9 Oceanside ✆ 743-2233

Gee whiz. Absolutely nothing went right on the day we visited the Cracked Conch Cafe. But everything looked perfect at their indoor dining area, bar, and outdoor dining room, enclosed by white-washed cement blocks. Lots of boughs of tropical green creep and poke around the room among little tables for two or four, and one table for up to six people. The waitresses are sturdy-looking gals with some good stories to tell—you just know it when you see them. This place was featured on *TV Diners*, a program that goes on location to feature curious culinary sites all over the country. Since you don't often see cracked conch on a menu, it is easy to imagine how the chewy mollusk that figures big on this menu, as well as in the name of the joint, caught the attention of the *TV Diners* scouts.

"Hey, is this the place that was on *TV Diners* on the TV Food Network on May 24, 1995?" I asked a waitress.

"It sure is," she replied proudly.

So after all that, we were expecting to eat one fine lunch. It was 1 p.m. and the place wasn't crowded. We had 2 'o clock plans. Surely enough time to have a quick sandwich, right? *Wrong.* Twenty minutes after we had ordered, our waitress came to the table to confess that she'd forgotten to put our order in to the kitchen. She brought us a couple of cups of nothing-to-write-home-about chowder to make up for the delay. "Men like red and women like creamy," the waitress said.

Finally, our sandwiches arrived. The deep-fried conch sandwich was chewy, but good. My poor friend's fish sandwich wasn't cooked all the way through. In fact, he realized after a couple of bites, the damned thing was very close to raw. Time was ticking away. The waitress took the raw fish sandwich off our bill. She would have taken it back to the kitchen and had it cooked through, she said, but we were running late for our 2 'o clock plans and didn't have any more time to spend at the Cracked Conch Cafe.

All things considered, we wouldn't go back. Oh, and *TV Diners* is off the air.

Crockogators Road Kill Cafe
MM 59 Bayside, Grassy Key ✻ 743-8282
Best-selling dishes here are two house specialties: Road Kill Stew, a thick soup of beef, chicken, pork, tomatoes, lima beans, corn, and whatever else is lying around. "We sell gallons of it," says Suzanne, owner of the cafe. Second favorite dish is Alligator Tail. "We marinate it, pound the hell out of it, flour it, and deep fry it," explains Suzanne. "If you've tried alligator before and found it not to your liking, it was probably not prepared properly," she says.

The Road Kill Cafe is not a fancy place. The outside is painted bright yellow, while inside, you'll find a cheery sunflower decor and a convenient roll of paper towels sitting on every table, along with the salt and pepper. The menu changes daily—except for that famous stew and the alligator, of course. The daily specials are written up on a display board and brought to your table. Breakfast, lunch, and dinner are simple and traditional, nothing fancy, because Suzanne got tired of putting up with persnickety chefs.

When you go, ask if Suzanne is still the boss. If she is, food is guaranteed good. If she's gone—the place is on the market as we go to press—forget everything you just read. If you want to buy it, you'll need $287,000, and more dedication than you ever dreamed of.

Grassy Key Dairy Bar
MM 58.5, Oceanside ✻ 743–3816.
Maybe this place was pretty spiffy when it opened twenty-five years ago, but it's not spiffy anymore. Instead, it looks and feels like what it is: a funky, family-owned-and-operated restaurant, bordering on run-down.

Decor is real Keys fishy: nautical-themed curtains and paintings, drift-wood art, framed awards, mounted fish, and photos of the proud anglers who caught them. Whoever decorated the back room is parrot crazy, but the cane furniture is nice. A small aquarium with a few tiny fish might entertain the kids for a little while. A small counter in the front room seats six, and when you enter the place, all six diners turn around to have a look at the newcomers.

Old-fashioned is often better than modern, and that's true with the good food and the great service here. A fish sandwich basket with French fries and coleslaw is $6.95. Bread, rolls and desserts are baked fresh in the kitchen. Key lime pie is $2.75. A fine lunch for two is under $20. The dinner menu is traditional—steaks, seafood. Charcoal grilled fish or chicken comes with a baked potato and veggies. Prices range from $10–$16. Heart-healthy dining program is available too. Their fish is smoked right in the back yard. Take a walk around the building and check out the hurricane shutters. These folks are ready to snap those shutters into place and close this place up tight at a moment's notice. Closed Sunday and Monday. Wine and beer only. No Credit cards. Cash only.

Herbie's
MM 50.5 Bayside ● 743-6373

A Key West friend says he always stops in at Herbie's on his way to or from Miami. So we figured we should try it, although there's nothing about the way it looks from the outside to entice you to go inside. Unless you're encouraged by long lines.... But it's a fun bar, and the fried fish sandwiches are yummy. Gee whiz, what else do you want? But around 8 p.m. on Friday and Saturday nights, people stand in line to get into Herbie's to eat, which might give you the idea that the food is extra fantastic. Why else would they wait when there are so many other places? The waitresses are super fast, but the prices are like fried fish prices everywhere else. It's one of those been-here-forever joints.

Hurricane Raw Bar
MM 49.5 ✹ 743-5755

It's Saturday afternoon at the Toucan Lounge. Disco music blares; a flickering strobe bathes the room with oddly shaped splashes of light. The dance floor is packed with tiny, barefoot people spinning and swirling. It's somebody's sixth birthday, and the place is jumping with moms and their tots. Next door in the Hurricane Bar, a Saturday crowd of locals are sipping beer and watching baseball on a giant television. A waitress is busy taking orders for the day's special: ribs and French fries with coleslaw. Food is not fussy, but it's great; we enjoyed every greasy bite.

On the menu we noted that the severity of the heat in the spicy-hot Hurricane Wings is rated by force, just like a hurricane. Get it? "Force 1" is mild. "Force 2" is not so mild, and so on. The menu states that, to order "Force 6," you must be over eighteen and willing to sign a release form. Other menu selections are fried fish baskets and Philly cheese steaks. The full bar features lots of beers. The waitresses are cool; the laid-back atmosphere is big with local, funky Keys characters.

Key Colony Inn
MM 53.5 Key Colony Beach ✹ 743-0100

Off the beaten path, but not too far off. The food here isn't ultra fantastic; it's just very good, very satisfying, kind of like Mom's home cooking. Prices are somewhat less than at comparable restaurants on the main highway. At this no-nonsense restaurant you can count on finding a good selection of nicely prepared, beautifully presented dishes based on American and Italian cuisine. Service is excellent and personable. Lots of variations on local seafood. Salad is served family style, in a big bowl with more than you can possibly eat. This place feels like a country club dining room up north; a little old-fashioned, but nicely so. And everybody knows everybody else. Order the Grand Fisherman's Platter, sauteed or fried, for $19.95. Or ravioli with tomato sauce and mushrooms, at $8.95. The well-designed children's menu has very good prices. Lunch and dinner only; full bar.

Weekends feature lots of weddings, so you'll see people in wilted wedding clothes wandering through the dusk, looking dazed and sort of beat, the way you feel at the end of a long wedding day. The Inn opens around 11 a.m. every day.

The Hideaway
MM 58 at Rainbow Bend Resort ☞ 289-1554

The newest personality chef at the Hideaway is Chef Bobby Pepper from Louisiana. In addition to the Hideaway's gourmet entrees like Beef Wellington, roast duck, lamb, fishes and pasta specials, Bobby Pepper serves up some real mean Cajun cuisine. House favorite of late is Chef Bobby's Jambalaya ($24.95).

Both Bobby and Brian, his assistant, generally visit every table to satisfy themselves that their culinary efforts are being appreciated. They'll even let you buy them a glass of wine. A great dinner for two, with wine, dessert and a tip will cost around $75. Lunch entrees are considerably less than dinner.

The Hideaway's advertising slogan is "The only thing we overlook is the ocean."

Little Italy
MM 68.5 ☞ 664-4472

The name of "Little Italy" is a bit of a misnomer because the place serves much more than just standard Italian dishes: fried conch and fish; Reuben and chicken parmesan sandwiches, and salads, each for around $4.95–$6.95. The same people who own this place also own the Key Colony Inn; They aim to appeal to locals, and they do. Regular customers are staff members from the nearby Dolphin Research Center. Area motels send more business, and regular Keys travelers know they'll find consistently good food and reasonable prices here. The Little Italy opens every day at 6:30 a.m., serving breakfast dishes like battered and fried dolphin with eggs and home fries for $4.25; blueberry pancakes and yummy stick-to-your-ribs standards. Lunch is served till 2:30 p.m. Dinner hours are 5 p.m.–10 p.m. The dinner chef makes a mean shrimp scampi for $14.95. Dolphin, prepared many different ways, is usually $12.95. This place closes only for Thanksgiving and Christmas. The parking lot is always full.

Porky's BBQ
MM 47.5 Bayside ✺ 289-2065

Perched between the Overseas Highway and a very tranquil saltwater lagoon, Porky's indoor/outdoor shack dining room is painted with fishes, moons and slogans like "swining and dining." Porky's may not look like an important restaurant, but it is. The atmosphere and the attitude here represent all that is sweet and goofy about the Keys. While you wait for your ribs or BBQ sandwich or beer, you may find yourself chatting with folks at the next table. They might be locals; they might be visitors. They might be Miami tourists who stop by every couple of weekends on their way into or out of the Keys. If you're looking to rent a boat, have a look at Captain Pip's selection on the right side of the marina. Ring a ship's bell and Captain Pip will appear to handle the arrangements. The reef, Captain Pip will explain, is about about five miles out.

Lunch or dinner for two—there's only one menu—is around $25. The food isn't as good as the atmosphere, although it's definitely good. Our gripe was that the ribs ($8.95, with French fries and cole slaw) were reheated. Same for the barbecued beef and pork sandwich ($5.95, with Porky's Famous Potato Salad). We've heard that some of the area's winter residents rush straight to Porky's as soon as they arrive back in town each season for some of Porky's southern-style barbeque. Porky's caters some of the best area parties, too. We'd like to go to a party catered by these folks. Beer and wine only. Porky's is open every day. They close only for bad weather. Bring cash because Porky doesn't take credit cards.

Seven Mile Grill
MM 47 Bayside ✺ 743-4481

Buy a T-shirt. See live Marathon characters like a very hungover guy picking up a to-go order in a shirt that says *If I'd known you were gonna care about me this long I woulda taken better care of myself*. The food complements the area's borderline shabbiness.

The foot-long hot dog with all the trimmings used to be special and terrific because of the old-fashioned grilled roll. Lately they've stopped grilling the roll, which seems like a sign of the times. Is nothing sacred? "The bakery doesn't send us those rolls anymore," a waitress, who I think owns the place, explained. The waitresses who work here have been around forever. Fried fish, stuffed crabs, burgers and a yummy shrimp

bisque are all specialties. (Long ago a Seven Mile Grill employee told me
the bisque is made of evaporated milk, Campbell's cream of asparagus and
cream of mushroom soups and tiny canned shrimp. You figure out the
proportions, she said.)

The Grill features traditional roadside, deep-fried food served at a
long, old-fashioned lunch counter. Decor is old diner—walls full of
license plates, wooden plaques with dumb fishing cartoons, and signs that
say stuff like "No Snowmobiling." Pitcher of draft beer is around $7.50;
also cans and bottles of beer, and wine.

We always stop at the grill for something or other; usually we eat. You
can dine in the air-conditioned dining room, but then you're missing the
point. Not so long ago, there were few other choices, and that's when my
family and I got hooked forever on the Seven Mile Grill. It's closed tight
as a drum on Wednesdays (Thursdays, too, during the off season) and
every fall from mid-August to mid-October, which starts the rumor each
year that the place has closed for good. Bring cash; that's all they take at
the Grill.

Shuckers Raw Bar and Grill
MM 47.5 Oceanside, in the 11th Street Marina ● 743-8686
My Aunt Marge, who winters in Marathon, likes Shuckers because it's a
great place to hang out with lots of company. You get a table on the outdoor deck overlooking the harbor. Then you order drinks, chat, eat a
bowl of steamed clams, order another round of drinks, chat some more,
and, eventually, order dinner. It would be difficult to do all that visiting,
eating and drinking in Aunt Marge's condo.

Shuckers' servers and bartenders are blond, tan, shapely, and incredibly nice. They'll very patiently answer your questions about what to do
and see, and where else to eat in Marathon. (That won't take long.)

You can pull up to the bar in your boat or Waverunner and tie up to
one of a series of skinny docks off the outdoor raw bar. Shuckers serves
food all day, and there are plenty of tables outdoors overlooking the
harbor, and plenty inside the air-conditioned dining room. Watch a small
fishing fleet coming and going, and several fishing charters arrive around
4 p.m. with the day's catch. A partially submerged wreck in the harbor
attracts several species of squawking sea birds. Enjoy spectacular views of

the endless vista of sky and the sea. Nice. And you'll find the prices very fair.

Silverado's Steakhouse
MM 48, at 15th Street Oceanside ☙ 743-5600
The early days of the American West are celebrated here with displays of chaps, guns in showcases, and "wanted" posters. Decor looks like the set from *Gunsmoke*. You expect Miss Kitty herself to slip behind the bar to take your order. Entertainment is important here. Something goes on at the Silverado every night: A trio of musicians, a couple of whom played with the Tommy Dorsey Band, are jamming them in each Friday night; Saturday night is Latin Night, with a fabulous band; Thursday is Country Night. Learn to line dance Thursday nights (or Tuesday, depending upon the time of year) when the Southernmost Dancers show up to host line dance lessons in the saloon on their good-sized dance floor. More theme-nights are planned, though business slows considerably in the summer months when the snowbirds are back up north.

When you're tired of Marathon's favorite food, fresh seafood, come to Silverado's where beef rules! Filet mignon, NY strip, T-bone, London broil, prime rib, teriyaki rib-eye, and sirloin steak soup. Other selections are blackened Caesar salad, scallops, and shrimp dishes; a kids menu with kid-sized meals and prices, too. Early bird hours daily. In the off season, May—November, the Silverado is closed Mondays and Tuesdays.

Village Cafe
MM 50, Gulfside Village Shopping Center ☙ 743-9090
Enjoy a terrific Sunday breakfast buffet from 8:30 a.m. to 2 p.m., with all the usual breakfast goodies, for $6.95. The Sunday dinner buffet, served from 5 p.m. to 9 p.m. for $10.95, is attractive, and the atmosphere is perfect for Sunday evening, when everybody is a little tired but feeling warm and fuzzy. The regular menu is very nice, and the food really well-prepared at this family operation. The waitrons here seem to be going crazy at lunchtime, but, in spite of the hubbub, they keep on smiling. They shouldn't be surprised it's so packed because this is one of the best places for pasta meals, and most reasonably-priced, in the Keys. The fresh pastas have terrific sauces, and the clam sauce is heavenly. The fresh tomato

and basil is good, too, and reminded me of New York Italian cuisine. Good salads, good service, and a very nice presentation. Considering all that, particularly as it stacks up against what else is available in the area, it's one of Marathon's best deals.

Wooden Spoon
MM 50.5 Oceanside ✹ 743-7469
The grill's on at 5 a.m. Heavy-duty fishermen's breakfasts attract many hungry locals and tourists. Crowded from the crack of dawn on. Buy a box lunch and take it on your fishing boat. The waitresses in here call you "Hon" and are so good at anticipating your needs, it seems as if they are reading your mind.

Nightlife

Anglers Lounge
MM 48 in Faro Blanco Resort ✹ 743-9018
Live entertainment nightly. Radio party 5:30 p.m.–6:30 p.m. every Friday. Many tourists staying in the sprawling Faro Blanco Resort show up here for a nightcap, so the mix of customers is always interesting.

The Brass Monkey Lounge
MM 50 ✹ 743-4028
Rock 'n' roll rules! Tonight and every night in this longtime-popular local bar. The Brass Monkey boasts live entertainment nightly and no cover charge. Happy hour daily, and on Friday, what has become a tradition: the Friday Happy Hour Buffet. House star is John Bartus, rocker, writer, businessman, wit. There's a liquor store, too, so the place is open all day and all night until 4 a.m.

Gary's Pub and Billiards
MM 50, Oceanside ✹ 743-0622
Open seven days, 11 a.m.–late. Twenty-one TV screens satellite-fed by eight dishes, featuring sports events from everywhere. Settle yourself in front of the screen of your choice, take a break from the sun and the

vacation fun and pretend you're back home. Only this time home is equipped with a waitress and lots of great food. Pizza, chili dogs, and a barbecued pork sandwich ($2.50!). The elegantly appointed interior, with a sixty-foot-long gleaming mahogany bar, is reminiscent of a private men's club in London. Of course, women are welcome here, too, and are invited to play pool, darts, fooseball, and pinball. Choose from sixteen brands of draft beer; the food, and remember it's far from gourmet, is basic and cheap—chili, $1.50; chicken or fish sandwich, $2.75; twelve-inch pizza, $8; chicken wings are sold by the piece, 30¢.

Sombrero Marina and Dockside Lounge
MM 50, Oceanside; on Sombrero Boulevard ✱ 743-0000
This dockside lounge with a full bar and live music, overlooks scenic Boot Key Harbor. The party-hardy atmosphere blends Caribbean music and limbo contests with Hawaiian luau food and hula dances. Patrons are encouraged to dress accordingly. The goal of the Sombrero Dockside Lounge is to make you feel at home no matter what side of the continental divide you're from—and to rent you a sailboat the following day.

Shops

Bougainvillea House
MM 53.5 ✒ 743-0808

Within this ancient, sun-silver wooden building, beneath an explosion of brilliant pink bougainvillea, you'll find handcrafted jewelry, sea grape, guava, cocoplum, lime, and hot pepper jellies created in a nearby Keys cannery, and local photography. Delicately-wrought earrings featuring bits of colored beach glass are called Mermaid's Tears, and with each pair of earrings comes a tag telling the history of the glass in those particular earrings.

BP Cargo
MM 49.5 Oceanside ✒ 743-0555

The first question every customer asks upon entering this shop is this: "Do you always play Jimmy Buffett music in here?" The answer is "Yes. Nine hours every day."

"Actually, fortunately, I like Jimmy Buffet's music very much," says manager Sandy Spear. "I can't imagine doing this if, say, Wayne Newton had an apparel line."

Merchandise here is CDs, tapes, trinkets and doodads, all inspired by Jimmy Buffett's music. Caribbean Soul is Jimmy Buffet's apparel line.

The store's latest item: Margarita Mix. Also, there are shirts here to fit tall and big guys up to size 4X. The store opens at 9 a.m. daily.

The Enchanted Elephant
MM 54, Gulfside ✒ 289-0646 ✒ 800-689-0646

A shop you'll never forget. This happy looking little gray and purple store is for folks who love cats, dogs, parrots, and kitschy, Keysy, beachy things like rayon sarongs, novelty picture frames, and objects d'art. The world's smallest museum pays homage to one of the world's largest creatures. The museum, a collection of elephants in all shapes, colors and sizes, is the heart and soul of this operation.

Food For Thought
Gulfside Village ✶ 743-3297
This is the largest bookstore in Marathon, which isn't saying a hell of a lot. Still, they do a good job of assembling a fine selection of reading into fairly small quarters. The bargain table always has something sensational like a giant book of photographs and trivia about the king of rock 'n roll: *Graceland: The Living Legacy of Elvis Presley*, which sold originally for $50. I got it for $9. Amazing, huh? Also bestsellers and books by Keys writers, and postcards and nice notecardy things. Check out the community announcement center posted in the window, with its great array of posters and ads for all sorts of events and services. It's a fun browse, and you'll probably find something crazy or interesting to do or see.

On the other side of the shop, you'll find a health food store with whole foods, organic beauty products, and vitamins. Food for thought…get it?

Kennedy Studios
MM 48 Oceanside ✶ 743-2040
This eclectic poster collection is appropriate for local decors. McKnight. Kiraly. Van Gogh. A wonderful collection of local art, it's probably the best representation of work by local artists in the Middle Keys. This shop, with its helpful staff, is part of a growing empire of Kennedy Galleries in Cape Cod and the Keys, including a couple more of their galleries in Key West. Bob and Michelle Kennedy prints and posters are wonderful and affordable, all prices are very reasonable. Great pirate treasure maps for the kids. Framing is done on the premises, but it's not such a great deal. Custom framing often costs more than the work. Open 10 a.m. till 5 p.m., Tuesday–Saturday.

Marathon Liquors & Deli
MM 49.7 ✶ 743-6350
Last summer our good friend Chuck found himself in a situation that necessitated frequent drives up and down the Keys. "At first the trip seemed a chore, a nuisance," Chuck said, "but I've actually grown to enjoy it! There's so much to see and do along the road." One of Chuck's big finds was the Marathon Deli and Liquor Store, with soups, deli salads,

and thick sandwiches-to-go that closely resemble the luscious, over-stuffed wedges of New York or Boston. In addition to the sandwich counter, their bakery bar is full of irresistible cookies, and coolers of fresh fruits and veggies. We sampled salads and cookies, too, but nothing compared with that Italian-style wedge. The place is full of goodies like DeCecco pastas, canned olives and imported sardines and sun-dried tomatoes. A browser's paradise. A necessity for gourmands.

The store is run by a group of stern-looking women who lighten up easily if you begin a conversation. I chatted with the cashier about Hurricane Donna, 1960, which she says she remembers in terrifying detail. Then we talked about the deli, how busy it is, how many tourists reappear year after year, and how much she enjoys her job. Finally I asked for her name, but she refused. "I'm nobody," she said.

Martha's Caribbean Cupboard and Dangerous John's Hot Sauces & Cigars
MM 54, Gulfside

Martha and Johnny were lovers. So they set up a tiny shop and set out their wares. Martha collects beautiful kitchen things, tie-dyed aprons, and cookie cutters shaped like turtles and lizards. John's passion is hot sauces, spiced jellies, and earthy cigars. How much heat can you take? You're invited to sample the goods laid out on a center table—dozens of jars and bottles of hot sauces that you spread on Cuban crackers. One taste of fat-free, red pepper and black bean dip will keep your mouth jumping for hours. You have my personal guarantee.

John Bartus, a local musician, DJ, jingle writer and columnist, creates Velvet Elvis, a smoldering hot sauce. Buy the sauce alone for $7; buy Bartus's album and a bottle of Velvet Elvis for $15.95.

The Purple Isles and
Their Number One Passion
Islamorada

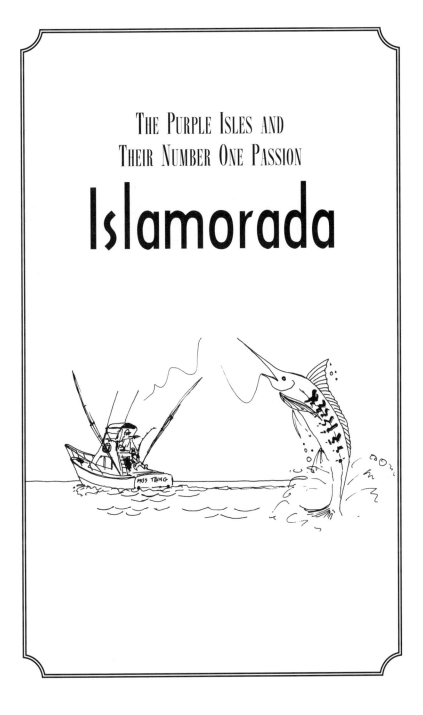

Mile Marker 90

Plantation Key

To
Key
Largo

Upper Matecumbe Key

Windley Key

Islamorada

Lignumvitae Key

Indian Key

Lower Matecumbe Key

Mile Marker 70

To Marathon and Middle Keys

*...Marlin fishermen suffer from a rare psychological
disorder that I call the Ahab Complex—
an obsession to pursue and conquer a monster
of the depths regardless of the consequences to
one's bank account, career and family life.*

– PHIL CAPUTO, PULITZER PRIZE WINNER

The Purple Isles
and Their Number One Passion

"THE PURPLE ISLES." That's what the early Spanish explorers called this little group of islands. But no historian is quite certain what purple inspiration those sailors saw. Flowers? Shrubs? Tree snails? Seashells? Like many of the descriptive names given these islands by Spaniards long ago, this is another without a clear-cut origin. All we know is they saw purple and, since Islamorada is such a pretty name, we're glad they did.

The area we know today as Islamorada is comprised of six islands also known as "the Matecumbes." The meaning of the word "Matecumbe" is also unclear. In some places you will read that Matecumbe is the mispronunciation of the word "Guarugumbe," which was the name of one of the islands. Another theory is that Matecumbe is a contraction of two Spanish words: matar, "to kill" and hombre, "man." Obviously, controversies over the meanings and origins of Keys names are quite common.

The six islands of Islamorada, or the Matecumbes, are Plantation Key, Windley Key, Upper Matecumbe, Lower Matecumbe, and the offshore islands of Lignumvitae Key, and Indian Key.

The fundamental differences between the Upper Keys areas of Key Largo and Islamorada spring from their respective primary tourist industries: diving and fishing. Consider the differences between people who dive and people who fish, the differences between communing with nature and, well, *challenging* it. Key Largo is a diving town, and Islamorada is a fishing town—the "Fishing Capital of the World."

Fishing can be an extraordinarily expensive passion. The guides, the gas, the gear, the vessels and the licenses all carry big price tags to be passed on to the tourist. But for devotees, the fat price tags are part of what makes it such a noble sport.

Hardcore anglers will find their heaven on earth in the fish-rich waters of Islamorada. The people of Islamorada understand the allure of angling—perhaps better than any other community you will find in the world. So the place feels kind of country-clubbish, and the theme everywhere, always, is fishing.

If, however, endless vistas of sea and sky tinged with the scent of diesel fuel and fish bait bring you no joy whatsoever, do not despair. There is much else to do on Islamorada's shores. Some of the Keys' most remarkable history happened right here. You can stay in some truly wonderful resorts, motels, and inns, visit great places to shop, eat and drink. Or just sit and read in the unbridled breezes of the mighty Atlantic.

The area of Islamorada covers the miles from Anne's Beach at mile marker 73, all the way up to mile marker 90, near where the big island of Key Largo begins.

Islamorada Chamber of Commerce
MM 82.5 Bayside ☛ 664-4503 ☛ 800-322-5397

It is quite amazing how much goes on inside this little red caboose. You might think this off-track caboose was perhaps part of the famous and doomed Overseas Railroad. It wasn't. The only thing this caboose has in common with the Overseas Railroad is the train theme. Donated to Islamorada some years ago by a man from Kansas, the sturdy caboose houses the busy Islamorada Chamber of Commerce and Visitor's Center.

Of the Florida Keys chambers of commerce, this one is probably the friendliest, and craziest. The chamber is run by a handful of industrious women, who call themselves "The Chamber Maids." These bright specialists are in charge of telling the world about Islamorada and keeping records on who wants to know what. They handle over one hundred telephone calls a day and answer thousands of in-person tourists' questions. They work very hard, for less money than you would think. Every last one of them is crazy about Islamorada, and it shows. If you're looking for a place to eat, sleep, drink, party or shop, these women, of varying ages, backgrounds and tastes, will come up with all the answers to your questions.

One of their more appreciated attributes is their honesty. They won't pretend to know about something if they don't. And when they do know about something, they will share the news with open hearts and minds.

Also in the chamber you'll find the usual selection of brochures and pamphlets, as well as several info sheets on most-asked questions like "Where's the beach?" and "What's there to do?" and "Where do we sign up to swim with the dolphins?" The info sheets are a good idea and will make you wonder why all the other chambers don't follow suit.

Don't forget to ask for the much advertised, free coupon book worth $1,000. "You should live so long to save all this money," laughed the chamber maid who handed me my coupon book. In other words, it would take a dedicated adventurer many days in Paradise to use up all $1,000 of the savings listed, and many of the discounts and reductions are good only on non-holidays and on weekdays. Still, it is surely worth a few bucks off here and there.

The Chamber Caboose is set back a bit from the road, so keep your eyes peeled for it. There are often traffic jams in the tiny parking lot, but find a good spot and come on in for a good time.

If you're not here yet, call ahead and they'll send you those info sheets, a list of charterboat captains, a coupon book, and a list of accommodations. But you've got to ask for each specific item.

A Bloody History

WE KNOW FROM SPANISH sea charts, dating from as far back as the 1500s, that the freshwater wells on Lower Matecumbe Key have long been of great importance to passing ships as well as to Indians who originally inhabited these islands. Archeological evidence points to several Indian communities having been here. Easily accessible from the Atlantic Ocean, the Matecumbes were visited frequently by seafarers who came ashore for fresh water.

It is believed that Indians began communicating and interacting with Cuban fishermen as early as the 1500s. Native Americans incorporated Spanish words, as well as Spanish names, into their cultures. The Keys Indians were proficient divers and were the first salvagers of ships wrecked on the dangerous reefs that run parallel to the island chain. The items they found on wrecked ships were often useless to them and their society. However, items like fanciful clothing were much appreciated, and, always, Indians were delighted to find barrels of rum. Sometimes the victims of the frequent shipwrecks were enslaved by the Indians, and sometimes they were killed. It is said that Keys Indians were tolerant of Spanish-speaking people, but suspicious and extremely hostile to others.

Just after the Civil War, Bahamian settlers arrived in the area and survived by raising cash crops of melons, limes and vegetables, which they transported by trade schooners to Key West or northern Florida. According to the census taken that year, in 1870 the population of the entire Keys outside of Key West was three hundred.

Early settlers of the Upper Keys faced unimaginable hardships: bugs and mosquitoes, poverty, isolation. Many settlers came to the Keys, settled on the open land, tried for a few years, and then went away again beaten by the harsh conditions.

In the 1820s and 1830s, however, a little community was founded, and it flourished quite remarkably on Indian Key. But the town was burned in 1840 by warring Indians during the Second Seminole Indian War.

The arrival of the Overseas Railroad in the early 1900s brought little change to the area. But the Overseas Highway, completed here in 1928, changed life in Islamorada forever, just as it would do everywhere in the Keys. Still, those changes came very slowly; the population figures from the mid 1800s through early 1900s are unbelievably small.

When the Matecumbe islands, where the ocean is always just a few feet away from anywhere on shore, became accessible by car, tourism slowly began as a trickle and then grew steadily. Besides the terrific climate, deep-sea fishing was the draw. Then in 1935, the United States' most devastating hurricane nearly wiped the Lower Matecumbe islands off the map, and so the area had to start up fresh from scratch once again.

Tourism was established as the Keys' most important industry by the time electricity was installed here in 1942; fresh water, via an extravagant pipeline stretching from the mainland all the way to Key West, came in September of the same year. Mosquito control began in 1952. Today, area jobs and businesses are nearly all tourist-related.

The Indian Key Massacre

There is scant record of anything going on in the Keys before the early 1800s. When the U.S. government began a settlement at Key West Harbor in 1822, the Keys were wild and ungoverned and filled with a handful of people who liked it that way. One of the few places outside of Key West to attract any settlement was Indian Key. The eleven-acre island was situated close to the treacherous reefs that brought increasing numbers of ships aground. It was also less than a mile from Lower Matecumbe Key and its important source of fresh water for seafarers. The island was a busy rendezvous for pirates, smugglers, privateers, and all sorts of rugged seamen on often nefarious journeys.

The first store in the Keys, outside of Key West, was founded on Indian Key around 1824 by a Spaniard. The tiny general-supply store was doing a brisk trade when an aggressive wrecker and scofflaw named Jacob Housman showed up on the island. Recognizing its many natural assets and its potential for development, Housman settled here with plans to take over.

The Infamous John Jacob Housman

Born in 1799 to a Staten Island, New York, sea captain, John Jacob
Housman grew up around the sea. His father was in the shipping business. When he was twenty-two years old, Housman was piloting one of
his father's schooners when he became struck with wanderlust. Without a
backward glance, he commandeered his father's boat and set sail for the
West Indies. But before he got to his destination, he went aground in the
Florida Keys.

Hanging out in Key West while he waited for his ship to be repaired,
Housman became intrigued with the lucrative business of wrecking, which,
in one way or another, employed every able-bodied man on the island.

Wrecking, at that time Key West's number one business, was the
exciting and extremely profitable business of salvaging goods from vessels
that had run aground, or wrecked, on the dangerous reefs off the Keys'
shores. Once ashore, owners of the wrecked ships would negotiate with
wreckers, in a wrecking court, for a share of the recovered cargo.
Wreckers were often awarded half or more of the salvaged goods, which
might not seem like such a good deal. But to a shipper, losing half his
cargo was better than losing all of it.

Jacob Housman ditched his plans to go to the West Indies and went
into the wrecking business. But the Key West wreckers didn't take kindly
to outsiders, and Housman felt the wrecking courts were unfairly bal-
anced in favor of the locals. He may well have been right. Even the
judges owned wrecking businesses!

After five or six frustrating years in Key West, Housman sailed to
Indian Key, 75 miles away from Key West's wrecking court, and 75 miles
closer to the most dangerous reefs in all of the Keys. There he prospered
with a wrecking business of his own. With the proceeds of his growing
business, on his 30th birthday Housman bought himself a very big gift:
the island of Indian Key.

During the years between 1831, when he purchased Indian Key, and
1840, when Indians destroyed the community, Housman turned the place
into a busy wrecking center. He owned four wrecking vessels, wharves,
warehouses, workshops and thirty cottages—most of it built by his twelve
Negro slaves. Eventually there was even an Indian Key post office. The
planned city was a tiny, breezy paradise, featuring paved streets, a neat
town square, and even a conventional inn, the Tropical Hotel, often busy
with guests.

One notable guest at the Tropical Hotel was bird artist John James Audubon, who visited the island twice in the spring of 1832. Indian Key is depicted in the background of Audubon's painting of the brown booby. In his journal, Audubon glowingly describes the island's many natural charms, as well as an evening at the hotel:

> The bouncing of brave lads and fair lasses shook the premises to the foundation. One with a slip came down heavily on the floor and the burst of laughter that followed echoed over the isle. Diluted claret was handed around to cool the ladies, while a beverage of more potent energies warmed their partners.

In spite of outwardly charming appearances, life on Indian Key was not so pleasant under the iron rule of power-hungry Jacob Housman. The citizens who lived here, mostly turtlers and wreckers, were dependent upon Housman's good will and, often, his charity. It was common practice for Housman to forgive debts at the general store in exchange for favors—many of them slightly illegal, or at least unethical.

In 1836, Housman came up with a scheme to give his settlement independence from Key West. He convinced a friend who was a representative in the territorial legislature to push through a bill that made Indian Key the county seat of a new county named Dade. Dade County, at that time, was vast, unsettled and very scarcely populated. To be the county seat of a barely existent county doesn't sound like much today, but to Housman, it was the first step in making Indian Key a port of entry, complete with its own courts, over which Housman imagined himself having domain.

For a while things went well for Housman and his tiny kingdom. Not only was his wrecking business reaping huge rewards; he also earned big bucks from his shoreside enterprises like rents on docks and warehouses. The general store, where ships routinely stopped for supplies, earned him over $30,000 annually.

In 1838 Housman, described at the time as "a man of unprincipled disposition," was finally busted, doing what many people believed he'd been doing all along. It was proven that he had embezzled goods and money from a vessel he'd salvaged. His wrecking license was revoked. Without the enormous income his salvaging business had provided and the decrease of commerce in his village due to the Seminole War begun in 1836, Housman's fortunes began to dwindle.

In 1839 Housman came up with yet another of his self-serving, money-making schemes for which he had grown famous. He proposed a deal with the government whereby he would "catch or kill all the Indians of South Florida for two hundred dollars each." The congress, however, did not go for Housman's proposal.

Perhaps the Indians learned of Housman's plan, or perhaps they were simply after Indian Key's store of gun powder. In any event, they attacked. On August 7, 1840, just after midnight, a band of warriors arrived on Indian Key in seventeen canoes. Their plan was to wait until dawn to begin the assault, but someone with insomnia spotted them well before daylight. Gunshots were exchanged and the raid was on, in the dark.

Jacob Housman and his wife escaped through their back door and into the water at the end of their dock, just as the Indians burst through the front door of their house. Their terrified dogs followed them into the water, barking and clamoring. When he could not calm them, Housman was forced to drown both dogs with his bare hands.

The next morning as the sun came up, the Housmans and a group of Indian Key survivors watched from a Navy schooner as Indians set fire to every building and wharf on the island.

Housman and his wife moved to Key West, where he auctioned off the remainder of his possessions: several boats and his Negro slaves. He went to work as a seaman on a wrecker and was killed in a freak accident at sea less than a year later, when he was only forty-two years old. Mrs. Housman took his body back to Indian Key and marked his grave with an elegant stone. Eventually the marker on his grave was smashed by vandals and even his remains were stolen.

Dr. Perrine

Botanist and physician Dr. Henry Perrine arrived on Indian Key with his family at Christmas, 1838. Like Jacob Housman, Henry Perrine was born on Staten Island, only two years earlier than the wrecking king, in 1797. Perrine had big plans to begin a settlement dedicated to agricultural experimentation on a six-mile square land grant in southeast Florida. However, until the Second Seminole War was over, he was reluctant to take his family into the Indian-infested wilderness. So they came to pretty little Indian Key to wait out the war.

Several of Perrine's children kept journals of life on Indian Key, and it is from these writings that we are able to piece together a picture of their lives when Indian Key was at the height of its brief glory.

The Perrines did not socialize with anyone on the island but the Charles Howe family. Mr. Howe was the postmaster; he had a wife, three children, and seven slaves. Dr. Perrine and Mr. Howe were business partners in a joint agricultural venture on nearby Long Key.

The Housmans were considered socially beneath the Perrine family—not because of Mr. Housman's famous loose morals, but because of Mrs. Housman's bad reputation, presumably brought all the way from her hometown of Charleston, South Carolina.

Modern-day descendants of the tropical seeds Perrine planted in the 1830s still thrive on Indian Key, Lignumvitae Key, Long Key, and even Cape Sable, where he reportedly risked confrontations with warring Indians to go ashore and scatter his exotic seeds.

On the night the Seminoles attacked Indian Key, Dr. Perrine hid his wife, two daughters and one son in an enclosed area beneath their dock where turtles were penned. Then he climbed into a cupola at the top of the house to hide himself. But the warriors soon found him and as his horrified family shivered in their hiding place, they listened to his screams as the Indians murdered Dr. Perrine.

Most of the inhabitants of Indian Key managed to live through the attack by hiding out in various spots around the island. Some died in their hiding places. One boy hid in a cistern under a warehouse and was presumably boiled alive before the burning building finally collapsed. An infant was torn from his mother's arms and thrown into the sea. His horrified parents were then scalped, their bodies left to burn.

One of the first things the Indians did when they invaded the village was to help themselves to the hotel's liquor supply. Consequently, the warriors grew progressively drunker, and progressively easier to duck, too as the night wore on.

After the massacre, in which eighteen people died, the island was briefly occupied by the Navy. Several barracks, warehouses and a hospital were erected. During an outbreak of malaria, fifty sailors died in the hospital on Indian Key.

At the time of the Labor Day Hurricane of 1935, Indian Key was operated as a fishing camp by two brothers. One brother left the island to seek shelter on the mainland before the storm struck. The other brother secured himself in a large cistern built nearly a century earlier by Jacob Housman. His body was discovered two days after the storm.

Later, Indian Key became a shipbuilding yard and, after that, a strange sort of tourist attraction. Tourists paid to be delivered to the abandoned island and given a shovel with which to dig for buried treasure that they imagined had been forgotten by pirates and/or the infamous Jacob Housman. But all their digging, and eventually, even dynamiting, failed to turn up treasure...or so history has it.

In 1972, the State of Florida purchased the abandoned island. Today it is part of the state park system, and it's open to the public.

The Killer Hurricane of 1935

No one knows for sure how many people actually died in the catastrophic Labor Day Hurricane that battered the Matecumbe Keys with 200 mile-per-hour winds and swamped the land with a tidal surge of over eighteen feet. The coroner's report said that 423 bodies were found after the storm, but there is no doubt that many, maybe even hundreds, of victims were washed out to sea.

The hurricane was a category five, so rare that only one or two occur in a century. Hurricane Andrew, the storm that hit the Miami area in August, 1992, was a category four hurricane. Andrew's winds were clocked at around 160 mph; the tidal wave was twelve feet. Damage from Andrew was estimated at $20 billion. But only 35 people died from storm-related deaths.

In the days after the Labor Day Hurricane, Red Cross workers and volunteers suffered through the heart-breaking job of sorting through the dead. Identifying the victims' bodies was often impossible. Most of the dead were so mutilated they barely resembled humans at all. Some were without faces, their flesh having been sand-blasted into raw pulp. Many of the dead were World War I veterans. President Franklin Roosevelt's New Deal had given 650 veterans both homes and temporary work. They were building the highway that would eventually link Miami with Key West. Their homes were makeshift work camps in Islamorada.

On the first day of September in 1935, few signs warned of the hurricane's approach or of its power. Storm-tracking was a very imprecise science then; forecasting the route a hurricane might take was pretty much hit-and-miss. Citizens of the Keys were given two days' notice that a hurricane was heading in their direction. Key West was prepared for the storm, but was spared the devastation that would savage the Matecumbes a day later. Only the outer bands of the storm, strong winds and heavy rains, passed through Key West on the night of September 1.

Then, as hurricanes often do, this one wandered a bit before resting for a day over the Atlantic Ocean. There it gathered power, expanding into a storm of enormous strength. The barometer dropped to 26.35 on the afternoon of September 2, indicating to natives that they were in for a horrific storm—a normal barometer reading is 30.00.

Murphy's Law

Overseas Railroad officials sent a train from Miami into the Keys to transport local families and the veterans to higher ground. But through a series of mishaps, bungled communications, and manpower shortages due to the Labor Day holiday, the train was tragically delayed. As the doomed train finally headed down the tracks toward Islamorada, people climbed on at stops along the way. Local legend has it that the clocks of Matecumbe stopped at 8:30 that evening. That's just about when the rescue train arrived in Lower Matecumbe, where it collided with the storm. Part of the train was tossed off the tracks and laid on its side by the 200-mile-per-hour winds. The engine remained upright, and it is there that several men survived the tempest. A monstrous tidal wave surged over the island, and then scraped nearly everything in its path into the water, leaving the ground clean, right down to its raw, white coral base.

Aside from the many vets who lived in workcamps, the Upper Keys were scarcely populated in 1935. Twelve members of the Parker family miraculously survived the storm in a small, sturdy cottage. They huddled under a mattress on an iron bed. The survivors were those who found shelter in houses that floated. After the storm, they found themselves, and their cottage, atop the bare, battered branches of a lime tree grove. Fifty members of the pioneering Russell family perished in the storm. Many of their bodies were never recovered.

Victims also died by being swept into the Florida Bay, or sucked into the Atlantic by the undertow after the wave passed. Others were struck by flying debris. Of the 423 bodies accounted for (according to a coroner's report), most were thought to be the veterans. It was suggested that the dead vets should be transported for burial at Arlington National Cemetery, but the idea was wildly impractical. The Upper Keys did not yet have electricity, or refrigeration, or even a train for transporting bodies. The Overseas Railroad had been destroyed by the storm, most of its tracks impassable. Finally, there was no choice but to burn the bodies in four massive fires.

The Hemingway Spin

Ernest Hemingway was living in Key West with his wife Pauline and two young sons at the time of the hurricane. In 1935 he was at the height of his famous literary career. He arrived in Islamorada by sea on the day after the storm. In an article for a socially conscious magazine called *The New Masses*, he described the sight of trees completely stripped of their foliage; once-developed land, raw and resembling a river bed; massive railroad cars toppled onto their sides. He wrote graphically of dead seabirds tangled in the mangroves; two girls who ran a sandwich shop and filling station hanging lifelessly in the trees, their bodies rotting in the sun; a man whose fingers had been eaten by land crabs; another man, out of his mind, walking through the devastation.

Later in the article, which was entitled "Who Murdered the Vets?" Hemingway lambasted the U.S. government for sending the bridge workers to their doom. He also made the following point about the Keys' natives who died in the storm:

"It is not necessary to go into the deaths of the civilians and their families since they were on the Keys of their own free will: they made their living there, had property and knew the hazards involved. But the veterans had been sent there; they had no opportunity to leave, nor any protection against the hurricanes; and they never had a chance for their lives."

There is a legend that in 1965 a car with 1935 tags and five skeletons inside was dredged up out of a coral rock quarry. For many years skeletons were found on mangrove islands in the backcountry. No doubt, more remain.

The Hurricane Monument

Historic Landmarks

The Hurricane Monument
MM 82, in the Median

A memorial to the hundreds of people who lost their lives in the Labor Day Hurricane of 1935, this monument was created in 1937 by artists and craftsmen as a Works Projects Administration art project. The art deco slab marks a community grave that holds the ashes of more than four hundred people.

When the Hurricane Monument was dedicated two years after the Florida Keys' worst disaster, 5,000 people showed up to observe the sad occasion. In March 1995, the memorial was added to the National Register of Historic Sites.

Whale Harbor Tower
MM 83 Oceanside ☛ 664-4959

The stone tower at the entrance of the Whale Harbor dining room still has the high-water mark established during Hurricane Donna on September 9, 1960. Go inside and explore the gallery of mounted fish and historical photographs. A sign in the tower says: "This tower served as a shelter for six people during Hurricane Donna's 200-mile-per-hour winds and seven foot tides."

The Pioneer Cemetery
Cheeca Lodge Grounds ☛ MM 82, Oceanside

In 1992, the Cheeca Lodge restored a tiny cemetery on its property and brought in a Miami historian named Josephine Johnson to research its history. Names on the grave markers—Pinder, Russell, and Parker—are from the area's pioneering families who arrived in the rough wilderness in the late 1800s. Some of the descendants of these families still live in the Keys today. In fact, many of them are employed by the Cheeca Lodge.

Tourists are welcome to visit this site and see the cemetery's most famous marker, the angel with the broken wing. In the 1935 Labor Day

Hurricane she was picked up and thrown over 1,000 feet to land on the Old Highway which runs parallel to the Overseas Highway. But she was soon returned to her rightful position as guardian to the grave of Etta Pinder, who died in 1914.

The angel with a broken wing at Pioneer Cemetary

The Pioneer Cemetery was recently dedicated by the Historical Association of Southern Florida. It is an easy walk or short drive from the Hurricane Monument. Go to the Cheeca Lodge—the entrance is just north of the monument—and head around to the back of the main lodge. The Pioneer Cemetery is on the beach, about fifty yards south of the pier.

Windley Key Fossil Reef State Geologic Site
MM 85.3, Bayside ✺ 664-5574

Around 1934 the WPA put people to work quarrying coral rock from this site for use by more people put to work building Key West's post office and federal building. Keystone from this quarry was used to face many historic buildings in Miami and out of state. Cut and polished slabs of keystone were used in the creation of Islamorada's commemorative Hurricane Monument.

Rock cutters left behind an amazing display of fossils formed by corals millions of years ago, making this one of the few places where it is possible to study the ancient coral reef formation without getting wet. The site was bought by developers in the 1980s. They planned to build a complex of condominiums here, but local environmentalists battled to save the quarry from development. Ultimately the environmentalists prevailed, and in 1985 the quarry was named a state park.

Little more has happened to encourage visitors to explore the geological wonder of long walls of fossilized coral reef. Park rangers and volunteers lead tours at 9 a.m. and 11 a.m. on the third Saturday of every month, but that is a small window of opportunity.

An alternative to waiting for the third Saturday is to stop in at the Long Key State Recreation Area (MM 67.5 oceanside), or at the Lady Cyana Divers (MM 85.9 oceanside) during regular business hours. They'll ask you to fill in a form to sign out a key that unlocks the quarry gates. Then you can guide yourself through the park.

Future plans for the park include buildings, facilities and staff. Also ahead: an environmental learning center at the quarry. What frustrates those environmentalists is the snail's pace at which the state moves toward completing its stated missions.

Each February the quarry site devotees hold an annual quarry picnic and nature party, where guests are invited to capture fossil images with rubbings, just as cemetery buffs carry headstone likenesses home with them.

Nature News

Florida Bay Research Radio broadcasts news of wildlife happenings and scientific research. Bulletins accompany National Oceanic and Atmospheric Administration weather reports every two minutes, around the clock. Tune in to 1610 AM (a program of Everglades National Park).

Helen Wadley Library and Hurricane Shelter
MM 81.5 Bayside ☎ 664-4645

Built as a hurricane shelter in 1936, the building that today houses the Helen Wadley Branch of the Monroe County Library has been a school, a church and a Coast Guard station. The structure was built to withstand winds of 150 mph, and did duty as a hurricane shelter in 1960 when Hurricane Donna passed directly over Islamorada. Both the building and many local residents who sought shelter in it came through the storm unharmed. During a recent face-lift and expansion, a 1,000 square foot meeting room and disabled-accessible bathrooms were added to the library.

Offshore Islands

Indian Key
MM 78.5

In 1972, the State of Florida purchased the abandoned island. Today it is part of the State Park system. Each October, Islamorada celebrates Indian Key's turbulent past with a weekend-long celebration. Boats ferry people from the mainland to the island for tours and history lessons led by guides dressed in period costumes of the 1830s, Indian Key's golden decade. During the weekend of the celebration, visitors can send postcards, hand-cancelled with the Indian Key postmark.

Indian Key State Park is open Thursdays–Mondays from 8 a.m. till sunset. Visitors pay $1 to tour the area. The island has no restrooms and no shops of any kind. Park ranger-guided tours leave the dock at 9 a.m and 1 p.m.

What remains on Indian Key are parts of the foundation of Jacob Housman's house and a replica of his original gravestone. Some unidentifiable rubble is thought possibly to be part of the Tropical Hotel or ruins of the Naval installation. Visitors to the island may be surprised at how little there is to see, considering its remarkable past. An imaginative and well-informed guide will make the place come alive. Otherwise, it can be a bit of a disappointment, particularly for kids, who expect so much....

How to Get There

Access to Indian Key and Lignumvitae Key is by water only. Robbie's Marina (664-9814) at mile marker 78 runs a state-sanctioned shuttle boat service to both Keys. Roundtrip boat service to either Indian Key or Lignumvitae Key is $15 per person; $10 for children 6 and under. To see both Keys, you'll pay $30; $15 for kids. Boats arrive at the Keys in time for daily tours. For further information on Indian Key contact the Florida Park Service at 664-4815.

Lignumvitae Key State Botanical Site
MM 78.5, Offshore, Gulfside ✆ 664-4815

Some say the best time to visit Lignumvitae Key is in the spring. Others say the worst time to visit Lignumvitae is in the spring. The 130 species of trees on the island bloom and blossom magnificently in the springtime; 130 million mosquitoes, also on the island, regenerate quite gloriously in the spring.

Because of its location on the Gulf of Mexico, and its thick, leafy canopy, Lignumvitae is ten degrees cooler than the mainland. Keep that in mind as you don your long-sleeved shirt and ankle-length pants. And don't forget the insect repellent. Any area of exposed flesh is fair game for these sub-tropical devils.

A wealthy Miami chemist named William Matheson bought the 280-acre island in 1919 for use as a family vacation retreat. Matheson had the house built of coral rock gathered on the island. Its power was generated by a huge windmill, still there, although today power is provided by a generator. The island's water comes from a 12,000-gallon cistern filled by rain falling off the roof. The cistern has run dry only twice since the State of Florida has been in charge of the place, beginning in 1970. Behind the house there is a small building where the estate's caretaking family lived, and behind that building a smaller one. It is not known what the small mystery hut was used for. The hurricane shelter beneath the house, our guide described as "scary and dark."

The house was damaged in the deadly 1935 Labor Day hurricane but not annihilated, like most buildings of the Matecumbes. The house is built at the island's highest point, sixteen feet above sea level, which is also one of the highest points within the entire length of the Keys. The winds of the 1935 storm tore the roof off the Matheson's house. It was reinstalled with steel rods—you can see them—that hopefully will hold the roof tight in future blows.

The Matheson house contains collections of shells, stones, colored glass, seafans, a turtle skull, and driftwood. In addition, a megaphone the family used to call to each other across the island.

At the beginning of the tour, visitors pass a small slice of lignumvitae wood from one to the next to experience its surprising weight and its remarkable gloss. You rub it briefly with your thumb to bring out its built-in sheen. Wood of the lignumvitae—Latin for "tree of life"—is denser and more resilient than iron, so it does not wear out, and it does not dry out or easily rot.

Lignumvitae wood has been used to make bowling balls and even false teeth. The wood of lignumvitae was used in making hinges for locks on the Erie Canal; these hinges remained functional for one hundred years. It is said that Columbus was so impressed with the amazing properties of the lignumvitae tree that he carried logs of it back to Spain after his second voyage to the New World. Indians believed that the gum resin of the lignumvitae was good medicine. One species of tree snail, liguus,

**Lignumvitae
leaf and flower**

prefers the lignumvitae tree over all others in the virgin forests of Lignumvitae Key.

Some of the plants and trees on this botanical preserve have been growing here for a thousand years. The settlers and pioneers saw some of these very same ones when they arrived in the Florida Keys so very long ago.

Visitors walk on the trails originally cleared for the horses, pigs, goats and chickens that were once raised here. Sisal, planted in the Keys by botanist Henry Perrine during his brief stay in the 1830s, is prevalent. Your guide will cut a piece from the plant and show you exactly why Perrine was so enthusiastic about sisal's potential as a cash crop for South Florida. Its leaves are laced with a strong, twine-like core. Until the 1940s and the invention of nylon, sisal was the main component of rope.

Park rangers are always anxious to point out the scary poisonwood tree, to spare anyone the misfortune of wandering too close to its treacherous leaves and bark. They compare its properties to those of poison ivy. Plenty of poisonwoods are scattered throughout the hammocks of the Keys, they say.

"So why don't they cut them all down?" asked an attentive seven-year-old.

"Because poisonwood berries are the white crown pigeon's favorite food," the ranger replied, launching a talk on the graceful symmetry of a successful ecosystem.

Other interestingly named trees you will encounter are gumbo limbo, mahogany, Jamaican dogwood, mastic, pigeon plum, stopper, wild coffee and strangler fig. Scattered throughout the trees are delicate tree snails, other-worldly in their design, and butterflies, swirling gracefully in the peaceful woods. All are protected from removal, even the pretty shell you believe to be uninhabited. That must stay, too.

Sisal

As the tour loops down by the shore, the types of trees change. You see buttonwood, which grows next to the shore up and down the Keys, wherever concrete has not taken over. You'll be introduced to red, black and white mangroves as the ranger explains the mangrove's unique filtering system.

Nearly a 3,000-foot coral-rock wall runs from the center of the island all the way down to the water, which is somewhat of a mystery to historians. Who built it? Why? The wall is not on the general tour, but a ranger is happy to take you to it if you ask. It resembles a stone wall you might see in the forests of New England.

Beaches

Anne's Beach
MM 73, Oceanside
Once known as Islamorada Public Beach and located on Lower
Matecumbe Key south of Caloosa Cove Resort, it is dedicated to local
environmentalist Anne Eaton. Anne began her life as Anne Kinder
Jones. She was a schoolteacher until she met and married wealthy indus-
trialist and banker Cyrus Stephen Eaton in 1957. Although polio left her
wheelchair-bound when she was only twenty-four years old, Anne and
her husband traveled the world, meeting politicians and international
leaders in science and industry. After her husband's death, Anne heard
about the Florida Keys, the only frost-free place in the continental
United States, and knew she had found her heaven on earth. Of all the
places the wealthy seeker of world peace had been, she is said to have
loved Monroe County best. Anne Eaton lived in the Keys until she died
in 1992. Her home in Lower Matecumbe, near the beach dedicated to
her, is called the Last Resort.

A small parking area is located at each end of Anne's Beach; the two
are connected by a marvelous boardwalk. At low tide the beach is alive
with crabs and other crawly creatures. At high tide, you might wade out
far enough for a swim. The public bathrooms are usually in pretty rough
shape—BYO soap and toilet paper.

Islamorada County Park
MM 81.5 Bayside
Locals call this the Library Beach because of its close proximity to the
Islamorada library. Located on a natural creek that runs from the Florida
Bay, the tiny park is on one side of the creek, and a line of mangroves is
on the other. You need to swim across some fast currents to get to the
mangrove's edge, but once you're there, the snorkeling is great. Many
wonderful fish babies hatch and grow to maturity here. There is nowhere
quite like the busy and complex worlds that exist in and around the roots

of the islands' anchoring mangroves. Meanwhile, back on shore there's a terrific playground for the kids, plus a few picnic tables.

The only drawback here is the current, which makes this not a very good place for kids to swim. There's a little, sandy beach good for wading, or water and sand play. For a change of pace, there's a nice children's reading room inside the library.

Plantation Yacht Harbor Beach
MM 87 Bayside

The Islamorada Chamber of Commerce lists the beach at Plantation Yacht Harbor as one of four in the area. Turn into Plantation Yacht Harbor and drive through a grove of mahogany trees. Follow the signs to the beach, which is on the Florida Bay. Parking is plentiful, and everyone is welcome at this gloriously funky beach that hasn't been changed or updated or overhauled in years. Walk out into the water and you'll soon come to good, deep swimming water.

A wonderful sense of old Keys permeates this place. The bathrooms are very funky, like beach bathrooms used to be. At the Lagoon Saloon you can buy a drink or basket lunches featuring beachy stuff like burgers, hot dogs, and chicken wings. The music selection is dreamy, too; you might hear jazz, big band, rock or pop. You might see folks playing volleyball on the beach or board games on the deck. Sunday afternoons beginning around 2 p.m. a live band plays. During weekend evenings, rock bands attract lots of partiers, too.

The Sandbar
Oceanside, off MM 84.5

On perfect Saturday and Sunday afternoons, you'll see dozens of boats crowded around a wide sandbar just offshore, right around mile marker 84–85. Locals call it "the Islamorada Beach." There's only one way to get to it—by boat. Rent one from a concession at Pelican Resort or at Holiday Isle Resort. Rent will run you around $70 to $100 for a very simple, motor-driven skiff—but you and four other friends will meet and play with Islamorada's most devoted partiers.

Fishing

I
SLAMORADA IS PROUD of the many high-profile celebrities who travel
regularly to this island cluster to partake in the world's best sports
fishing. But you don't have to be a big shot to fish in the same ocean
as President George Bush, Vice President Al Gore, and Miami Dolphins
football coach Jimmy Johnson. Everybody is welcome in the Fishing
Capital of the World. Earlier visitors to this area were President Herbert
Hoover and British Prime Minister Winston Churchill.

The area's wonderful proximity to the Gulf Stream has spurred the
development of a number of fine enterprises—tackle shops, concessions
and marinas—and the largest concentration of fishing boats in the
Florida Keys. Some of the sports fishing related businesses here have been
passed down through several generations of islanders. These people know
their stuff.

First time visitors are sometimes surprised to learn just how much it
costs to drop hooks in the Gulf Stream. Chartering a boat, captain and
crew who will devote themselves exclusively to your comfort and happiness will cost up to $600 a day. A much less expensive way to get out on
the water is to buy aboard a party boat (around $30 for a half day), in
which the heavy charter fees are divided among a crowd of anglers. Some
folks enjoy either mode, and fish according to what is available each day.

People catch plenty of fish off bridges, too. All you need is a fishing
rod, a license, and lots of patience. Buy a license in any bait and tackle
shop. There is no thrill comparable to catching your own fresh seafood
dinner. Many area restaurants understand this and will happily cook your
catch for a small preparation fee.

A Big Deal of a Tourney

President George Bush, the most famous angler at Cheeca Lodge, hosts
an annual bonefish tourney every August. It's a high stakes, all release
fundraiser. Entry fee is $1,000 per angler. As part of the tourney, partici-
pants—who are some very, very high rollers—rub elbows with the former

Marlin fishing

President during the kick-off dinner and several other events. The whole of Islamorada looks forward to this very important, and always spectacular, fish party.

Proceeds go to the Everglades Trust, a non-profit organization formed to restore the Florida Bay and the Everglades. Info: 664-4651.

Florida Keys Fishing Tournaments, Inc.
P.O. Box 420358, Summerland Key, FL 33042 ✒ 872-2233
"Tourneys Are Us." Christina Sharpe, a member of one of the Florida Keys' most important fishing families, runs this very busy year-round organization. If competitive fishing is your bag, this is an important resource for you. Christina and her staff will direct you to all the fun. It is a rare weekend when something isn't going on in the area, or at least somewhere in the Keys. For an extensive list of local and Keys fishing tournaments and events, write for a free brochure. If you can't wait, phone them during business hours.

How To Find a Fishing Captain or Guide
Go for a walk through a marina—they're easy to spot—and get a first-hand feel for the place. Nobody is friendlier or more helpful than a captain or a guide trying to put together a party for a day of fishing. Can you think of a better way to make a living?

The Islamorada Chamber of Commerce (800-322-5397) has a list of fishing charterboat captains and backcountry fishing guides. Call or write ahead, and they'll send the list; then you can do the research before you get here.

Florida Keys Fly Fishing School
P.O. Box 603, Islamorada, FL 33036 ♦ 664-5423
Learn casting, fly selection, fly tying, and knots and leaders from a staff of instructors that reads like the Who's Who guide to the world's most famous saltwater fly fishermen. If you're a fly fishing enthusiast, you'll recognize the names of these champs: Chico Fernandez, Flip Pallot, Sandy Moret. At the Florida Keys Fly Fishing School, these stars and more will be your teachers.

The structured fly fishing course is on six times a year. Included in the cost of the course is a Friday-night reception at the glittery Cheeca Lodge, and breakfasts and lunches, as well as the nuts and bolts of fly fishing, and rods and reels. In the eight years since it was founded, the Florida Keys Fly Fishing School has graduated 900 fly fisherpeople. This course is the fastest way to learn this sport of cunning and finesse.

Cost of the course is around $750, without lodging. Packages that include five nights of lodging and a couple of post-graduation fishing expeditions are also available. Call or write for a spiffy brochure that tells you all about it.

Some Marinas

Bud 'n' Mary's Fishing Marina
MM 80 Oceanside ♦ 800-742-7945 ♦ 664-2461
You'll probably notice the huge, fiberglass replica of a 417-pound shark, hung by his tail and glistening in the sun, just at the door to Bud 'n' Mary's tackle shop. Caught in the late 1980s off the coast of Australia, this great white shark once held the record for being the largest fish ever caught with a rod and reel. Alas, the record was broken mere weeks later! If you don't stick your head into the shark's mouth and have your picture taken, you're no fun.

The Gulf Lady, a 65-foot, air-conditioned party boat is docked in the
marina. Day trips are $45 and push off at
9:30 a.m.; dock at 4:30 p.m. Night fishing
trips are $40; from 7:30 p.m.–12:30 a.m.
You bring your own food and drink. Rent
on the rod and reel, $5. On a party boat
like this, the captain and mates will bait
your hook and help you reel in the big
fish. *The Gulf Lady* is also available for
sunset cruises and private charters. Group
rates are available, too.

Also, fourteen off-shore charter boats
available for deep-sea fishing; thirty backcountry boats with guides. Don't be
surprised to see a political or media or
sports star here. This is the place where
they can feel comfortable because here
everybody is treated exactly the same.
"Famous people really like that," one guy
behind the counter told me, referring to
the swarm of secret service men who had
just left the dock after depositing their
famous politico boss on a boat bound for
the Gulf Stream for a day of sport fishing.

**Bud 'n' Mary's
replica of a
417-pound shark**

Catch and release is popular these days, but if you do want to eat your
catch, they'll clean it when you get to shore. Then you take it to a local
restaurant to have it cooked. If you want to have a spectacular catch
replicated in fiberglass, they'll know where to send you for that, too. (Fish
are no longer stuffed and mounted in the old-fashioned way. Nowadays
your prize fish is replicated.)

Rent an unsinkable fiberglass boat and take it out to the Indian Key
or Lignumvitae Key. Bud 'n' Mary's rents rooms, too. Boat rental for half
a day is around $75. A whole day is $100. Weekly rates are available.

Bud 'n' Mary's Fishing Marina, in business since 1944, is open seven
days; 7 a.m. to 8 p.m.

Holiday Isle Marina
MM 84 Oceanside ✦ 664-2321 ✦ 800-327-7070

You may have to park your car in the lots across the street because this place is always very crowded. A fleet of sixteen off-shore fishing charter-boats, and fourteen backcountry fishing boats and guides are lined up at this busy marina. Also, party boats, which are the least expensive. Best time to go shopping for a charter is before 8 a.m. or after 4 p.m. because most boats leave the dock for the day between those hours. Many visitors find that a good way to chose a captain and boat is to observe anglers arriving back at the dock after a day of fishing. Do they look happy? Disappointed? Friendly toward their captain? Holiday Isle is a very friendly, very informal place. The offshore charters at Holiday Isle Marina charge between $475 and $600 for a full day of fishing. Back-country guides charge around $325 for a full day; $225 for a half day. They'll supply the fishing gear; you bring food and drinks. Each boat sets its own prices. They are all privately owned and operated, renting space at the marina.

Papa Joe's Marina
MM 80 Bayside ✦ 664-5005

Directly across the street from Bud 'n' Mary's Marina, it's the place to go to find a guide for backcountry fishing. Twelve skiffs are available for private charter-flats fishing daily, and tours to Indian Key, Lignumvitae Key, Horseshoe Key and a sunset cruise as well. Sturdy Papa Joe's T and sweat shirts and bill hats are available in the tackle shop, as well as fishing licenses. There's a nice bar atop Papa's Marina, from where you can gaze upon the ocean and the bay.

Robbie's Marina
MM 77.8 Bayside ✦ 664-9814

Robbie's is located beneath the Lignumvitae Bridge, home of the hungry tarpon dock where you feed the fish, and the Hungry Tarpon Restaurant, where you feed yourself. Rent a boat for a ride into the backcountry, or take yourself to Indian Key or Lignumvitae Key. (Lignumvitae Key is closed to the public on Tuesdays and Wednesdays.) Boats from 14 to 25 feet rent from $80 to $195 for a full day.

Or take a shuttleboat to Indian Key and Lignumvitae Botanical Site State Parks for $15, adults; $10, kids.

Whale Harbor Marina
MM 83.5 Oceanside ✻ 664-4511

You'll find up to sixteen offshore sport-fishing boats at the Whale Harbor docks. They charge anywhere from $400–$500 for a half day; $600–$675 for a full-day trip. Best time for a visit is early mornings or around four in the afternoon when the fleet returns with the day's catch.

Two 65-foot party fishing boats at Whale Harbor are the *Tradewinds* (664-8441) and *The Caloosa* (664-2248). Both charge about $30 per person for a half day.

On most fishing excursions you take along your own food and drinks for the day. Buy it at the ship's store or at the Harbor Bar & Raw Bar, a neat dockside bistro with a great view of the marina and the ocean. They'll sell you a box lunch and/or breakfast from 6 a.m. Raw bar menu served from noon til midnight. Live entertainment every evening, except on Sundays. The Whale Harbor Inn was once a hotel made popular by radio personality Arthur Godfrey, who vacationed here often in the '50s. Remember him?

Diving

Some Famous Islamorada Dives

Alligator Reef Light

In 1823, the USS *Alligator*, part of an anti-pirate squadron commanded by Commodore David Porter, battled with pirates near Indian Key. The battle was won by the anti-pirate forces, but Naval Commander W.H. Allen was killed in the fray. In honor of his dead comrade, Porter went back to his home port of Key West and renamed the settlement "Allentown." A year later the USS *Alligator* went aground on the reef where the Alligator Light now stands. Porter's attempt to rename Key West failed, too.

Pickles Reef

Pickle barrels containing a mortar-like construction material ended up on this reef in the 19th century. The wood of the barrels rotted away in the saltwater, but the barrel-shaped blocks of solid mortar are still visible on this 10–25 foot deep reef.

The Eagle

One of the first big artificial reefs created in the Keys, the *Eagle* was sunk in 1985. Since then, the *Eagle* has become gloriously encrusted with numerous corals. It is a popular hangout for many large fish, and a terrific and very popular dive for scuba divers.

Hens and Chickens Reef

Tourists from everywhere in the world ask to visit and dive the Hens and Chickens Reef. This reef is excellent for snorkelers because it is shallow, and it contains enormous coral heads full of caves and holes; it's also veined with narrow valleys of sand.

Horseshoe Reef
Another Jesus guards this reef. Several born-again Christian divers stuck this little Jesus into a car tire full of concrete.

Davis Reef Ridge
A small, fat Buddha smiles benevolently at the south end of this ledge that rises six to eight feet from the flat sandy floor. Schools of sergeant majors here can be so dense they block your view. Underwater photographers say this reef is the most picturesque in the Keys.

Cheeca Rocks
About 600 yards straight out from the Cheeca Lodge, a comfortable dive for snorkelers.

San Pedro Underwater Archaeological Preserve
Located 1.3 nautical miles south of Indian Key, the *San Pedro* was part of the Spanish fleet that sailed from Havana Harbor in 1733. A few days after it took to sea, it was driven into the reefs by a powerful hurricane. Today the remains of the *San Pedro* anchor a shipwreck park dedicated in 1989. A popular underwater nature trail features varied populations of fish, crustaceans, mollusks, and corals, as well as bricks and pieces, much picked over by now, from the doomed *San Pedro*.

Dive Into History/The School
852-1690
It's summer school for wreck-diving enthusiasts: a marine archaeology field school conducted and supervised by Duncan Mathewson, an authority on historic shipwreck archaeology. Each summer one wreck is selected for research. Participants collect data which will be added to a shipwreck database to be used in a sanctuary management plan. All divers receive PADI specialty diving certification in Orientation to Marine Archaeology and Archaeological Research Diver I from Shipwreck Research. Non-divers provide surface support.

More than 300 shipwrecks along the Florida Keys are to be classified and added to the database. In July 1996 the school prepared a detailed archaeological survey and scientific excavation of the 1822 wreck of the USS *Alligator*.

Some Dive Charters

Holiday Isle Dive Center
MM 84.5 Oceanside ✶ 664-4145 ✶ 800-327-7070
Whoever books the trip first gets to choose the reefs visited on that trip.
Holiday Isle's 35-foot powerboat carrying scuba divers or snorkel divers,
or both, departs at 9 a.m. and 1 p.m. to visit two reefs. If you are hoping
to visit specific reefs, tell the dive center and they'll book you on the
appropriate trip. A minimum of two must sign on for the trip to go out.
The maximum is twenty-two people.

A snorkel trip with gear rental is around $30. A two-tank scuba trip
is $40; to rent scuba gear, you'll pay around $30 more. No discounts for
kids; no babysitting service on board the boat while parents are diving.
The trip is roughly three-and-a-half hours long.

Lady Cyana Divers
MM 85.9 Oceanside ✶ 664-8717 ✶ 800-221-8717
Visit the Lady Cyana Divers on Saturday or Sunday for a free lunch of
BBQ grilled hot dogs and hamburgers and a social hour with divers and
dive masters. Lady Cyana trips are at 8:30 a.m. and 1 p.m. every day of
the year, including Christmas. Dives are around $30, including equip-
ment rental, for snorkelers; around $60, with equipment rental, for scuba
divers. Divers with their own equipment pay $20 and $40, respectively.
Trips last three-and-a-half to four hours.

Where will you go to dive? Once again, whoever books the trip first
gets to call the locations. If you're the first reservation, have a good look
at the video of locations that runs inside the dive shop.

Lady Cyana offers a bonus reservation service, too; call ahead and ask
for tips on accommodations. Book your dive trips and your room at the
same time. You'll receive a parcel of brochures on hotels and local features. This reservations service can do what the Chamber of Commerce
cannot do—recommend a place best suited to you, the diving enthusiast.

Big Fun

Coral Bowl
MM 83.5 Bayside ✆ 664-9357
Bowling in Paradise? Sure. You'd be surprised how popular these air-conditioned lanes are on steamy summer afternoons, where relief from the heat is worth more than gold. Coral Bowl, which has been serving bowling enthusiasts for twenty years, is the only public bowling available in the Keys. Open bowling on weekdays is from 3 p.m. till midnight; weekends, noon till 2 a.m. League nights (wintertime only) are Wednesday, Thursday and Friday, 7 p.m.–9:30 p.m. Snack bar, seven pool tables, and video games, they've got it all. Summer prices are a bit lower, and the hours a bit shorter; and kids always get reduced rates. Enjoy live entertainment in the Buckets Bar on Friday and Saturday nights, and all sorts of games and activities. Fun, fun, fun!

Islamorada Tennis Club
MM 77 Bayside ✆ 305-664–5340
Everything you could want or imagine in a tennis club is here—where you'd least expect to find it—in the fishing capital of the world. The owner is longtime tennis pro, Sonia Stock, who prides herself on her talent for matching up tennis partners. If you are wandering around solo, itchy for a game, call the tennis club, and Sonia will hook you up on the six courts, five of them lighted, both clay and all-weather. Figure to pay around $5 an hour to play on the hard courts; $7 to play on clay, both season and off-season rates. The enormous pro shop is full of the latest state-of-the-art goodies. Private, semi-private and group lessons are available. Open from 8 a.m. till 8 p.m. every day of the year, including holidays.

Swings over the Water
MM 72.1 Bayside
Keep your eyes peeled. Between Channel 2 and Channel 5 bridges look for two rope swings. Park in the wide grass shoulder. Watch for a while,

and if you're brave, get on line for a ride on one of the rope swings. Often a picnic will be going on here, too. How long this free treat will be available nobody knows. But for now, it's a treat worth stopping for.

Feed the Tarpons/Robbie's Marina
MM 77.5 Bayside ✻ 664-9814

As long as the sun is bright, and the tarpons are hungry—and the tarpons *always* seem to be hungry—there's something wild to do at Robbie's Marina. Buy a bucket of fish for $2. Pay $1 for each person in your party to walk out to the end of the dock. Feed the bucket of little fish to the big fish. Once the tarpons figure out it's feeding time again—it goes on all day—you'll have dozens of the huge, glittering fish swarming frantically beneath the dock. Some of these guys are up to six feet long. Pelicans are a bit of a nuisance, though. They're so used to humans that they'll take a tiny fish right out of a little kid's hand. Don't worry, pelicans don't have teeth. Usually the marina dog chases pelicans away. If you're lucky, whoever's in charge of taking the money will let some of the smaller kids go for free. Lots of fun. For tots, it just doesn't get any better than this.

Pelican Cove Boat and Waverunner Rentals
MM 84.5 Oceanside ✻ 664-4435

Keith and his beautiful assistant watch their customers very carefully to be sure that Waverunners are operated safely and respectfully. Basic fee for a half hour of wet and wild thrills is $40. You must be 18 years or older and be able to prove it.

Rent a 16-foot, flat-bottom skiff from Keith for $70 for half a day. Again, Keith will have to convince himself that you know what you're doing before he'll let you go. He'll show you where to find the channel, and how to avoid hurting turtle grass. Only five people at a time on the boat. Hours are...well, put it this way: when you need him, Keith will be there.

Theater of the Sea
MM 84.5 ✻ 664-2431

When the Overseas Highway was completed in 1938, and traffic picked up real well in these parts, it seemed a good plan to create a tourist attraction based on the natural resources at hand—the sea and its remarkable inhabitants. And so this marine park was created on the site of several abandoned quarries dug at the turn of the century during the construction of the Overseas Railroad. The family that established this 14-acre park in 1946 owns and operates it still. Over 100,000 visit the park annually.

Marking the entrance to the bustling theme park are the masts of a pair of tall ships. On a wide, grassy plot in front of the park are shrubs sculpted into mermaids and leaping dolphins. A treasure ship will titillate your imagination, and inside, all sorts of wonderful creatures of the deep will charm and delight children as well as their grateful parents.

Inside the park's three acres is a saltwater lagoon, home to dolphins, sea lions, sea turtles, tropical and gamefish, sharks, and stingrays. The lagoon is also a refuge for several endangered species who, due to injuries, would not survive in their natural habitats. You can also observe a blind American crocodile, who lost his sight as a result of shotgun wounds, and several sea turtles, most of them missing flippers from disastrous entanglements with monofilament fishing lines. The aim of the park is to educate as well as to entertain with these rare creatures.

Since 1987, the Theater of the Sea has been offering several human/dolphin swim programs for various groups. The most popular swim-with-the-dolphin experience costs $80. Participants must be 13 years or older. The thirty-minute swim is preceded by a thirty-minute educational orientation. Two very special groups, Make-a-Wish and Children of Dreams Foundations, whose patients are undergoing critical care or who are terminally ill, work in cooperation with the park to help their clients realize life-long dreams of swimming with dolphins. In addition, an intern program for college students is designed to award college credits after completion of an intensive course in marine animal care.

Continuous ninety-minute tours of the park begin at 9:30 a.m.; the last tour starts at 4 p.m.; the park closes at 5 p.m. Admission is $14.25 for adults; $7.95 for kids ages 3–12.

Write to the Theater of the Sea (P.O. Box 407, Islamorada, FL 33036) for specific information on any of their programs or for an enormous amount of information on the park. Also, get good fact sheets on dolphins, handy for school reports!

Tours by Land, Sea and Air

Carousel Boat Tours
Papa Joe's Marina ❧ MM 79.7 Bayside ❧ 664-5005 or 800-539-8326
State Park tours or sunset cruises aboard the Osprey. A brochure invites you to step back in time to relive the famed 1840 Indian Key massacre. And while it probably wouldn't be much fun to relive such an infamous event, Indian Key's history does make for a fascinating afternoon—especially with a guide as good as the ones you can hire at Papa Joe's Marina. The kids will thrill to the images of Indians in warpaint, gruesome murders, and children boiled alive in cisterns when Indians burned down the town.

Meanwhile, on the Florida Bay side of the narrow Overseas Highway, Lignumvitae Key has its own interesting, though certainly softer, charms: flowering plants, trees, and mangroves. And a coral-rock house built in 1919. Unfortunately, excitement-wise, it doesn't hold a candle to Indian Key's grisly past. So don't take the kids on this trip. They'll probably be bored silly.

Horseshoe Key is an island encircled by a bigger, horseshoe shaped island, or key, creating a rookery, or safety zone for many species of birds—some migratory, some local. See how this place got its name. Watch the sunset. Identify the birds you see.

All tours are $26 for adults; $15 for kids. Make reservations at Papa Joe's Marina between 7 a.m. and 5 p.m. daily. No tours to Lignumvitae Key on Tuesdays and Wednesdays.

Coral Sea Glass Bottomed Boat & Snorkel Tour
Bud 'n' Mary's Marina MM 80 Oceanside ❧ 664-2461
The Coral Sea Glass Bottomed Boat afternoon tour is an opportunity for everyone in your crowd to visit area reefs like the Crocker, the Davis, and the Islamorada Coral Gardens. Weather and people permitting (that is if the weather is good and enough people signed up to go), the Coral Sea heads out at 1:30 p.m. every afternoon for a visit to two reefs. At each stop snorkelers are in the water for 25–30 minutes, while their less

adventurous boating companions view the reef through the Coral Sea's plexiglass windows. The trip takes approximately three hours. Cost: $15 for non-swimmers; $20 for swimmers. Basic snorkeling equipment rents for $7.50. Kids ages seven and under go for half price.

Dolphin Wildlife Adventure Snorkel Cruise
Theater of the Sea, MM 84.5 Oceanside ✺ 664-2431

This four-hour tour visits sites of environmental and historic interest in the waters of the Atlantic Ocean and the Florida Bay. Tour destinations are sometimes altered to accommodate weather conditions but generally take you to historic Indian Key, the Alligator Light Tower, and Cheeca Rocks Reef. A naturalist on board describes the ecosystems of ocean, backcountry, and the plants and creatures that thrive therein. Dolphins hopefully will appear somewhere along the way in their natural habitat, which is a treat and a bit of a revelation: these creatures are natural born showoffs! Dolphins in the wild are often as entertaining as dolphins in captivity! A snorkel dive of at least 30 minutes is included during the tour. Gear is provided free.

The Adventure Cruise departs at 9 a.m. daily from the Theater of the Sea; dock time is 8:30 a.m. Adults: $49.95. Children 6–12: $29.95. Make reservations.

Land and Sea Tours
Cheeca Lodge ✺ MM 82 ✺ 664-3666

Tour historic Islamorada in an air-conditioned bus. The narrated tour drives through Islamorada's historic district and past the Hurricane Monument where you stop to hear the grisly tale of the most ferocious hurricane in recorded history ever to hit the United States. From the bus you'll gaze out at the historic Indian Key, where Indians once burned down an entire village, and Lignumvitae, one of the most peaceful and unspoiled islands in the Keys. The tour is $15 for adults. $10 for kids.

Sunset Waverunner Tour
Pelican Cove Resort ✺ 664-8892

An hour-and-a-half guided tour on Waverunners for up to eight people— two to a Waverunner. (Larger groups can be accommodated.) Guides are master storytellers, well versed in island lore and legend, as well as current events. The cruise winds out of Pelican Cove, under the Snake Creek drawbridge, and into the flat waters of the Florida Bay. Points of interest are inlets once prowled by pirates, Indians, and modern day smugglers. You sort the fact from the fiction. Also, nature treats like osprey nests, and the tale of an osprey who swooped right out of the sky to steal a big old snapper right out of a fisherman's hands. Just before sunset, the tour ends up back at the Pelican Cove dock.

Cost is $100 per Waverunner. One to two people fit on a Waverunner. Call for reservations.

Ultralight Plane Rides
Pelican Cove Resort ✆ 664-8892

For a bird's-eye view of the skinny islands of Islamorada, take a fifteen minute demo flight aboard an ultralight plane. Carol O'Donnell, a licensed and insured member of the United States Ultralight Association, pilots a Quicksilver Sprint II with full Lotus floats. Take off and land on the water; soar through the air at 30 to 50 miles per hour. Call for reservations. 18 years or over, 14 or over with parent's signature. Open 9 a.m till sunset, weather permitting. Prices begin at $50.

Accommodations

OTELS, MOTELS, INNS AND GUESTHOUSES around here follow some
mighty complicated guidelines when it comes to figuring their rates.
Generally you can't stay for only one night of a weekend. On holiday
weekends they'll often only sell three-day packages. Off-season rates do
not apply on holiday or big Keys events weekends. At those times, expect
to pay full high-season fare. (Check the Annual Events chapter in this
book. We celebrate holidays down here that you haven't even heard of!)

Remember, the sales tax and the bed tax, all together, add 11.5% to
your bill.

Unfortunately, a shortage of B & B-style accommodations exists in
the Upper Keys. Possibly, by the time you get around to visiting, more
options may be available. If you're a B & B person, phone the Islamorada
Chamber of Commerce at 1-800-FAB-KEYS and ask for information on
area B & B's. Call around before you make reservations. Know what
you're looking for, and ask for it. Pets? Kids? Handicapped? Do you want
sand on your beach, or will a fabulous pool with a spectacular sunset view
do? Sunset is bayside; sunrise is oceanside. Don't bother asking for coffee-
ice-cream-colored sandy beaches because we don't have them here in
Islamorada…o.k., sometimes you'll find a bit of sandy beach—but the
sand is imported. It comes. It goes.

Bed & Breakfast of Islamorada
81175 Old Highway, MM 81 Bayside ✶ 664-9321

Dottie Saunders is a high-energy woman whose dedication to aerobics
keeps her trim, enthusiastic, and tough enough to trek the world armed
with nothing but a backpack, camera and endless curiosity. One of her
sons is a pilot, and that's how Dottie gets all those plane tickets to the far
corners of the world. She says she doesn't mind roughing it, and neither
should you if you choose to stay at her laid-back bed-and-breakfast.
Dottie smokes, so you can, too. If you don't like smoke, don't stay at
Dottie's. Each of the three rooms has a TV and a clean, very modest
bathroom. That's it, amenity-wise. It's not on the water, and there's no

pool, but it's inexpensive, $50–$65 (less if you pay with cash, Dottie says), and lots of information about the area is conveniently collected in several looseleaf notebooks in the living room, including menus, brochures; and numbers to call (Dottie charges 25 cents per call). Dottie has fished, snorkeled and partied in the area for many years and names the Lorelei as her favorite watering hole.

Ask to see Dottie's collection of news clips, too. One travel writer from the *Washington Post* wrote that Dottie reminded him of "Ava Gardner in her role as innkeeper in *Night of the Iguana*," which, frankly, isn't at all far-fetched when you consider that Tennessee Williams also roamed these Keys for many years...he had to get his inspiration for those characters from somewhere.

The Bed & Breakfast of Islamorada is located behind Sid and Roxie's Green Turtle Inn at mile marker 81. After dark, when the lights go on and the green neon turtle begins his nocturnal laps above the doorway to the restaurant, it's real easy to find the turnoff to Dottie's.

Caloosa Cove Resort
MM 73.8 Lower Matecumbe Key * 664-8811

Over sixty years ago, this was ground zero when the worst hurricane ever to hit the United States tore through Lower Matecumbe Key and wiped it clean of vegetation, buildings—and people. Even centuries before that, several Caloosa Indian settlements also thrived here, so these grounds are steeped in history. Oh, if these coral rocks could talk!

Today, the Caloosa Cove is a particularly lovely arrangement of thirty oceanfront condominiums, built with care and lots of closet space. Every unit has a spectacular view of the ocean, and the resort is far enough away from the busier sections of the Overseas Highway that you don't have to see or hear anything other than the soothing sights and sounds of Paradise.

If you don't want to buy a luxury condo in Islamorada, you can rent one—when they're not booked by time sharers—for a day or a week or longer. Efficiencies start at $125 nightly and $750 weekly; they are comparatively spacious units, certainly as big as a deluxe New York City efficiency. The bedroom suites with dens have couches that pull out, and kitchens, modern, very clean, and well-equipped. Rates are $175 nightly and $1,050 weekly. And if you can't see your way clear to the coffee machine, starting at dawn, the office serves a daily continental breakfast of coffee and Danish pastries.

For a rundown on what the people around here are up to, check out the bus trip schedule outside the office. You can visit a bingo parlor on a Miami Indian Reservation, Sawgrass Mills Shopping Mall, west of Fort Lauderdale (one of the biggest in the world!), and Miami happenings like the annual boat and home shows.

The Safari Lounge pays homage to somebody's trip to Africa. On display are photos of a white hunter posing between two dead lions; a Masai warrior, posing proudly for the camera; antelope antlers; and carved wood, evocative of the dark continent. Lazy paddle fans and a great view of the ocean make it everything a tropical Keys bar should be. Cool, dark, spacious, kind of mysterious. Where is everybody?

Back out in the sunshine, explore the long, good-for-a-walk beach; enjoy the BBQ pit and picnic tables, or a game of volleyball, tennis or ping-pong. Or swim in a very big, heated pool. Very inviting. And not a crowd anywhere.

The Caloosa Cove Marina, a place that looks quite a bit spiffier than most marinas in Islamorada, is a nice marina to wander (check out the yachts and charter boats). *Poverty Sucks,* a 53-foot Hatteras Sportfisher-man offshore charter fishing boat, is popular with tourists. They like standing next to it and having their pictures taken. Phone 664-9256 to schedule a trip. Also, an industrial-strength party boat called *Deep Adventures* is surely the largest fishing boat anywhere. It looks like a luxury cruise ship.

Cheeca Lodge
MM 82, Oceanside ❧ 664-4651 ❧ 800-327-2888
Simply the best, better than all the rest. When money is no object, you might want to stay here. Then again, you might not. A well-known travel writer from San Francisco told me that in January she stayed in a $525 suite with all the amenities. It had everything, she said, and not a speck of dust. But, she sighed, it was so damned sterile.

The original hotel on this location was the Olney Inn, comprised of 22 bungalows, built in 1946 by a hotelier from Washington, D.C. The inn's very first guest, Cheeca history has it, was President Harry S Truman. In 1960, after Hurricane Donna nearly demolished the place, it was sold to Carl and Cynthia Twitchell. A&P heiress Cynthia's nickname was "Chee," and from that, the Cheeca Lodge got its name. The Twitchells built the four-story lodge that stands today, and operated the inn with 86 rooms. In 1987 a Chicago concern bought it and invested a reported $33 million into a massive up-date and expansion of the property.

Today the Cheeca features both fresh and saltwater pools, six tennis courts, a three-hole golf course, several restaurants, watersports, and 203 units, and there's even a heliport!

If you can't afford to stay in a room or villa at the Cheeca Lodge, you can still visit the place, have a cocktail in the Light Tackle Lounge, and dine in the palatial Atlantic Edge dining room. Have lunch at the indoor/outdoor Ocean Terrace Grill, or come for the spectacular Sunday brunch. In the lounge, notice the room-rate card from 1962, way before the Cheeca became so intensely posh. Room rates then were $25–$40 a night. Also on display: snapshots of the rich and famous who have come to the Cheeca Lodge to fish and be photographed with members of the Twitchell clan.

Members of the Islamorada Chamber of Commerce staff will tell you that President George Bush stays in the Cheeca's $1,000 presidential suite. Each summer Bush comes into town to head up a very high-stakes fishing tourney, the proceeds of which go toward preserving the endangered Everglades. The Bush connection is one of the Cheeca Lodge's many claims to fame, and Cheeca employees say that the former prez is a dream to work with, "a real nice guy."

The Cheeca Lodge sprawls on 25 acres of oceanfront property that once was one of the Upper Keys' earliest settlements. You'll find substantial beachfront and a long, narrow, sun-and wind-worn wharf jutting into the Atlantic that is quite irresistible—you *have* to walk to the end of it. A neat, sandy beach on a small, safe lagoon is perfect for families. During the winter season, as well as most weekends, kids can take part in an in-house children's program that is something like a day camp at a country club. The theme of the program is marine environmental awareness and responsibility. Kids are taught by four counselors with some pretty spiffy credentials and degrees.

All this luxury costs plenty, but the Cheeca really does have just about everything you could ask for in a resort. Cheeca employees are known for their friendliness. Many of them are descended from those founding families represented in the Pioneer Cemetery out on the beach of the property. Guests at the Cheeca Lodge are treated very well indeed. And they match the surroundings: sleek, elegant, and with not a speck of dust!

Holiday Isle Resorts & Marina
MM 84, Oceanside ✺ 664-2321 ✺ 800-327-7070

The penultimate spring breakers' resort, this massive complex of bars, restaurants, shops, concessions and motel rooms has it all, and more. It jumps! It swings! It stops traffic! The size of the traffic jam on the Overseas Highway outside the Holiday Isle complex indicates how busy the resort is that day. Weekends it is always packed; sometimes it's packed to capacity, and people are turned away.

A young crowd features people who look stunning in bikinis. If you don't look so good, you'll be happier elsewhere. Even the Monroe County Sheriff's deputies eat lunch here. Oceanside barbeque hamburgers and hot dogs are the same here as anywhere, but, oh, the view.

This complex has extensive facilities for watersports, including wreck diving and windsurfing, five restaurants and nine bars, including a tiki bar, shaded by palm fronds. Bimini Walk is an array of shops featuring art and posters, and swimwear and T-shirts, the clothes you need to fit in at this very hot beach. For information and reservations call 800-327-7070 and ask for a brochure. There's so much here! The Horizon Restaurant is on the sixth floor; just take the glass-sided elevator. Guests are curious women and their patient husbands. The college kids can't afford to eat up here—they're doing hot dogs and hamburgers on the beach. Who cares how the food is? It's a novel place to dine.

Holiday Isle goes all out for the spring break crowd in March and April, with lots of parties, specials, and a couple of bikini contests with big cash rewards.

Oh, and you can sleep here, too. The marina has boats for fishing, diving, and sunset cruising. Printed information on the Holiday Isle could fill a small book. An information person on duty on the beach can help you, just in case you're looking for something to do.

The Islander Motel
MM 82.1 Oceanside ✒ 664-2031

The Polynesian arch over the driveway hearkens back to the '60s, and it might discourage travelers looking for more modern digs. Right, it's not sleek and modern. It's sleek and funky, but oh-so-charmingly so. The family-owned Islander Motel maintains a style of old-time Keys seaside resort that is becoming more and more difficult to find. The place is very attractive, that is—it attracts you, and the ocean breeze beckons. Broad expanses of white coral rock, stark beneath the hot, tropical sun, make you feel like pinning a hibiscus in your hair and wandering around in a flowing cotton gown on the very pretty, very long white beach. O.K. There's no real sand to speak of, but that just makes the 1,100-foot beach earthier. Lots of slouchy beach chairs rest at the edge of the seawall. The twenty-five-acre grounds are absolutely opulent by local standards. You could almost get lost.

In all 114 units of the Islander, you'll get good beds, refrigerators, telephones and televisions; some have fully equipped kitchens. Villas with screened-in porches are popular with families who rent them for weeks at a time at very reasonable rates. In fact, this is surely one of the best deals in the Keys. Help yourself to simple, complimentary breakfast every morning in the lobby. The freshwater pool and the saltwater pool are heated. Snorkeling or fishing right off the 200-foot lighted pier is good fun, not to mention shuffleboard. (Does anybody actually play shuffleboard anymore?), basketball, and volleyball, all near the BBQ patio.

When you stay in this family-oriented vacation resort, you're close to all the local sights, but you may not want to go to all the trouble of seeing them. A true sense of being well away from it all may be enough for you. Venture to the front office, however, it's worth a visit: several shelves of books, a bunch of board games, and oodles of brochures promoting area highlights—maybe these will inspire you.

The hotel switchboard is on twenty-four hours a day, so if you need to be telephone accessible, you can be here. Sorry, no pets. The reservation desk is open weekdays only, from 10 a.m.–3 p.m. Otherwise, FAX them: 305-664-5503.

Islamorada Motel/Inn
MM 87.8 Bayside ❦ 852-9376

This small, clean mom-and-pop joint on the highway—no ocean, no bay—is operated by a real mom and a real pop. All thirteen units, rooms and efficiencies, are on a deep, pleasant property. The furniture, including the beds, is perfectly preserved, '60s-era cane, wicker and rattan, all in good shape. A good-sized saltwater pool, a BBQ pit, and a diving gear clean-up station with a hose are all out back. Also, a nifty, thatched-roof tiki hut out front, sheltering a round wooden table and a bunch of chairs, looked like a very fine place for six or eight people to have a lot of fun. The circulating pump was on the fritz on the day we visited, so the pool was leafy—but not gross. All in all, the grounds of the Islamorada Motel were not as pristine as the interior but certainly comfortable enough. A long clothesline in the sun looked like a very good idea.

Prices at the Islamorada Motel aren't as low as the purple brochure from the Chamber of Commerce says they are, but, all things considered, prices are fair enough. The rooms are equipped with televisions and air conditioning and dial-out phones. The maid proudly told us that all linens are changed every day! One small unit for one person is around $70; otherwise, the prices start at $79–$99, with additional charges for more than two people.

Pelican Cove Resort
MM 84.5 Oceanside ❦ 664-4435 ❦ 800-445-4690

Found: one sandy beach, the sandiest beach we saw anywhere in the area. Maybe they just brought it in; they do buy sand here and spread it on the beaches. Anyway, if you're longing for the kind of sand you sink in up to your ankles, this is the place for you.

Every room in the Pelican Cove has an ocean view, including hotel rooms, efficiencies and suites. The beach, the oceanside pool and the jacuzzi behind the hotel are all meticulously tended. They've also got a boat ramp and dock, tennis, a poolside cabana, and a bar and cafe. The watersports concession on the beach is run by some truly lovely young people who are as nice as they look.

If your parents suggest a family week in the Keys, tell them you want to stay at the Pelican Cove Resort. They'll love it and so will you because here's the deal: You check in, get the folks settled. Then you put on your

best swimsuit and head over to the Holiday Isle—it's right next door!—
where you immerse yourself in the thick of the Keys' wildest party scene.
It rocks around the clock. Then, when it's time to check in with the
folks, come back over to the beautiful, genteel Pelican Cove Resort. Boy,
are you smart!

Your parents will love their balcony overlooking the ocean. Every
room has one. Sweet jazz or show tunes from the Pelican Cove's beachside cabana float up to the balconies. The ocean glitters in the distance.
Room rates are on the expensive side here, but guests lulled to sleep by
palm fronds rustling in Caribbean breezes believe it's worth it. It's fair to
call this place luxurious—and expensive.

Plantation Yacht Harbor
MM 87 Bayside ⚓ 852-2381

For a while in the 19th century, this property was a pineapple plantation.
More recently it was a conference and teaching center for a manufacturer
of medical equipment, with classrooms, rooms and villas, and several vast
dining areas. Students of medical technology would come on Monday,
leave on Friday. On weekends, the area was rented out to tourists.

The Plantation Yacht Harbor is no longer used as a teaching center,
but the Coulter Corporation still owns it. Little has been done to bring
the place up to 1990s-era grandeur, but that's not to say the place isn't
clean and sufficient. It is both of these. And since the rooms weren't
designed as motel rooms, but rather as comfortable quarters for valued
employees, they're spacious and just a little bit grand. The Plantation's
rambling and somewhat-faded charm suits lots of folks just fine. It is popular with families who appreciate the resort's self-containment, and with
boaty types who prefer to dine in areas from which they can watch their
yachts floating peacefully in the nearby harbor.

The grounds are expansive, including tennis courts, a big pool, swings
for the kids, and a beach with a bar and a hamburger stand. The Lagoon
Saloon is still like Keys bars used to be. The docks on the Florida Bay are
full of yachts that you can get a good look at from a coral rock promenade and seawall that encloses the harbor.

Several acres of wide-open space are used for events like an annual
seafood festival held around the third weekend of January, boat shows,
and concerts. Willie Nelson and Bertie Higgins both performed here.

The lawn is so spacious, in fact, that local pilot Jackie Barnes, on a dare, once landed his Piper Cub plane on the Plantation grounds.

Nearly as broad as the grounds are the dockside dining rooms including a horseshoe bar, and a large dance floor. The Chamber of Commerce holds luncheon meetings here, and wedding receptions go on nearly every weekend.

The dining room never looks busy, but how could it? Even an army couldn't fill it. Breakfast, lunch and dinner are served daily, the food being surprisingly good and fairly priced. Key lime pie and other goodies are baked on the premises. The Coulter Corporation apparently puts no pressure on the friendly employees to increase the Plantation Yacht Harbor's business. And so it remains a sort of modern white elephant resort with relatively old-fashioned room rates.

Ragged Edge Resort
MM 86.5 Oceanside ✺ 243 Treasure Harbor Road ✺ 852-5389

Jackie Barnes, of Barnes-storming fame, a cheery guy in a straw hat, may be the first person you meet when you arrive at the Ragged Edge Resort. Jackie is proud as punch of the place and will patiently show you around until you find the accommodation you really want. All ten units are built with guests' comfort and safety in mind. For instance, the tiles on the floors of one newly remodeled room have non-skid surfaces; one little apartment is wheelchair accessible and right on the water. All the screened-in porches are perfect perches for taking in sea breezes. The kitchens are conducive to serious food prep. They're certainly not the barely equipped kitchens you often encounter in other Keys apartments and efficiencies. "We even supply the filters for the coffeemaker," says Jackie, opening the cupboard to show us. Also on the premises are a washer, a dryer, and a clothesline. The phones are for out-going calls only, so don't stay here if you're waiting for a phone call because you'll miss it. Outdoors, by the dock, lucky anglers will appreciate the fish cleaning area.

"Don't even think about cleaning your fish in our kitchens," Jackie says, "Your mama won't let you clean fish in her kitchen, and you can't do it here, either."

Jackie then shows us a little marina, sheltered and calm, and a boat launch, a few yards down the street. A freshwater pool overlooks the

Atlantic, and a lookout tower is a popular setting for weddings performed at the very crack of dawn. From the dock you can look out into the distance and see the light slash of turquoise against the horizon that marks Crocker Reef, some four miles out.

Jimmy Lee has owned the Ragged Edge for twenty-two years. He likes sitting at a picnic table in the yard and talking about the people who have stayed at the seaside lodge through the years. The Ragged Edge got a whole chapter in a travel book by a London writer who recorded his adventures in a book called *Hunting Mr. Heartbreak*. Ask Jimmy to show it to you.

Both Jackie and Jimmy know what's going on in the area. Jackie knows the kitchen crews in area restaurants and can often call ahead to the bistro of your choice to find out the specials of the evening. Knowing Jackie is like having a best friend in Islamorada.

During season, a nifty studio or efficiency goes for $109 a day. Off season it's 30% less. Weekly and monthly rates are 10% off that. Rates here are among the best in the area.

"We haven't caught up with the rest of the world," Jimmy Lee explains, "and we don't want to."

Coral Bay Marina Houseboat Rentals
MM 81.5 Bayside, on Blackwood Road ✷ 664-3111
At Coral Bay Marina you can rent a little (34'×12') houseboat, complete with propane energy, a kitchen with a refrigerator, a toilet and shower, and fresh water. Also a private stateroom with a double bed, and sleeping room for a total of six people. (Six is maximum allowed on the boat.) A 90 hp Johnson outboard motor powers your house into the Florida Bay, where you luxuriate for a three day or week-long stint in Paradise.

But don't get too lost...Somebody in your party needs to be experienced enough to operate a boat of this size and to read navigational charts. The waters of the Florida Bay are very shallow, its seagrass meadows delicate and vulnerable. The bay is also vast and seemingly endless. Walter Collins, who owns the operation, auditions potential commanders for seaworthiness before he turns over the keys to the floating castles. If you're not confident enough to set out into the watery wilderness, you can still enjoy the novelty of houseboating because you never have to leave shore. Houseboaters are welcome to stay right at the Coral

Bay Marina dock whenever they like. Some people go out into the bay to fish and sun by day, then tie up at the marina by night. At the dock you can hook up to electricity to run your air-conditioning; you can't do that in the bay, and, yes, it can get mighty warm out there in the summertime; buggy, too. Off shore, boats are powered by generators.

Minimum stay is three nights: Week-night rate is $450; weekend rate is $500 for three days. Rental for a week is $850. Also figure in the cost of the fuel. The 50-gallon tank is full when you leave the dock; that's the way it has to be when you return it.

Dining

Bentley's
MM 82, Oceanside ✺ 664-9094

People who work here seem to be having a good time serving the fish and pasta platters. People who run the hotels in the area often recommend this place. The bar here is full of beer posters and neon slogans, kind of like a frat rumpus room. Prime ribs, a house specialty, are so huge they barely fit on the plate. An appetizer called "drunken sweet potato," with brown sugar and dark rum, butter, cinnamon, and nutmeg, is so wonderful you'll try to recreate it when you get home. Dinner samplers feature shrimp or fish served in several different sauces on the same plate. Kind of weird, but they seem to please Bentley's customers. The place is packed every night. And don't forget to bring cash, because they don't take credit cards here.

Coral Grill
MM 83.5 Bayside ✺ 664-4803

Two ways to dine here: the first, and most famous, is an amazing all-you-can-eat buffet: fish, meats, veggies, salads and desserts, presented in two gigantic, usually packed upstairs dining rooms. Downstairs is a smaller, more subdued dining room with table service. Each week the Coral Grill sells six thousand pounds each of shrimp, prime rib, and chicken. Up to five hundred people dine here daily.

Lee and Judith Pieretti have been running the Coral Grill since 1946. On the rare slow night, Lee, a former professional musician, might be talked into playing the piano in the lounge. But usually he's much too busy yelling out names over the public address system: "Jones! Table for sixteen!" They don't take reservations at the Coral Grill, but half the fun of eating here is hanging around waiting for a table. You meet fellow tourists and compare notes on how the vacations are going. Sometimes Miami football teams show up during summer training, and you might get an autograph. The dining rooms are so huge that nobody waits for long, but if you're the impatient type, ask to eat downstairs. The menu there is a la carte, but the salad bar has plenty of offerings, with almost as many goodies as upstairs, only it's less expensive and certainly less crowded. Lots of locals eat downstairs at the Coral Grill. Some of the waitresses have been working here since the beginning of time, and yet they're still in high spirits.

The place is open only for dinner, except on Sundays when it opens at noon. It's closed Mondays. Early-bird buffet, from 4 p.m.–6 p.m., is around $16. After six, the buffet is $18. Downstairs entrees start at $9 and include soup, salad and dessert.

Green Turtle Inn
MM 81.5 Oceanside ⋆ 664-9031

This landmark restaurant coasts slowly but surely along on its reputation. Mostly tourists, but very few locals, eat here. The place was established way before green turtles were an endangered species. Visitors to the fishing capital of the world are intrigued and thrilled to eat exotic turtle meat, but they may be surprised to know that the turtle is not saltwater turtle and not green turtle at all. It's taken from farm-bred snapping and soft-shell turtles raised in Central Florida. They may order beef, chicken, and fresh seafood dishes.

Built in the twenties, it was blown apart by the 1935 hurricane, rebuilt, and then reopened in the '40s. The neon sign out front is spectacular, but the piano player is the best part of the whole deal.

Right across the street is the Green Turtle Cannery, where the young guys behind the counter are endearingly enthusiastic about their Florida Keys products. An old guy named Jimmy Woods cleans fish at the cannery. Jimmy is a survivor of the '35 hurricane, when he was just nineteen. The shop is great fun, full of islandy cans, bottles and jars of hot sauce, Key lime juice, and assorted seafood accompaniments. The guys behind the counter swear their Key lime pie is the best anywhere, but they couldn't be more wrong. We found it ghastly, with an aftertaste reminiscent of a green popsicle. You know—the last one in the box to be eaten because nobody really wants it....

Grove Park Cafe
MM 81.7 Oceanside ☏ 664-0116

Fine food in a funky little conch house—this is another of those fairly new places that you hope and pray will survive. Everybody in the Upper Keys is talking about how great it is. Also, people from the area who worked for many years at other places own and run this place, so everybody's rooting for them.

The panini sandwiches at lunch are different and sensational; the soups, too. Eggplant, veggies and cheese on foccacia bread is memorable, and much more impressive than the pork sandwich-special featured on the same day. Go for the panini. The dinner menu includes New York strip steak, Yellowtail Tropicale with mango-papaya salsa, Pasta Calabria with hot and sweet sausage, and grilled veggies, a no-fat dish served on pasta, spa-style. The wine bar serves micro-brews and wines by the glass. There's also an espresso bar, and unforgettable ice cream. You'll be happy to pay these moderate prices for food this good. The decor at the Grove Park Cafe, featuring bright paint, flowered fabrics, and swirls and splashes of bright color, looks good enough to eat, too. The place is small; a large person might feel larger in here. Grove Park's executive chef Carole Genevish used to chef up the road at the ritzy Cheeca Lodge. The food here is just as satisfying as it is at the Cheeca, but the prices here are much easier to swallow.

Hog Heaven
MM 85.3 Oceanside ☏ 664-9669

Imagine twenty-two televisions in two bars tuned to nothing but sports in a funky marina with great food and a laid-back atmosphere. They've got it all here: sports bar, restaurant, late-night club with live music on weekends. Otherwise, DJs Dave Extraodinaire and Dirty Ernie provide the music. Open daily from 11 a.m. till 4 a.m. serving lunch, full dinner till 4 a.m. The big draw is the 20-ounce porterhouse steak for $9.99. On Mondays and Wednesdays the special is a 12-ounce prime rib, with baked potato and salad, all for $9.95. Catfish dinner is $7.24. Lunch specials like meatloaf or pita pockets of chicken or crab salad are $4.44. Meet the two-year-old pot bellied pig with painted toenails named B.L. Dinner.

No particular happy hour because, "We're happy here all the time," says bartender Nancy. Fun, not frantic, sort of like the bars in *Easy Rider*.

And very clever menus, take one home. Use any credit card except Discover.

Interesting photo ops: Airplane tail sticking out of the second story of the building, as if it had flown directly into it. This might traumatize the kids if you don't explain it's rigged. Pose Granny next to one of the jazzed up Harleys out front. Most bikers here are so friendly they'll loan you a helmet for the shot.

Holiday Isle
MM 84, Oceanside ✱ 664-2321
In the Holiday Isle complex, it is possible to do some serious bar-hopping without ever leaving the premises. Remember the song "Kokomo" by the Beach Boys? Originally, it was a fantasy place, nonexistent, but when people began arriving in the Keys, asking directions to the mysterious and wonderful-sounding place called Kokomo, the folks at Holiday Isle quickly rushed in to answer their dreams, and a bar named Kokomo was born. So there you are—in Kokomo till the wee hours. There's live island music—reggae, Caribbean, rock—at Kokomo, and more of the same at the nearby Tiki Bar. Rum Runners, a triple-decker thatched-palm tower featuring bars and cocktails on breezy alcoves and terraces, is the very hottest watering spot in the Keys, a must-visit, according to one of my more dedicated fun-chasing friends. By the way, one of the owners of Rum Runners is songwriter Bertie Higgins, whose song "Key Largo" commemorates the seaside splendor of romance in the tropics. There's dinner and dancing five stories up in the Horizon Club, where the view of the ocean after dark, when the stars and boat lights are twinkling on the vast horizon, may inspire *you* to write a hit song.

The Hungry Tarpon
MM 77.5 Bayside, at Robbie's Marina ✱ 664-0535
You've heard of grunts and grits, the staple dish of the Florida Keys Depression-era diet, but have you ever tried it? Folks who frequent the Hungry Tarpon Cafe will tell you that eating grunts and grits is no hardship. In fact, they return again and again to this whitewashed, lace-curtained bistro for this legendary treat. Other specialities at George and Vanna's Hungry Tarpon are Pirate's Caviar—a melange of dolphin roe,

cheese grits, and scrambled eggs, and a smoked fish omelette, prepared with Smokin' Joe Re's smoked kingfish. A mess of smotherin's—onion, pepper, and garlic bits—sizzle in a perpetual pile on the griddle, just like they did on Vanna's Cherokee mama's stove when she was a little girl.

You can choose your own CD and slide it into the player, but heed the handwritten sign: "No Jimmy Buffett music will be played here. Violators will be fed to the tarpons."

It's not that George has anything against the man from Margaritaville. It's just that he's been sailing most of his life. And when you're a sailor, you hear a lot of Jimmy Buffett.

"From Nova Scotia to the Caribbean, Jimmy Buffett music is blaring on the waterfront," George says. "So now it's a house rule. I'm hoping Buffett will hear about it and show up so I can get his autograph or something."

People from all over the world come into the Hungry Tarpon. The restaurant is open Wednesday–Saturday from 7 a.m. till 3 p.m. There's a fish fry on Friday nights 6 p.m. till 9 p.m.; and on Sundays, a breakfast buffet from 8 a.m. till 2 p.m. A little pricey. Charm ain't cheap.

Islamorada Fish Company & Bakery
MM 81.5 and 81.6 Bayside ✹ 664-8363 (the bakery)
664-9271 (the fishhouse) ✹ 800-258-2559 (to order fish)
Dixie Cream Donuts and a restaurant serving breakfast and lunch from 6 a.m. to 2 p.m. are located at MM 81.6. The little building that used to house the popular Lovin' Dough Cafe, which my crazy family renamed the Peace and Love Cafe, is where you go for donuts, breakfast and lunch. Also, cinnamon rolls with hot icing on top, or sticky rolls, which is the same thing without the hot icing. They're $1.75 apiece, and with coffee—spectacular. Other bakery goods are also delectable, and the pancakes are particularly delicious. In fact, all breakfast items are nicely prepared and presented.

A few blocks away at MM 81.6, you'll find the Fish House, located a bit farther back from the road. There's a retail fish business there as well as the restaurant. Lunch and dinner are served in the back on a bayside sun deck or, on windy days, a deck out front. The lunch and dinner menus are the same, and everything is served on plastic or paper. Prices are moderate, but there are several fresh salads—nice alternatives to the fried fare. Twin lobster tail dinner with fries and coleslaw runs around $25, depending upon the market price of lobster. Salad with fresh shrimp is $12. Salad with grilled chicken is around $10. The Fish House is open six days a week, from 8 a.m.–7 p.m; Sundays, 9 a.m.–5 p.m.

If you're feeling guilty about all the fun you're having in Paradise sampling the wonderful bounty of indigenous seafood, why not ship a slab of fish or a couple of Florida lobsters or a pound or two of ground conch to the folks back home? It costs around $60 for packing, shipping and handling up to five pounds of fish anywhere in the continental United States; the fish you pay for separately. The packing room is always busy. At Christmas time it's a madhouse, so order early.

Lazy Days Oceanfront Bar & Grille
Mile Marker 79.9 Oceanside ☎ 664-5256

We tried the Lazy Days Restaurant for the first time on a Saturday afternoon in March. "Sorry–No Vacancy" signs were posted on every hotel, motel, and inn in the area. The restaurants were packed, too, and traffic was bumper to bumper. We'd had a busy day and felt we owed it to ourselves to seek out the best fish sandwich the area had to offer. And guess what? We found it. The crunchy yellowtail sandwich at Lazy Days Bar and Grille was spectacular. Several area restaurants are now adding crunchy yellowtail sandwiches to their menus, too. This one is the original. We ordered fried conch, too, but we wouldn't order it again for two reasons: first, because of the many other truly tasty choices on the menu, and second, because it was so tough that all the chewing in the world wouldn't tenderize it. (Everybody knows the trick to succulent conch is to thoroughly tenderize it and then to cook it very briefly.) Considering the business of the day, the cook may have forgotten it on the fire for a few minutes too long. Or something. The French fries at Lazy Days are terrific. They're worth the visit, hand-cut, not frozen, amazing. You won't ever want to go back to the other yucky kind.

The television program *TV Diners* came to film at the Lazy Days when they did a program on great waterfront restaurants. The show aired in July, 1995. While you're waiting for your food to arrive, check out the view. To the right you'll see a point of land with a heliport and a row of magnificent palms. No, it's not a public facility; it's the multimillion-dollar retreat of a Chicago businessman. To the left is Bud 'n' Mary's Marina.

Lazy Days offers what every hungry tourist is hoping to find: ocean-front dining and good, fresh seafood. Of course, you pay a bit more to get things so exactly right. Because the entire restaurant is about a story-and-a-half up from the ground, there's a soft breeze that you can probably count on finding year-round. Otherwise, eat indoors. Prices are fair—for two, around $25 for lunch; $40–$50 for dinner. There's a big bar and great servers. Lazy Days is open 11:30 a.m. to 10 p.m. Closed Mondays.

Lorelei Restaurant and Cabana Bar
Mile Marker 82 Bayside ▪ 852-4656
Lorelei was the legendary German mermaid who haunted the Rhine River. Lorelei's plaintive songs lured sailors and fishermen into destruction on the rocks that lined the river. Nice gal, huh? And who knew rivers had mermaids? Eventually Lorelei was carried away by the currents, but her sad singing is still heard late at night along the banks of the Rhine, some believe....

Lorelei, the place on the Florida Bay, evokes a much happier mood than its namesake. Lorelei herself is recreated outside in a glittery splash of all-weather sequins.

On a walkway leading into the complex a plexiglass photo gallery contains pictures of President Bush arriving for dinner; and a barefoot couple getting married: she in a white swimsuit and veil; he in a black bathing suit and bow tie.

Dining in the Lorelei Restaurant is dockside, or indoors in a rather elegant dining room. The restaurant opens for dinner only, from 5 p.m. till 10 p.m., 10:30 p.m. on weekend nights. Early bird specials from 5 p.m. Food is pricey; quality is rather inconsistent, but you don't go to the Lorelei for the food. You go for the ambiance. You go to celebrate sunset on another day in Paradise with people who make their living on the water.

At the Cabana Bar, breakfast and lunch are served daily. Fishing guides, sailboat captains and dive masters come to the Cabana Bar to unwind in the late afternoons. Live music plays about always. And on Sunday afternoons, local celebrity Big Dick plays.

Once locally owned and operated, the Lorelei is now part of a New York-based corporation that owns thirty-five properties around the world. Here's one you might have heard of: The Tavern On The Green in New York City's Central Park.

Manny and Isa's Restaurant
MM 81.6 Oceanside ✶ 664-5019

The people who have been running this place for over thirty years own a rare orchard of Key lime trees. (Key lime orchards used to be a cash crop in these parts, but hurricanes and economics blew most of them into oblivion.) Each morning, local legend has it, Manny Ortiz squeezes fresh Key limes and bakes a batch of genuine Key lime pies to serve in his world-famous restaurant. He also serves seafood, Cuban food and American fare. The house salad dressing is not to be missed, but the Key lime pie is the big draw. It's been written up in numerous newspapers, and the articles, yellow with age, are on display on the walls. Manny's Key lime pie is a lighter, less tart version of the denser, richer original recipe, and some people prefer it that way. The pie is $2.75 a slice, and it's Manny's claim to fame.

Miami Herald reporter Susana Bellido described this joint as "the kind of place where waitresses announce out loud that a fresh pot of coffee is brewing." Not on the day we were there. That day, a Saturday morning around 11:30, the sole waitress seemed preoccupied and barely aware or concerned about our presence. As she tended to her lunch prep chores, she chatted with a single diner who lingered long over coffee and that famous Key lime pie. "Does he mind that you cut your hair?" the customer asked the waitress. "He understands my lifestyle," she answered.

Marker 88
Guess where? Bayside ✶ 852-9315

Dinner only; 5 p.m.–11 p.m. Boy, does this place get mixed reviews! Some say the food is strictly gourmet, extensive list of fine wines, complete bar, creative menu. Others say the tables are too close together, it's too noisy when it's full, way over-rated, take plenty of money. Entrees range from $14 to $34, mostly a la carte. Food critics praise the Key lime baked Alaska dessert. Closed Mondays, reservations strongly suggested on weekends.

Papa Joe's Landmark Restaurant
MM 79.7 Bayside ✻ 664-8109

Recently named a Historic and Cultural Landmark by the Monroe County Board of Commissioners, this seafood restaurant and bar sit pretty as a postcard on the dock o' the bay. Interior has low ceilings and lots of cedar beams, and a nautical theme with no apologies. The outdoor bar is really the nicest place to eat, if the weather permits. Yet another great view of the sunset. A good place where a party traveling together can split up for a spell to pursue separate endeavors. Maybe all you want to do is sit at the bar and watch the sun glitter off the waters of the Florida Bay. Your more ambitious companions are cruising out to Indian Key or Lignumvitae Key for a local history lesson. Papa Joe's is just the place from which to launch this perfect afternoon in Paradise.

Food is not gourmet or trendy, just simple fare, well-prepared and nicely served, and a great children's menu with terrific prices. If you've got kids, ask for a table near the aquarium. Lunch is from 11 a.m. till 3:30 p.m. Daily specials, like country fried steak with mashed potatoes and gravy for around $5, are popular. Early-bird dinner specials are famous, too. From 4:30 p.m.–6 p.m. prices on lobster, shrimp, or prime rib dinners are around $10. There's always a crowd at Papa Joe's because the food's good, and the prices are right. Plus—it's on the water!

Closed Tuesdays. All major credit cards accepted.

Whale Harbor Inn
MM 83.5 Oceanside ✻ 664-4959

Attention, hungry whales! The world famous seafood buffet, featuring troughs overflowing with shellfish, roasted beef and hams, and seventy-five accompanying hot and cold dishes, caters to the early bird crowd from 4 p.m. till 5:30 weekdays and Saturdays, and noon till 4 p.m. Sundays. Buffet prices: $17.95 for early birds; $19.95 otherwise. Kids always cost $9.95 if they're under ten; $4 if they're under four. It is interesting to imagine how the Haitian workers who dish out the endless servings of food—shrimp, oysters, clams and roast beef—must feel as they watch the excess and the waste. The food looks quite a bit better than it actually tastes; even the shrimp, which you peel for yourself, loses its appeal a lot faster than you might think. When you get tired of eating, go for a walk. The gift shop is a terrific place to wander through, and the prices are affordable on stuff you might need, like a bigger sweatshirt.

Tour buses stop here, so don't be surprised to see one, but do consider going elsewhere and returning at a less riotous time. Certain bus loads, one waitress told me, are comprised of particularly demanding and pushy tourists. If you are a part of a bus load, make reservations and find out from Darlene about discounts for parties of twenty or more.

Ziggie's Conch Restaurant
MM 83.5 ✷ 664-3391 or 664-4590

Whenever we drive by Ziggie's, my husband and I have a little, traditional chat about the name of the place. "There's Ziggies Conch Restaurant," I say. "No. It's Ziggie's—The Conch Restaurant," my husband says. Which is it? Also, no one in the area can decide whether it's real good or real bad. One travel writer said she wouldn't eat the Key lime pie at Ziggie's if they were giving it away. Wow. A la carte, expensive; dinner only, 6 p.m.–10 p.m.

Woody's Saloon and Restaurant
Mile Marker 82 ✷ 664-4335

And now, for something completely different! Advertised as Islamorada's hottest night spot. Karaoke starts at 6 p.m. At 9 p.m., the house band, Big Dick and the Extenders, goes on. At 10 p.m., lead man Big Dick, a Don Rickles-type comedian, does his famous hour-long harangue, one of the area's most notorious attractions billed as "adult entertainment." You are warned not to sit in the front row unless you want to swap witticisms with Big Dick. One Islamorada resident told me that Big Dick is "really dirty." Another says, "Big Dick is obnoxious, but you gotta see him once."

Woody's also has sensational Chicago-style pizza and very good Italian dishes. By the way, Big Dick takes Mondays off, and on that night the karaoke goes on all evening. Also, Big Dick and his Southern rock and blues band never turn down requests to appear, for no pay, at local fundraisers, and in the Keys, there are plenty of those. With a heart that big, how bad can Big Dick be? Big Dick also performs at the Lorelei on Sunday afternoons.

Shops

Cover to Cover Books
MM 90 Oceanside, on the Old Highway ✴ 852-1415

Former teachers Joy McIntosh and Linda Johnson had what Joy describes as "a very horrible, awful, terrible, no-good year" in Miami a while back and decided to find a softer, easier way to stay close to their love of working with kids. They decided to become entrepreneurs and run a bookstore. To learn the business, the team traveled to Boston and took an American Booksellers Association-sponsored course in book selling. Shortly thereafter, the bookshop Cover to Cover went on the market, and in March of 1995 the teachers bought it. Things have been wonderful ever since. Wednesdays are special events days. Over fifty kids are enrolled in the "Goosebumps Club," and there's also an adult discussion group. Local writers read and sign new works frequently.

"Our store specializes in children's literature and educational games, as well as Florida books. We're former teachers, and that influences the atmosphere of the store," Linda says.

The strong, hot coffee and sweet snacks from the Cover to Cover coffee bar is a big influence, too.

Treasure Island Village
MM 86.5 Oceanside ✴ 852-0511

It all started with a replica of a Spanish fort built in 1949 by treasure hunter Art McKee, who is known around the world as the father of modern treasure diving. McKee's guests were invited to view McKee's collection of recovered loot and then to climb the winding stairway to a lookout at the top of the fort. All went well, local legend has it, until someone fell from the top of the fort and broke his neck. A long litigation followed, the details and results of which have been lost in time. Eventually, however, all was apparently settled and the fort changed hands to open in its next incarnation as an anchor store for a spiffy, new, leafy shopping complex filled with island goodies.

As you encounter the 37-foot spiny lobster replica at the entrance to the Treasure Island Village Shops, imagine how the lobster feels when the tables are turned and he is facing a hungry human diver on the ocean floor. Surely this is the biggest spiny lobster replica in the world. As you gaze upon the Spanish tower, imagine how fine it must have looked to tourists in the 1950s. Also remember: the bathrooms are located in the tower.

The shops of Treasure Village are arranged on a boardwalk that encircles a shady courtyard, with picnic tables and open space for antsy kids. The courtyard provides a lovely time-out zone for those in need of a break or some quiet time. Half your party can shop while the other can sit in the courtyard digging on the reggae that never seems to quit.

The Rain Barrel Artisans Village
MM 86.7 Bayside ◦ 852-3084
The mood here is serene, soft and green, and very friendly. If you're the sort of person who likes to schmooz a bit with the artist before you buy the art, here's your chance. Shops and boutiques feature artistic expression in pottery, clay, glass, custom frames, airbrushed T-shirts, paintings, stained glass, jewelry, with more saleable items being created all the time. Works are displayed in a main gallery as well as in a series of smaller shops that radiate from the center.

Creations here are on the expensive side but look and feel as if they will last a long time. Clearly more dear than schlock.

Usually in the late winter or early spring the Rain Barrel artists stage an arts festival. In addition to resident craftspeople, there are live demonstrations by visiting artisans; live music and food. Admission is free, but food will cost you.

Why is this gathering place of artisans called "The Rain Barrel?" Owner Carol Cutshall says the arts and crafts center is named after the 5,000-gallon rain barrel in the center of the garden. "Because rain is water and water is needed for the existence of life," she says.

Everybody in this little enclave talks like that. Open 9 a.m. till 5 p.m. daily.

Islamorada
. . .

Hooked On Books
MM 82.6 Oceanside ✻ 517-2602

Long time Keys visitors, Jean and Kevin Kelley always had the dual
dream of one day moving to the Florida Keys and owning a bookstore.
Married at the Cheeca Lodge in Islamorada, their dreams came true in
1998 when they left the straight life behind and opened Hooked on
Books. Kevin is a yacht captain, Jean runs the store which offers New
York Times bestsellers, books on local subjects, CD's, and for vacationers
for whom reading is a mainstay of their holiday, there is a large selection
of pre-owned paperbacks which they sell or trade. Open Tuesday through
Saturday 9 a.m.–5:30 p.m.

SOONER OR LATER,
EVERYONE COMES TO

Key Largo

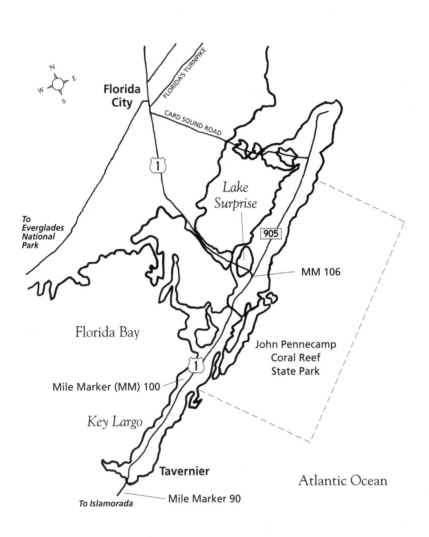

George was right.
The Keys are different from anything
I've ever seen—and hotter.

– Humphrey Bogart's first line
in the film *Key Largo*.

Sooner or Later, Everyone Comes to Key Largo

KEY LARGO is a sun-baked and weather-beaten island, built on bleached coral rocks and populated by people often as sun-baked and weather-beaten as their surroundings. Key Largo feels dry and flat and windswept. It is the first island you come to when you drive into the Keys, and the last one see when you drive back out.

Key Largo is the longest, largest, and easternmost island of the Keys chain. It is bordered by the Florida Straits and the Atlantic Ocean on the south and the Florida Bay and the Gulf of Mexico on the north.

Since no natural fine-grain sand beaches exist here, local folks working in the tourist industry spend a lot of time and energy explaining to disappointed visitors that Florida's sandy beaches do not extend all the way down to the craggy shoreline of Key Largo. The rest of Florida's coast has beaches, while the Florida Keys have the living reef, the only one in the continental United States. The community of Key Largo seems a support system for that reef, and that's not a bad thing; it gives the place a purpose it would not otherwise have.

Much of the upper part of Key Largo is federally protected land and unsettled wilderness, encompassing the Crocodile Lake National Wildlife Refuge. The refuge is a 6800-acre hardwood hammock and lake that has become the primary breeding ground for the endangered American crocodile. Other endangered species in the refuge are the indigo snake, wood rat, Key Largo cotton mouse, and Schauss' swallowtail butterfly. Because crocodiles are timid, particularly around matters of reproduction, this area is closed to the public.

Visitors, however, are invited to roam the Key Largo Botanical Site on upper Key Largo and, on lower Key Largo, the Wild Bird Sanctuary for an up-close and personal visit with some remarkable species of Keys birds.

Aside from these sanctioned areas, the island of Key Largo is quite heavily populated. Its main street, which is the Overseas Highway, is lined with motels, shops and restaurants. Several shopping centers attract residents from several Upper Keys communities. In spite of four lanes, the highway here is curvy, and traffic is often thick and slow.

Key Largo's biggest attraction is John Pennekamp Coral Reef Park, the first underwater park in the United States, and Florida's most popular state park. It's the largest diving destination in the world, receiving over two million visitors each year.

Diving is very big business in Key Largo. Everywhere you look you see dive shops offering to sell or rent just about anything you need for a day, or a week, of reef or wreck diving. One shop advertises, "We supply everything but your bathing suit." Endless combinations of dive packages are available, too, and every motel and resort in Key Largo is ready for divers, pretty much assuming that's why they've come.

Like everywhere else in the Keys, fishing guides and charter captains are easily available in Key Largo to take you to the quiet, shallow waters of the backcountry, where cagey anglers, such as former President George Bush, go to outsmart snook and bonefish, or out into the deepest, scariest part of the ocean—the Gulf Stream—where burly sportsmen do battle with leaping marlin and sailfish.

Hollywood director John Huston, back in 1948, filmed several brief scenes for the movie *Key Largo* in the Caribbean Club in Rock Harbor, a small settlement on the island of Key Largo. When the film *Key Largo* was released in 1952, area businessmen saw an opportunity to cash in on their island's sudden glamour, spread far and wide via the silver screen by Humphrey Bogart and Lauren Bacall. Promoters decided to drop the name Rock Harbor and call the place Key Largo. Some folks didn't like the idea of the name change, but business interests prevailed, and Key

Largo has been promoting itself in relation to the film classic of the same name ever since.

For purposes of this guide, the area of Key Largo begins roughly around MM 90 and ends at MM 106, where the Overseas Highway splits into two roads, U.S. 1 and Card Sound Road. Either one will take you, in under a half hour, to the beginning of the Florida Turnpike or the Everglades National Park. Take Card Sound Road; the other way is much too hectic and, statistically, much more treacherous.

The Key Largo Chamber of Commerce
MM 106 Bayside ♥ 451-1414 ♥ 800-822-1088

If you're home, and your trip to the Keys is still in the planning stages, call ahead and tell a Chamber staff member what you're most interested in doing in Key Largo. Someone will answer your questions and send a comprehensive list of the area's features.

This center is often the first stop for folks arriving for the first time in the Keys. One chamber woman told me that many people come to Key Largo to see the living reef but are confused about how to find it. At least once a day, she says, she must explain that the reef is located miles offshore and beneath the water. "You can't see it from the road," she explains. "You can't drive your car to it. It is only accessible by boat."

You Are Here

On a blustery Saturday afternoon in January, business is brisk at the Key Largo Chamber's Visitors Center. Planted among the milling crowds are a half dozen telephone stations from which travelers may phone ahead to reserve rooms for the night. Each station is equipped with a pencil and a tiny pad of paper. Couples are busily conferring, and it appears that nailing down a room reservation is a man's job, for it is usually the men who are doing the negotiating with the motels. The men repeat what they are hearing to the women: "He says we're still two-and-a-half hours away," a man says. "They say the room is definitely on the water," another assures his wife, "but it's $30 more."

Yes, Key West is only a hundred miles away, but those are hard miles. Late afternoon is not the best time to head into the Lower Keys; it would be better to settle in for the night at one of Key Largo's funky motels or sleek resorts. At the very least, stop for an hour and enjoy the setting sun from some cozy vantage point on the bay. It's no fun at all driving straight into the blinding sunset, and that's exactly what you'll do if you head out for Key West around 6 p.m. on a January evening.

History

EY LARGO (in Spanish, Long Island) was named by Spanish sailors in the early 1500s. It is one of the oldest named places in Florida. However, for centuries, having a name did not lead to having a population. The isolation, lack of fresh water, mosquitoes, sand fleas, and heat prevented much of anything at all from happening until several pineapple plantations got the civilization ball rolling in the later half of the 1800s.

Archaeologists have uncovered evidence of an Indian village site in North Key Largo that dates back almost 3,800 years. Thought to be a ceremonial altar, it is a high mound made entirely of coral rocks, each measuring from eight to twelve inches in diameter. The site has been plundered by curiosity seekers as well as campers from a nearby campground, who use the rocks for encircling camp fires. In the 1950s, before the rocks were pilfered, the mound was 15 feet high, 100 feet long, and 15 feet wide, with a flat top and several wide ramps leading to it.

In the mid-1800s, several families received land grants to settle in the Key Largo area, but not one of them survived the harsh environment, and the area remained unsettled.

Then in 1866 a successful Key West wrecker named Ben Baker, perhaps growing weary of the seafaring life, planted 6,000 pineapple plants on a large piece of property he owned in then-desolate Key Largo. Baker reaped a very profitable harvest from that first crop, which encouraged other farmers also to begin growing pineapples. For the next forty years, pineapple farmers slashed and burned huge areas of tropical hardwood trees to make way for the pineapple plantations that provided jobs and livelihoods for the area's sparse citizenry. Pineapple workers were often native Bahamians who were accustomed to the harsh environment, and were unable to find work on their own islands.

One acre of land yielded nearly 7,000 pineapples in eighteen months. But making a harvest pay was not always easy. Ripe pineapples were transported to Key West on small schooners and then loaded onto larger ships bound for northern cities. Transporting perishable cargo in the days before refrigeration was an often frustrating business. Getting the fruit to market before it began to rot depended mainly upon favorable weather conditions.

In 1906, the Overseas Railroad linked the Upper Keys communities to the mainland. Plantation owners had hoped that the railroad would help overcome their shipping problems, but in that same year a hurricane destroyed enormous tracts of pineapple plants, then came a devastating blight. Those events marked the end of pineapple farming in the Keys.

The Overseas Railroad linked the Upper Keys communities with the mainland, but having a train station didn't promote a population boom in Key Largo. Even after the turn of the century, panthers, crocodiles, alligators, bobcats and huge populations of mosquitoes and sand flies continued to proliferate. Without jobs or fresh water or electricity or telephone service, the Upper Keys were understandably unappealing to settlers.

But all of that began to change when, in 1942, fresh water flowed into the Keys via a pipeline from Florida's mainland. The pipeline, built by the U.S. Navy, ran 130 miles all the way to Key West. Electricity also became available in Key Largo through a private enterprise around the same time. With those amenities in place, and property selling for as little as $110 an acre, Key Largo began to attract developers.

Meanwhile, far away in the south of France, Jacques Cousteau and Emile Gagnan were testing the world's first self-contained underwater breathing apparatus or, SCUBA. The invention was to revolutionize the sport of underwater diving. Before 1950, skin and scuba diving were known to very few people because of the expense and scarcity of equipment. As the development of sport diving equipment evolved, making the reef more available to the general public, so did Key Largo's fame as one of the world's most important diving centers.

In 1952, mosquito control arrived in the Keys, wiping out the most profound of the Upper Keys detriments to development. Homes, schools and churches were built; businesses, particularly those serving the tourist trade, were established to respond to the burgeoning trend of middle class folks seeking out vacation getaways. From the late 1950s onward, Key Largo's population and business community boomed.

Key Largo, The Movie

Humphrey Bogart plays a good guy. Edward G. Robinson plays a bad guy. Lauren Bacall is a beautiful young war widow. Lionel Barrymore is a lovable old gent, father of Bogie's army buddy who died in the war. Bogart has come to Key Largo to meet his dead army buddy's dad and wife, who run a hotel. Guests at the hotel are a gang of bootleggers, who take the other people in the hotel hostage when a hurricane threatens and their plans are blown off course. After the storm, the bad guys kidnap Bogart and force him to pilot the boat full of rum. But Bogart is too smart for them, see. He quickly knocks off the bootleggers and turns the boat around for Key Largo.

In the last scene of the film, Bacall gets word that Bogie is on his way back. She joyfully rushes to the windows, pushes aside the curtains, and lustily slams open the shutters. Bright sunlight pours into the Key Largo Hotel. The storm is over. The sun is shining. Happy days are here again!

All this, and neither Bogie nor Bacall ever set foot in the Florida Keys. Most of the movie *Key Largo* was shot on a sound stage in California. But that's beside the point to the people of Key Largo. Never have you seen a town so thoroughly milk an opportunity.

Key Largo, The Song

In 1980, songwriter Bertie Higgins's girlfriend Beverly told him she wanted to end their romance. "I figured the only way I could get her attention was to get a song on the radio," Higgins says. So he wrote the song "Key Largo," based on the couple's many romantic times here. In 1982, the song was a smash hit. Beverly married Bertie and they now have two kids.

Higgins grew up in Tarpon Springs, Florida, where he lives still. But he has been coming to the Keys since he was a little kid, and he still comes here often to fish and to check on his business, the Rum Runners Bar at the Holiday Isle Resort.

Other Bertie Higgins songs are "Just Another Day in Paradise" and "Casa Blanca." What he needs now is another song on the radio… Beverly has left him again.

Historic Sites

The African Queen & The Thayer
Holiday Harbour Marina, MM 100 Oceanside ✶ 451-4655

You've got to admire the people at the Key Largo Holiday Inn for taking a couple of boats with illustrious pasts—the *African Queen* and the *Thayer IV*—and blending them into a theme that is used again and again throughout the resort. The gift shop carries black-and-white poster-sized photos of Humphrey Bogart and Katherine Hepburn. You can buy hats and shirts like the ones they wore in the film *The African Queen*. And after you look through the gift shop, you can have a sandwich at Bogie's Cafe.

If you remember watching the the *African Queen* floating through the jungle in the film, you probably remember the boat as being a bigger vessel than it actually is. When you see it in real life, it's quite small and

The African Queen

plain. Sometimes the *African Queen* goes on the road to make guest appearances in other places. Sometimes her aging engine is out of order, but other times when everything is working just fine, she will take you for a ride. An older friend of mine went for a ride on the *African Queen* and thought it was one of the high points of his life! Others will find the trip quite tame, no matter how illustrious the stars who once occupied it may have been.

Charter groups of up to fifteen can rent the 1912, thirty-foot English steam-powered *African Queen* for a party or wedding or whatever they like for around $250. A simple ride is $15 per person.

The battered-looking Chris Craft baking in the sun in the white pea-rock yard by the Holiday Inn pool is supposed to be the *Thayer IV*, which appeared in the Oscar-winning film *On Golden Pond*. But recently one of the ladies at the counter in the Bogie, Bacall and Katherine Hepburn-themed Holiday Inn gift shop, told me that the real *Thayer* is in storage because the tropical sun was frying it into oblivion. The one in the yard is the real *Thayer's* movie double.

The Community Center
MM 91.7 Oceanside ☎ 451-9401

Originally, this neat little building was a Methodist church, located somewhere on the other side of the street. Later, when it was a masonic lodge, the masons moved the building to the oceanside of the Overseas Highway where it still stands today. It was built, the current lessee says, of debris following the 1935 hurricane, and indeed the beams are old and battered but also substantial looking.

Jan Gonzalez has turned the place into a cleverly decorated shop that women love. Local artists supply good jewelry and leather belts. She also has for sale a collection of antique fabrics and a couple of signed Keith Haring posters. In fact, everything you see here is for sale.

The Albury House
MM 91.7 Oceanside

When a Key Largo postmaster named Albury built his island home in 1913, he used huge beams at the foundation so that, in the event of hurricanes, the house would float. And that's exactly what it did when the

1935 Labor Day Hurricane hit the Upper Keys. Albury's house knocked the Key Largo train station over on its side, and then, when the waters receded, ended up sitting squarely on top of it. They don't build 'em like that anymore.

For more stories about Albury and other historic figures from Key Largo's legendary past, start up a chat with the merchant who sells antiques, collectibles and good junk in Albury's famous house.

Caribbean Club
MM 104 Bayside ✹ 451-9970

A nostalgia stop, since one or two exterior scenes for the movie *Key Largo* were supposedly filmed here, although the majority of the film was shot on a Hollywood sound stage. Still, a big sign out front says: "Where the famous movie *Key Largo* was filmed." A serious drinker's bar, this place opens daily at 7 a.m. and stays open until 4 a.m. If you show up for a Bloody Mary first thing in the morning, no one will look twice. Why not enjoy your eye-opener at a picnic table out back with everybody else? Live music some nights is enjoyed by a mixed clientele of locals, tourists, and curiosity seekers. You're as likely to spot a bona fide Keys character here as anywhere else. At the Waverunner rental place next door to the Caribbean Club, we spotted a topless girl sunbathing as the traffic on the Overseas Highway sped past. Also, bikers! Happy hour is a busy time at the Caribbean, so prices must be very good, because not one person came outside to ogle the topless girl in the yard next door. Filming for a new movie entitled *Blood & Wine*, starring Jack Nicholson and Michael Caine, closed the Caribbean Club down for a week in January 1996. And this time, the stars themselves showed up, unlike Bogie and Bacall.

John Pennekamp Coral Reef State Park

John Pennekamp Coral Reef State Park
MM 102.5 Oceanside ☎ 451-1202 or 451-1621

The gates to this hugely popular state park open daily at 8 a.m., often to a line of waiting cars. On particularly busy days, the park has been known to reach capacity crowds and shut its gates as early as 9:30 a.m. At first glance the park might seem small, but actually it is quite large, encompassing 53,660 acres of submerged land and 2,350 acres of uplands. You can see just about the entire above-ground areas of the park from the observation tower. Well over a million people visit the park annually.

This is America's first and only underwater state park. We can thank *Miami Herald* newspaper editor John Pennekamp for alerting his readers and government leaders to the importance of preserving America's only living coral reef. Before the 1960s when Pennekamp began writing his fiery editorials urging Washington to take a stand on maintaining South Florida's unique natural assets, tourists and divers were well on their way to destroying the reef's population of queen conch, live coral, and tropical fish. Aggressive visitors carved, tore or even dynamited chunks of living coral for souvenirs, perhaps believing that what they were taking away would be replaced by nature. Or perhaps not thinking at all.

In 1963 a gift of several million dollars was anonymously donated to the Florida Park Service for use in acquiring the location of the park's headquarters.

The Coral Reef Theater

A very comfortable visitor center features a giant reconstruction of a living patch reef in a floor-to-ceiling circular aquarium. It is the first opportunity most people have to observe the bright, little inhabitants of the underwater world—swimming, eating and resting, just as they do at the reef. Visitors can then check out several topnotch natural history exhibits, too.

Perhaps later your kids will have questions about sharks, eels, and other scary creatures of the deep. Find the park marine biologist in the theater, who will be happy to answer them.

In the Reef Theater a terrific slide show provides an enormous amount of education and much that you need to know to negotiate the reef. You learn how delicate the living reef is and how you can do your part to preserve it for future generations: simple stuff like not touching the coral and using diving buoys instead of anchoring; these make a big difference. After you visit the Reef Theater, you'll understand why reef etiquette is so vitally important.

Warning: nothing will whet your appetite for a visit to the reef like a visit to the Reef Theater first.

The coral reef

Pennekamp Diving

The living reefs are spectacular aquatic gardens of hard and soft corals. The reef is home to 600 species of tropical fish—more fish by far than in any other reef in the world, thanks to its proximity to the grasslands and mangroves of the Florida Bay, spawning grounds to hundreds of species.

These reefs provide 75% of the sport fish and 90% of the commercially-harvested sealife in South Florida.

Along with the 600 varieties of tropical fish there are more than fifty species of hard and soft corals live there too, with fanciful names like stag, elkhorn, brain, and tree. Soft corals are the fans and whips that undulate in the soft currents. Diving trips to the reef are managed by the Coral Reef Park Company. Snorkeling tours depart three times a day and cost around $25 per person. Scuba trips leave twice a day and cost a few dollars more. Combined snorkeling and sailing on a half-day combo tour aboard a 38-foot catamaran are around $32 per person. Diving instruction and equipment are available for an extra charge.

Bill Barron manages the dive shop inside John Pennekamp State Park. Like many of the people who live and work in Key Largo, Bill has enormous enthusiasm for diving America's only living reef and truly loves getting people out onto the ocean and into the water. As a kid Bill remembers watching the television show *Sea Hunt*, which starred Lloyd Bridges as a scuba diver for hire, facing both perils and triumphs beneath the sea.

"That show started it all for me," Bill says.

He learned to dive in California but found his way to Key West where he worked as a diver for Mel Fisher's Treasure Salvors. One of the things he recalls about those days is how Mel would rouse the divers each morning, saying "Hey guys, today's the day." Bill says that Mel's daily pep talk always worked, and, eventually, they found the treasure.

"Diving never gets old," he says. "It's always different, every time you go."

Pennekamp Beach

For the non-diver there are beaches, albeit man-made, and not at all wild or rugged, or terribly tropical. Still, they're nice enough for a couple of hours. Look for a sunken Spanish galleon off one beach where beginning snorkelers can practice and even go home with true stories of wreck diving. You can enjoy swimming, picnicking, and fishing, and boat ramp access on the beach, too. If all you want to do is lie in the sun while the rest of the gang heads out for the reef, fine. You'll be happy here—and close to shelter, food and water.

Pennekamp Camping

Pennekamp Park Manager Bob Wilhelm grew up in South Florida. Because he loves camping and the natural world so much, he majored in park management at college. He's been the manager at Pennekamp for nearly four years and is still in awe of his good fortune in landing a job he thoroughly enjoys. "This is what I love to do," Bob says. "And now I'm getting paid to do it."

In all of the state parks, half of the sites are reserved for up to, but not more than, sixty days in advance. The others are left open and available daily on a first-come, first-served basis. During the summer months your chances of finding a site are quite good, but during the season, from around mid-December through April, procuring a camping site in the state park without a reservation is a hit-or-miss affair. Sign the waiting list at the rangers' station in the morning, then at 3 p.m. the park ranger will announce how many sites are available, and to whom they will go. It is not uncommon to turn away fifty camping parties in a day.

The maximum stay in a state park campground is two weeks. Yes, some campers stay for two weeks, drive out of the park, and then drive in again to get around the regulation. But such maneuvers don't work very easily in wintertime.

At the Pennekamp Park, you'll have a dump site but no individual sewer hookups. Forty-seven campsites for tents or RVs each cost around $25 per night. Electricity is an additional $2 per day. Scouts or school groups can stay in the youth camping area which features water only but is quite inexpensive at $1 per person, for up to twenty-four people, providing most of them are kids.

Camp bathhouses are pristine, and the campsite areas are also clean and well maintained. The majority of the campers are in long, sophisticated RV campers; a few are in tents. During summer months tents are hot; bugs are hellish. Summers are when those big, mobile campers make the most sense. Pennekamp campers have 24-hour access to the beaches and the areas throughout the park that are often mobbed by day. Imagine a full moon rising over the sandy-edged lagoon....

All can enjoy the interpretive programs, nature walks and talks at Pennekamp. An ever-popular theme is the "Delicate Balance of Nature" series. Friday evening presentations during January and February are open to the public. Audiences of well over a hundred nature lovers turn out to hear these free lectures. To get a list of Friday night talks scheduled during your visit, phone the ranger station during daylight hours.

Bob Wilhelm advises tent campers to bring air mattresses for more comfortable sleeping. Remember, the Keys are actually the gnarly spine of an ancient coral reef. In the summertime, sign on for an electricity hook-up, and bring a fan. If you're lucky, the fan will blow off some of the bugs.

To Know More

The brochures and charts created for John Pennekamp Park are translated into German, French, and Spanish. Write John Pennekamp Coral Reef Park, P.O. Box 487, Key Largo, FL 33037. Phone the Coral Park Company at 305-451-1621, for diving tours and boat rentals. For camping information and reservations, phone the ranger station at 305-451-1202.

Diving

Getting Your Divers License

The Professional Association of Diving Instructors, or PADI, has designed a Discover Scuba Diving course for tourists. Local instructors call it the resort course. The course begins early in the morning, breaks for lunch and then boats out to the reef for two instructor-accompanied dives. The course costs $150 each for two or more students, and $200 for a single student.

It is not uncommon for people to take the resort course and then decide that they want to take the (usually) three-day certification course. Most dive shops will give resort course grads a break on the price of the PADI certification course, which generally costs around $350 each for two students, $400 for one.

PADI certification is recognized all over the world. Some people will take the preliminary instruction for certification in their hometowns and then complete the final diving segments of the course here in the Keys.

It is important to understand that hours spent on the resort course do not count toward a full certification course, the driver's license of diving. The resort course is a one-shot deal—instant gratification for people in a hurry. If you are unsure whether or not you are interested in diving as a lifelong avocation and have only a day or two in the Keys, the resort course is probably for you. If you're certain that you're going to scuba frequently, skip the resort course and plan your visit to the Keys around the certification course, or take it in your hometown, if possible, before you get here.

For information about becoming certified, or about taking a resort course, contact any dive shop.

Some Famous Dives

Key Largo Dry Rocks and The Christ of the Abyss Statue
"This is as close as most of you will ever get to Jesus," the dive master says as you prepare to enter the water for a look at the submerged Christ of the Abyss statue. The 4,000-pound, nine-foot sculpture stands in twenty-five feet of water; it's a replica of a statue of the same name located in the water off Genoa, Italy. This underwater sculpture, located six miles east-northeast of Key Largo's South Cut, is said to be the most photographed underwater sculpture in the world. The famous statue was donated to the Underwater Society of America by an Italian diving group in 1961, but it wasn't until 1965 that it was placed in the park. Christ's hands are raised toward the surface, gesturing a welcome to hundreds of daily visitors. It's the area's most requested snorkel dive, and it really is dramatic. Several diving lovers have been married here.

Molasses Reef
It's the most popular dive destination in the world! Five miles straight out from Key Largo, the Molasses Reef features a classic spur-and-groove pattern. (Spurs are the high towers of coral; grooves are the areas of sand that run between them.) This spectacular and radiantly healthy reef covers around seventeen acres, and contains several variant types of topography. The Molasses Reef begins near the water's surface and slopes away from the light to a depth of fifty-five feet. Schools of spadefish, permit, goatfish, and horse-eye jacks share the reef with turtles and manta rays. Molasses Reef is the sole destination of area glass bottomed boat tours as well as many smaller dive boats. Visibility is usually good here, thanks to a regular flushing from the north-flowing Gulf Stream current.

French Reef
North of Molasses, about four-and-a-half miles southeast of Key Largo's South Cut, the reef sits below forty-five feet of water and is marked by a black piling. Scuba divers swim through cave-like passages filled with small fish; a favorite is Christmas Tree Cave.

The Elbow

Where the reef makes a sharp turn back toward the shore, this part takes on a crook-like, elbow formation. The water is clear here, thanks to its proximity to the Gulf Stream, so you can see a couple of moray eels as well as angelfish, filefish and barracuda. The *City of Washington* wreck is located in this area, too, about twenty-five feet below the water's surface. Also, Mike's Wreck—which is not actually the true name of the sunken ship. It's unknown, so a diver named Mike decided to name it after himself. A third wreck nearby is the subject of much controversy. Nobody knows its true name either, and no one has come along to name it in the meantime.

Grecian Rocks/White Banks

About three-fourths of a mile south/southwest of the Christ of the Abyss area, this dive is popular with snorkelers because the water is shallow, twenty-five feet at deepest. In fact, in some areas the corals nearly touch the surface, so watch your belly. Don't touch the corals; just look!

The Carysfort Light

Because this area is so far north—nearly five-and-a-half miles from Key Largo Harbor—few dive boats travel here. It just takes too long to get to it. Divers, after all, would rather be in the water doing what they came to do rather than cruising over the water on their way to some far-flung area of the reef.

The Carysfort Lighthouse marks a reef that is treacherous for boats but divine for divers. The shallow waters around the 112-foot lighthouse are rich with hard corals and schools of grunts, angelfish, parrotfish, butterflyfish and pufferfish. It's also rich with great history.

In the early 1800s, the Carysfort Reef, which got its name from the wreck of the HMS *Carysfort* that went aground here in 1770, was considered the most dangerous to shipping of all the reefs in the Keys. In 1826, the U.S. government anchored a lightboat here to warn vessels away from the treacherous shoals. The seven men who lived aboard the lightboat one day rowed to the shore, and then to an unsettled wilderness, to plant a garden of vegetables and fruit. That garden is believed to have been in the area that is today the headquarters of Pennekamp State Park.

In June 1837 during the Second Seminole Indian War, another group of men from the lightboat rowed ashore for some fresh supplies from their garden and were ambushed by a band of Seminole warriors. Two men were killed that day; one was Captain John Whalton, whose descendants live in the Keys today.

In 1852 the lightboat finally was replaced by the Carysfort Reef Lighthouse, the first of the six iron screw-pile structures that light the Florida Keys reefs today.

The Duane and Bibb

Two Coast Guard cutters were sunk intentionally to form an artificial reef a mile south of Molasses Reef. The twin 327-foot boats were laid to rest on a white sand bottom in 1987. The *Duane* landed upright with its crow's nest just sixty feet below the surface; the *Bibb* lies one hundred feet deep. Visibility is good, but the current is sometimes strong enough to make diving inadvisable. This is a dive for expert scuba divers, not because of the depth—although it is deep—but because of that powerful current.

Aquarius Underwater Habitat

For scuba divers only, this underwater habitat rests in sixty feet of water and, for up to nine days at a time, is home to researchers working for the marine sanctuary. A support barge on the surface marks the location of the *Aquarius*.

City of Washington Wreck

Just offshore of the Elbow reef lies the remains of the ship *City of Washington*. The wreck, in twenty to thirty-five feet of water, is known for its abundant and friendly fish population. Besides the wildlife, the scattered wreckage provides an excellent backdrop for underwater photography.

The Benwood Wreck

The Benwood was a 285-foot-long freighter, accidentally rammed while running without lights during WWII, and then torpedoed by a German submarine as it attempted to ground itself for later salvage. Its hull now lies in around fifty feet of water and is home to several huge groupers.

Key Largo Undersea Park's Emerald Lagoon
MM 51 Shoreland Drive ✹ 451-2353

On windy days, the Emerald Lagoon is the busiest dive site around because it's protected from strong winds so the water doesn't get choppy or stirred up. That's why people say, "There's no such thing as a bad day in the Emerald Lagoon." But that's not the only reason to visit the lagoon; because the habitat is so different here from that of the reef, you will see different sealife as well as a shipwreck and several archaeological sites. Sometimes a manatee finds its way into the lagoon, to the great joy of staff and visitors alike.

Dive Shops & Charters

Amoray Dive Resort
MM 104.5 Bayside ✹ 800-4-AMORAY

Amy Slate has been performing underwater weddings for eighteen years. She'll supply tuxedo T-shirts, veils, pearls, and conch shell bouquets to couples taking the big plunge. Receptions are often held on the *Amoray Diver*, a 45-foot catamaran. If you want to do it beneath the surface, call the Amoray Resorts wedding coordinator, who will arrange for dive photographers and videographers, entertainers and caterers. In an average week during season, Amy Slate performs two to three weddings.

By the way, you'll also find standard diving services at the Amoray Dive Resort.

It's a Dive
MM 102.5 Bayside, at the Marriott Key Largo
451-2377 ✹ 800-809-9881

What a name, huh? But it was recognized as the number-one day-boat operator in the February 1996 readers' poll of *Scuba Diving Magazine*. "It's a Dive" also ranked number three for best operation in the United States. We spent an hour talking to a wonderfully kind and helpful young woman at the It's A Dive and came away thinking she was the nicest person we'd ever met. Then we wandered through many more dive shops and discovered that dive people are simply a wonderful bunch!

John Pennekamp Coral Reef State Park
MM 102.5 ✺ 451-1621
Here's a great dive concession with terrific employees, and these state park prices seem a tad lower than private businesses. See the John Pennekamp Park Diving section for more on this shop.

Sharky's Dive Center
MM 106.2 Bayside (and two more nearby locations)
451-5533 ✺ 800-935-3483
In four short years Danny Stahl has expanded his business from a one-man, one-snorkel boat operation into a small fleet of vessels run by twenty-eight employees. Today, Sharky's is headquartered in a 3600-square-foot shop, its walls and shelves lined with fascinating dive stuff. The people who run the place are enthusiastic and helpful and full of information. Sharky's offers dive tours, equipment rentals and sales, and all kinds of merchandise related to reef and wreck diving.

Sharky's Machine, the double-decker dive boat that started it all is still going strong. A couple newer vessels are the *Mean Machine* and the *Extreme Machine*. Sharky's dive boats are equipped with freshwater showers and offer on-board refreshments. Prices are competitive with other dive-tour operations in the area.

Why Sharky's? "We have the fastest and newest toys," one happy Sharky's employee says.

Caribbean Shipwreck Museum and Research Institute
Maritime Museum of the Florida Keys
MM 102.6 Bayside ✺ 451-6444
Across the street from the entrance to John Pennekamp. Listed in at least one free guidebook as two attractions, these two names are actually one place. Dedicated to the pursuit and the romance of sunken treasure, the museum sets the mood for the Keys. Exhibits are rare maritime artifacts like bits and pieces of tools, Chinese blue and white porcelain,

jewelry, and such dubious treasures as ancient cargo hooks and hull scrapers, all plucked from the ocean floor.

Historical exhibits tell of the arrival of Columbus and his discovery of the native Americans named "Indians" by Chris and his crew. Gruesome descriptions create images of Indian tortures perpetrated upon doomed explorers and sailors: pouring molten gold down their throats is one. Also on display are tales of wicked lady pirates, raised as boys and just as tough as any guy pirates; quotes from a book of treasure stories by Howard Pyle, called *Dead Men Tell No Tales*; a whale's skull; and stories of fleets of wrecks, lolling for centuries under the sea, strewing their fantastic treasures for miles and miles around. If you're fascinated by the very real possibility of recovering sunken treasure off Florida's coast, you'll enjoy the displays and information you see here. View a 20-minute film about the discovery of coins from the 18th-century Spanish fleet that sank off the coast of Sebastian, Florida, during a fierce hurricane; that will get your treasure salvor's blood boiling. At the beginning of the film, Mel Fisher himself grins into the camera and says: "There's plenty of treasure here for everybody!" Finding it is the hard part, right Mel?

Don't miss the small but fascinating exhibit of items from the wreck *Henrietta Marie*, the first documented slave ship discovered in the Florida Straits in the 1970s. The display shows arm and leg shackles and an artist's rendering of the arrangement of the ship's hold, where hundreds of humans were transported from Africa to North America. This partial exhibit is a vivid reminder of what went on in the world not so terribly long ago. A much larger exhibit of the *Henrietta Marie* is currently touring America.

What little amusement kids will find in this double museum is quickly exhausted, one employee told me. But they all love the gift shop. Museum admission is $5 for adults; $3 for kids under 12; kids under 6 go in free.

Dolphins In Paradise

DOLPHINS ARE WONDERFUL, mysterious and very much at home in the waters of the Florida Keys. For many people, there is no greater thrill than to see dolphins up close and enjoy their remarkably sweet vibes. Many tourists list their interest in dolphins as a prime motivation for visiting the Florida Keys, where dolphins are as much an icon as palm trees.

For centuries man has been intrigued with the sea's most popular denizen. Dolphins are playful, sociable and smart, and they appear to enjoy humans as much as humans enjoy them. Do dolphins have a natural affinity for man? No, says one trainer, but, he adds, dolphins in captivity do come to associate humans with fun, toys and food.

Caring for dolphins is a much-coveted job in the Keys. Dolphin trainers who often have degrees in psychology or zoology, are dedicated and passionate about their charges, and very patient.

"You don't get a five-hundred-pound animal to do anything it doesn't want to do," says one.

Dolphins, who are very trainable, have excellent long-term memory which enables them to use past experiences to form new judgments. They have highly developed sonar or ultrasound-like mechanisms they use to find objects as small as coins tossed into their areas, and they even have the ability, many trainers believe, to detect tumors in humans.

Dolphins are sexy creatures, too. Males denied sex by the objects of their affection become frustrated and irritable. Dolphins in captivity are taught that sexual excitement, as evidenced by erections that grow to an average length of eighteen inches, is not appropriate when swimming with humans.

Play between dolphins can be surprisingly rough, but they are gentle and cautious with humans, particularly so with those who are physically or mentally challenged. Therapists working with autistic children find that dolphins are inexhaustible when coaxing disturbed children to respond to them. Long after humans have run out of endurance and

patience in dealing with this strange disorder, dolphins will continue
activities to stimulate a child.

This hypersensitivity is one of the dolphin's most remarkable and
endearing charms. Nonetheless, pregnant women are generally not
allowed to swim with dolphins for two reasons. First, a dolphin detecting
two heartbeats in one human may become intrigued and curious and,
sometimes, wholly fascinated with a pregnant woman, ignoring everyone
else for the duration the swim. Second, a startled dolphin can propel
itself at speeds of up to twenty-five miles per hour; this torpedoing dol-

phin could, conceivably, do great harm to a pregnant woman. Though chances of this happening are slim, no one wants to risk it.

Here in the Keys we have Atlantic bottlenose dolphins, which are found along the east coast from New Jersey to the Gulf of Mexico.

Female dolphins tend to stay together, while bachelor males also form their own groups, as do adult males. A lone dolphin in the wild will often seek out human companionship.

When dolphins give birth, they are assisted by companion females, who often stick around to help raise the calf. Dolphins nurse their young up to three years. A mother dolphin is very protective of her first calf, less so with her second, even less with her third, and so on. An adult male dolphin can weigh up to 600 pounds and grow to nine feet long. Females are slightly smaller. Dolphins live for around thirty to forty years.

Dolphins do not drink sea water; they absorb water from the fish they eat. They do not sleep because they do not breathe involuntarily. Instead, they put themselves into a resting state and shut down half of their brains while the other half remains conscious to attend to matters of survival.

The brains of dolphins and humans are about the same size. The odd sounds dolphins make, a series of clicks and whistles, may or may not be a form of dolphin communication. Scientists are not sure, although they do know that each dolphin makes its own distinct sounds, just as humans do.

Because dolphins are such an important part of what makes the Keys wonderful and unique, many opportunities exist here for visitors to observe dolphins, learn about them, and experience a truly rare encounter—a swim with the dolphins.

Since this is one of the most popular activities in the Florida Keys, reservations for classes or swims with dolphins at marine and dolphin centers should be made six to eight weeks in advance at the three facilities listed below. These are the only places in the Keys, at this time, offering the opportunity to swim with dolphins.

A final opportunity, and the one purists like best, is to encounter dolphins in their own territory, the open sea. You might see an impromtu dolphin show performed by dolphins in the wild. We saw one in January at Marathon's Sombrero Beach. Some charter boat captains specialize in knowing where to go to encounter dolphins. Dolphins in the wild socialize when the whim strikes and then disappear in a split second if they catch an odd or threatening vibe.

Dolphin Swims

Dolphins Plus Research Center
MM 100.5, Key Largo ✱ 451-1993

Not a theme park or a show, Dolphins Plus is a research and educational center. How dolphins relate to humans and the dolphin's role in zoo-therapy with disabled children is studied here. The center claims that their dolphins are not captive, since several times each month, they are given the opportunity to swim out of the canal and into the ocean. They *choose* to live at the center.

An hour of education precedes the thirty-minute swim. Before entering the water you are warned that dolphins will not approach if they sense that you are uptight or in an aggressive mood. You are instructed not to reach out to them, but to swim as if there were no dolphins around. Trainers will tell you that dolphins like children best, women second, and men, a distant third.

Because these dolphins are untrained, they do only what they feel like doing. So you won't see them gobble tossed fish, leap into the air for rewards, or perform tricks on demand. There is no guarantee that you'll make contact with a dolphin here. Only nine people swim in the dolphins' canal at a time and, since there are seven dolphins, chances for an encounter are good.

If you don't want to swim with dolphins but are curious about them anyway, it costs only around $8 to take the hour-long pre-swim class and stick around to watch your classmates swim with the dolphins. Kids ages 10–18 must swim with an adult guardian. To take the class and the swim that follows (you *must* take the class to swim) costs around $80. Reservations are definitely a must, but during the off season you have a good chance of reserving a space on short notice. You'll be asked for a deposit to secure your reservation.

Dolphin Research Center
MM 59, Grassy Key ✶ 289-0002

This is the oldest dolphin facility in the Keys, founded thirty-seven
years ago as a marine educational facility called the Porpoise School.
Swimming with dolphins started here over thirty years ago. The giant
statue of a bottlenose dolphin out front is a replica of Mitzi, who starred
in the feature-length movie *Flipper*, the forerunner of the television
series. Mitzi died in 1972, but her daughter and grandson are still at the
center.

Dolphin swims go on in a natural lagoon of the Gulf of Mexico. The
trained dolphins are retained by plastic mesh fencing. Here, as in all dolphin facilities, before you swim with dolphins you must learn about them.
You'll be briefed on how to conduct yourself and what to expect of them
during your twenty-minute swim. The rule of thumb is always this: swim
as though there were no dolphins in the water at all. Play innocent. You
will also be advised to use your arms as little as possible to avoid alarming
the dolphins. No other creature swims like a human, instructors warn.

Cost of the training and the swim is $90. Special arrangements can be
made for children under twelve. You should plan on spending three-and-
a-half hours on this trip, since the training is considerably longer at this
facility than at the others.

Theater of the Sea
MM 84.5 Oceanside, Islamorada ✶ 664-2431

Pregnant women, people under age thirteen, and those who do not
speak, read and understand English are not allowed to swim with the
dolphins here. Thirty-minute dolphin swims are preceded by a half-hour
of instruction. Swimming is in a natural ocean water lagoon with trained
dolphins. Cost is $80, and includes admission to the park's many fine
marine shows.

An alternative to a swim is a three-hour dolphin trainer-for-a-day
program. For this, you don't even need to get wet, but you might get
splashed a little when you feed the dolphins their lunch. You'll learn to
prepare fish for dolphins to eat, and discover why and how dolphins do
the quirky things they do. You'll have the opportunity to show off your
dolphin training skills at a regularly scheduled dolphin show—just like
a real trainer! You must be ten years old or older to do this, and it costs

$75. There is no guarantee that you will not beg to sign up for a swim with the dolphins after you spend a few hours learning about them.

So many people contact the Theater of the Sea about jobs as dolphin trainers that they have a pre-printed sheet of information. Write for it or any other information about the dolphin programs.

A four-hour dolphin adventure diving trip, in which you'll cover thirteen miles of coast, snorkel for thirty minutes at a nearby reef, and learn an enormous amount about the history and biology of the Keys ecosystem, is available for $35, which includes snorkel gear. There is no guarantee that you'll see dolphins on this trip, but seeing them is what everybody is hoping for. If the vibes are right, you just might catch a thrill, but even if you don't meet a dolphin, it's a neat trip anyway. The boat leaves at 9 a.m. daily.

Dolphin Encounters

Dolphin Watch
Key West ● 294-6306

Captain Ron Canning has been introducing people to his dolphin friends for nine years since he's been visiting a particular pod of around thirty male, female and baby dolphins for nearly a decade, he is extremely knowledgeable about them. Captain Ron bases the decision on where to go to look for his pod of dolphins on a number of factors each day: the weather, the phase of the moon, the tides, and the number of children in the party. Dolphins love children, and they're usually curious to know whom Captain Ron has brought to meet them.

The best time of the year for encountering dolphins in the wild, Captain Ron says, is between April and October. Captain Ron takes up to six people on four-hour charters aboard his 31-foot catamaran. He charges $65 a person, and there is a four person minimum. It is important to call ahead for reservations; call also for a brochure or for more information.

Captain Vicki Impallomeni
Murray's Marina, U.S. 1, Stock Island ✆ 294-9731

Wilderness guide Captain Vicki knows where the dolphins are likely to be. Once you get to the dolphin playground, the captain turns off the engines and waits to see if the dolphins are in the mood to come out and play. Music attracts them, and so Captain Vicki often coaxes them out with bouncy stuff like a polka or a spirited Strauss waltz. Dolphins swim under the boat and around it.

Each time she visits the dolphins, Vicki says, they respond differently. Sometimes they disappear as suddenly as they appeared. Other times, they stick around while snorkelers gingerly don snorkel gear and slip into the water to watch them and listen to their strange language of whistles and clicks. You will be warned by Captain Vicki not to touch the dolphins. Remember, these are natural, free dolphins, swimming with you for fun, not for a reward. They like to see you laugh; they enjoy making you happy. Sometimes, if they're in the right mood, and you're keeping their attention, they'll perform. Just remember: the sea is their environment. You are the guests.

Captain Vicki charges $275 for four-hour charters, $375 for eight hours, in her boat, which holds six people. Her popular trips are booked months in advance, so it's best to make reservations. If she has no openings available, her answering machine will direct you to some of her fellow wilderness guides.

Hawk's Cay Resort & Marina
MM 61, Duck Key ✆ 800-432-2242

The Chicago Zoological Society maintains a dolphin training and breeding facility at Hawk's Cay Resort. Dolphins are fed daily at 10 a.m.,1 p.m. and 4 p.m., and they're required to perform for their meals. The show is free. Dolphins live in a fenced-in, saltwater lagoon along the coast of Hawk's Cay. You do not swim with the dolphins here; you only observe them.

Natural Wonders

Harry Harris Park
MM 92.5, Oceanside

Follow the signs to the park and, on the way, as you pass through a residential area, you'll see where the waitresses, fishing guides and shopkeepers of Key Largo actually live. (This is a good destination for bicyclists—a chance to get away from the noisy, beaten path.)

Harry Harris Park is the site of one of the Upper Keys earliest settlements, the town of Planter. In the late 1800s, Planter had seven farms, a chapel, a post office, a general store and several piers. Pineapples were the main crop. But in 1906, and again in 1909, Planter was hit by devastating hurricanes. When the pineapple business began to fail due not

Pineapple

only to these hurricanes but poor agricultural procedures, and blights, people began leaving for higher ground and easier lives elsewhere. By the end of 1942, nothing was left of Planter but memories.

This same site is now Harry Harris Park, which is a pretty super little park containing a man-made lagoon with clear ocean water, a well-maintained beach, a kid-pleasing playground, and restrooms, picnic tables and BBQ grills so clean you'll want to run out and buy charcoal and hamburgers. Pay phones are available for those who can't quite give in to getting away from it all. The park, rarely crowded, opens at sunrise and closes at sunset. On weekdays it's free and open to the public; on weekends and holidays, visitors from outside of Monroe County—your license plate gives you away—must pay $5 per person to enter and $10 to use the recently upgraded boat ramp. All kids under 12 always enter for free, no matter where they're from.

The county employee who sits in the booth at the park's entrance will kindly entertain your questions about the beach, the birds and the islands you spot from the shoreline. Maybe he doesn't know all the answers, but he's friendly and helpful, and he's happy for the diversion.

Dolphins Plus Research Center
MM 100.5 Oceanside (Call ahead for directions) ✆ 451-1993
"Experience the thrill of swimming with the dolphins" says the brochure. Understand that this is not an amusement park or a dolphin show. And unless you take a mandatory class, you won't see a dolphin at all. It's important to make arrangements well in advance if you're planning a swim with the dolphins. But always check. Sometimes you can get lucky and find there are lots of slots open and find yourself in the swim by that afternoon. Either way, you pay in advance. (See the chapter on Dolphins.)

Everglades National Park
242-7700
Florida's river of grass is a 1.5-million acre ecosystem and the only one of its kind in the world. The park runs west from the bay side of Key Largo, around the southwest corner of the Florida mainland and then north all the way to Everglades City. Much of the Florida Bay is within its nearly

10,700 square miles. Within the park live 300 species of birds, plus alligators, crocodiles, deer and bobcats. Mosquitoes can be horrific, especially
in the spring and summer. You'll definitely need bug repellent if you venture into these amazing marine wilds. Eco-tours and fishing expeditions
easily access the park via the Florida Bay. While it is possible to rent a
skiff and head into the Everglades National Park on your own, it is not
advisable. Hire a guide and leave the driving to the experts. The park is
a huge labyrinth of creeks, lakes, rivers and shallow plains of seagrass.

State Road 9336 is the main road into and out of Everglades National
Park. To get to the closest entrance to SR 9336, you must go to
Homestead, approximately twenty-two miles north of Key Largo.

For a list of available guided tours as well as canoeing, fishing, camping and hiking information and accommodations inside the park, call
242-7700. Or write: Park Headquarters, 40001 State Road 9336,
Homestead, FL 33034.

Geology Lesson at MM 103

For a look at the geological makeup of the Upper Keys' fossilized coral
rock, stop at the bridge that crosses over the Marvin D. Adams waterway.
The banks of the man-made cut, a neat cross-slice through the island,
provide a look into the make-up of the coral rock foundation of the
Upper Keys: staghorn coral, coral heads, and other formations are petrified in the walls. It's really difficult to slow down enough to see anything
close up, so stop the car, get out, and walk—carefully, with an eye out for
traffic.

Wild Bird Rehabilitation Center
Mile Marker 93.6 Bayside ☎ 852-4486

Although the primary purpose of the center is to provide emergency and
recuperative care to injured birds, the bird center has evolved into a popular nature information center. Several daily tours through the area and
on a boardwalk along the Florida Bay feature plants, mangroves, and
berry trees that are food to birds, but poison to man! The five-acre sanctuary is kept as close to the sea birds' natural habitat as possible.

Injured birds are brought to the center for rehabilitation. Pelicans,
which are quite comfortable around people, are the center's biggest cus-

Pelican

tomers. Director and founder Laura Quinn says that birds who hang around humans a lot get into lots of trouble. Most of their injuries are from baited hooks and fishing line carelessly tossed aside by fishermen. You'll recognize the birds' broken wings by the bright blue "casts" they wear on the injured appendage. The center is also a convalescent center for cormorants, egrets, herons, and the rarely seen roseate spoonbills. It's easy to see why the fantastic pink feathers of the roseate spoonbill were so attractive to hat designers in the years before the world understood that the supply of birds was finite.

With no admission fee, they hope you will donate whatever you can after you've seen the significance of the operation to Florida's natural world. The center is not government-funded and not likely to be in the near future. It is solely supported by private donations. Quinn started the bird sanctuary in 1991. Since then, she says, the Keys environment has become more and more perilous for birds.

Great white heron

Laura's seven cats and one dog share the grounds with a lot of birds here, and all seems to go well. You can see Laura's artwork, wooden bird carvings, in the gift shop. Laura Quinn is a special woman, and so are the others who work with her. A favorite volunteer is Marvin Galanty, father of four, grandfather of seven, whose natural affinity for birds, and children, makes him an invaluable source of information on the natural world. Marvin delivers his lessons in easily understood terms. And he never, ever runs out of energy or enthusiasm.

Key Largo Hammocks State Botanical Site
Route 905, Upper Key Largo
451-1202 (Pennekamp Park Ranger Station)

It's located less than half a mile before or after U.S. Route 1 and SR 905 converge in Key Largo, depending upon which way you're headed. One thousand acres of tropical hardwood forest were partially developed before the State of Florida began acquiring the property for the formation of the present Key Largo Hammock in 1982. Port Bougainvillea was planned to be a massive community of pink stucco condos smack in the heart of a natural habitat to nearly all of the Keys twenty-two endangered species. Environmentalists fought wildly to keep the place holy. And what a glorious battle it was! You can still see the entrance gate and the proliferation of bougainvillea planted there by hopeful developers. Today, it looks a little like the faded entrance to an abandoned southern plantation.

If you take a good look at the fountain just past the beginning of the trail, you'll get some idea of just how grand a place Port Bougainvillea was to have been. Now, that fountain is a gigantic birdbath serving several species of birds. The turkey buzzards seem not to mind a human or two walking by, but the great blue herons mind very much and lift off into the sky with a noisy and dramatic shudder of their wings the minute you approach.

On Wednesdays and Saturdays at 10 a.m. during winter and spring, Pennekamp park rangers lead nature walks through the botanical site. Otherwise, brochures at the entrance will lead you on a self-guided tour. Plants and animals that live in the area include poisonwood, lignumvitae, dollar orchid, prickly apple cactus, golden leatherfern, American crocodile, and Key Largo cotton mouse. For information about the area and the guided tours, call the Pennekamp Park Ranger Station.

A Very Cool Library

Key Largo Library
MM 101.5, in Tradewinds Plaza ✹ 451-2396

As libraries go, this one's quite large and plush, with soft-carpeted floors and comfortable reading tables. Good surplus books are on sale for 50¢; surplus magazines and softcover books are free. On exhibit are a huge shell collection and a tiny raft made of canvas and rope and inner tubes that carried four Cubans to Florida. It seems unbelievable that the flimsy raft did the job.

Don't miss the racks with pamphlets and brochures on local attractions and natural wonders. A family could easily spend a hot afternoon cooling off in the air-conditioned environs of the Key Largo Library and, as part of the deal, come away a bit wiser. The library is open every day except Sunday from 10 a.m. till 6 p.m. and until 8 p.m. on Monday and Wednesday. Call ahead for information on Saturday morning children's programs.

Big Fun

Biking

A fifteen-mile bicycle and walking path begins at MM 106 and runs beside the Overseas Highway all the way down to MM 91. The trail is paved and makes for good traveling in northern Key Largo, a little rougher as you move south. It becomes treacherous in places where cars are pulling on or off the road, driving across the bicycle path in a big hurry. Every year somebody—a biker or pedestrian—dies in Key Largo from being hit by a car.

Key Largo Bikes
105 Laguna Avenue (turn at MM 100, Oceanside) ● 451-1910
Simple island cruisers rent for around $10 a day and $40 a week. Emmett Wattignoi, owner of the shop and super nice guy, says he knows a few more bike trails—some beside the road, some not—that will take you all the way down to Lower Matecumbe Key at mile marker 78.

Tavernier Bicycle Depot
MM 92 Bayside ● 852-2859
Another place to rent a bike, it's located at the other end of the Key Largo area. Rental for a day: $10; a week: $49. The people here will also direct you to bike paths; particularly popular is the one that winds around to Harry Harris Park. Baby seats and helmets are available. The Bicycle Depot is also a bike repair shop and a hobby shop featuring remote control planes and boat models. Hobbyists like to poke around this shop. They've recently increased their bike rental business in response to many more requests. Seems like more people are interested in riding around on bikes than they used to be.

Watersports

Caribbean Watersports
MM 97 Bayside, at the Sheraton Resort ℱ 852-4707
Why take a lonely parasail when you can pair-a-sail? That's right. Now
two people at a time can take to the air for 15 minutes of thrills and
views—providing their combined weight is less than 300 pounds.

Also at Caribbean: sailing lessons, Waverunners and Waveblasters
and wind-surfers. They'll also arrange for your snuba lesson and dive trip.
Snuba? It's simpler than scuba, because you don't have to worry about all
that equipment. You breathe air through a tube, or hookah, connected to
a tank of compressed air on the water's surface. But before you're ready to
go out to the reef, you take a lesson in a pool and swim around until you
get used to snuba equipment. The lesson is around $35; the trip to the
reef is $70. Snuba enables you to dive to thirty feet, where you'll see
more sealife and coral formations than you can from lesser depths.

Enviro tours of the Florida Bay aboard a 17-foot Zodiac with a very
quiet electric motor, depart four times daily. The two-hour tour featuring
a close look at the lovely and serene world of the backcountry, is $40.

The Movies

Tavernier Towne Twin Cinema
MM 91.5 Bayside ℱ 852-2023
This is the only movie theater in the Upper Keys. Two newly released
movies roll at 7 p.m. and 9:45 p.m., 365 days a year. No matinees.
Tickets: $6 for adults; $4 children 11 and under. Monday–Thursday are
Senior Citizens nights when tickets are $4 for ages 65 and over with ID.
In addition to the regular movie house concession stand junk, the Twin
Cinema serves some damned fine pizza from a nearby restaurant.

Fishing

A<small>T THE</small> H<small>OLIDAY</small> I<small>NN</small> M<small>ARINA</small> at mile marker 100, you can find out just
about anything you want to know about Key Largo fishing: Deep sea,
backcountry, party boats, private charters. Follow the canal-side
harbor walk, which continues around to the Marina Del Mar boat basin,
and you'll find dozens of boats for hire. Charter people never mind telling
you about their services. And if you hang around and watch for a
while—boats generally come back to shore around 4 p.m.—you'll soon
get the gist of how things work around here.

Otherwise, check with the Key Largo Chamber of Commerce for a
comprehensive list of fishing boats and guides.

Rent A Boat

The Boat Renters Guide to the Florida Keys
800-553-5591

Boating enthusiast and knowledgeable sportswriter Jeff Kelly has published a nifty little book that answers any questions you might have
about renting a boat in the Florida Keys. *The Boat Renters Guide to the
Florida Keys* ($5.95) tells how much it will cost to rent, based on boat
type, engine size, and electronic equipment, as well as where you are
allowed to operate your rental boat. This isn't a book of boating
philosophy; it's hard facts, and much-needed information assembled in
geographical order from Key Largo to Key West. After all, you're choosing from over 500 rental outlets in the Keys—power, sail, houseboats and
kayaks. Although rental rates in the Keys run about the same, what you
get for the same amount of money differs greatly from one outlet to the
next. You'll save yourself not only money but lots of time by zeroing in
on what you really want and need. Also included is a list of boating tips
that could save your life. Order the book using the 800 telephone
number above, or look for it in dive, bait, and tackle shops throughout
the Keys.

Tours by Land and Sea

Captain Ray Cramer's Airboat Tours
852-5339

Ray Cramer will take you on an Everglades airboat ride and nature tour. Ray will point out birds, plants, blooms and alligators. But what many folks like best are his Indian stories about the Tequesta and Caloosa warriors who once ruled the 'glades. Call Ray for times and rates, which vary according to the number of people in your party, and the time of the year. Also, nighttime frogging trips!

Everglades Ecology and Nature Tours and Safari Tours
MM 102, in the Quay Marina ⬧ 451-4540 ⬧ 800-959-0742

Captain Sterling Kennedy and his wife and first mate, Jill, have been taking folks on nature tours of the Everglades National Park for eight years now, and they're still crazy about their work. They operate their fleet of several 25-foot deck boats, and custom built 48-foot pontoons out of the Quay Docks. The boats are designed for the one-to-two-feet-deep shallows of the Everglades and the backcountry.

The Kennedy's offer several ecology and nature tours in the liquid fringes of the Florida Keys. One is a two-hour tour for a maximum of six people or a minimum of two. The tour takes you into the shallow, clear waters of the Everglades where you may see manatees and dolphins, and a rare crocodile. Crocodiles are endangered, and tours are not allowed to enter areas where they are most prevalent. You'll be in the saltwater portion of the Everglades, so you won't see alligators. They're only in fresh water. The tour visits two bird rookery islands, where pink roseate spoonbills, herons, pelicans, cormorants and dozens of species of migratory birds are plentiful.

There are three tours daily in the wintertime, and four tours in the summertime, when the days are longer. Cost is $35 adults, $25 for children. A one-hour abbreviated version of the tour is $20 for adults and $15 for children.

A daily sunset cruise departs at 5 p.m. in the winter, and 7 p.m. in the summer. The champagne sunset cruise is about forty-five minutes long and costs $15 for adults, $10 for kids.

The Kennedys perform many weddings on their large pontoon boat that holds thirty people. Several wedding packages range from $175 to $375, and you are invited to design your own. All weddings include a ceremony performed by Captain Kennedy, and a video of the nuptials, recorded by Jill.

An increasingly popular tour is the mangrove tunnel safari where you boat into the natural cave of the dark interior of a mangrove island. You'll think you're in a far-away jungle. It's even freakier at night, when the Kennedys light up the dank, quiet spaces with a huge spotlight. This is only for the most daring and strong of heart. The tour is about an hour long, and costs $20 for adults. Private charters are also available.

Florida Bay Outfitters Kayak Tours
MM 104, Bayside ✽ 451-3018

Enjoy half or full-day kayak or canoe rentals as well as guided tours of the Florida Bay. Frank Woll has been running this place for five years, and along the way he's learned what tours people like best; what tours go untaken. A very popular trip is overnight camping at North Nest Key with a guide to show the way. For around $140 a person, you get the guide, all the camping gear, food and supplies. Also on self-guided tours, they'll give you a map and rent you the camping gear. They offer discounts for kids, but not all kids are interested in communing with nature in the backcountry, and several other tours with overnight camping to places as far-flung as the Dry Tortugas, which you and the kayaks travel to on a big boat. Frank and his guides are always designing new trips and packages. Call or stop by. Frank can FAX you information, too.

Witt's End Sailing Charters
MM 100 ✽ 451-3354

An utterly romantic getaway for fairy-tale types. Sail from mile marker 100 in Key Largo at sunset. Cruise to an uninhabited island and anchor for the night. If you like, you can get married; just bring the license and the Witts will take care of everything else. Later enjoy a sumptuous wedding dinner and sleep in your own private stateroom. The next morning, enjoy a gourmet breakfast on deck. The overnight wedding package runs around $350. But you don't have to marry, you can just cruise and enjoy. Witt's End, by the way, is renowned for its fine food.

Glass Bottomed Boats

This is one of the most popular attractions in the Keys. The beauty of glass bottom boat tours is that you get to see some of what divers who actually get into the water see—but not all of it. The boats don't really have all-glass bottoms, of course, it's more like they have plexiglass windows that slant from the floor outward, giving you a series of windows into the sea and the reef beneath. For younger or non-swimming children, older folks, or anyone interested in not getting wet, glass bottom boat tours allow for a pretty remarkable glimpse at the other world below the surface of the deceptively calm-looking sea.

It's a good show, especially since, unlike a snorkeler, you'll have a skillful and enthusiastic guide to point out the highlights and to tell you what you're seeing. Often, a trip to the reef will convince you to don snorkeling gear yourself and go for a longer look. All of the glass bottom boat tours in the Key Largo area go to Molasses Reef, which is marked by a 50-foot tower, so you'll know when you're getting close.

Key Largo Princess
Mile Marker 100, Holiday Inn Docks ☛ 451-4655
Up to 123 people can be loaded onto the *Princess,* and it takes forty-five minutes to get out to the reef. You spend twenty-five minutes looking at the Molasses Reef. Then, you turn around and begin the forty-five minute trip back. Adults $14; 11 and under $7. Boat departs at 10 a.m., 1 p.m., and 4 p.m. Aboard the two-hour cruise, hot dogs, sodas, full bar, and bird snacks are available. Most people enjoy feeding the seabirds, which swoop down for a treat when they see the boat coming.

San Jose Glass Bottom Boat
Mile Marker 102.5 at John Pennekamp ✶ 451-1621
Carries 98 people out to the famous and popular Molasses Reef, which has been named by one dive magazine as America's favorite reef. It takes almost an hour to get to the reef. Once there, you and 97 other passengers float atop the waters of the reef, gazing at the sealife below through fiberglass plates for around a half hour. Then you head back to the park. The *San Jose* shoves off every day at 9:15 a.m., 12:15 p.m., and 3 p.m. Set aside three hours total for the trip. When the wind is blowing and the water looks rough, you can be sure that the ride will be rough. Some people will become quite seasick. (Not you, of course.) If at all possible, take this trip on a calm, clear day when visibility is good; hot, soft summer days are best. Otherwise, we recommend a seasick remedy before the fact. Prices around $14 for adults; $9 for kids 11 and under.

Casino Cruises
MM 100, Holiday Inn Marina ✶ 800-THE-KEYS
Gambling is okay on this boat, which cruises to a place just beyond the legal limit, anchors, and remains there all day and late into the night. Main departure is at 2 p.m. daily from Holiday Inn docks at mile marker 100. If you miss the first trip, you can take a water taxi out to the the the boat six times daily. Day trips are $7; evening trips are $11. This 100-foot-long vessel holds 150 passengers and features blackjack, roulette, slots, craps, shipboard lotto, and other games of chance. Minimum bet allowed is $5; maximum is $500. Once you're aboard you're invited to stay as long as you like. There's a full cash bar and a brief a la carte menu. If you're not into gambling, enjoy the upper deck where there's usually a pianist to entertain you. Discounts for senior citizens and, from time to time, other specials. Operates daily, 365 days a year.

A Motor Tour
Best Transportation Company ✶ 451-7027
Here's the trip: You board a nine-passenger van in Key Largo—they'll also pick you up in Islamorada—and head for Key West. Along the way you listen to a taped history of the Keys. Then you make three stops: The first is at Sombrero Beach in Marathon, which really is a great place to

stop. "You gotta let people go to the bathroom," says the guy who sells the tour. "And the bathrooms are clean here." Next stop is Big Pine Key, with the hope of catching a glimpse of a Key deer. At the Blue Hole, a freshwater pond, you're likely to see a couple of very friendly-looking alligators. Don't feed them! Finally you arrive in Old Town, Key West, where you are on your own for four hours. Then, it's back on the bus for a straight trip back to Key Largo. The entire trip covers over 200 miles in ten hours; it's a long day.

"I guarantee that when you finish this tour, you'll know more about the history of the Keys than the people who live here. Otherwise, there's a money-back guarantee. I've never had to give anybody their money back. In fact, people say I don't charge enough," says the guy who sells the tour.

The van doesn't go anywhere until at least four people willing to pay $40 each come aboard.

Accommodations

Y OU CAN HAVE IT ALL in Key Largo, of course, but is that what you really want? Stay at a Sheraton, a Marriott, a Holiday Inn or a Howard Johnson's. You know what you'll get in those places. And often the small, funky places are just as much fun as well as considerably less expensive.

A rule of thumb is this: the closer you get to Key West, the more you'll pay for accommodations that are basically the same, with one big exception. In Key West, only the very finest, most expensive rooms are on the water. In Key Largo, most motels and hotels are on the Florida Bay or the Intercostal Waterway. Either way, what's all-important is that waterfront and that amazing sunset every evening. You might be surprised at how soothing the Upper Keys' subtle charms can be.

"No B & B's in Key Largo." At least that's what someone said at the Chamber of Commerce. When I asked why there are none, he explained it this way: "Hurricanes have destroyed all the big Victorian houses, and so there are very few B & B's in this area." Wrong answer—Key Largo's relatively brief history contains no Victorian houses—but nice try. A woman told me a few days later that B & B's are illegal in Key Largo; zoning laws don't permit them. And that is the truth. Still, mom and pop joints line the bayside of the Overseas Highway, and the moms and pops who run them know their area well. Staying at one of these is almost as much fun as a B & B. Often the continental breakfast is part of the room rate.

Remember when you are quoted a room rate to add on the 11.5% tax. And it is wise to check on deposit and cancellation policies and amenities like telephones in the rooms—some of the nicest places don't have them. If you have children, say so because some places don't take them. You will find reservationists to be patient and friendly, so question them carefully.

Here, in unbiased alphabetical order, is an arbitrarily chosen list of some inns, lodges and resorts of Key Largo.

Bay Harbor Lodge
MM 97.7 Bayside ☙ 852-5695
The Bay Harbor Lodge is popular with tourists from Germany and
England because owners Laszlo Simoga and his wife Sandra are from
Germany and England, respectively. Prices are very fair for comfortable,
super-clean, air-conditioned and well-equipped efficiencies and cottages.
Here you'll find good swimming, sunning, and free use of row boats,
paddle boat, canoes and kayaks along a 150-foot-length of bay front.

Barbeque grills and tiki huts are well utilized by appreciative guests. Big news at the Bay Harbor lately is the brand new, 40-foot-long heated pool. Heated! Lots of the guests here return year after year. You'll find lots of places like this along the Florida Bay in Key Largo, and each one of them has its own special personality. Rates vary according to time of year and what's going on, but they're very fair.

Frank's Keyhaven
Mile Marker 92, Bayside ☎ 852-3017 ☎ 800-765-5397

Here's another tiny gem of a joint in a long, crazy string of them. In this small waterfront retreat, you'll find standard Keys amenities like a heated pool, BBQ facilities, and a 200-foot lighted dock for fishing, snorkeling and sunset watching. Units are one-room efficiencies, adjoining family units, and one-or two-bedroom apartments, all equipped with kitchens. Rock-bottom price for a no-frills room in mid-January was $89, I was told when I phoned to inquire. "Anything less expensive?" I asked. "You won't do better anywhere in the Keys," the woman replied sweetly. "I know one place that's cheaper, but I wouldn't recommend it."

In fact, you can find a better deal. We did. Still...you've got to admire the attitude.

Holiday Inn
MM 100, Oceanside ☎ 800-THE-KEYS

You're in the heart of the tourist zone here, in a four-block area of piers, hotel rooms, great bars and excellent restaurants. But...no beach. Some people like the comfort of staying with a known and trusted host. This is it. Though Key Largo's history is a very short story, the Holiday Inn pays it homage with endless references and spins on the Bogie and Bacall theme. The Holiday Marina is home to the original *African Queen*, from the film of the same name, the *Thayer*, an outboard that appeared in the film *On Golden Pond*, and Bogie's Cafe, named for the actor who starred in the film *Key Largo*. The gift shop sells Bogie and Bacall and Katherine Hepburn-related novelties.

Room rates at the Holiday Inn begin around $130 for a standard room with two double beds; king-sized beds cost more; harbor views cost even more. Two pools, and guests get free passes for the casino boat, which is owned by the same guys who own the Holiday Inn. Get it?

Jules' Undersea Lodge
MM 103.2 Oceanside, at 51 Shoreland Drive ≋ 305-451-2353
Earn your aquanaut certificate. Spend an entire night in this space-age, self-contained habitat five fathoms under the sea, and join an elite army of 4,000 who have slept here too. Several couples have married in this underwater lab-turned-novelty inn. It's a popular nest for honeymooners, too, and with people who were children in the 1950s and remember coming home from school in time for the TV show *Sea Hunt*, featuring Lloyd Bridges as the dauntless diving master of the deep, Mike Nelson.

Like Mike Nelson, you must be in good health and be confident in the water. If you're not certified in scuba diving, you're required to take a three-hour diving course ($75 or $125 for two) before you enter the hotel. To get to your room, you wear fins and a mask and breathe via a 120-foot-long hookah connected to compressors on the surface. The lodge is located in a mangrove lagoon, birthplace of many species of fish.

You'll want your wits about you, so there's no drinking allowed at Jules' and, certainly, no smoking.

The air-conditioned lodge sleeps four in two bedrooms, with a stereo, telephone, TV and VCR; hot showers and a full galley. The most popular video: *20,000 Leagues Under the Sea*. Lots of portholes keep you from getting claustrophobic. Certified divers are allowed to slip out for a dive whenever they please, but others must schedule buddy dives with the operations manager, Mike Smith.

For $50 per person, couples or groups may visit Jules' Undersea Lodge for a three-hour mini-adventure during which they have unlimited use of the amenities and opportunity to experience life in an aqua-habitat. The European plan for around $195 per person, however, provides the room, amenities, and a dinner and breakfast that guests prepare for themselves. Check-in time is 5 p.m.; check-out is 9 a.m. The most elegant and expensive package is the Ultimate Romantic Getaway, which costs a couple $1,000 per night. The big package includes romantic music, flowers, caviar, and a gourmet dinner prepared by Mike Smith, this time wearing his chef hat.

Lifestyles of the Rich and Famous featured Jules' Undersea Lodge in a program taped in 1987 and has rerun the piece many, many times. Most insomniacs have seen it at least once. Jules does not advertise his bizarre undersea lodge. The world's one and only underwater hotel attracts a lot of attention, though; with all the publicity, Jules doesn't need to buy ads. Call for reservations or to learn more. The woman who answers the phone, manager Agnes Newcome, is so enthusiastic you'll sign right up.

Key Largo Bay
MM 103.5, Bayside ✻ 453-0000 ✻ 800-932-9332
This Marriott Beach Resort soars four stories into the sky and features white-washed walls, lots of white wrought iron and coral rock fences. The gorgeous man-made beach is as good as man-made gets. A bayfront pool is in the middle of seventeen majestic acres of finely landscaped waterfront. The gazebo is as big as a house while several tiki huts on the edge of the Florida Bay contain hammocks and tables. What a place to watch the sun go down! Don't miss the blue dolphins statue, another great photo opportunity. Attractive stone tiles take the place of pavement, and a suspension bridge connects restaurants to rooms—Whoa!—one hundred and fifty rooms, suites, or penthouses tropical luxury all the way. Rates $139 to $189 for bayview; $209 for deluxe bayview; lower on weekdays, lower still in summer.

Tropical decor. White wood. Bold, flowery prints all over the place. A setting strongly evocative of *Fantasy Island*. Any minute, you expect to see Ricardo Montelban step out from behind a royal palm and say "You look marvelous."

Kona Kai
MM 97.8, Bayside ✻ 852-7200 ✻ 800-365-7829
In 1994 Ronnie Farina and Joe Harris took over this fine, small resort, which they're renovating. The former New Yorkers are madly enthusiastic about their new roles as modern day mom and pop innkeepers. Even their dog Roxy is crazy with joy. Imagine her earlier life in a tiny N.Y. apartment compared to her new life today. Nick, the great white heron who hangs around the dock, has become a member of the family.

Sunset is a community time at the Kona Kai. Joe and Ronnie pour wine and watch the sunset with their guests. To the right and to the left are other bayside beaches, just like this one. The little boats, the sleepy ambiance, the shapes on the docks in the distance, all remind you of a lakeside community. Or the song "Sitting On the Dock of the Bay."

All eleven units in the Kona Kai are at ground level, with varying numbers of beds and amenities in each. The heated pool and jacuzzi on the waterfront are new. The beach really is the nicest man-made white-sand beach in Key Largo. Guests are free to use the paddle boat and kayak and to fish right off the 150-foot dock. In the summertime many guests arrive by water, Joe says; several diving and nature tour boats stop by to pick up tourists right off the Kona Kai pier.

Rates vary: price range from $84 during the low season to $207 at the peak of the high season. Expect rates to increase when the Kona Kai renovation is complete.

Largo Lodge
MM 101.5, Bayside ▪ 451-0424 ▪ 800-IN THE SUN
Little has changed here in the thirty-plus years since the Largo Lodge opened for business in the late '50s. The Largo Lodge has got what many people are coming here to find: peace and quiet beneath a canopy of swaying palms. Three duplex cottages containing two units, each with three rooms: living room, bedroom with two beds, and kitchen with whatever equipment you need to cook; private screened-in porches and entrances. No continental breakfast, no phones, no kids under sixteen years. Apartments are all still in the '50s mode—owner Harriet Stokes collects ashtrays and fixtures from the period to keep them that way. They'll remind you of the motor court cabins of your childhood.

Besides the cottages, two rooms with queen-sized beds and color TVs aren't advertised. Harriet might put you in one of them if you ask nicely and she likes you. The unadvertised rooms are $75 in the winter; less in summer. Cottages are around $95 in winter; $75 in summer. But be warned: prices haven't budged in ten years at the Largo Lodge and, much as she regrets it, Harriet says she may have to raise her rates soon.

"The mom and pop days are gone forever," she sighs.

The grounds at Largo Lodge are wonderful and tropical-lush. You really feel as if you're very far away from the rest of the world. Orchid lovers will go nuts here: brilliantly colored orchids are everywhere. Squirrels scurry up and down the thick trunks of coconut trees. Waterfront is typical bayside: funky, breezy, wondrous at sunset.

And there's something sort of ageless and wonderful about Harriet Stokes, too.

Marina del Mar Resort and Marina
MM 100 Oceanside ☏ 800-451-3483

and

Marina del Mar Bayside
MM 99.7 Bayside ☏ 800-242-5229

Let's get this straight: Two locations are called "Marina del Mar"—one on each side of the Overseas Highway in Key Largo. The one that is a marina is on a deep-water canal a short distance from the Atlantic Ocean. Don't let that "Oceanside" in the name fool you, because it's definitely not on the ocean, and there's no beach either; there are, however, a deep-water marina, a dive center, a gym, tennis lessons, a giant pool and whirlpool spa. Also, Coconuts Restaurant and Cocktail Lounge with indoor and outdoor dining. After dark, Coconuts is one of the area's hottest night spots. Sharkey's Bar on the water has pool tournaments. At Benny's Galley upstairs choose reasonably priced indoor and outdoor dining. If you're a sports-minded person in town for a vacation of fishing by day and carousing by night, this is the place for you.

The Marina Del Mar Marina is connected to the the Holiday Inn Marina via a long canal-side walkway. Take a stroll along the water and have a look at some of the vessels tied up at the Del Mar docks: grand old wooden yachts from Norfolk, and Philadelphia, and Charleston, that make you think old money; and deluxe fishing boats with flying bridges nearly three stories high. We peeked through the open door of a fishing boat and were amazed to see fat, flowered chintz chairs and dark mahogany—an English sitting room!

You'll see some very serious-looking charter fishing boats, captained by former Navy officers. Should you wish to hire one of them, phone numbers are posted on signs near the boat. And so as to not waste your time or anyone else's, prices are posted, too. A day's fishing on such a splendid vessel as this will cost around $600 for between one and six people.

Every once in a while the *African Queen* glides down the canal, crying her tremulous steam-engine toot. She looks quite fine from afar— actually quite a bit better than she does tied up at her dockside spot at the Holiday Inn Marina.

Standard rooms, with queen or king-size beds, refrigerators, TVs, and continental breakfast start around $110 in the early fall and go up to $270 at the height of the season. More expensive suites with one to three bedrooms are also available.

Marina Del Mar Resort, Bayside

The sister property on the Florida Bay is a West Indies-style resort a quarter mile down the road from Marina Del Mar Resort and Marina. But this is a rough quarter mile over a busy highway, so, in other words, you wouldn't want to send your kids across the street alone. Nonetheless, you are invited to make your way across and use all of the amenities there— the pool, the whirlpool, the gym, the canal-side path, and so forth. So why would you stay bayside instead of oceanside? Well, how can we say this delicately? It's for people of more limited means, more modest tastes. You fish off the pier, not off a million-dollar boat. Room rates are somewhat less expensive than across the street at the Marina Del Mar Resort and Marina.

Marina Del Mar Bayside Resort has a swimming pool and a sandy beach dotted with cabana chairs. For action, there's a volleyball court in the sand. The sun sets on the Florida Bay, and it's truly memorable. Those are the kinds of natural charms people who stay bayside love; they seem to want little more than a comfortable cabana. Call and ask all the questions you like, and then decide where you want to stay. Room rates are between $104 and $270.

Westin Key Largo
MM 97 Bayside ☞ 852-5553 ☞ 800-228-3000

Two hundred balconied rooms and forty-four suites with marble vanities, coffeemakers, and fancy hotel fixtures, are all located in a hardwood hammock where you can wander along footpaths that lead past wild coffee plants and mahogany trees. Dine at three restaurants and lounges.

A separate swimming pool for families with kids keeps the quiet, adults-only pool always serene. Other features: a little beach, a jacuzzi, and tennis courts; Waverunners and hobie cats; diving, guided fishing trips, and parasailing. A snorkel charter leaves from the Westin docks every morning at 10 a.m. and again at 2 p.m. The three-hour trip visits dive sites on the shallow, calm bayside of Key Largo, then cruises through a connecting cut and over to the ocean for some stopovers there. The trip is around $25 for adults and $21 for kids. An environmental-awareness tour leaves right from the Westin.

On weekdays in season, prices on the Westin's basic rooms with two queen-sized beds overlooking the Florida Bay or a tropical hammock start at $200. When you call for reservations, ask for information on off-season specials and packages. If the reservationist has a strong Canadian accent, you're probably talking with John Strong, from Halifax, Nova Scotia, who is the rooms division manager, and a very happy resident of Key Largo.

Sunset Cove Motel
MM 99.5 Bayside ✶ 451-0705

A neat, old-timey joint with very reasonable prices. Many guests reserve rooms from one year to the next, so if you're planning on staying at Sunset Cove, book early. No-frills cottages on the bay are in demand, and some Sunset Cove guests have been coming for seventeen years! Even the staff is familiar year after year. It's located in that busy some-thing-for-everybody center of Key Largo, near diving, fishing, bars and restaurants, and owned and operated by terrific folks who seem to thoroughly enjoy their mission, which is to keep you happy in the Keys. Manager Ilene Drennan came to the Keys in 1967; in thirty years she's seen a lot and come to the conclusion that Key Largo is the best place to live, and work. She loves her job, and it shows.

The Sunset Cove and the Hungry Pelican next door recently became one property, which is good news for guests. The property now has forty clean and reasonably priced units in all, six with back doors that open onto the Florida Bay. All rooms have refrigerators and TVs. Some units have kitchens and enough beds to sleep a baseball team. No phones in any of them. Also, no pool on the property. Futons are being added in some places to make room for even more guests, a big improvement over

Accommodations
...

pull-out couches and cots. Complimentary continental breakfast and kids are welcome.

Three fishing piers, a glass bottom paddle boat and a couple of other fun boats are free to guests. Hand-woven Jamaican swings, suspended from the top of thatched chickee huts are perfect nests for napping or watching the sunset. Lockers and dip tanks for divers, a talkative parrot named Bart for the kids.

Room rates are based on double occupancy. Additional people in a room cost $10 more. A basic room—double bed, fridge and TV—is $50. Most expensive units are around $130, year-round. Certainly no one should be surprised if they are adjusted upward sometime soon. (My warning. Not theirs.)

Tavernier Hotel
MM 91 Oceanside ❦ 852-4131 ❦ 800-515-4131

In the early '30s a Miami schoolteacher named McKenzie moved to Tavernier and built a movie theater of cinder blocks, a practically unheard of building material in the Upper Keys in those days. The movie theater was a pretty bizarre undertaking, too, considering the tiny population. But the theater operated for a couple of years. McKenzie's cinder block building even survived the Labor Day Hurricane of 1935 and was turned into an emergency hospital by the American Red Cross. McKenzie also built a drugstore, which is now the Copper Kettle Restaurant. In 1938, after the Overseas Highway brought cars full of tourists to the Keys, he added a second story onto the original building and turned it into a hotel.

The seventeen rooms in the Tavernier Hotel are small and very simple: double beds, private bathrooms with showers, TVs and dial-out phones. You'll have to do your daily calisthenics in the gym downstairs. Rooms go for around $70 weeknights; $80 weekends. Discounts after a couple of days; also weekly rates. It's not the kind of place where you'd spend your entire day: no beach, no pool, just clean, no-nonsense rooms tended by clean, no-nonsense hosts.

Margaret Thompson began refurbishing the Tavernier Hotel in 1991. She's done a great job, but she'll tell you herself she's far from finished. The refurbishment is still in the works. Margaret hopes to get the place in the National Historic Register because it would certainly qualify.

The Serendipity Cottage next door houses a tiny bakery run by a French pastry chef who makes real Key lime pies for $12.95. (Everybody says their Key lime pie is the best, so get used to it.) Also the Serendipity Cottage is a gift shop that Margaret Thompson tries to fill with whimsical things that she hopes you haven't seen anywhere else. She does a good job, too. The Serendipity is a good place to do gift shopping for the folks back home.

Camping & RV Parks

There are many camp and RV parks in the Key Largo area. Call the Chamber of Commerce at 800-822-1088 for a complete list of campsites and RV sites of the Keys.

America Outdoors Campground
MM 97.5 ✽ 852-8054

154 sites, RVs and tents mixed. It's very comfortable, not rustic camping with air-conditioned bathhouses, hot showers. In operation for twenty-five years with a 700-foot sandy beach on the Florida Bay, a marina with non-motor boat rentals, grocery, dockside restaurant serving breakfast and lunch, laundry facilities. Mostly RVs from mid-December to mid-March. March and April are spring-breaker months, but don't worry about rowdy crowds or big noise. Students must give manager Laurie Comeau their home phone numbers when they check in. In the case of bad behavior, their parents are contacted. Honest. "We are their parents while they're here," Laurie says.

Rates are based on two people in a camping unit—tent or RV. Additional people cost $3 each per day. Kids under six camp for free. Water, electric and TV cable hook-up per tent or RV is $33 per night. Full hook-up, which also includes sewer, is $38. Ten beachfront sites are $45 per night. Monthly rates for two, including cable TV, water and electricity: $670 (don't forget the additional $77 for sales tax). With sewer, $740 (plus $85 sales tax). No beachfront sites available by the month. Summer program for RV's features much lower monthly rates.

Vacation Rentals

Condos, homes, mobile homes, cottages on the Florida Bay or the
Atlantic Ocean. Pay from $700 to $3,000 a week for a fully equipped
home. Don't forget to figure in taxes and the security deposit.

Bayview Properties
800-226-4577

Century 21 Keysearch Realty
800-210-6246

Loveland Realty
800-454-5263

Dining

Copper Kettle
Mile Marker 91.5 Oceanside ☎ 852-4113

This restaurant adjoins the historic and charmingly unpretentious
Plantation Hotel. The food is good enough to attract a full dining room
by 8 p.m., at least on the night we were there. In fact, the host was turning people away or asking them to wait at the little bar, which they did.
Our waiter was a very handsome, polite Russian fellow. If he'd understood
English, too, he would have been perfect! The menu is standard fare,
with a tiny bit of exotic flair. Spinach pie in filo dough is delicious and
makes you feel Popeye-powerful; veggies and salad were not out of the
ordinary; baked goods are prepared at a tiny bakery next door. Pray the
baking here never ends—fresh-baked goods for breakfast separates this
place from the others doing breakfast. They serve only twenty-three
diners at a time, so everything runs smoothly. The full bar seats only a
few drinkers. Reservations for this small, popular cafe are probably a
good idea.

The Cracked Conch
Mile Marker 105, Oceanside ☎ 451-0732

When the people who work in a restaurant are as enthusiastic as the
people in the Cracked Conch, it seems a good sign that the food will be
very good. And it is. But the waitresses, and the beers, are the best thing
about the place. The beer selection must be the largest collection of
imported brews in the Keys: pale ales, brown ales, scotch ales, and barley
wine; cream stouts, malts, porters, and tap beers; even spiced beers. The
beer menu is actually longer than the food menu. You can get the island
food you want here, too, stuff like deep-fried fish, excellent cracked
conch, good conch chowder. Try the alligator and find out for yourself
why this rare delicacy never really got off the ground. Key lime pie is
frozen and very refreshing. Dinners are Caribbean, Cajun, and Mexican-
influenced with a different menu of specials every night and very
reasonable prices.

A note on the menu says, "This establishment is run by a very close staff and family...Close to broke. Close to insanity. Close to killing each other." Guests staple their business cards to the wooden walls. (Makes you wish you had one...well, maybe you do.) Stapled next to my table was the business card of a local realtor. Someone had drawn a mustache and beard on her tiny business-card photo, and then, in wee, little letters, had written, "Let me sell your house so you can move back up North."

The inside is much bigger than it looks from the outside, which seems to be a trend around here, huh? You can sit outside, too, if you don't mind the traffic on the Overseas Highway a few feet from your table. Open noon till 10 p.m. Closed Wednesdays.

Denny's Latin Cafe
Mile Marker 100, Bayside ✹ 451-3665
Denny's is open 24 hours a day. The Cubans in the Upper Keys love to hang around talking and drinking strong cafe con leche at Denny's. (By the way, this Denny's is not even remotely related to Denny's, the chain.) Plenty of hardcore Key Westers rave about Denny's, too. It's a favorite stop on the road to, or from, Amerika. They tell you that they wouldn't dream of skipping a trip to Denny's. Cuban food: Do you have any idea what a deal beans and rice is? And we're not just talking money; we're talking nutrition, too. Try Denny's—if you can get near it. Sometimes, if you're not too far away and he's got a man to spare, Denny's will deliver.

The Fish House
MM 102.4 Oceanside ✹ 451-HOOK
You gotta go to the Fish House because, when you ask where to go for fresh fish, this is where everyone will send you. It's the hottest seafood joint in town. Lunch from 11:30 a.m. to 4 p.m., then dinner till 10 p.m., with beer and wine only. The children's menu is really no bargain—a kid's hamburger is $4.25. All the prices are pretty steep, perhaps because the food is served on real dishes, not paper. The forks and knives aren't plastic, and you drink your wine from real glass, but you pay for elegance like this in a fish house. Chowders, stone crab claw appetizers, shellfish, and local fish, cooked a dozen different ways. Nice, big, tasty meals are served with boiled potatoes and corn on the cob; and steaks and garlic

butter and oil pasta for the landlubbers. A bread basket is 75¢. Desserts like Key lime pie are $3.25. Watch out though, for the sharing charge, a wine corking charge, and the 15% gratuity added onto the bill for parties of six or more. Attitude is important at the Fish House, where owners promote themselves and their employees as "fun, friendly, and Keysy." Anybody who has eaten here raves about the food.

Ganim's Country Kitchen
MM 99.5 Bayside, and again at MM 102.5 Bayside
451-2895 and 451-3337
Isn't it weird there are two of these? One would have been plenty.

Harriette's Restaurant
MM 95.7 ✿ 852-8689
Lots of folks love Harriette's for breakfast. Some mornings you see them lined up outside the door waiting for one of Harriette's wobbly, worn-out tables. Why? Perhaps it's the gritty atmosphere or the cozy aroma of grill-fried food. The scrambled eggs, pancakes, French toast, grits and coffee at Harriette's are certainly all right, but the service is lightening-fast, maybe too fast…. Our waitress was in no mood for questions the Saturday morning we showed up for breakfast. Our meal was a wham-bam deal, in and out. That's Harriette's for breakfast; lunch, too. No dinner. Open 6 a.m. till 2 p.m. every day except Christmas and Thanksgiving. No credit cards!

Italian Fisherman
MM 104 Bayside ✿ 451-4451
A really huge dining room; you'll be surprised. The statue of the naked, net-pulling Italian fisherman outside is majestic. He and a couple of less spectacular white statues mark the doorway to the restaurant. You can't get anybody in the area to say much about the food. It's o.k., they say, but that's about it. Early-bird specials starting at $7.95 are served from 4 p.m. to 6 p.m. every evening. Tuesday is pasta night—pasta dinner for $5.95!

The Italian Fisherman is one of those places where people have been going for so many years they don't think of changing their routine and trying some place new. The fish dishes are better than the Italian dishes;

Attempts at combining the two result in weird results like Conch Parmigiana. Great sunset dining—but then, every place on the gulfside of the island has a great view of the sunset. Big marina behind the outdoor decks and terraces provide even more to watch. This place has been bustling like this for years and years.

Jim and Val's Tugboat Restaurant

2 Seagate Boulevard, corner of Oceanside Drive • 453-9010

All the local color and atmosphere you could ever hope to find is right here at the Tugboat, and if that weren't enough—the food is the best around. Locals eat here and tell only the very nicest, most special tourists about it. Why? "If we tell the tourists everybody will know about it, we'll ruin it for ourselves," a local shopkeeper told me.

From the screened dining area you'll see a couple of tropical hardwoods—mahogany trees—that do not grow farther north than South Florida. A very talkative parrot named Pedro is a permanent fixture. Val adopted the bird many years ago, when her kids were babies, so she figures Pedro to be anywhere from 38—43 years old, which means he's almost half as old as he might grow to be. A little bar, featuring a mesmerizing portrait of Humphrey Bogart, serves beer and wine only. The whole place is small—a full house would be around fifty customers.

Lunch and dinner specials change regularly, but look for fish or crab chowders, roast pork, pan-fried yellowtail or grouper, all served with black beans, rice, and cornbread. Also big salads and open-face sandwiches. Lunch prices range from $5 to $8. Dinner hour starts at 5 p.m., and the place closes at 9 p.m. Prices at night are a few dollars more, but the food is just as good. Special mention: cracked conch is done just right and priced just right, too. Key lime pie is the best for miles around, in this weary traveler's opinion, and also, strangely enough, the least expensive—$2 a slice! During winter the Tugboat is open weekdays from 11 a.m. to 9 p.m. and weekends from 8 a.m. till 9 p.m. All major credit cards are accepted. Phone for specials of the day.

The Pilot House
13 Seagate Boulevard ✍ 451-3142

Turn onto Seagate Boulevard and drive past a couple of boatyards on your right before you come to the Pilot House's spacious parking lot. It's a country-clubbish place on a harbor where the air is scented with diesel fuel, not fish. Sometimes you find a place that looks as good as this—lots of polished wood, serious carpet, brass-rimmed porthole windows—and then the food is only so-so. But not so here. The food's very good, and the cocktail lounge, as well as a long chain of cozy booths, is absolutely inviting. Otherwise, you can dine right on the water on a spacious outdoor deck. Young greeters and servers are attractive—polite and perky.

The lunch menu includes a fruit salad with a center scoop of raspberry sherbet and huge, bright strawberries ($7.95) that was quite spectacular, and the famous fish sandwich—deep-fried dolphin, grilled with cheese, tomato and lettuce on whole wheat—served all day, every day, since 1950, for $5.95.

At dinnertime a fried shrimp platter with twelve fried shrimp, rice, and veggie is $9.95. And there's fish, of course, prepared in a variety of ways; pastas, chicken, and steak, too. Most dinner prices fall between $10 and $20.

At the bottom of the menu, a note says: "If you are a visitor and it is customary, we will add 15% gratuity to your check." What does that mean? Probably that people with accents, or from places like Europe or Canada where service is included in the check, should expect to see the gratuity added onto their check here, too. All cards except American Express are accepted. Brunch on Sunday is big with locals. Open daily from 11 a.m. till 9:30 p.m.

Mandalay Marina and Tiki Bar
80 E. Second Street, turn at MM 97.5 toward ocean ✍ 852-9019

At first look, you'll think you're in the wrong place. But look harder. Looks, after all, aren't everything. This place, many locals say, is not to be missed. Wednesday is fried chicken night—all you can eat for $6.95. On all-you-can-eat nights, the waitresses encourage you to eat, eat, eat. Other menu items include good, hearty stuff like scampi and half or full rack of lamb. Great prices. Call for daily specials. Lunch and dinner.

Mrs. Mac's Kitchen
MM 99.4 ✺ 451-3722
When the Key Largo well-to-do go slumming, this is where they eat lunch. Mrs. Mac's is the kind of place you came to the Keys to find. From the road it's a shack, but it's quite big once you get inside. Filled with attractive, spunky girls, one of whom reminded me very much of actress Crystal Bernard from television's *Wings*. The menu is long and colorful; the decor is funky. Big fat sandwiches on pita bread, good chili, steaks and different themed specials—Italian, meat, seafood—each night. Frankly, you come here for the atmosphere, not the food, which is nothing to rave about. But it's a lively, friendly, stop with diner prices. Beer and wine only, cash only. Closed Sunday. Call for specials.

Num Thai
MM 103.2 Bayside, in Central Shopping Plaza ✺ 451-5955
Ahhh. A soft, serene oasis steeped in Far Eastern tradition. It's located in a short, neat strip of shops; just look for the sign. Thai, Japanese, and sushi. Owners are Bangkok natives who lived first in Miami and then in the Keys. Lunch on weekdays only, from 11:30 a.m.–3 p.m. Dinner seven nights from 5 p.m. to 10:30 p.m. Owned and operated by Panyaporn Russmetes ("Num" is his nickname, which means "forever young"), and his wife Tiki. Num's family opened and ran the first Thai restaurant in Miami. Tiki is a Japanese cook so their restaurant Num Thai is a monument to their many years in the food business. Big menu: eighty-three Thai dishes, sixty Japanese dishes, children's meals, curry special each night, and Thai and Japanese beers and wines, also a sushi bar. Grilled chicken with rice and veggies, $11.95; Key Largo sushi roll, $7.95; live lobster, $23.95. Moderate prices for exquisitely prepared food and, what makes it all so wonderful, lovely people doing their best to please their guests. The people at Num Thai understand good service and fine dining. It's well worth the money and what a find for vegetarian gourmands!

The Old Tavernier
MM 91.8 Oceanside ✺ 852-6012
My friend Thorn Trainer, who lives in this area, says we can't write a guidebook to the Florida Keys without mentioning the Old Tavernier

Restaurant. "The garlic rolls are wonderful!" Thorn says. Ilias Kofinas has owned the Old Tavernier for eight years now. He is Greek, so occasionally you'll find a traditional Greek dish among the evening's dinner specials as well as great Italian and American dishes. At the Tavernier Twin Movie Theater down the road, pizza from the Old Tavernier is sold in the lobby. How novel!

The Old Tavernier serves dinner only, from 4 p.m.–10:30 p.m. daily. Full bar, and entrees come with soup or salad, and bread: fish, steaks, lamb, chicken, and traditional Italian dishes. Some sample prices: veal parmesan, $12.95; yellowtail provencal, $17.95; New York strip, $18.95.

South of the Border
MM 103 Bayside, in the Pink Plaza ❦ 451-3307
A waitress told us that the same people who own Mrs. Mac's Kitchen own this place, too. It's good Mexican food served in a place with a city-ish atmosphere, which is to say, it ain't feeling real Keysy—yet. Maybe after a few more years it will find itself a personality. The big bar has notably comfortable chairs; soft drinks are served in quart-sized mason jars. Fair prices on the standard Mexican restaurant dishes that are quite tasty and certainly quite generous. If you're mad for Mexican, you'll be happy. But you can't use your credit card unless your bill is over $15. "There's a sign on the door," the waitress told me. Sorry, I didn't see it. Later, I checked with my Visa card issuer, who told me credit cards are good for any amount. So insist!

Snooks
MM 99.9 Bayside ❦ 453-3799
Snooks is difficult to find because their sign, right next to Key Largo Honda, is not the easiest to spot—but the search is well worth the trouble! Press on. This qualifies as one of the most relaxing restaurants in the Keys, with a cozy piano bar and a terrific waterfront view of the Florida Bay. The bar inside Snook's boasts a large saltwater aquarium, a unique bartop made of hammered copper to resemble fish scales, and a baby grand piano. The piano player shows up at 6:30 p.m. on weekends and plays until 10:30 p.m. or so. You'll meet lots of locals as well as tourists here. Several way-cool boats are always tied up at the dock. Sunday

brunch is popular with locals as well as tourists. The dazzling brunch buffet is $14.95; entertainment then is a guy playing reggae guitar. Lunch entrees range between $7 and $10; dinner $18–$25. Sunday brunch, served from 11 a.m. till 3 p.m., is lazy and wonderful. In a tiki hut down by the water's edge, you'll find Patrick's Waterfront Bar, from where the sunset is splendorous, and you can watch it from a place that is sort of high-scale laid-back.

Night Life

There isn't a hell of a lot of club activity in Key Largo. Sunset and happy hours, with cocktails and conversation, signal the end of another day in Paradise. Your best bet for after-dark activity is bars and lounges in local restaurants and the bigger hotels.

Coconuts
MM 100 at Marina del Mar Marina Oceanside ✹ 453-9794
Monday night features comedy; Tuesday, blues; Wednesday is Ladies Night, a top-40 band plays Wednesday through Saturday, and Sunday is reggae. How can you not dance with that big, inviting dance floor gleaming there beneath the strobe lights? A walk outside takes you to the water's edge or to a table under the stars where a beautiful waitress will serve your cocktails. Young tourists like this place a lot.

Shops

Banana Hill
MM 98.3, on the median ✻ 852-6161

"Take a vacation from your vacation" the yellow Banana Hill brochure cleverly suggests. Not a bad idea. The gentle people at Banana Hill embrace a holistic approach to relieving stress and recharging body and soul. The healing center offers massage therapy, chiropractic, acupuncture, shiatsu, reflexology, herbal body wraps and more. Other forms of therapy include artistic healing: arts and crafts classes. All of the therapists are fully licensed and insured. (Massage therapists have to be in Florida.)

Visiting artisans might check out the pottery and stained glass studio. Local artists buy supplies here, and there are frequent classes.

There's a meditation room, and readings that foretell of all good things in your future. Magic Merlin sells magical books and games, tapes and CDs. Also there's a shop called the Earth Boutique that features spiritual jewelry, incense and oils, lotions, potions, cards, crystals and gems. Tai Chi, yoga and meditation classes are held some evenings. The occasional psychic fairs here are very popular.

The Book Nook
MM 100, Oceanside, in Waldorf Plaza ✻ 451-1468

Anyone who's been here once will come again. On a counter at the front of the shop, proprietor Joel Carmel stacks his free monthly newsletter, a rundown on what new books are on the scene. Joel's even-handed reviews are terrific, helpful, even funny. His opinions are so well respected that Keys writers hope to have his comments on the covers of *their* books. Occasional booksigning parties are good opportunities to meet some big-time writers.

The Book Nook carries the *Wall Street Journal*, the *New York Times*, *Barron's*, and the *Daily Telegraph* and *Daily Mirror*; also audio books that you can buy or rent. Joel is very well versed on his local-book section both titles and authors. He's familiar with just about any book you might name, but that doesn't mean you'll find it in his store because he carries only books that he believes will appeal to his customers. You might be surprised by what's not there because Joel has deemed it to be without merit. The readers of Key Largo trust him, and you can, too. If you are a bookshop browser or a world traveler who wisely hangs around local haunts to understand a community better through its people, Joel won't mind a bit. In fact, you're welcome.

Caribbean Cigar Factory
Mile Marker 103, Bayside, in the Pink Plaza ✦ 453-4014
A couple of Cuban cigarmakers are busy at work rolling cigars just as they did in Key West in the 1800s. You'll find at least one cigarmaker on duty most of the time. Visitors are invited to watch the process up close. Most of these gentle artisans don't speak English, but they occasionally smile and make you feel welcome. Check out the table, the tools, the way their graceful hands move as they wrap and roll the tobacco. It's so soft and supple, it looks like thin, moist suede. Imagine. Around the turn of the century, Key West's cigar industry produced over 100 million cigars a year, all hand-rolled by Cuban and Spanish men and women working at tables with tools just like these.

Select a handmade cigar from a room-sized, walk-in humidor that sends puffs of vapors through ducts in the shop's ceiling. The odor is intoxicatingly delicious. Open late every day.

Florida Keys Handbag Factory
MM 93.6, Oceanside ✦ 800-462-7112
The Florida Keys Handbag was invented by a former boat cushion maker. The purses are made of the same incredibly durable vinyl used in boat cushions, and then last for many, many years. What keeps the place in business is referrals from satisfied customers and a very successful mail-order program: a woman buys a handbag and likes it so well she decides to give handbags to her mother, her sister, and her best friend, so she calls the 800-number and orders them. And there you are: a hot business. Half the fun of designing your own monogrammed purse is choosing from, literally, a thousand design possibilities.

There is a local story of a Key Largo woman who was in a small-plane crash in the area. All that survived the crash, besides her and her boyfriend, was her Florida Keys Handbag, which she carries still.

Grant Gallery
MM 90, on the median ✆ 852-8776
Here is a schlock-shopper's heaven. There are clothes, tables, chairs, antiques, collectibles, and whatever else has caught the eye of the gallery's owner, former Delta flight attendant Nancy Grant.

If you visit the gallery, please be careful not to criticize the merchandise. If you don't like the arty clothes, or the secondhand furniture, or the pottery Nancy Grant collected in Africa or Europe, and especially if you don't care for Tom Grant's paintings, just keep your opinions under your hat.

"A store is a very personal thing," Nancy explains. "I cringe if I hear a customer say they don't like something in here. This store is my art. The building is my canvas. The stuff in it is my medium."

Nancy and her husband Tom have a ball running the business. Tom is the company delivery man and also accompanies Nancy on buying trips to Georgia. They travel in a camper with Jack, a chocolate brown standard poodle.

"Just like *Travels With Charlie*," Nancy says.

Key Largo's Secondhand Rows

Josie's Junk Alley
MM 99.5. on the median

Pink Junktique
MM 99.5 on the median

Salvation Army
MM 99.2, on the median

Talk of the Town Thrift
MM 92.4 Bayside

Upper Attic Thrift
MM 103.2 Bayside, in the Central Plaza

Tavernier Towne
92.5 Bayside
Don't miss this open-air mall; just remember to turn at McDonald's.
You'll find a whole world back there behind the hamburger store! The
McDonald's at Tavernier Towne is where the tour buses stop, probably
because this is one place where they can find plenty of spacious parking
spots for the brightly painted, air-conditioned tour buses. And it's so
familiar, and inexpensive, and all-American.

Also look for this fascinating exhibit of local color: at the Winn Dixie
Food Store, a huge bulletin board is covered with hundreds of intriguing
messages. A cleaning woman with a "French touch" wants to clean your
house or boat, or both. Houses, condos, and boats are for sale or rent;
cars, bikes, pool tables, plants; photos, sketches and portraits of available
items. Also posters about up-coming events: bingo nights; community
theater presentations; and a poster for the Keys Players production of *Kiss
Me Kate*. (You missed it.)

Just when I'd finished reading all the notices on the board, a woman
with a bizarre shade of red hair came along and asked me if I knew where
she could go to have acrylic nails applied. Huh? Me? She was new to
town, she explained. "This is a hard place to stay beautiful," she said,
scanning the bulletins for an acrylic nail applier. She didn't find one, so
she launched into a diatribe about her trials as a new resident. "I was
treated like public enemy number one when I tried to open an account at
the bank and at the library when I tried to get a library card!" she said.
"When I was a tourist, it was a whole different scenario. Now that I live
here, they treat me like a member of a crime family!"

Index

Bull & Whistle Bar, 33, 252
Burton, Philip, 37, 52
Burton, Richard, 38

C
C.B. Harvey Rest Beach Park, 173
Cafe des Artistes, 223-24
Cafe Marquesa, 224-25
Café Solé, 230
Caloosa Cove Resort, 444-45
Camille's, 225
Cape Air, 134
Captain Bob's Grill, 225-26
Captain Hook's Marina, 367
Captain Tony's, 48, 82, 253
Captain's Corner, 158-59
Caputo, Phil, 50, 52, 405
Caribbean Air Charters, 134
Caribbean Cigar Factory, 535
Caribbean Club, 478-79
Caribbean Gallery, 86
Caribbean Shipwreck Museum, 490-91
Caribbean Spa, 164
Caroline Street Books, 58
Carousel Boat Tours, 440
Carson, Johnny, 112
Carey, George, 81-82
Carysfort Light, 487-88
Casa Antiqua, 34
Casa Grande, 314-15
Casa Marina, 185-86
Castaway Restaurant, 389-90
Cayo Hueso Y Habana, 101

Center Court, 200
Chapel by the Sea, 274
Charles Rivers Labs, 286
Charter Boat Row, 160, 167-68
Chart Room, 78
Cheeca Lodge, 441, 445-47
Cheeca Rocks, 435
Chico's Cantina, 226
Christ of the Abyss, 486
Christmas by the Sea, 155-56
Cinema Shores, 90
Cinema Six Theater, 90
city cemetery, 97
City of Washington, wreck, 488
Civil War Days, 140
Clinton Market, 30
Club Body Tech, 164
Cocoa Plum Beach, 355
Coco's Cantina, 319
Coconut Grove, 212-13
Coconuts, 533
Coffee Mill Center, 165
Coffins Patch Reef, 368-69
Conch Flyer, 253-54
Conch Republic Cigar Factory, 47
Conch Republic Days, 142-43
Conch Train, 121, 123
Conchs, 25-27, 242
Consigning Adults, 268
Copper Kettle, 526
Coral Bay Marina, 452-53
Coral Bowl, 437
Coral Grill, 437
coral reef spawning, 150
Coral Sea Glass Bottom Boat, 440
Coral Tree Inn, 215

Courtney's Place, 201-02
Cover to Cover Books, 464
Cracked Conch Cafe, 390
Cracked Conch, The, 526
Cramer's Airboat Tours, 509
Crane Point Hammock, 353, 360
Criss Cross, 44, 187
Crockogators, 391
Cuba! Cuba!, 261
Cudjoe Key, 285
Curry Mansion, 33, 99, 202
Curry Princess, 125
Custom House, 30, 100
Cypress House, 34

D
Davis Reef Ridge, 435
Deer Run, 315-16
Deli Restaurant, 226-27
Delivery Service, 227
Dennis Pharmacy, 79, 227
Denny's Latin Cafe, 527
Dippin' Deli, 319-20
Discovery Glass Bottom Boat, 129, 166
Diva's, 254
Dive into History, 435
Dog Beach, 171
Dolphin Marina Boat Rentals, 299
Dolphin Research Center, 496
Dolphin Watch, 497
Dolphin Wildlife Adventure Cruise, 441
Dolphins Plus, 495, 500
dolphins, 492-98
Dos Passos, John, 52
Duane/Bibb, wreck, 488

Index
...

Index

• • •

Order Form

Palm Island Press
411 Truman Avenue • Key West, FL 33040 USA
800-763-4345 for toll-free orders
305-294-7834 • 305-296-3102 for fax orders

Send _____ copies of *June Keith's Key West and The Florida Keys* at $18.95 each

Send _____ copies of *Postcards From Paradise* at $19.95 each

Send _____ copies of *More Postcards From Paradise* at $19.95 each

I understand that I may return any books for a full refund—for any reason, no questions asked.

Add $4.50 Priority Mail postage and handling for the first book and 75¢ for each additional book. For books shipped to Florida addresses, please add 7.5% sales tax per book.

Please charge my ☐ VISA ☐ MasterCard #_____

Expiration date: _____ Name on card: _____

Signature: _____

Enclosed is my check for: _____

Name: _____

Address: _____

City, State, ZIP: _____

☐ This is a gift. Please send directly to:

Name: _____

Address: _____

City, State, ZIP: _____

☐ Autographed by the author
    Autographed to: _____